# WAY OF THE
# WORLD

# INTRODUCTION

I first joined the *Daily Telegraph* as a stripling of 21 in December 1960 to be a junior reporter on the Diary column, then called London Day by Day by Peterborough. Easily the best thing in the newspaper – perhaps the only good thing in those far-off days – was the Way of the World column written under the pseudonym of Peter Simple by Michael Wharton. It was a mixture of satirical fantasy and acerbic comment, taking a balanced view of politics and world events which I found congenial, and already peopled by a huge cast of caricature figures who, over the years, established themselves firmly in the imaginative awareness of the million-odd readers who had the opportunity to consult it four times a week.

Within a year of joining the *Telegraph* I had applied to Wharton to be taken on as his apprentice. The column had previously employed two people. I would tend his flocks, polish the shoes of his aldermen, pour sherry for his bishops, tea for his clergymen, whisky for his journalists, sit goggle-eyed at the feet of his Hampstead left-wing *penseuses* and read haikus in Japanese to his captive aesthete down a disused lead mine in (I think) Derbyshire . . . . Michael Wharton heard me out with the exquisite politeness of an older generation, and with the same politeness, showed me the door.

He later wrote in his autobiography that he was nervous I would try to steal his thunder. The column was his creation and his life. It would have been bitter for him – and most unjust – if by virtue of a more recently celebrated family name, I seemed to take it over. I drifted away from the *Telegraph* – to the *Mirror*, then *Spectator*, eventually achieving a degree of fame, if not fortune, on *Private Eye*. It was during my 16 years on the *Eye* that a shared friend told me Wharton had jocularly confided he had a sealed envelope, to be opened on his death, appointing me his successor to the title and estates of Peter Simple.

For many years I waited in dread anticipation of the Call, worming my way back into the *Telegraph* apparatus in 1981 with a leader-page column on the Sunday newspaper under the editorship of J. W. M. Thompson (later of Peregrine Worsthorne). That column ran for nine years, while Peter Simple grew from strength to strength. I never mentioned to Wharton that I was awaiting my moment. His remark might have been misreported, uttered entirely in jest, he might have changed his mind, lost the letter, forgotten about it . . . my only hope was to wait around, trembling for the awful Event which must one day occur.

Then I observed a sinister development. Wharton had not died, thank God, but had decided to write the column less often. A usurper had moved in, and was writing the column twice a week under the pseudonym Peter Simple II. Enquiry revealed he was someone of about my own age, whom I had known for 20 years or so. Somehow, he had wormed his way into the sacred precinct, although I observed that he did not dine at Simpleham, entered by the back door and was never permitted to play with any of Wharton's artefacts: (Major) Jack Moron, the fearless journalist, General 'Tiger' Nidgett, of the Royal Army Tailoring Corps, Mr Julian Birdbath, the man of letters, Dr Spacely Trellis, Bishop of Bevindon . . . Instead we had a thin, indignant voice preaching to us about the ecology of diving beetles and earthworms.

It was an awkward situation because this Peter Simple II had been a colleague for many years on *Private Eye*, we had been to each other's houses. I had even offended his wife by something I had written about him. All these things form a bond, and insofar as journalists can be, we were friends. Moreover, he was much poorer than I was, and had no other source of income. He had a young child or young children . . . I could not, in conscience, agitate to take his place merely because I coveted the job.

My problem was solved in a fortuitous way when, perhaps feeling my hot breath on his neck, or intercepting my baleful glances, Peter Simple II suddenly launched himself into a violent and entirely unprovoked attack on me. It was a wonderfully happy moment.

The final settlement, however, may be seen as a Pyrrhic victory. Wharton, still burning with the holy fire which inspired him for nearly 40 years, took all his flocks, his servants and artefacts to the lush pastures of *The Sunday Telegraph* where he continues to delight and amaze the same readers – if slightly fewer of them, and less frequently than before. He reasonably claimed that the name of Peter Simple was morally his own, by virtue of long usage, and all the characters who adorned the column were also his own property, by virtue of his having created them.

It would have been unthinkable to have used these characters without his blessing, and almost as unthinkable to have used them even with his blessing in parallel with his own continuing output. My choice was between inventing a new set of characters, to complement or rival the Simpleham menagerie, or write an entirely different sort of column. I suggested the pseudonym of Paul Sly, possibly an illegitimate son of the great Simple, brought up in a cottage on the Simpleham estate by a gamekeeper's wife, and now going into the world as a cynical young opportunist, an Essex man whose acquaintance with the gracious life of Simpleham sharpens his awareness of the opportunities available to those who are selfish and ruthless enough. . . .

This seemed to find favour with everybody but then the Editor of *The Daily Telegraph*, Max Hastings, put the kybosh on it by saying that if he was paying for an established name he would use the established name. When I eventually arrived on 1st May, 1990, I was not sure whether I would be trying to start the Peter Simple column again, with a new set of characters or whether it would turn out to be a slightly up-market version of the style made famous by Ms Glenda Slagg – a gentler account of the world than was given by my opposite number on the *Sun*, Richard Littlejohn, and more touched, perhaps, by irony, but essentially covering the same ground.

Whether it was the result of some uncertainty of purpose on my part, or uncertainty of expectation on the part of others, the new Way of the World did not find universal favour when it appeared with a great fanfare of trumpets in May 1990 – least of all with Max Hastings, the Editor, and those who stood around him. This was partly because it was wobbling between identities and struck one or two embarrassingly false notes, but partly, as I believe, because it took time for others to adjust. Reading through the early months in order to prepare this book, I decided they were not nearly so bad as everybody said they were at the time, and that with the spectacular failures removed, some of them were really rather good.

The great complaint – apart from snobbery, occasional cruelty, and ignorance – has always been of gloom. It is my contention that gloom, if genially presented, and without rancour, is an enjoyable emotion, as well as being quite plainly the best approach to our national predicament. I see my role as that of a comic, raising morale by making merry jokes as the country goes to the dogs. It is not the most important role, nor the most admirable one, but I cannot see that it does any harm, and so long as it keeps some people happy, I hope to be allowed to continue with it.

The column has its admirers, but I have no idea how many. It also has its opponents, one of whom wrote to say that he much enjoyed the *Telegraph* but it made him sick to think of his money contributing to my wages. Again, I have no idea how many of them there are. There are many horrible things happening in the country, but by no means everything that happens is horrible. I would guess, in fact, that we are living in the happiest, most prosperous and carefree society in the history of Britain. Various conspiracies exist to pretend otherwise, of which the most interesting comes from the displaced intelligentsia, ranting against the standards of the new mass entertainment culture in all its undeniable ugliness and nastiness, as it replaces the humane bourgeois liberal culture of the last 150 years. Another major ingredient in the general gloom is the national propensity to whinge: although workers and unemployed alike are, for the most part, more comfortable and freer than they have ever been before, there is a general feeling that we are all missing out. If this book is seen as a celebration of the national gloom, I hope it also has the effect of cheering us up.

I should warn that the density and richness of the material make it unsuitable for prolonged reading. Perhaps the best plan is to have a copy in every room for immediate relief in moments of desolation, as well as several at your place of work to impress colleagues and visitors.

## Coup latest

AFTER a week of turmoil in the course of which the rest of the world held its breath and averted its eyes, the following joyful message has been received from Way of the World's Columnar Wireless Broadcasting Station at its new headquarters in Combe Florey, Somerset.

'Fellow British citizens, on behalf of the patriotic and well-meaning peoples of the middle belt and southern parts of this country, and the surviving pockets of civilisation in northern Britain, I happily wish to inform you of the successful ousting of the oppressive, malign, vituperative, inhumane, sadistic, deceitful, insanitary, longhaired, polygamistic, insect-infested and unpatriotic administration of the maggot-worshipping usurper known as Peter Simple II.

'Will all supporters of the overthrown pretender and pilgerist kindly report to the nearest Post Office, where arrangements will be made for them to be shot?'

As far as the eye can see, the West Country is ablaze with bonfires as villagers celebrate the news. From distant Kent we hear of an African elephant roasted outside Canterbury Cathedral. In Cornwall, where there are few elephants, the simple country folk have been turning bats inside out in their time-honoured Cornish way. Messages of congratulation and gifts of monkey skins have been received from the heads of all civilised nations and from many savage tribes.

## *9th May, 1990*

## New danger

I WONDER if any thought has been given to the possible threat to our British monarchy from this new Channel Tunnel. The worrying possibility occurs to me that our beloved Queen with her consort and all the Royal Family might get stuck in the middle of it during the grand opening ceremony. There they would remain as a permanent obstacle to the free movement of terrorists, drug dealers, paedophiles, horse-meat, rabid animals and all the other wonderful traffic we are expecting out of it.

Has anybody considered the constitutional implications of a monarchy stuck permanently under the sea, in territory which belongs to neither country, half-way between Britain and France? Many Britons are very worried about this.

# 14th May, 1990

## Nature queries

JUST as the Greens propose a universal 50 mph limit to reduce emissions of green-house gases, we learn that another villain is the domestic cow. The average cow emits 400 litres of deadly methane gas every day, we are told. Cows and other ruminants account for between 12 and 15 per cent of all methane emissions, or so the US Environmental Protection Agency claims.

Must we then slaughter our cows to stop the polar caps melting? I hate to point out, but if a cow emits 400 litres of gas a day, it stands to reason that an African elephant emits at least 2,000 litres. Can we still afford the luxury of contemplating these agreeable but useless beasts? What, if anything, should be done about the present epidemic of vegetarianism in young women?

## Panic stations

THE NEWS that a five-year-old cat in Bristol has died from bovine spongiform encephalopathy ('mad cow disease') may be a cause for sorrow, but is no proper reason for panic, according to the Ministry of Agriculture's chief veterinary officer, Mr Keith Meldrum. Despite their best endeavours, scientists have been unable to uncover any evidence that the disease is transmissible between species.

What these Ministry of Agriculture spokesmen fail to realise is how much we all enjoy a little panic now and again. The information that there has been no known case of bovine spongiform encephalopathy among human beings is not reassuring so much as deeply boring. I prefer the approach of the *Sun*'s doctor, Vernon Coleman, who informs us of a similar, if rare affliction among humans called the Creutzfeld-Jacob Disease:

'Mad Cow Disease could be the biggest threat to human health since the Black Death plague that killed millions in Europe in the 14th century . . . Over the last 15 years, my predictions about health hazards have invariably been right . . .

'Nearly 4,000 members of a tribe of cannibals in Papua New Guinea are believed to have died from the disease after eating a missionary who was infected with the virus . . . '

The message is clear. We must choose very carefully which missionaries we eat. Also, we should watch our cats very carefully for the fatal symptoms: sleepiness, loss of balance and irrational behaviour. If we have any reason to suspect our cat has caught the infection, we should play safe and refrain from eating it.

## Think sausage

I WONDER if the nation's politicians have any idea how very few Britons give a sausage for Parliament, its sovereignty, its time-honoured rituals, or anything else about it. This is a discovery I made during five years as a political correspondent, although I am not saying Britons are right. My only criticism of the House of Commons as it now emerges on our television screens is that the fig leaf has worn indecently thin and it no longer succeeds in its traditional role of covering the naked ambition and power urges of its Members.

I draw attention to this unpleasant and unwelcome development simply to beg Conservative politicians and their journalistic supporters to stop using the threat of reduced parliamentary sovereignty as an excuse for keeping us out of Europe and denying us the benefits of cheaper drink and tobacco and free movement. It won't work.

If they can't tell us the truth – that they want to go on bossing us around and exerting power over us – they might at least fall back on patriotic defence of the Good Old British Banger. Somebody must like the filthy things.

## *16th May, 1990*

---

## Bishops' move

SNIGGERS can be heard here and there at the publicly expressed opinion of Mr Brendon O'Friel, governor of Strangeways Prison, Manchester, that the Easter riot there was

probably the result of direct intervention by the Devil.

For many years it was unfashionable to believe in the existence of the Devil, but there is now evidence of a growing cult on both sides of the Atlantic, probably in reaction to recent developments in the Christian church, where bishops must act the part of kindergarten play leaders and Mickey Mouse is God.

The general response has been to seize any available kiddies or pets and sacrifice them in brutal black magic rituals. Adrian Berry, in *The Daily Telegraph*, quotes a deputy sheriff in Chicago as estimating that there are as many as 50,000 human sacrifices a year throughout the country, 'mainly of transients, runaways and babies conceived solely for sacrifice'.

In Britain, we were warned to lock up our pets on Walpurgis night, at the beginning of this month. On Thursday, in the House of Commons, Sir Geoffrey Howe had to restrain the Conservative MP for Littleborough, Mr Dickens, who wished to call an urgent debate on the growth of Satanism and devil worship.

I do not know whether the Bishop of Manchester, the Rt Rev Stanley Booth-Clibborn, who has so many interesting ideas

4

about the poll tax and social reform, also believes in the Devil. Whether he does or doesn't, he and his fellow bishops have their stipends to earn. Next time prisoners start sitting on prison roofs, a flying posse of bishops, armed with croziers and holy water, must be sent up to join them.

## Environment News

'BALLOONS are among the latex rubber products that are under fire. At least four billion are released in the United States each year, many settling on the sea, where sea animals eat them and choke to death' – *The Independent on Sunday*.

This means that every man, woman and child in the United States released, on average, more than 17 balloons a year, and about 11 million are released on average every day. Is there, in fact, a single recorded instance of a sea animal's death from trying to eat one?

Never mind. Let us have a national registration of balloons, with balloon wardens to enforce a £2,000 fine on anyone who cannot produce his balloon licence or registered balloon on demand, and a 10-year sentence for anyone who releases a balloon out of doors. That will show the world which country is greatest.

## *19th May, 1990*

---

## No kids

AT A specially summoned press conference in Community Liaison House, Det Chief Supt David 'Dave' Davey, Community Liaison supremo, introduced a typically British couple, Mikey and Dikey Domingo – he's 17½, she's a stunning 27 – who had a narrow escape when sick perverts called at their typically British home in Mandela Mansions, Tottenham.

Mikey described how three well-dressed strangers, two women and a man, came to the door and demanded to intimately examine their innocent children, saying they knew the Domingos had 2.03 of them. When asked how he had responded, Mikey replied: 'I said, "No way".'

Afterwards, he began to wonder whether they might not have been sick perverts from the evil network of fiends, and telephoned the picture desk of a national newspaper.

'I thought there was something odd,' explained Mikey, 'because although we are a typical British couple, we don't actually have any children. Dikey feels that Thatcher's government discriminates against single parents who cohabit.'

'I hate him, anyway,' explained Dikey. 'If I could afford to, I would move out tomorrow. I seriously regret having met him in the first place. We make love on average only twice a week.'

For once, the fiends seemed to have picked the wrong house. They may not be so unlucky next time.

## Federalism explained

SINCE it was launched in Monday's Way of the World, the movement to concentrate Common Market debate on the single issue of the British sausage has gone from strength to strength. At last people are beginning to understand what fancy words like 'federalism' really mean.

Federalism comes from the German word *Federalismus*, which, roughly translated, means a total ban on British sausages *even in Britain*, where they come from. Many people in Europe seem to forget that we fought two wars this century to stop people – mostly the Germans – from trying to make us 'federate', or eat foreign sausages, particularly German ones.

After the defeat of Hitler, when all the Huns, Krauts and Nazis had to pretend to be respectable, they decided to call themselves the German Federal Republic. The idea behind this was that they could continue to federate behind their frontiers, if they wanted, but they would never again try to force any other country to change its habits with regard to British sausages. All this seems to have been forgotten.

FACT: the German word for sausage is *wurst*, because even the Krauts know they are the worst in the world.

Order your exclusive Way of the World T-shirts now: SOS ('Save Our Sausages') for the hunky guys, GOBB ('Good Old British Bangers') for super-chicks.

## *26th May, 1990*

## Horrifically clear

THIS evening, at a time when most intelligent people are sitting down to dine, BBC2 will broadcast an immense international rock concert which is planned as the crowning glory to a week of debates, lectures and children's poetry readings on the subject of the environment.

The admirable idea behind this is to save the world from pollution. At a similar rock concert in Central Park, New York recently, environmentalists left behind 44 tons of litter, but that is not really the point. The theme of the week's events, which claims to have the Pope's blessing, is 'One World, One Voice'.

To speak in one voice – 'una voce' – was the traditional aspiration of the great Church over which Pope Wojtyla presides, although traditionally the voice was expressed in the beautiful cadences of medieval Latin. What sort of voice will we be hearing this evening, I wonder, under the Papal recommendation that we should all adopt it? What sort of 'one world' will we be offered to replace the infinite and exquisite variety of our present one?

The great and good Bob Geldof explains: 'To me, it is horrifically clear that if we don't make some drastic global environmental changes, the human race isn't going to be around that much longer.'

Such a risk might, indeed, be clear to him. I have a feeling that if I could bring myself to watch television this evening, listen to the terrible noises and contemplate the monstrous sights on offer, I might find it easier to reconcile myself to his presentiment. A new peace of mind may be born.

## Sporting news

AN ADVERTISEMENT for British Gas which showed a baby swimming under water has come in for heavy criticism from the Royal Society for the Prevention of Accidents, on the grounds that many mothers will now attempt to teach their babies underwater swimming at a time when insufficient research has been done on the effect of water pressure on babies.

So it looks as if we will have to cancel the babies' underwater swimming race at Combe Florey's Church Fete this year.

Attempts to introduce the new sport of rottweiler racing at the Crayford greyhound track in Kent have been frustrated by the track's owner, Ladbroke's, who feared it would be bad for their image. The rottweilers were to have chased an electrically-operated baby doll, in place of the more usual hare. The race had to run behind closed doors in Hackney stadium.

Even the tortoise race has had to be cancelled at the Combe Florey Church Fete as a result of this Government's insanely bossy 1982 ban on importing tortoises. Secret plans are being made for a Crawling Babies Race. The babies, when let out of their traps, will be invited to chase after a Pekingese puppy. Now we must expect objections from the new pressure group, Parents for Safe Food. I can only say that during the war, when coal was rationed, we British babies ate odder things than the occasional Pekingese puppy – and, at the and of the day, succeeded in giving Herr Hitler a thrashing from which he never quite recovered.

## Her loveliness

IN THE same week that two American academics – one of them a mathematician – have published their discovery that Queen Elizabeth I was the true author of Shakespeare's poems and sonnets, a group of muck-raking English journalists has suggested that *Budgie and Bendick's Point*, the Duchess of York's sequel to her masterpiece of children's literature called *Budgie the Little Helicopter*, is a plagiarism, copied from Arthur Baldwin's *Hector the Helicopter* published in 1964.

Only Americans, it seems, are nowadays prepared to treat royalty with proper reverence. It would serve us all right if Her Loveliness the Duchess went to live in the United States with her handsome, hunky husband and their two delicious children.

The charge, of course, is utterly baseless. Apart from anything else, the books are about two different helicopters, one called

Budgie, the other called Hector. They may have had much the same adventures, but they are totally different helicopters.

Even if Her Loveliness had copied out Baldwin's book word for word – which she certainly didn't – that would have been quite a creditable achievement, when one thinks how many other calls there must be on her precious time, and how many millions of young people nowadays would be unable to do it.

On the question of Shakespeare's plays, I have always favoured the theory that they were written by Queen Elizabeth the Queen Mother. Nobody else, I would venture, has ever possessed the same lightness of touch.

## *28th May, 1990*

### Call to arms

CAN IT really be true that Labour victors on Bradford City Council have decided to cut back on rubbish collection in the better parts of the city as a blow against the rich, who are thought to be doing well out of Poll Tax?

Ever since the news came through, bells have been ringing in caves deep in the Somerset countryside. Hidden stock-piles of weapons left behind by the retreating Americans at the end of the last war are being taken out of their grease. In the Operations Room of a secret underground headquarters, beautiful long-legged young women await instructions given in crisp, patrician voices to move flags across the map. The Class Vengeance Brigade has been mobilised at last.

A first step will be to contain the Bradford peril. The city's town hall will have all its exits and entrances blocked by bags of rubbish collected from the homes of Bradford's better class of citizen, as well as from various ducal residences on the route.

Next the homes of Labour's councillors shut inside the Town Hall will be razed to the ground, and the sites turned into municipal rubbish dumps. Those who voted socialist in the municipal election will be permitted to buy certificates declaring they have broken with their past and will never vote socialist again. After taking an oath of allegiance to the House of Lords, they will be allowed to resume the dipping and dyeing of sheep's wool with no further mention of this sad episode in the history of Britain's working class.

## Defiance

IT CAN scarcely be a coincidence that Mr 'Chris' Patten chose this week to hurl defiance at the bureaucrats and busybodies of Europe in his defence of dirty British beaches. Monday, as many people will be pointing out, is the 50th anniversary of Churchill's famous speech marking another occasion when Britain stood alone:

'We shall fight on the beaches, we shall fight on the landing grounds, we shall fight in the fields and in the streets, we shall fight in the hills; we shall never surrender.'

Chris and his Department of the Environment team have been every bit as brave in their defiance. 'The Government's position will be that we should expect to mount a vigorous defence,' said the Department. And here it comes from Chris:

'I believe we will be able to demonstrate we are doing everything we should to meet the standards people in this country quite properly want. I don't think we can go any faster.'

That's the boy. Let them have it, Chris. It is the only thing these foreigners understand. Let them listen also to Mr 'Phil' King, Southport's chief tourism and attractions officer, who challenged anyone from the so-called EC to find out what a real British resort is like: 'And while they are here, I will glady jump in the sea and go for a swim.'

A George Medal for Phil. Chris for Prime Minister.

## Visitors

I WRITE with some authority on the subject of coastal pollution, being an acknowledged expert. A few weeks ago, I received a deputation of loyal burghers who came from distant Taunton to ask my advice about a large oil slick which had been reported on the north Devon coast.

'We hates to inconvenience your lordship,' said a trembling spoksman, 'but we'm be troubled for knowing what to think about he. There's them as says 'im be bad for fishing, like, but us has been thinking your lordship be mighty in favour of pollution for keeping 'm grockles away.'

They watched me anxiously while I pondered the question. Eventually someone at the back saw what can only have been a ray of benevolence pass over my brow, and misinterpreted it:

'Three cheers for oil slick. Hip, hip,' he piped. A ragged cheer went up, before I silenced them with the merest hint of a frown.

Oil, I told them, was an unpleasing substance of foreign origins. We should not rejoice when it arrives on our beaches. What we Britons expect to find at the seaside is untreated sewage which, with home-made industrial effluent, creates the pleasing bubble bath effect even while it adds colour and pungency to what might otherwise be a dull and inert liquid.

So there was no need for them to ambush or obstruct the volunteers coming down from unmentionable places like Sheffield and Leeds to clean up Devon beaches. Such people were much better ignored, I said, indicating that the audience was at an end.

They thanked me profusely as they were led back into the kitchens  where they would be given sausages and ale  in preparation for the long return journey to Taunton.

## 2nd June, 1990

### Now why

ANTI-JAPANESE feeling is running high in Camberley Heath, Surrey, by an account in Thursday's *Sun*. It tells how a Japanese electronics company bought the local golf course for £7.3 million, and allegedly refused corporate membership to an English consultancy firm. The club's manager insists British firms can apply.

Keith Appleby, who runs the firm, is quoted as having told the *Sun*'s Jamie Pyatt: 'I never thought a Jap would tell me where to play golf. There is now [sic] way we should stand for it.'

This reported statement marks a major development in written English, which will no doubt be of particular interest to Oxford's new Rupert Murdoch Professor of Language and Communications, when appointed.

For some years I have remarked that where an ordinary Englishman would say 'we will not stand for it', the New Brit feels bound to prefer: 'there is no way we should stand for it.' I had also noticed, without commenting on it, that in spoken English, this usually came across as 'there is now way.'

In fact the Murdoch phonetic grammar may already be out of date. What the New Brit more often says, nowadays, is: 'there is *now why* we should stand for it.'

These developments in written English, if they pass into general acceptance, may make it harder for us to communicate with other English-speaking nations, but then there is no particular reason to suppose that Americans, Canadians, Australians, Indians and the rest of them will have much interest in what we have to say.

Perhaps I should apply for the Rupert Murdoch Chair. I have an uneasy feeling that nobody else is much interested in these developments.

## *4th June, 1990*

### English made easy

FURTHER to my note about defending the British sausage, a correspondent suggests that the German exclamation: 'Das ist mir Wurst!' – I couldn't give a d\*mn, literally 'That's sausage to me' – suggests that not even the Germans have much regard for their loathsome travesties of a sausage.

By contrast, in Britain, whenever we read a beautiful poem, hear some beautiful music or see a beautiful woman, we are as likely as not to exclaim: 'Pure sausage!', 'Almost sausage-like in its multi-layered tonality!' or 'What a fine piece of sausage we have here!' (Way of the World Simple English Guide for Foreigners).

## *23rd June, 1990*

### Bless them all

WE MUST not laugh at the Bishop of Gloucester for his suggestion that there should be a Church of England ceremony to mark a divorce, as well as one to witness a marriage. He does not propose that divorce should be recognised as a sacrament, and anything which gets religion into the newspapers is surely to be encouraged.

A few years ago we heard proposals for a religious service to bless an abortion, but that proposal seems to have petered out. One obvious gap in the existing liturgy, it seems to me, is for a service to bless a sex change operation.

More and more people are adopting this response to the pressures of our times, and churchmen cannot be happy to see themselves left out of the act. There are those who have suggested that it might offer a temporary, side-door compromise solution to the vexed problem of female ordination. Male clergymen who really want women priests could volunteer to blaze the trail.

As a member of the Church's Board for Social Responsibility, Bishop Yates should be particularly concerned about the fate of trans-sexuals who are sent to prison. Under the present dispensation, they are sent to prisons catering for their original gender. After the Strangeways riot, this does not seem a particularly good idea, although I cannot for the life of me think what would be the best solution. Even the notion that life should consist of nothing but an ongoing religious ceremony does not seem a particularly good idea after Strangeways.

## Bite the children

ONE schoolchild in three has been attacked by a dog, the majority being bitten, according to a survey in the *Indy*, a weekly magazine for young people, which claims to have consulted 7,500 children.

My first reaction was to wonder whether our dogs may not be trying to tell us something about our children. Would the little dears not be happier with a tiny bit more discipline? Since we obviously can't impose it ourselves, perhaps the dogs feel they might lend a hand.

My second reaction was to suppose that it illustrated the enduring gullibility of grown-ups. Not all children are liars, of course – many of them are extremely truthful, especially when speaking to Esther Rantzen on Childline – but no self-respecting child is going to tell the truth when filling in a survey questionnaire.

But the RSPCA, the National Farmers Union and other interested bodies have seized upon the survey as further evidence in support of their Hitler-style plans for the national registration of dogs, whereby, for a fee of £15, every dog in the

country would be put on an enormous list and supervised by a new army of officials, administrators, outreach welfare visitors and canine experts.

Although I am not a member of the RSPCA, I am a member of the National Farmers Union and a Patron, I think, of the National Canine Defence League. Nobody has asked me for my opinion. How dare these bodies claim to represent my views?

In my home I have three pekingeses and a Lhasa Apso, as well as a floating population of spaniels, red setters, whippets and assorted mongrels. This is not the time to ask ourselves how having their names on a national register will prevent them from biting any schoolchildren who visit. We should rather ask whether we should not be prepared to bite the schoolchildren ourselves.

### Historic moment

THERE was much fearsome talk of the New Conservative Woman at the 60th Conservative Women's National Conference, but I was happy to see none of them in the Royal Horticultural Halls in Vincent Square this weekend. Conservative women are the most delicate and delightful creatures alive, and I was not seriously alarmed to hear the chairman, Mrs Wendy Mitchell, announce that it was time to put an end to the lie that Tory women always have silver spoons in their mouths and flowers in their hats.

I had never heard this lie uttered, but it is a fact that flowers generally improve a woman's hat, and I have always been in the habit of wearing them on my annual visit to the Conservative Women's Conference, as well as putting a silver spoon in my mouth.

When I am asked why I do this, I reply that with my small group from the Somerset branch of the Surtees Society – mostly retired majors - I feel that the simple joy of moving among so many Conservative women justifies the risk of exposure and humiliation. There can be no other gathering in the world where a loyal motion which congratulated the Government on introducing the community charge would be unanimously approved.

When at the end of the day we take off our flowery hats and frocks, remove the silver spoons from our mouths, we all have the feeling of having somehow taken part in the unfolding history of our times.

### What you eat

'DIS moi ce que tu manges, je te dirai ce que tu es' wrote the illustrious Brillat-Savarin in that crowning achievement of the French 19th century, *Physiologie du Gout* (1825). The German epicurean philosopher, Ludwig von Feuerbach summarised it somewhat brutally five years later: 'Der Dimensh ist, was er isst' ('Man is what he eats') – but nobody could pretend it was a new thought.

Now a Californian criminologist, Stephen Schoenthauer, is advancing what he believes to be the revolutionary idea that criminal behaviour is determined by diet. Cut out sweets and the various toxins contained in junk food, he argues, and the most hardened criminals will take to knitting, tapestry *petits points* and other benevolent pursuits.

Of course he is right, but like Feuerbach he ignores the influence of taste. However much we urge our children to eat fruit and bran, there will always be those who head straight for a diet of fishfingers, hamburgers, sweets, lighter fuel and other solvents, just as there are babies who will ignore all the nourishing coal laid out for them in the grate and head straight for any elastic bands and dog messes which have carelessly been left lying around on the carpet. Hence our crowded prisons.

## *27th June, 1990*

### Hard lesson

AFTER three days of driving rain I stare out over the Somerset countryside and begin to understand Mrs Thatcher's reluctance to send aid to the Russians. If they are starving, they have only themselves to blame. Perhaps the whole Gorbachev phenomenon is a gigantic trick to persuade us to lower our defences.

Why, otherwise, do the starving Russians continue to spend a daily £50 million increasing their military strength? According to the *Sun*, the Soviet Union adds two supersonic fighter planes, six tanks and one short-range nuclear missile to its arsenal every day, a £1 billion nuclear submarine every six weeks.

But perhaps that is a lie, too, put out by our own Ministry of Defence in order to discourage military spending cuts. At such bleak moments, we might be excused from asking ourselves the age-old question: what is truth?

A few weeks ago, the *Sunday Correspondent* decided to announce that Britain faced the worst drought this century. This week it explained why the end of the universe may be at hand. I understand that this pleasant and upright newspaper is in some sort of trouble, and I grieve for it.

In the same way, I feel our own perceptions of truth may be influenced by the weather, as we stare out over our sodden acres and curse the rain. Come another peep of sunshine, and I shall make up a litle parcel – baked beans, pork luncheon meat, fresh eggs, instant coffee, soap, toothpaste – and send it to the poor

Russians. What a hellish time they have been having these last 80 years or so! I am sure they have learnt their lesson, and will never vote Labour again.

# 30th June, 1990

## Recognition

I HOPE that the unknown woman who reported Major Peter Phillips, father-in-law of the Princess Royal, to the police for allegedly having alcohol on his breath at 12.30 pm is proud of her day's work. The  major has been fined and banned, and photographed in all the newspapers.

In parts of the United States, offenders who are convicted of driving over the limit are required to carry notices on their cars: 'Beware. I am a drunk driver.' Or so I have been told. One hears so many disgusting things about the United States nowadays that I will almost certainly never visit it again to find out the truth.

Our English weakness is not so much for drunk driving – we have one of the lowest records in the world – as for informing on each other to the police. Would it not be a good idea if informants were awarded a medal for each successful report to the police, which they could then wear whenever they went out of doors? I am sure this would encourage the rest of us to behave better, as well as to treat these model citizens with the respect they deserve.

# 2nd July, 1990

## So intelligent

IN THE *Spectator* this week we learn of a shocking practical joke played on the Royal Family while it was living at Windsor during the 1939-45 War by the late Sir Osbert Sitwell. Queen Elizabeth was worried about her children's education, so Sir Osbert arranged for a poetry evening, with readings by himself and his sister, Edith.

Finally he produced a 'rather lugubrious man in a suit', who turned out to be the American T.S. Eliot, to read *The Waste Land*, What might have been a most embarrassing occasion was turned into a riot of fun by the Royal Family's excellent sense of humour.

'First the girls got the giggles, then I did, and then even the King', reveals Her Majesty in a private conversation with A.N. Wilson, the novelist and biographer.

This seems to me a tribute to the Royal Family's education, as well as to its natural intelligence. How many students today could be relied upon to see the absurdity of this gloomy nonsense read by a portentous American in a suit? Nowadays, they would all sit goggle-eyed with their mouths hanging open, trying to look sensitive.

I wonder if I might persuade the Queen Mother to present the Literary Review's Grand £5,000 Prize for Real Poetry in August. It promises to be the main cultural event of the summer.

## *7th July, 1990*

### Biscuit days

IN ALL my West African travels, I never had occasion to visit Cameroon, where French and English are spoken interchangeably in the elegant cafés and beer gardens of Yaounde among the streams and shaded avenues for which the country's capital is famous.

Why, then, did I find myself burning with sudden Cameroonian patriotism on Sunday? Why did I cheer every forward movement of their brave footballers, shining black against the Italian turf in the World Cup Quarter-Finals, why did I groan every time they were beaten back?

Odder still, large parts of Somerset seemed to be infected with the same enthusiasm for Cameroon, even among people who had never heard of the united republic before – or, if they had, tended to confuse it with macaroon, the delicious almond-flavoured biscuit. In London literary and artistic circles I found that support for Cameroon was more or less solid, with one or two licensed eccentrics, as was only to be expected, supporting the other side, apparently called 'England'.

The reason, I suspect, was resentment at the idea that these sweaty, incompetent louts and their grotesque supporters could possibly represent the country we know and love and call our own, the country of Shakespeare and Hardy, of Johnson, Wordsworth and Chesterton, Barchester, Grantchester, Wimbledon and *The Daily Telegraph*.

# 9th July, 1990

## Hail the chief

A 10ft high bronze statue of Lord Mountbatten of Burma which has been unveiled in Southampton, near his home at Broadlands, has an unusual feature. The former chief of defence staff is portrayed standing informally in naval uniform while his left hand would appear to be engaged in either scratching his bottom or lifting the back of his tunic.

I am the last to hold forth on the subject of modern art, which is a closed book to me, but I cannot help wondering if the sculptress, Greta Berlin, was aware of the ribald association which the British Services attach to this image of the left-handed shirt-lifter.

Almost certainly not. Even so it might be a good idea, to save general embarrassment and distress, if the statue could be shipped to somewhere east of Suez – possibly Calcutta – where the Indians are bound to have fond memories of their last Viceroy, and where it would almost certainly not bear the same symbolic loading.

# 11th July, 1990

## Confession

IT IS seldom, in the pampered world of the chattering classes, as we newspaper commentators are called, that a genuine, raw emotion breaks surface. I hope our readers will credit the genuineness of our feelings as we contemplate the unspeakable behaviour of our colleague, the novelist A. N. Wilson, in revealing his conversations with the Queen Mother at a private dinner party.

All civilisation may be at an end as a result of Wilson's action but that is a minor matter. Civilisation comes to an end most weeks. We can't feel very emotional about that. The emotion sweeping us all is not one of terror or outrage, but the far more terrible emotion of jealousy.

I must confess to feeling it myself. I am jealous that Wilson was seated next to the Queen Mother at a dinner party. I am jealous that she regaled him with so many delightful anecdotes.

I am jealous that he put them to such good use. Above all, I am jealous at the furore he has excited, the bitter denunciations, the anathemas, the mocking profiles, the revelations of his marital difficulties by one of our most high-principled Sunday newspapers.

I will fight against this unworthy emotion. But I feel I should warn the world that if ever, in the future, I make a slighting reference to this exceptionally gifted writer, it should be disregarded. Jealousy is a most destructive and reprehensible feeling. Forgive me. I bleed.

## 16th July, 1990

### Aren't they sweet?

A NEW biography of Anthony Trollope, by Richard Mullen (from Duckworth) makes the point that Trollope could educate his two sons privately on five per cent of his income as an employee of the Post Office. Anyone reckoning to educate two sons on five per cent of his income nowadays would need to earn about £400,000 a year after tax.

One of the great scandals of our time is undoubtedly the extravagant increase in the cost of private education. Oddly enough, one hears few complaints from middle-class parents as they beggar themselves to provide their indifferent offspring with physics laboratories, language laboratories, computer laboratories and such-like foppery.

Instead, we hear a great wail from the so-called poor, who have these things provided free. Last Monday, the Child Poverty Action Group solemnly announced that it costs at least £164,000 for the average couple to raise a child to the age of 16, of which £122,000 is made up of wages the mother might have earned if she had not been raising children.

Perhaps it would be a good idea if the working class gave up having children. There was a time when these 'kiddies', as they were called, made themselves useful in various small ways as well as striking picturesque attitudes and keeping the rest of us on our toes with their ribald, irreverent, laconic wit. But it could well be that the entire British working class has become something that we, as a nation, can no longer afford, like French chefs, *premier cru* Bordeaux and Easter eggs from Fabergé.

# Existential

LONDON children, or 'kids' as they are rudely called, have taken to crawling down sewers, where they could be overcome by lethal gases and pick up infections, according to Thames Water authority. Its spokesman, Peter Jakes, who reveals that they have had to seal sewer entrances with cement, adds 'it is an extremely dangerous thing to do'.

Experts think the new craze is brought about by a children's television programme showing some mutant turtles who live in the sewers, apparently without harm to themselves.

This explanation strikes me as unlikely. Children who watch television all day seldom have time to do exciting things like explore sewers. A possible explanation is that they are trying to escape from television, but I doubt that, too. The terrible thought occurs to me that if there has indeed been a significant migration of London kids and kiddies into the sewers, it could be the result of a dawning existential suspicion that this is their destiny, this is where they really belong.

# *4th August, 1990*

## Happy hour

IT IS quite true, as the Employment Secretary, Mr Michael Howard, has pointed out, that nearly all the historic monuments and beauty spots of England are swamped by hordes of tourists. Like starlings, they disfigure wherever they settle, destroying its peace and serenity with their noise and their mess; like locusts they strip its vitality, leaving a wilderness of car parks and toilets behind.

But the phenomenon is not confined to Britain. It is a worldwide product of mass prosperity, which has made me reluctantly decide to stay at home. People can think of nothing to do with their money except to move from place to place, spending it as they go. I do not honestly think that many of them really wish to see Wells Cathedral, or the Roman baths at Bath, or the Oxford and Cambridge Colleges. They have simply been told of these places – all, now, ruined, – as possible destinations for their journeys.

It was a brave idea of Mr Howard's to send them instead to the industrial wastelands of the north: to Liverpool's moribund docks, to the empty workshops of the Clyde, the cold furnaces of Consett, the despoiled housing schemes of Birkenhead and Kirkby New Town, where they can inspect the unemployed, feeding them with sweets and buns, if they wish.

I have no doubt that many will find this just as interesting and rather more instructive than treading the Quantock footpath once trod by Wordsworth and Coleridge. But many others resent having to see anything, and derive their enjoyment simply from being part of a crowd, like the hundreds of thousands who flock to Wembley Stadium without any chance of seeing Madonna except on the large television screens provided.

These people could surely be catered for on various desert islands around the world, where they can be delivered and taken away in cruise ships and huge aircraft, to sit for a few hours in a stadium with fizzy drinks and loud music and large television screens. I am thinking only of the greatest happiness for the greatest number, but there should be a quid or two in it for someone.

## You, the jury

SINCE 1981 it has been a criminal offence to disclose anything that happens in the jury room of an English court, if the revelations can be associated with a particular trial. Whatever the reasons behind the 1981 Contempt of Court Act which established this offence, its effect has been to draw a veil over the simple fact, plainly stated by the Recorder of London on his retirement last week, that the jury system no longer works in this country.

An excellent article in Monday's the *Sun*, by one of that newspaper's female writers, described her own jury service in an unidentified drugs trial: how the jury divided into two warring groups, those who would believe *anything* the police prosecution said, and those who would believe *nothing* the police prosecution said; how, after five hours of heated and shambolic arguments which had little to do with the evidence, much more to do with prejudice, emotion and simple stupidity, the jury allowed itself to be bullied into returning the wrong verdict.

Concern is often expressed about the number of unjustified acquittals, but I would have thought that unjustified convictions were almost as much a danger. Under the circumstances, it is strange that in the wake of Ian Gow's murder, a phone-in poll of *Sun* readers revealed 21,928 in favour of restoring the death penalty, only 432 against.

History has shown that it is not the typical *Daily Telegraph* reader who is most in danger of being hanged in error. Victims are always working class, nearly always mentally retarded. Perhaps it would save time and trouble if we abandoned the jury system and hanged 30 or so randomly selected *Sun* readers, every year.

This should satisfy their low taste for drastic punishment, while convincing the rest of us that something was being done to make the world a better place.

# 6th August, 1990

## Say please

THE NUMBER of people claiming sickness benefit, after being ill for over six months, has trebled in the last 12 years, according to the Social Security Advisory Committee. Of the 1,185,000 now claiming sickness benefit, it is reckoned that some 500,000 are simply long-term unemployed who have switched their claims.

One advantage is that the invalidity benefit of £46.90 a week is tax-free; another that the claimant does not have to be available for work. It helps to convince us that the government is winning the battle against unemployment.

But it is bad from another point of view, as it makes the nation seem to have suffered a dramatic deterioration in health, opening the door to every fanatic or quack remedy. It is also undignified for genuinely unemployed people to have to pretend they are ill. By no means all of us are very good at acting, and this is only slightly preferable to the earlier indignity, of having to pretend to apply for rotten jobs we did not want.

Any tinkering with welfare payments will always come up against the competing claims of need, entitlement and incentive. My own solution would be towards the idea of a discretionary entitlement, whereby anyone who sincerely does not want to work will be entitled to draw, say, £50 a week from his local post office whatever the state of his health, *but only if he asks for it politely*. It is the *rudeness* of New Britons which makes them so unattractive rather than their idleness or their ill-health.

## Never walk alone

MR JUSTICE Hidden's ruling at the High Court in Liverpool that, in certain circumstances, people can claim damages for psychological trauma incurred when watching television, may well herald a new golden age for the legal profession. I can think of few occasions when I have switched on the television without suffering some psychological trauma.

On this occasion, the claims are against South Yorkshire police from relatives of victims of the Hillsborough football disaster. Obviously, it would be thought very shocking in Liverpool if relatives of victims could not cash in somehow. But I wonder whether High Court decisions given in Liverpool should be allowed quite the same weight as High Court decisions given elsewhere – even whether Liverpool is a suitable place to hold a High Court. The two do not really seem to go together. Liverpool is so very special in so many ways . . .

## Treats

THE QUEEN Mother's 90th birthday on Saturday was an occasion which no one who lived through it can possibly forget. Where were you when you remembered it was Queen Elizabeth's birthday?

I was in the bath with a window open, listening to the birds singing outside and wishing that somebody would close it. To celebrate the occasion, I got out and closed it myself, reckoning that we all deserved a little peace on such an auspicious occasion.

Now it is all over. Next we must wait for the Princess of Wales's 90th birthday in 61 years' time. Then I really intend to let myself go.

## *8th August, 1990*

## Enough trouble

FOR 70 years the leaders of the Soviet Union protected its citizens from any knowledge of what was happening in the rest of the world by the simple expedient of preventing them from travelling abroad. They could never compare the freedom and prosperity of the West with their own poverty and oppression for that reason.

I wonder if the present government's reluctance to allow open frontiers with the rest of Europe is similarly inspired. There is a burgeoning awareness in this country of various awkward facts: that we have the most incompetent railway system in Europe, and possibly the most expensive in the world, for instance; that our public places are dirtier, our economy worse managed, our education system, road network, employment and inflation records are inferior, our environment more despoiled and families less protected than in any of our neighbouring countries.

Perhaps the solution is to close our frontiers and prevent all movement of people, goods or ideas. The first can be justified by the war against terrorism, the second by the war against drugs, the third by the need to protect us from child pornography and other unpleasant foreign enthusiasms.

## *11th August, 1990*

### Nature notes

ON MAY 13, 1988 I was amused to read a report in *The Daily Telegraph* that the Royal Society for the Protection of Birds had erected a mesh fence to keep bird-fanciers away from a colony of little terns on Great Yarmouth beach, whose numbers had grown from 20 pairs to 70 pairs in three years.

On August 2, 1990 I was interested to read a report in *The Daily Telegraph* as follows:

'Britain's biggest breeding colony of little terns, on Great Yarmouth Beach, Norfolk, where 201 pairs were nesting, has been largely wiped out by two hedgehogs and a kestrel.'

Kestrels, of course, are fanatically protected by all the high-tech and paramilitary resources of the multi-million pound RSPB, which on this occasion seems to have been hoist with its own petard, as they say. It is hard to know with whom we should sympathise most in this tale: the ordinary bird-fanciers, who were kept away from fancying little terns by a mesh fence put up by the superior bird-fanciers of the RSPB bureaucracy, or the unfortunate little terns, condemned to twitter away unseen.

My own sympathies are with the hedgehogs. They are delightful, if slightly flea-ridden, animals, with whom it is sometimes possible to hold an intelligent conversation. Has

25

anybody ever had an intelligent conversation with a little tern? Hedgehogs do not demand a whole apparatus of repression to survive. Every time a hedgehog wipes out a little tern, it is a blow for freedom.

# 13th August, 1990

## Glorious Thirteenth

TODAY the grouse-shooting season opens, a day late owing to the Glorious Twelfth having coincided with the tenth Sunday after Pentecost, or ninth after Trinity, according to taste. Normally this column would be devoted to a round-up of prospects on the various moors where Japanese and Arab sportsmen will be blazing away, with carefully veiled racist hints about the superiority of Japanese marksmen over their Arab colleagues.

But the noble sport is under attack from two directions. The Royal Society for the Protection of Birds accuses sportsmen and gamekeepers of mistaking hen harriers for grouse. Hen harriers are common and voracious birds of prey which eat grouse eggs in preference to any other sort of food, and are savagely protected by the bird fanatics, despite having quintupled their numbers in the last five years. They are easily mistaken for grouse, especially after lunch, but do not taste so good.

The second attack comes from firebrands in the Ramblers Association, who are demanding the right to ramble over all the country's grouse moors, thereby disturbing the grouse and destroying the sport. It is almost as illegal to shoot Ramblers as it is to shoot hen harriers, although Ramblers do not have the gigantic resources of the RSPB, with its electronic surveillance systems, to protect them.

But I am not suggesting that Ramblers should be shot at. They are clumsy, slow moving creatures, and there would be no sport in it. The best thing to do with Ramblers is to arrest them on suspicion of worrying hen harriers in the course of their rambling and hand them over to the RSPB, who will know what to do.

# 22nd August, 1990

## Sensible precaution

ARMY surplus stores have reported an enormous run on gas masks, as American tourists in this country prepare for an all-out war with the mad dog Butcher of Baghdad. Fortunately, I have been able to put my hands on three old civilian gas masks, carefully tidied away in an attic at the end of the last war, complete with their webbing satchels. I have no doubt they are better constructed and more effective than anything made nowadays.

It is not that I am anxious about Saddam Hussein's chemical weapons reaching London or Somerset. But I have noticed that since British Rail stopped travellers smoking throughout most of its overpriced and vilely incompetent service, people have taken to stuffing themselves with egg sandwiches.

I often carry my gas mask on the train between Taunton and Paddington against the foul smell of these refreshments, but have never dared to put it on in case it hurt people's feelings. Some of them might have a rare illness which requires them to eat egg sandwiches day and night.

Now we can all travel in gas masks, pretending to be frightened by the situation in the Middle East. This may prove one of the most useful foreign policy initiatives we have seen for a long time.

# 25th August, 1990

## Thought

'NOT A lot of people nowadays have two hot meals a day,' said a health service spokesman, explaining why hospital patients are to be fed on sandwiches. 'It is quite common just to have a hot meal at lunchtime and sandwiches and fruit in the evening,' said another.

I suppose this may be true. For years we have been told that technology was making us richer, but we eat less and drink less than we did 100 years ago, so where is the improvement? I remember when nearly everyone had three cooked meals a day *and* a substantial tea with cakes and scones and butter and jam.

Perhaps people lived less long, but at least there was some purpose in their lives.

If we ask ourselves where all the so-called money goes, I suppose we must decide that it goes on satellite dishes, on idiotic video machines which no one over the age of 45 can work, and on medicine. If satellite dishes, as I suspect, give you Legionnaire's Disease, and video machines drive you mad, there is growing evidence that most medicines do you no good at all.

It must surely make sense to cut down on medical treatment – which, if it has any good effect, can only prolong life into miserable old age. Then we can concentrate the vast resources of the National Health Service (which will soon employ one in three of the labour force) on providing four square meals a day for hospital patients.

# 27th August, 1990

## Open mind

A CURIOUS report from the *Telegraph*'s Scandinavian correspondent, called Julian Isherwood, in Friday's newspaper, announced the setting up of an international three-day brains trust on the anatomy of hate. The conference is held under the auspices of a Nobel Peace Prizewinner called Elie Wiesel.

It will be attended by the Presidents of France, Czechoslovakia and Lithuania, by former President Jimmy Carter, future President Nelson Mandela, by Henry Kissinger and Lech Walesa, by Nadine Gordimer and Gunther Grass. The organiser, Mr Michael Melchior, describes it as 'a sort of mental therapeutic jam session'. I hope they have remembered to ask Lady Antonia Pinter and her husband, the gifted playwright.

My only contribution is to keep an open mind about Saddam Hussein. Two years ago, we were told he was an absolutely splendid fellow, bulwark of moderation against the bloodthirsty tyrant Khomeini. Personally, I have never much liked the look of King Fahd of Saudi Arabia, but then I have never supposed that it matters very much what I think about these unpleasing, hairy people.

Why are so many people concerned to make us hate them in the right order? What does it matter? If the Conservatives don't try a little harder than this they are going to lose the next general election. That is all I know and all I need to know.

## *29th August, 1990*

---

### Rock of ages

THE OPEN mind which I am struggling to maintain on the subject of the next Archbishop of Canterbury (no less than on President Saddam Hussein) suffered a setback on Monday when I read a report from the *Telegraph*'s religious affairs correspondent Jonathan Petre that Bishop George Carey has suggested the word 'church' should be replaced by the word 'movement'.

Changes of this magnitude need very careful thought. He hopes to transform the Church of England into a 'unified Jesus movement', which sounds exciting. But what does it mean? A more familiar image of the Church is of a rock. Are we to see it as a rock in constant motion, swimming around like some monstrous whale?

In my copy of *The Grapevine*, official newspaper of the Bath and Wells Diocese, Bishop George refers to his new appointment as 'the hottest job in the Anglican Communion'. Bishop Nigel, his assistant, affirms that whatever Bishop George has set in motion at Bath and Wells will be continued. Perhaps it will, perhaps it won't. At least the village church at Combe Florey at the bottom of my garden seems to be anchored, as we tearfully wave goodbye to the unified Anglican Jesus movement.

## *11th September, 1990*

---

### Firm action

I WAS in Africa for the recall of Parliament and Emergency Debate on the Gulf crisis, but I am relieved to learn that the House of Commons was at its best. I had feared it might be otherwise.

In the event, our legislators rose to the occasion by creating a new imprisonable offence: British citizens can now receive up to seven years or be made to pay an unlimited fine for sending food parcels to anyone in Iraq.

As the news pages informed us: 'The government is

29

determined that food shall be allowed in only when the UN is satisfied that there is evidence of serious shortages leading to probable starvation.'

Whether or not a blockade is likely to work under those conditions remains to be seen. But the important thing is for the Government to be doing something. This invariably means creating new imprisonable offences for British citizens.

## Tell us more

SOUTH African newspapers are full of Iraqi atrocity stories: how in one day in Kuwait 120 people, including children, were shot in the neck and their bodies dumped as a warning on their families' doorsteps.

All these stories were date-lined London, which has obviously become the international clearing house for Iraqi atrocity stories. The more sober newspapers produced them as evidence that the propaganda war between the two sides was warming up, but none gave us the complementary Baghdad versions.

How many children is Mr Hurd alleged to have shot in the neck? How many female torsos have been discovered in Mrs Thatcher's deep freeze? One hopes there is no truth in any of these stories, but I would like to hear both sides. It is hard to escape the impression that some things are being held back.

# 12th September, 1990

## Highly effective

WHEN I was a boy I was taught it was cruel to shoot small birds and frogs, and shooting foxes was even more wicked. Certain birds were protected, and it was illegal to shoot them, but one thing you could never shoot was a poacher. This was partly because poaching was no longer a capital offence, but even if it had been, sportsmen were not allowed to take the law into their own hands.

All this has changed now that conservation, rather than sport, is all the rage. I learn from the *Guardian* that the World Wide Fund for Nature has supplied a helicopter gunship to the Zimbabwean national parks department, which flies around taking pot shots at people believed to be poachers after a herd of

black rhinoceros. At the last count, 57 alleged poachers had been killed in this manner which, according to the WWF, has proved 'highly effective'.

I suppose we should count ourselves lucky that in this country we can only be fined £1,000 for frightening or disturbing a bat, £2,000 for killing one. But I wonder how long our luck will last, as the Green frenzy grows. Any day now I expect to find a duffle-coated animal fanatic hiding in my attics or cellars and brandishing a pistol.

## *15th September, 1990*

### Vibrate elsewhere

THE CHURCH of England report called *Faith in the Countryside* is a beautiful, unworldly document. It might usefully be incorporated in the liturgy and intoned through the noses of the faithful at prayer.

At first glance, its proposals may seem to divide into pious supplications for more taxpayers' money, and more general exclamations of desire for endless new study groups, councils and reports: a Government transport review 'taking in social and economic needs, environmental pressures and the greenhouse effect'; 'training and enterprise councils for difficult rural areas'; 'new strategies' etc.

But at least two solid proposals emerge – that the Church should 'make available' (i.e. sell) rural land for low cost housing development, and that rural clergymen should receive a massive pay increase, with a further 'annual honorarium' for their lady wives.

The two obviously go together. There is even more money to be made in low cost, high density housing than there is in high cost, low density retirement homes. I was delighted to learn, from the example given in Wednesday's *Telegraph*, that local councils still refuse the Church planning permission to develop its land in this way, despite all the pious references to new strategies and our very serious concern with the greenhouse effect.

The Rev David Streater, of Kingham, west Oxfordshire, argued his case with passion/and conviction. Young people were moving out, he said; some couples were having to put off their wedding because they had nowhere to live. 'The district council could be more flexible with its village plan.

Villages should be vibrant communities . . . '

I suppose this is a reference to the amazing noises the young people will make out of their stereo systems once the Church has been able to spoil every village in the country with hideous new housing estates for them.

I have lived in country villages all my life. Perhaps average ages have increased, in line with the great retirement explosion, but I have never detected a great demand for vibrancy.

Perhaps it is just that young people are happier vibrating elsewhere.

## *19th September, 1990*

### Baffled

A WAXWORK of the Duchess of York in a York museum has been sexually molested by so many drunken Yorkshiremen that the curator has been forced to put it behind glass.

We in the South of England can comfort ourselves that Yorkshire is a long way away, and its most famous son, the Ripper, is safely behind bars, but then we read from a survey conducted in Sloane Square that one in eight women walking through that once-respectable area is ready and willing to pay for sex.

Now we learn that the BBC is preparing a film which will show passionate lesbian scenes involving a former gardening correspondent of the *Observer* and the daughter of a royal mistress.

Have we always been a nation of sex maniacs, or is this a new development? Are we being driven to this behaviour by lubricious newspapers and television, or is it our new predilection which shapes our television and press? Which came first, the chicken or the egg?

If waxworks are threatened, can Britain long be a safe place for chickens? When the last chicken has disappeared we may, perhaps, learn the answer to these baffling questions.

## *22nd September, 1990*

### Use of Liberalism

I HOPE that delegates at the Liberal Democrat conference in Blackpool this week do not feel they have been wasting their time. There were moments in the history of the old Liberal party when the whole gaggle of simpletons, exhibitionists and sexual deviants seemed a waste of time. But now they would appear to have found a new role, and a thoroughly useful one.

This is to debate some of the silliest ideas going the rounds – this week they proposed a higher rate of income tax for graduates and an elected House of Lords – and then, after due deliberation, defeat them resoundingly. Any other assembly might have thought the proposals too silly to discuss, but if these ideas are never properly debated, we never have an opportunity to agree how silly they are.

Next year I would like them to debate a motion that children at state schools should be required to drink a quarter of a pint of camel's milk every day, and also that children of parents who smoke should be taken into care by the local council.

These proposals may seem far-fetched, but they are exactly the sort of ideas adopted in secrecy by committees within the Department of Health, or Education, or the Environment and then implemented with all the gigantic powers of the state, without our knowledge, let alone our consent.

Those who feel it absurd that smoking should ever be considered reason enough for children to be taken away from their parents may reflect that a similar rule already applies in effect to adoption. By the decision of some committee, unreported at the time, it is virtually impossible for a couple to adopt a child if one of them smokes. Nobody outside that committee, wherever and whenever it met, had a chance to discuss the matter, let alone approve the decision. We were never even informed that it had been taken.

If only it had been proposed as a bright new idea at a Liberal party conference, we could all have had a good laugh at it and that would have been the end of the matter.


## All together

BUT there is a new and sinister threat which should be of concern to Liberals. They after all invented racism, sexism, ageism. The new threat can best be described as stoutism.

At first I thought it was only in the buffet at Taunton station, but now I realise there is a nationwide campaign to instal dining tables in railway buffets with benches immovably fixed to them, so small that they might have been designed for primary school children at their first lessons in making Plasticine worms.

The result is that those of a fuller figure have great difficulty in sitting down, with no chance at all of getting up. I suppose we shall have to form ourselves into a pressure group – Defence of the Fuller Figure (DOFF) under the chairmanship of Sir Cyril Smith.

It is an undignified and oppressive thing to be forced into joining a pressure group every time they think of a new way of annoying us. Politicians and administrators love pressure groups, as being part of a decision-making process over which they preside, but I have never met Sir Cyril Smith and am not at all sure that I wish to meet him. They say he is not so nice as he looks – nobody, perhaps, could be quite so nice as that – and stout parties do not necessarily rejoice in the company of even stouter ones. I see an evil conspiracy to force us all into pressure groups.

But if the fatties do not stick together, nobody else will stick up for them.

# 24th September, 1990

## Bald statement

WHEN I read in last week's *Sunday Telegraph* that a new injection brings hope to dwarfs, that dwarfism may be on the point of being eradicated, I resolved to hold my tongue. I am not a dwarf myself, and it must be quite disagreeable for those dwarfs who do not relish the state.

The fact that I like dwarfs is an irrelevant and selfish consideration. I saw one on the platform at Paddington station on Monday, and the sight made me happy all week. It has long been a secret ambition of mine to decorate one of the rooms at Combe Florey after King Philip's closet in Lepanto:

*The walls are hung with velvet that is black and soft as sin*
*And little dwarfs creep out of it and little dwarfs creep in.*

But to obstruct the whole march of science and humane medicine in the interests of a home decoration scheme would be inexcusable. Then I read in Friday's *Telegraph* that a new electromagnetic apparatus developed by scientists at the University of British Columbia brings hope to the bald; baldness, too, may be on the point of being eradicated.

The time has surely come to call a halt. I may not be a dwarf, but if I am slightly bald I am happy and proud to remain so. These scientists are trying to create a world where everybody is of a standard size and identically hairy. Only neurotics and social inadequates wish to look exactly the same as everyone else. In their struggle, they will destroy all the joy of creation.

# 26th September, 1990

## Circus time

AS SOCIALISM collapses in East Europe, most of the land, houses and other property taken over by the socialist states without compensation in the name of the working class is gradually being handed back to its rightful owners. I never thought I would live to see it. It is almost too wonderful to believe. But the complications involved, after more than 40 years of expropriation, must be truly horrifying.

Let us thank our lucky stars that the British never really took to socialism. We never suffered a Spartacist or proletarian revolution, and our respect for each other's property is so profoundly ingrained in our natures (except among a tiny criminal underclass) that we have not, traditionally, needed even a law of trespass.

I wonder how long this tradition can hold with the generation of New Brits, as ignorant of history as they are of politics, philosophy, economics and everything else. It would be a sad irony if socialism, after proving itself unworkable among all the lesser breeds without the law, next raised its brutal, grimacing head in the cradle of the free.

The Ramblers' Association, an organisation of 78,000 members, has announced a campaign of mass trespass on other people's property in order to establish its right to trample where it chooses. A statement, in the disgusting language of the times, said:

'We are firmly committed to maximising public enjoyment of our land and amenities. We have made massive inroads in improving the lot of ramblers.'

In one phrase, 'our land', these people shrug off the entire concept of private property and 2,000 years of human experience with a little shake of their cagoules. There are many more than 78,000 property owners in Britain – probably about 15 million of them. Such people tend to look unkindly on attempts to trample over their rights, as the original Spartacists discovered when 6,000 of them were crucified by the Roman consul, M Licinius Crassus, along the Appian Way to the resounding cheers of the Roman mob in 71BC.

If the Ramblers' Association is really committed to maximising public enjoyment, its future role seems clear.

## *29th September, 1990*

### All fall down

IN WHAT list of busybody voluntary organisations, government watchdog committees or quango in-betweens can I learn about the British Safety Council? This was the body which chose to use a photograph of the Prince of Wales trussed up after

his recent polo accident to adorn one of its posters.

The Prince, obviously in pain, with his arm in a sling, appears beside the word 'ouch' in red letters, over the caption: 'One in three of all accidents are [sic] caused by falls'.

Perhaps the illiteracy of this message will be found endearing in Gazza's Britain, but surely not the rudeness. The council's representative explained: 'The poster is a legitimate use of a current news story to reinforce a public safety message. We do not intend to withdraw it. This is a news photograph being used to make an important safety point, and I cannot believe the Prince would object.'

In the event, the Prince *did* object, through the Lord Chamberlain's office. I hope nobody is impressed by the council's self-important claim that 100 people die and 20,000 are injured each year through falls at work, which cost industry 'more than £1 billion'.

Ever since mankind learnt to walk upright, members of both sexes have tended to fall over from time to time and injure themselves. The idea that the process will be ended, or significantly reduced, by sending these posters of the Prince of Wales in pain to 100,000 factories and offices in the British Isles is not even laughable.

The vulgarity and impertinence of many people who feel they have a good cause behind them are major features of the age. Why did they not use photographs of the Lockerbie victims to make the same important safety point?

## *6th October, 1990*

### Cry for help

AN EXCITING new group announced its formation in an advertisement on the front page of Tuesday's *Guardian*. It is called 'Quiet Desperation', a title which so exactly sums up the attitude of most civilised people to the modern world that one can see it sweeping the country. I decided to investigate further:

'We are a group of concerned citizens – professional, media, academic – who view the future with grave foreboding,' it began. No 'workers' you note. Not even any insistence on women or inner cities. Sounds just the thing. But immediately it starts to strike a wrong note.

'The natural environment is collapsing around us, under the combined weight of over-populated and misued technology,' it announces. I imagine this is the way the *Guardian* prints 'overpopulation and misused technology':

'Without firm action at government level the crisis could well be terminal.'

Oh dear. They propose a sort of intellectual task force which will propose policies when the natural environment has collapsed, rather as Col David Stirling once proposed a task force of volunteers to assist the government when law and order was thought to be about to break down in the Seventies.

Translated into plain English, the manifesto should read: 'We are a group of useless intellectuals who have just discovered that socialism does not work and are desperately in need of another issue to make us feel morally superior and self-important. Please help.'

If only their mothers had taught them how to play bridge, or canasta, or even racing demon.

# No help needed

'TWO teenagers were shot dead and two wounded in a fight in Dallas, Texas, over a gold tooth that had dropped from a boy's mouth' – AP report in Thursday's *Daily Telegraph*.

The grim truth is only beginning to emerge about conditions in the United States as its citizens reel under the effects of Saddam Hussein's oil blockade coming on top of the $500 billion Savings and Loan scandal, a record trade deficit and gigantic government debt.

Refugees reaching Baghdad before communications were cut off, tell of a country where 1,000 people are murdered every week, where rapes are so frequent that one woman jogging in New York's Central Park was raped eight times before completing the course. The fatal plague of Aids, whose growth was thought to have slowed down, has surged again.

Can it be long before the country collapses altogether? The fact that there are no reports of Americans eating their zoo animals is probably to be explained by the vegetarian madness which has also swept large sections of American society, making no small contribution to the nation's enfeebled state.

I hope the British embassy in Washington warns all Britons still stuck in that country to take good care of any gold teeth they may have. The best advice to them would probably be to stay indoors, and never to smile at strangers. But I do not think we can talk about American society having collapsed. It was never put together in the first place.

## 13th October, 1990

## Monumental folly

PETER Palumbo, the millionaire developer and much-loved chairman of the Arts Council, was in Holland the other day to address the first conference of an organisation called DoCoMoMo (Documentation and Conservation of Modern Movement).

He told delegates from 20 countries that 'indifference, inaction and inattention' threaten surviving examples of the Modern Movement in architecture. I should have thought that disgust, impatience and shame were graver threats to their survival.

Those that have not fallen down or been replaced by something even uglier and shoddier stand as monuments to human stupidity and affectation.

Perhaps there is a case to be made for documenting this aberration, and even conserving one or two examples as a terrible warning of what can happen to a culture when so many intelligent people lose interest in the arts. But the fight to restore aesthetic standards has scarcely started. In building development, the forces of stupidity and affectation have been joined by those of idleness and greed. The Modern Movement must be well and truly dead and all its horrible smells suppressed before it can be stuffed.

## *22nd October, 1990*

### All the Harolds

THE STRANGE, self-appointed committee of inquiry into Harold Macmillan's involvement in the forcible repatriations to the Soviet Union after the last war consisted of a former Foreign Office official, Lord Brimelow, two former professional soldiers and a journalist. They approached the matter, we are told, from an independent viewpoint, with entirely open minds, and paid all expenses of the four-year inquiry, including the printing of a 700-word 'report', out of their own pockets.

One of the former professional soldiers resigned after it was pointed out that he was deeply involved in the forcible repatriations from Austria. Lord Brimelow, it appears, worked in the department of the Foreign Office involved in implementing the Yalta agreement with Stalin, by which these unfortunate refugees from socialism were clubbed and trucked back to the paradise awaiting them.

Of all the motives involved in this 'independent' inquiry, the most inscrutable would appear to be those of the other soldier, Brig Anthony Cowgill, who would also appear to be the moving spirit behind the enterprise. Why is he so concerned to establish the Army's complicity in the planning of these events, when most of those who took part are ashamed enough of the Army's role in their execution?

For my own part, I keep an open mind about Harold Macmillan, as I do about Harold Wilson, Harold Hobson, Harold

Evans, Harold Pinter and Harold Saddam Hussein, although it is becoming harder and harder to keep an open mind about Harold 'Kim' Philby, whose innocence Macmillan once proclaimed. However, I cannot understand why, if Harold Macmillan was as innocent as every instinct tells us he must have been, it was necessary to hold this extraordinary shrill charade of 'independence' to pretend to prove it.

## Warning

IS IT all a practical joke, or is it something more sinister? On top of the discovery that lead-free petrol causes cancer, we learn that the new catalytic converters which will become compulsory on new cars by 1993 will convert car exhaust into hydrogen sulphide, a toxic, foul-smelling gas which stinks of rotten eggs and kills humans in a concentration of one part in a thousand.

One proposed solution is to add nickel to the mixture. This will produce emissions of nickel carbonyl, an established carcinogen or cancer-promoting agent.

People complain that the Germans never bothered to read *Mein Kampf* before acclaiming their new leader in 1933, although it had been freely available since 1925. The Greens make no secret of the fact that their aim is to reduce the human population on what they are pleased to call planet Earth. This information is freely available in their manifestos and pamphlets for anyone who can be bothered to read them. The ecological movement has seen some strange converts recently.

I hope the 553 foolish people who voted Green in the Eastbourne by-election knew what they were doing.

## 27th October, 1990

## Agony

LONDON this week has been entirely devoted to the State visit of President Cossiga of Italy. I find I have shaken his hand no fewer than four times. It is surprising anyone manages to get any work done.

My own chief anxiety has been whether or not to wear a black silk hat at my son's wedding next week. In favour of the motion is that they are very beautiful objects, there are   few

opportunities in life to give them an airing and, as with the Crown Jewels, them as has 'em wears 'em.

Against the motion is the fact that very few people still own them – mine is 60 years old, and new ones are prohibitively expensive – and it might be thought ostentatious or, even worse, divisive.

My problem is that I have no one to whom I can turn for advice. On this intimate matter, I can think of nobody alive whose advice I would particularly value. Perhaps the best thing would be to ask the advice of John Pilger, or Karl Miller, or Peter Palumbo, and then do the opposite.

## *31st October, 1990*

### An idea

THE GIGANTIC army now assembled in Saudi Arabia to defend that noble Kingdom against the evil republicans of Iraq bears many resemblances to the Crusades of old. One difference is that its bibles have been seized by the Saudi authorities in deference to whose susceptibilities the Cross may not be displayed, nor may any Christian services be held in public.

I wonder if the Saudis have heard about this new happy Christianity, where we all clap our hands, shut our eyes, smile sweetly and declare that Jesus loves us. If not, they are surely missing something.

It occurs to me that if President Bush decides, on balance, not to wage war against Iraq this time round, he might use his enormous military presence in the area to reclaim Saudi Arabia for Christendom. How happy everybody would be! The Americans would not have been wasting their time, nobody would have lost face, and we would have the comfort of knowing that our oil was blessed.

Perhaps this will be judged rather a tactless suggestion at the present time. It is just a thought.

## *7th November, 1990*

### Too few

FEWER than 69,000 out of the National Trust's two million members voted for a ban on deer hunting, while 64,000 voted against. Both sides had presumably been whipping up support, but the 93 per cent who did not bother to vote surely spoke loudest, declaring they were not interested in the squabble and were reasonably happy with things as they are.

If the Council decides to pay any attention to the vote, it will mean that 5,000 infiltrators – a quarter of one per cent of the membership – will have been able to impose their will on two million members. They will have been able to gain control of 625,000 acres of land and most of the finest buildings in the country for whatever foul purpose they chose, whether as bat farms or fox sanctuaries, in disregard of the wishes of those who gave it to the National Trust in the first place.

It is one of the weaknesses of democracy that those who make most noise generally get their way. Tightly organised pressure groups will take over the world, unless somebody does something to stop them.

We who live on the Quantocks, and on Exmoor and the

43

Brendons, know perfectly well that the deer will go mad and die if they are not hunted. They expect it with every fibre of their being. A wild deer which is not hunted does not become a fat, waddling contented thing which can be fed egg sandwiches by cooing animal lovers from the cities and suburbs. It instinctively realises there is no further point to its existence, develops various unthought-of diseases, turns up its toes and dies.

## *10th November, 1990*

### Colour problem

IS IT possible that the Sir Donald Maitland who appeared in Wednesday's newspapers as the chairman of the Health Education Authority is the same Foreign Office man who was once principal press secretary at Downing Street under Edward Heath? I feel we should be told.

His anxiety on Wednesday was that the BBC might be breaching a ban on tobacco advertising by showing sporting events which had been sponsored by tobacco companies. This ensured exposure of brand names and cigarette pack colours which, he felt, was as effective as direct advertising.

What a wonderful thing it must be – if it was indeed the former consul in Baghdad who was addressing us – to have reached the age of 68 and to have as your chief worry that British kiddies, watching sport, might be exposed to the brand name of a cigarette, or even to a colour of the sort used on a cigarette packet.

The problem is easily solved. A ban on all television coverage of sport would remove one danger, while a ban on all colour television would remove the other. This might reduce enjoyment of games like snooker on television, but Sir Donald's men have discovered, according to the *Independent*, that 'identifiable brand colour combinations are used in snooker competitions'.

Certain words like 'gold' or 'smooth' or 'flake' might also be thought to have tobacco connotations, and should therefore be banned. Perhaps fields of corn should be painted green in the summer to avoid confusion. What fun it must be to be chairman of the Health Education Authority.

### Have a good time

THE MOST terrifying aspect of modern America concerns relations between the sexes. A 27-year-old waitress in somewhere called Oshkosh, Wisconsin, who claims to have 46 different personalities, accepts that one of her personalities agreed to have sex with a 29-year-old supermarket worker, but charged the man with rape after the event because her other 45 personalities had not been consulted.

Much more alarming than this, she found Oshkosh police prepared to press the charge, and an Oshkosh court prepared to convict. Four of these 'personalities' were sworn in separately, and the court heard different evidence from all four. The wretched man now faces up to 10 years in prison.

Perhaps he can count himself lucky not to be convicted of 45 rapes, for which he would face 450 years in prison. A simple moral from this tale might be for visitors to the United States to avoid anywhere called Oshkosh, but I mention Oshkosh only to illustrate how the madness which we knew to exist in places like New York, San Francisco and Los Angeles has spread throughout the whole country.

I worry for the fate of ordinary English couples who find themselves visiting the United States. The Form of Consent which British law will soon require husbands and wives to sign before each and every act of marital love (or gross indecency, as the law prefers) will not begin to save them from prosecution in the United States, where multiple personalities will be expected to sign separately.

How many personalities are expected to sign? Must every personality of each partner consent to intercourse with every personality of the other? By my arithmetic, this would require anything up to 4,232 signatures before the first amorous advance could be contemplated. Married couples planning to visit the United States would be well advised to insist on separate bedrooms.

---

## Decline and fall

IT COMES as no surprise to learn that Pablo Picasso was regarded as a 'possible subversive' by the FBI, dedicated to the overthrow of the United States. My own suspicions were first aroused when I discovered that he was a reasonably competent draughtsman who could perfectly well have done proper pictures, if he had wanted.

With most 'modern artists' one feels that they must have been born with some terrible disability which prevents them from seeing things properly. Alternatively, they are victims of the Shirley Williams revolution, and have never been taught to draw, or to distinguish between what is beautiful and what is ugly.

But Pablo (or 'Harold' as I always called him) had no such excuse. He knew exactly what he was about. One of the founders of the Modern Movement in art, and one of its cleverest exponents, he saw quite clearly that its main purpose was to drive the Americans mad.

Now, 17 years after his death, we learn that the FBI's J. Edgar Hoover was on his trail as early as 1945, when he ordered an agent in Paris to keep him under surveillance in case he ever tried to come to the United States.

By 1945 it was already too late to save America's sanity. Harold's revolting 'pictures' were already changing hands in New York for tens of thousands of dollars. In no time at all, they would reach respectable art galleries in Lincoln, Nebraska and Oshkosh, Wisconsin. The United States was doomed.

## Ho!

A NEW piece of evidence from that deeply disturbed country appeared in one of the Sunday newspapers. It emerges that in order to counter the excesses of the feminist movement in America, American men are joining together for Wildman Weekends where they hope to rediscover their lost masculinity.

They spend their days running, dancing and talking about themselves before retiring to a 'sweat lodge' – a sort of heated wigwam – where they cram together to sweat out the 20th century.

In conversation, the men (most aged between 35 and 75) try to come to terms with their failure to relate to their fathers, breaking off to hug each other 'as an expression of warmth and respect, but never pity'.

They honour older men by beating drums and shouting 'Ho' at them by way of verbal support as Indian warriors used to do. Gracious, how Picasso must be laughing in his grave!

## *17th November, 1990*

### And so farewell

THEY telephoned me in the early hours with the news that Muggeridge had finally died at the age of 87. I knew him first as a boy in Portofino, Liguria, when he was a sprightly 50-year-old, taking his first lessons in water-skiing.

On our last meetings, he talked incessantly of death, saying how much he was looking forward to it. This struck me as being rather rude to the living – not least to his dear wife, Kitty – and I rebuked him for it.

It cannot have been in order to prolong his life that in old age he became a teetotaller and vegetarian, renouncing all but the most spiritual of life's pleasures with a vehemence which seemed to repudiate everything he said about the vanity of seeking the Kingdom of Heaven on earth.

I urged that we must all decide whether we are on earth or not. If we are, there is solid comfort to be derived from good wine and cooked meat. If not, of course, we will have to make do as best we can with pleasures of the spirit.

When I put this point to him, wise old bird that he was, he fell asleep. Perhaps his death illustrates the unimportance of the transition from life to death. I do not know. Like many wise old birds, he attracted the attention of ornithologists from all over the world, who may or may not have been a nuisance to him. Now he has finally dropped from his perch, they will have to go away. There is nothing to be said about him which he has not said himself, rather better, many times over.

## 19th November, 1990

### Folly diverted

BEST news of last week was surely that Sotheby's has been left with a huge debt of $21 million, repayable to the estate of Henry Ford II, after a 45-minute sale of Impressionist and Modern pictures in New York failed to realise the prices which Sotheby's had guaranteed.

Perhaps it will be thought curmudgeonly to wish a pox on the whole market in 'modern art' and all who earn their bread in it, but we are bound to rejoice in any evidence that the Americans may be regaining their sanity.

The present collapse of the market in modern art is attributed to the Gulf crisis, however. For the life of me, I cannot see any connection between the two. The American government's readiness to send 40,000 troops across the world and risk an atrocious humiliating defeat in defence of a former trading partner's interest, is one thing; the readiness of American individuals, charitable foundations and investment trusts to spend millions of dollars on hideous modern rubbish is another.

Perhaps there is only a limited amount of foolishness available. If so much of it is devoted to political causes, there is less available to waste on repulsive travesties of art. If this is the true explanation, one at last begins to see some point and purpose to the Gulf crisis.

## 21st November, 1990

### Clouds of glory

IN MY early manhood I spent large amounts of time in the surgical wards of various National Health hospitals. One of the nicest things about them – and what succeeded in convincing me that the hospital service was inspired by genuine kindness rather than by the frenetic bossiness which has overtaken most aspects of the welfare state – was their attitude to smokers.

Patients were allowed to smoke almost anywhere. Junior doctors and nurses would join them for a quick, furtive cigarette. It was generally acknowledged in that friendly, easy-going atmosphere – many of the nurses were of Irish or West Indian

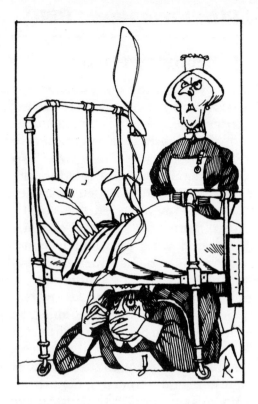

extraction – that more misery than benefit would result from a ban.

Now the heavy-booted fanatics of the Health Education Authority are moving in. A blacklist has been drawn up of 29 out of the 190 district health authorities which still allow tobacco to be sold to patients and staff in hospitals. Voices are raised saying that patients should be prevented from smoking even in specially set-aside areas.

The usual questionable statistics are trotted out. It is claimed that treatment of smoking-related diseases costs the NHS more than £500 million a year. In fact, the extra taxes paid by smokers – in excise duty and VAT – pay for half the entire hospital service. No doubt they pay for the Health Education Authority, too. That might be a good reason for giving up, except that the hospital service deserves whatever support we can give it.

## 24th November, 1990

### Dropping the pilot

ON THURSDAY the weather in Somerset was of a prelapsarian magnificence. Humming birds flitted through the bracken with little yelps of excitement, crocodiles croaked gratefully in the warm autumn sunshine, while on Exmoor I saw a female black panther gambolling with her cubs. There was a serene happiness in the air, as old age pensioners shuffled from thatched cottage to thatched cottage carrying their little bottles of champagne. It was no moment to be talking about politics.

Only an occasional distant scream told of a bird-fancier from Solihull who had fallen down a disused silver mine, or been set upon by a troupe of the giant toads which terrorise the Quantock Hills. On a footpath by Bicknoller Combe we found the grisly remains of a Friend of the Earth, come all the way from distant Frankfurt to demonstrate against the Quantock Staghounds. He had been much chewed by foxes, unless it was the staghounds which accounted for him first.

Retired bank managers and colonial servants and their wives took off their clothes and danced naked in their gardens, rejoicing in the timeless glory of creation. As evening drew on they resumed their clothes and settled beside their fires to discuss the events of the day.

## 26th November, 1990

### Cumberbatch

YOUTH and beauty are the most distinctive characteristics of women shown on television advertisements, according to a huge new survey undertaken by Aston University for the Broadcasting Standards Council.

This disgraceful fact, which none of us would have been able to guess without a two-year academic survey, is described as 'the very unacceptable face of sexism' in a report which describes this discovery as 'lending strong support to the concern that women exist in what is essentially a man's world'.

Perhaps most damning of all, the author of the report, Dr Guy Cumberbatch, concluded that 'women occupy a decorative role

50

far more commonly than is the case with men'.

Dr Cumberbatch also discovered that men outnumber women by two to one on television advertisements, but only one in 10 men (as opposed to one in three women) was slim, model or 'ideal' in appearance. Although men were more likely to be shown cooking than women, Dr Cumberbatch observed that when men cooked it was shown as a special and skilled activity. In one example, an Oxo advertisement, where the man cooked, there were even candles on the table to signify that it was a special event!

Or so I read in the *Guardian*. Life is too short to spend any moment of it reading Dr Cumberbatch's report. The world is full of earnest, ugly women who see the whole of human civilisation as a conspiracy to insult and humiliate earnest, ugly womanhood. Let us offer up a little moan of sympathy and think of something else.

## For the Chope

AN EDICT has gone out from someone called Mr Chope, Minister for Roads and Traffic, that from July 1 next year everybody travelling in the back of a car must be tied into it with a safety belt. He claims that this will save 100 lives a year.

One may doubt whether it will save anything like that number. The impressively low figure of 5,200 road deaths every year is made up almost entirely of pedestrians, bicyclists and motorcyclists in the first place, drivers and front-seat passengers in the second. Back-seat fatalities are comparatively rare, and few of them would be saved by tying passengers to the seat.

Even if it did reduce the figure of 667,000-odd people who die in this country every year by 100, one may doubt whether it is really worth the inconvenience and humiliation to everyone else to achieve this modest gain. Even more lives might be saved if passengers were required to wear full suits of armour made of tungsten carbide and lined with foam rubber.

One might even query why the Government makes it its business to force back-seat passengers to live longer, when overcrowding and excessive longevity are the major problems of the age.

But none of these anxieties is likely to trouble Mr Chope. He has done what every politician yearns to do, which is to press a little button and watch us all jump. If the exercise gives him an additional little thrill of self-righteousness, so much the better.

## Polite

EYEBROWS have been raised at Mr Major's decision to exclude all women from his Cabinet after 11½ years of successful female leadership. I suggest there are three possible explanations.

1. It would be unfair, humiliating and even insulting to any woman to expose her to comparison with Mrs Thatcher.

2. Tory womanhood has decided to renounce Cabinet office for all time in tribute to her leadership, rather as ratings in the Royal Navy still wear black silk in mourning for Lord Nelson.

3. The problems facing the economy are now so simple and so small that they do not need a woman's gigantic intellect, powers of concentration or fearlessness to tackle them. Would-be political saviours should now apply these dazzling qualities to the much greater problem of sorting out the nation's young.

## Faster, faster

THE LATEST issue of *Police* magazine has a story in it which will touch a chord among many motorists. It appears that last September PC Michael Batey stopped a driver on the M25 who seemed to be driving too slowly. The driver asked him if he was near Durham.

PC Batey replied no, Durham was about 300 miles away. The driver was visibly shaken. It appeared that he had left his home, near Rochester, Kent, 10 hours earlier, to drive to Durham, and had been driving round and round the M25 ever since. When stopped, he was 20 miles away from his home, but thought he must be near his journey's end.

It is not just all motorways which look alike in modern Britain. Even destinations tend to be indistinguishable, unless you happen to catch a glimpse of some surviving landmark, like the cathedral or castle in Durham, or the old Players cigarette factory in Nottingham.

Perhaps one day it will occur to all these people scurrying around that there is very little point, nowadays, in going anywhere. With all these wonderful new machines, we can communicate instantly with anyone, anywhere. Even this seems a questionable activity, when few of us have anything of interest or importance to communicate.

People differ very little between Rochester and Durham. Perhaps those in Durham are slightly smaller; but even this difference is disappearing. On the other hand, I suppose there are worse ways to spend the time than driving round and round the M25.

# *5th December, 1990*

## Nursery revolt

THERE is no formal notice advising you when you step from the British part of the newly opened Channel Tunnel into the part which has been dug by French engineers. Instead, you are assailed by the smell of Gauloise cigarette smoke and the sharp tang of coarse red wine in which French workmen delight.

This is because, unlike the British, French workers are allowed tobacco and wine underground. The British workers are expected to survive on tea and coffee. They are even not allowed to take their own food with them to work, for fear they drop crumbs.

I would not be so unpatriotic as to suggest that the French part of the tunnel is likely to be better constructed and last longer. But I do rather wonder what has happened to the British workman that he is prepared to put up with this sort of bullying from his employers, and what has happened to the British employer that he is prepared to accept such orders from the nanny state.

In my own profession, journalists working for the Murdoch empire in Wapping have accepted an absolute ban on drinking and face determined attempts to stop them smoking. It took the Russians over 70 years before they grew restive under the iron heel of socialism. I wonder how long it will take the English to turn on their persecutors and throw them into the Thames.

## Fair target

PARLIAMENT will soon vote for a fifteenth time since the abolition of the death penalty on a motion to restore it – this time for the murder of a policeman in the execution of his duty.

I imagine the same penalty will attach to the murder of a policewoman, but I wonder how the Bill will define 'duty'. Is a policeperson executing its duty when it stops a car to congratulate the driver on his good driving?

This is what police have been doing in Cumbria. They are the only circumstances in which I can imagine murdering a police officer. I hope there will be a specific exclusion on this point.

# *8th December, 1990*

## Toughest ever

NOW THE Christmas Misery campaign has started with a vengeance. Mr Christopher Chope, the junior Roads Minister, urges us all to inform on each other to the police if we suspect anyone of having had a drink before returning home from a private function – we are already accustomed to the unseemly scramble for the telephone whenever anybody leaves a pub.

It is all part of the Government's 'toughest-ever crackdown' to cut the number of alcohol-related road deaths over the Christmas period. Nothing is being spared in this £1 million campaign, from prolonged exposure of the genuinely bereaved to fictional horror sequences showing pretend-kiddies crying in their bedrooms.

Fortunately, the nannies have insisted that the horror sequences should be kept back until after nine o'clock when, with a bit of luck, kiddies have gone to bed and the rest of us will have had time to fortify ourselves against the horror of it all. Can any of us remember a Christmas which did not mark the Government's toughest ever crackdown? Isn't this what Christmas is all about?

# *10th December, 1990*

## The way ahead

THE House of Commons Select Committee on Home Affairs seems determined to scrap the 20p piece, or double florin, which has always struck me as the only successful innovation in the modern coinage. Many will disagree with me, saying that coins should be heavy and imposing things, even if they are worthless, but I have never seen the point of this argument.

My own proposal would divide coinage into the old decimal system, for paupers and sentimentalists to play about with, and for sounding impressive when put in the church box, and a new binary system for serious monetary purposes.

The old decimal system would thus include a 2½p coin (or 'tanner'), a 5p coin (or 'shilling') and the existing 10p coin (or 'florin'). The new, streamlined binary coinage would start with a 12½p coin (or 'half-crown') of small size but pleasing design rather like the old Indian 5-anna, a 25p piece (or 'crown') like the present heptagonal double florin but with milled edges, a 50p coin or half-sovereign like the old 5p coin but gold-coloured and with a raised, serrated rim, and the pound, or 'sovereign', as it is now but with a hole in the middle to aid identification and reduce weight.

As the coinage was debased, sovereigns could be used to make necklaces which would then be sold to tourists from Japan, Korea and Taiwan at an enormous premium. This is why children in our schools should at least be taught how to tie knots.

## *12th December, 1990*

### Kiddies' corner

NEW YEAR'S DAY will mark the beginning of National No Smacking Week, organised by a pressure group called Epoch ('End Physical Punishment of Children') as a prelude to making all forms of physical punishment unlawful, as they already are in Sweden and Austria.

I wonder how many parents will refrain from smacking a child after reflecting that it is National No Smacking Week. Will enthusiasts for corporal punishment – who seem to outnumber everyone else if I judge by my postbag – organise a contrary movement?

In National Smack a Child Week, everybody over the age of 35 would be expected to chastise at least one child every day. The purpose of this would be to teach the young that there is no justice on earth, and that they must learn to adjust themselves to other people's convenience.

## Joys of guilt

MARGARET DRABBLE, the gifted novelist, advances a new idea in her recently published pamphlet on the housing problem, that part of the enjoyment we all (or very nearly all) derive from home ownership is to be explained by unconscious gloating over the plight of the homeless, those asleep in the street.

'I have quite a lot of house of my own, and I am very attached to all of it,' she writes. 'I paid a lot and worked hard for my property, it has appreciated, it is mine and I enjoy it.'

Yet she, at least, finds no pleasure in contemplating the plight of those who worked less hard. My own theory is that the spectacle of the homeless may be necessary to keep the rest of us on the straight and narrow, to encourage our young people to be reasonably civil while they are still living at home and to get them out of bed in the morning.

This consideration obviously does not apply to the poor mental patients cruelly turned out of their hospitals into 'community care', but where the young and able-bodied are concerned I should have thought some sort of spur is essential.

Drabble sees them as victims of Mortgage Income Tax Relief, which, she thinks, discourages the provision of rented accommodation. But what discourages landlords is the certain knowledge some vote-seeking politican will come along and freeze the rents. This makes the provision of rented housing a mug's game.

'Are they also getting what they are asking for, do you think?' she asks of the homeless. 'Are they not rather the victims of our subsidised greed?' I should give the answer 'no' to both questions. They will have to do better than just ask for things. But it would be a terrible world if there was nothing we more fortunate folk could feel angry about. That is what adds spice to our enjoyment of the life for which we have all worked so hard.

## Merry-go-round

THIS WEEK's *Independent on Sunday* devoted a large area of its first page to the harrowing account of a London couple who are threatened with having their 20-month-old son taken away from them by Islington council on the grounds, apparently, that he has not put on sufficient weight.

The difference between this case and the many others we have read about in places like Cleveland and Newcastle is that on this occasion the father is a graduate in social administration and the mother a consultant community paediatrician who routinely diagnoses child abuse.

With the enormous growth in the child abuse industry I suppose it was inevitable that the experts would start confiscating each other's children before very long, just as a Nottingham policewoman posing as a prostitute once booked a police chief from another force for kerb crawling.

There simply aren't enough people for police and welfare services to arrest or spy on unless they start arresting or spying on themselves. But when we add to their huge numbers the new army of civilian informers – the Islington couple were victims, originally, of an anonymous denunciation to the NSPCC – then we begin to have the spectacle of a society chasing itself in circles.

One of the disagreeable things about hanging people of whom we disapprove is that it puts an abrupt end to the merry-go-round.

## *22nd December, 1990*

### The answer

BIT BY BIT, news begins to trickle through from the United States, now given over to rape, murder and unspeakable disease while the rest of the world averts its eyes.

One always supposed that some such fate awaited any country which allowed its working class to become too prosperous and too influential in the running of its affairs.

But the most terrifying news from behind the Gauze Curtain concerns what has happened to the country's so-called intelligentsia.

According to Charles Bremner, whose despatches appeared in *The Times* this week, more than 130 universities have now issued edicts laying down what subjects may or may not be freely discussed. Among the forbidden subjects at the University of Michigan are: 'race, ethnicity, religion, sex, sexual orientation, creed, national origin, ancestry, age, marital status, handicap or Vietnam-era status'.

At Smith College, 'lookism' – the belief that appearance may give some indication of a person's character or value – is expressly forbidden.

The University of Connecticut has given a warning against 'inappropriately directed laughter'.

In New York, epicentre of the national insanity, members of the University's law school refused to take part in a debate about lesbian rights on the grounds that any arguments allowed against them would be detrimental to the cause.

## The solution

AT PRESENT the illness is more or less confined to America. Supporters of the black teenagers convicted of raping and mutilating a jogger in Central Park argued that the accused could not be guilty of anything because they were the victims of centuries of oppression.

Anybody articulating such idiotic sentiments in Europe would be laughed to scorn, and it is not surprising that an element of anti-Europeanism has begun to surface in the American lunacy.

The study of Milton, Socrates, Racine and other great writers of the past is discouraged on the grounds that they belong to a rejected category of Dead White European Male.

The great task for European leaders is to make sure this epidemic never takes hold across the herring pond. I am no scientist, but I understand that many Americans are suffering from a form of Humour Immune-Deficiency, for which there is no cure.

Many experts believe you do not even need to share a lavatory seat with an American to catch it. A sneeze or a soulful glance is quite sufficient.

The next step must be to place the entire American continent out of bounds for Europeans and ban all traffic across the Atlantic. At the very least, visiting Americans should be kept in quarantine for nine months, under observation for any of the symptoms.

While in quarantine they should be subjected to laughter, inappropriately directed from every angle, to see how they react.

## *24th December, 1990*

### Keep honking anyway

THE SMARTEST and best-selling fashion accessory this Christmas season in Harrods has been the condom ear-ring set, according to Gail Counsell of the *Independent*. They come in packs of three – 'two to clip on and one to slip on', as the sales blurb puts it. At £7.95 a pack, 'they're just like chocolate money – you simply unwrap the gold foil and away you go,' according to an attractive young Harrods spokesperson.

Harrods customers, apparently, cannot get enough of them. The store has had to re-order them three times, and was running out for a fourth time when Gail Counsell called.

All the sparkiest, most daring young women will be wearing them this season, as if advertising their broadmindedness. But I wonder how many of these ear-rings will in fact ever be unwrapped.

It is a gloomy and possibly unpatriotic notion of mine that the whole idea of Bonking Britain may have been a myth, that the Eighties saw no more sexual activity than has always taken place, and possibly rather less.

Those car stickers saying: 'Have You Had It Today?' and 'Honk if you Bonk' always seemed to me to have a wistful air about them. But what really proves my point is the way each and every act of sexual intercourse by any star of stage or screen – and often by humble members of the public – has to be heralded in huge headlines by all the popular newspapers.

Even these widely proclaimed instances of sexual activity often turn out never to have taken place, as we later read in the law reports.

# Hero

IT MUST be making some incomprehensible statement or other about the alleged sexual revolution that these things should be worn by women, and worn on their ears.

I would hate to think it was another example of the woeful ignorance of the young, the failure of our teachers to impart even the most simple, practical information on any subject.

The Benedictine school in Somerset where I was educated did not advertise any course of instruction on where condoms should be worn, or by whom, but I left it with a pretty shrewd idea that they were not designed to be worn on the ears, or by women.

Under present circumstances of ignorance and mis-understanding, it would need a heroic man to wear them in public even as ear-rings, and there are very few male heroes around.

In order to foster what heroism remains, I have decided to appoint a columnar Hero of the Year annually at about this time. This year's award goes to the Right Honourable Michael Ray Dibdin Heseltine, Secretary of State for the Environment.

To crown a year of heroic endeavour, Heseltine has single-handedly won a reprieve from the European Commission which will enable us to keep our beaches dirty for another seven years. His junior Minister, Mr David Trippier, has described the concession as a 'great Christmas present' for the Government, but it is far, far more than that.

By defeating the European Environment Commissioner, Signor Carlo Ripa di Meana, on what we must all see as a crucial point of principle – our right, as Britons, to cover our beaches with sewage, cigarette ends, dog messes, and sweet papers as we see fit – Heseltine has shown that national identities can and will survive in a united Europe. He provides us all with a beacon of hope for the future. I will present him with the award – a handsome pair of ear-rings from Harrods – when next we bump into each other.

## The Terror

PERHAPS only a minority of voters will wake up to the threat when they read of Labour's detailed plan to outlaw the hunting of foxes, deer and hares for the first time in our island's 2,000-year history of modified tyranny. This measure will be enacted as a matter of urgent priority in the first session of a new socialist government, even as it grapples with the problems of a collapsed pound, a flight of savings, an IMF takeover and a general strike.

But an even more vivid picture of what the Hattersley-Kaufman Terror will involve is given by Roy Hattersley's Saying of the Year, quoted in Saturday's newspaper:

'If you cannot identify with 'Coronation Street' you are either profoundly insensitive or simply peculiar,' said Hattersley. I do not suppose I have watched this boring television programme more than twice in its 30 dismal years, but this was quite enough to convince me that anyone who claims to 'identify' with the programme must be either a backward working-class northerner over 65, or a misguided Labour politician who thinks that such people still make up a majority of voters.

But the menace in Hattersley's words is unmistakable. Anybody who is not prepared to toe the line in the moronic proletarian society he hopes to lead will be regarded as either 'insensitive' – i.e. potentially criminal – or 'peculiar' – i.e. insane.

The threat of this Hattersley-Kaufman Terror may have been averted, but I would not be too sure. It seems a lot of hope to repose in a single pair of phantom, vanishing moustaches.

## Gauze curtain

IN A breakdown of America's record year of violence – it is possible that more than 23,040 people will have been murdered by the time the final figures are in – I was interested to see the statistic that one in 1,000 young black men is now killed every year in the United States. This is 10 times the rate for whites.

In some areas of the country, according to a report in *The Times*, 'it is now more likely for a black male between his 15th and 24th birthday to die from homicide than it was for an American soldier to be killed on a tour of duty in Vietnam.'

At the time of the Vietnamese war, I remember it was

fashionable for visiting English journalists to express shock and dismay at the extraordinarily high proportion of blacks in the United States army. The suggestion was made that they found it harder to evade the draft than white middle-class boys, and were thus the victims of discrimination.

Now we know that in many cases they were having a lucky escape. When I have spent a few days in the United States in July for my nephew's wedding – I shall travel in bullet-proof armour, with protection against every known form of germ warfare – I may be in a position to write a book about what is happening there. It is odd that nobody else seems to be interested.

# 5th January, 1991

## Gruel is off

IN A late attempt to counter the dreadful problem of obesity among schoolchildren, Somerset County Council has stopped serving free meals to all and has put the poorer children – paradoxically the most prone to obesity – on a diet of cold food.

The menus look delicious to me: sandwiches of meat, Marmite and cheese, sausage rolls, quiche, cake, bananas, milk shakes. But Labour's education spokesman, Mr Jack Straw, takes a dim view: 'This menu is worse than workhouse food doled out in 1911,' he is quoted as saying. 'At least people in the workhouse got a hot meal.'

I am too young to remember the even more delicious food served in workhouses in 1911, but it is undoubtedly true that few things have improved since that crucial year, when Britain hovered on the brink of revolution and the Lords gave up their right to veto legislation emanating from the Commons. It is absurd for Jack Straw, who is even younger than I am, to suppose the country's poor will be as well fed now as they were at the beginning of the century, when Britain was so much richer, harder working and better governed than it is now. Hot meals? Hot meals? Let them eat Crunchie bars.

## Butterfly tax

AS WE shiver and groan in the icy winds sweeping across the country, we learn that Britain is pressing for the development of

Europe-wide 'green taxes' to reduce global warming from car exhausts.

If it takes 10 years for politicians in Westminster to assimilate a new idea, it takes 20 for them to get rid of it once it has been proved wrong. The myth of global warming has been exposed. A sun-spot cycle which gave us warmer weather for 11 years has ended. We are now destined for a cold spell. No human activity can make the smallest difference to the weather, compared to the effect of the sun's behaviour.

But once they have decided on a new way of raising taxes, of course we will be stuck for ever with the myth of global warming. If it does not warm the planet, carbon dioxide will be said to threaten the survival of cabbage white butterflies in built-up areas.

## 7th January, 1991

### Important members

THE GOVERNMENT'S insane decree of last week, making it a criminal offence to kill or injure an adder (or viper), might be seen as the reduction to absurdity of previous decrees, making it, for instance, an offence punishable by a fine of £1,000 to frighten or disturb a bat.

In a highly satirical moment, about eight years ago, I even suggested that the Government might make it a criminal offence to disturb or frighten vipers, wasps and horse-flies. Gracious, how we all chuckled at the time. But the Nature Conservancy Council is not remarkable for its sense of humour, and it may well be the horse-flies who are laughing now.

But I fancy that viper protection is a lunacy imported, like so many others, from the United States. There they herald the presence of rattle-snakes – considerably more lethal than adders – with notices:

'Rattlesnakes are important members of the local community. They will not attack, but if disturbed or cornered, they will defend themselves. Give them distance and respect.'

In America, it will soon be illegal to refer disparagingly to any serpent. Great chunks would have to be cut out of Shakespeare – 'O villains, vipers, damned without redemption' – except that soon Shakespeare will be banned in that demented country as being a Dead White European Male.

We may worry about Gazza and his generation of Shirley Williams victims, but goodness knows what the world will make of the new generation of young Americans. These poor creatures are the ones being sent in their hundreds of thousands to the Gulf.

## Feelings of dread

AS THE time for President Bush's ultimatum in the Gulf approaches, I have very little impression of excitement or dread or even of very keen interest in this country. Perhaps it is felt that the odds are sufficiently in our favour, with the United States (pop. 231 million) against Iraq (pop. 16 million) even before the rest of the world joined in on the American side.

Nevertheless, I have a dread that the Americans will somehow disgrace themselves. Everything would seem to depend on morale in the US Army. Since entertainment of any sort is forbidden in Saudi Arabia, the US authorities have hired five luxury cruise liners to be moored out in the Gulf, and are hiring English striptease artists from places as far apart as

Bournemouth and Bradford to entertain them there.

The Bournemouth entertainment agent who is arranging it all explains: 'I think they asked us because the Americans like English girls and because their own are stuck up. Anyway, stripping is a very English sort of thing.'

I suppose we should be proud that this little old country of ours is making whatever contribution it can, but I feel a certain hesitation. While I am reasonably confident that our troops can look after themselves against the Iraqis, I tremble for the fate of our English strippers among all those American soldiers.

## 14th January, 1991

### Meditation

AT LEAST once a year I feel we should all sit down and meditate about waste disposal. According to a report in the *Independent on Sunday*, the age of the long-haul dustbin has arrived. So short of dumping sites have we become that rubbish left out in London is liable to end up in Snowdonia, while Cardiff sends its rubbish to be dumped in Bedfordshire.

According to the National Association of Waste Disposal Contractors, the industry is being 'paralysed by Nimbyism'. This is the attitude identified by Nicholas Ridley, a bit of a Nimby himself, as an acronym for Not In My Back Yard.

Of course, none of us wants a rubbish dump in his backyard. Nimbyism is common sense. It may yet be identified as the ultimate democratic virtue. On the principle that if every householder sweeps the street in front of his house, then the street is clean, so if we all prevent rubbish dumps being allowed in our areas, the country will be dump-free.

The obvious solution is to send all our waste to the South Pole. Nobody lives there and nobody in his senses would ever want to live there. If half the energy put into such admirable causes as the CPRE were diverted into a new organisation, Enemies of the South Pole, England could become a green and pleasant land once again.

It need not be much more expensive than sending London waste to Snowdonia. Great ships carrying rubbish to Antarctica could return with delicious Australian and New Zealand wines, rabbit and kangaroo meat for our pekingeses, koala skins for our women, and old Australian mutton for boiling in caper sauce and feeding to the poor.

## Sian and Piers

SATURDAY's newspaper carried a report by Ross Clark which described two typical British university students of today. Sian and Piers live as a married couple, having teamed up after meeting at a party where they could not see or hear each other properly because of the darkness and loud music. That night they visited the Student Union condom machine for the first time, and have been together ever since.

They spend all their time swotting for their examinations, but have no interest or curiosity in their subjects. 'They do not argue, and will speak only when spoken to. They receive ideas but generate none,' wrote Clark.

All the brave, silly notions of 30 years ago have congealed into a peer-group consensus to which they rigidly adhere. 'If they do show any fire during their academic careers, it is likely to be when they accuse their lecturers of being "sexist" . . . ' When they have left, they will look back on these years at college as the best of their lives.

Is there nothing we can do for this dismal couple? Would electric shocks be of any help? Perhaps the university statutes could be amended to require all undergraduates to share their baths with an electric eel, in the interests of energy conservation and saving the ozone layer.

# 26th January, 1991

## Revênge

THE ENGLISH language has never, so far as I know, possessed a circumflex accent, and we are all the poorer for it. In ancient times, these agreeable things were used to warn of a rising or falling pitch in the vowel beneath; later, they merely indicated a strong vowel or they might, as in French, apostrophise an absent 's'.

In modern French, their function is entirely ornamental. This week the Académie Française (the sister organisation of our own Academy in Beak Street, London, but with a more official responsibility for the protection of the French language) firmly rebuffed a political attempt to abolish the circumflex accent, as well as to remove the 'i' from *oignon* and perpetrate various other outrages against public decency and established practice.

This action by our French colleagues – who are fairly elderly, for the most part – was all the more admirable because it transpired that at a meeting some months earlier, which most of them were not aware of having attended, they had unanimously approved the changes.

I have often observed how the French age better than we do. Would it be possible to find a group of distinguished old men in England who would lift a finger to protect the spelling of 'onion'?

It seems unlikely. They would argue that 'unnion' was more relevant to the young, the homeless, the unemployable northern working class, single mothers, victims of child abuse and the rest of it.

I begin to wonder whether perhaps in some distant, golden, long lost Arthurian past, written English did not indeed once boast a decorative, functionless circumflex accent. Then some ghastly committee of elderly academics, judges, alchemists, magicians and quack doctors met to decide that it was irrelevant and divisive, robbing the English once again of their ancient birthright.

## Save the children

ENOUGH has been said and written about this atrocious war in the Gulf. Every possible opinion has been thoroughly aired. Now that battle has been joined, the time has come for everyone to rally round and demonstrate support for allied war aims, which are no less than the full restoration of His Highness Sheikh Jaber al-Ahmed al-Sabah to the emirate of Kuwait, with all his 80 wives and as many of their children or kids as he chooses to acknowledge.

For this purpose, Way of the World is proud to provide a flag of Kuwait, which readers may cut out and display in various ways. Here are 10 ways to fly Way of the World's Flag of Kuwait.

1. Stick it on your car's rear window – making sure it does not obstruct your view.

2. Staple it between plastic sheets and fly it from a post in your garden or your car aerial.

3. Show it proudly from your bedroom or drawing room window.

4. Give it to your wife and ask her to embroider it on your waistcoat.

5. Hunting people can wear it on the ribands on their top hats.

6. If you are bald, you can stick it on the crown of your head.

7. If you have a secretary, ask her to glue it to her chin.

8. Ask your jeweller to make enamelled breastplates for your Pekingeses to wear on their harnesses.

9. Suggest to your children that they stick it on their cellular telephones for waving around at school.

10. Cover it with syrup of figs and force-feed it to anyone who does not support the Emir of Kuwait, his wives and kids, in their heroic struggle against overwhelming odds.


# Office jokes

IT IS a wonderful thing to find that a sense of humour has returned to public life. In Wednesday's newspaper, Sir Peregrine Worsthorne revealed that when a voice on the telephone purporting to be a Miss Simper from No 10 asked him if he would be interested in the idea of a knighthood, he assumed that it was a practical joke.

'Not surprisingly, I suspected a hoax . . . by Auberon Waugh,' he wrote. 'The name Miss Simper sounded too good to be true.' So he asked his secretary, Susan Small, to telephone Downing Street and check up with Miss Simper.

Practical jokes are cruel and beastly things, and I am ashamed to admit that on this occasion it was indeed I who had telephoned, pretending to be Miss Simper. But it all ended happily. When the telephone rang in Downing Street and a voice said it was Susan Small, secretary to Peregrine Worsthorne, wishing to speak to Miss Simper and confirm the offer of a knighthood, they immediately suspected this was another of my amusing impersonations. The name Susan Small seemed too good to be true.

Entering into the spirit of the thing, they roared with laughter and said of course it was all true. Luckily, the Queen is a kindhearted person. When she saw Perry clanking up to Buckingham Palace in his best suit of armour, she knew what had to be done.

## 2nd February, 1991

### War briefing

AT THE time of the Lockerbie disaster, we were told that half a pound of modern high explosive could blow up a PanAm airliner. At a specific point in the Gulf War, we were told that American pilots had flown 5,200 sorties, dropping an average of 1,000 pounds of high explosive on each sortie, making 5,200,000 pounds in all. In the same breath, we were told that they thought they had blown up a total of 145 Iraqi soldiers.

If these figures are true, it means that with all the devastating precision of their superior technology, the Americans now require 35,862 pounds of high explosive to blow up one Iraqi soldier.

One explanation may be that their devastating accuracy is more theoretical than empirical; another that American pilots are simply jettisoning their bombs and missiles over the desert and then scuttling back to the security of their bases. Either of these is possible. A third is that we are being deliberately misinformed, but I do not think Americans are capable of deliberate misinformation. A fourth is that nobody has the faintest idea what he is talking about, or what is happening.

On balance, I lean towards the last explanation. Every hour, it seems the previous hour's information is contradicted; sometimes to be reinstated, sometimes not. There is no point in listening to any of the news, or reading any comments on it. The only thing to do is to wait and see which side wins at the end of the day, and hope there was some point to it all.

## 9th February, 1991

### Not forgotten

TOMORROW marks the seventh anniversary of the sad death of Mr Fred Hill, the motorcyclist, who died in Pentonville Prison on February 10, 1984 while serving his 31st sentence for refusing to wear a crash helmet.

Hill was a retired school teacher, war veteran and friend of the Sikhs – during the war he had been motorcycle instructor to a Sikh regiment. However, when the Sikhs were exempted by law from having to wear crash helmets in 1976, he started his campaign on the principle of equality before the law.

Motorcyclists all over Britain will remember Fred Hill tomorrow for his opposition to the oppressive and nannyish law which requires them all to wear these helmets. A party from London and the Home Counties will meet outside Pentonville Prison at 1.30 pm, where it will lay a memorial wreath before driving in decorous and seemly procession to the Department of Transport headquarters in Marsham Street, arriving at about 2.30 pm.

Fred Hill's actions harmed no one, yet he was treated as a criminal. As another motorcyclist T.B. Trood, has put it, 'unless we are prepared to act to save our liberty, it will be syphoned away into the bottomless pit of totalitarianism'. The nation's non-motorcyclists should also honour Fred Hill's memory. His sacrifice was on behalf of us all.

# 11th February, 1991

## Greenhouse watch

EXPERTS were arguing last night about whether the present blizzards and icy conditions which have paralysed the country were the beginning of the expected 11-year cold spell in our solar flare cycle, or whether they marked the start of a 1,000-year mini-Ice Age, which will bring most life in Western Europe to an end.

If the latter explanation proves to be the true one, it will probably emerge that this drastic and unprecedented climatic change  was triggered off by the extreme effectiveness of government measures against the alleged 'greenhouse effect'.

In  Somerset,  we have taken Government warnings very seriously indeed. After spending £140 billion on researching the problem, scientists advised us that in order to reduce carbon dioxide in the atmosphere, we should either push our cars ourselves or drive them on the gas to be derived from fermenting grass with black treacle in large tanks on the back seat.

Similarly, to avoid damaging the ozone layer we should collect all the methane gas emitted by ruminant cows from their front and rear parts, and use it for cooking, heating and lighting our homes. It is absolutely essential that we have efficient heating systems in our homes as temperatures outside drop to minus 60 degrees Centigrade. A problem may arise when we run out of cows, but scientists are working on that one.

Without these urgent measures, there was a very real danger that bananas and pineapples would have started growing on our traditional Somerset apple trees, producing cider which looked and tasted like Coca-Cola.

## *16th February, 1991*

---

### Love in blue genes

'WOMAN'S HOUR' on St Valentine's Day featured a debate on the nature and mechanics of falling in love: is it a process determined by natural selection of a breeding partner, as scientific tradition might suggest, or does it also provide an avenue for those transcendental feelings which people used to derive from the practice of religion as that great expert on love, Sir Peregrine Worsthorne, maintained?

Sir Peregrine and his inamorata, Lucinda Lambton, were introduced as 'this year's most publicly romantic couple' to explain what the presenter described as the exquisite pain and pleasure of falling in love. Having set the scene for the moment when Cupid's darts struck, Sir Peregrine seemed prepared to consider the scientific explanation, that 'what was happening in that room was genes talking to genes'.

This provoked a peal of delighted laughter from his nymph, who averred that she had felt a surge of magic and extraordinary power, leaving her with an irresistible urge to blow trumpet after trumpet, light flame after flame. 'The rest is history, as they say,' said Sir Peregrine.

How wonderful it would be if, when the history of our times came to be written, it concerned itself chiefly with the love story of this enchanting couple, the nation's darlings, its Daphnis and Chloe, its Orlando and Rosalind. Alas, I fear that the history books will tell us more about futile and disgusting events in the Middle East, which should never have concerned us in the first place, than with the story which really caught our imagination and captured our hearts.

## *20th February, 1991*

### Exorcist required

IT MUST have been most encouraging for our troops in the Gulf to read in their copies of the *Tablet*, the Roman Catholic weekly, that Cardinal Hume has decided their war is not immoral, that allied forces are 'genuinely contributing to the establishment of peace'.

What the world would really like to see from him, I suspect, is an authoritative pronouncement on a point which has been raised and discussed in many quarters, most notably by Neal Ascherson in the *Independent on Sunday* and by our own Christopher Booker: is Saddam Hussein actually the Devil?

His habit of drinking a pint of blood for breakfast and eating two Christian babies for luncheon every day certainly points to some abnormality of background. It would not have been beyond the ingenuity of Iraqi plastic surgeons to have removed his horns and tail. With a little help from BBC Television's make-up department, the deception would then be complete.

If he really is the Devil, then it is a sobering thought that the allies may have dropped about a million tons of high explosive to no avail on this small desert state, incorporating within its boundaries not only the sites of Nineveh and Babylon, the Ziggurat at Ur and the Tower of Babel, but also, it is thought, the site of the original Garden of Eden (before it moved to Disneyland, Florida).

Perhaps Iraq did indeed plan to take over the world, with its

15,500,000 shivering inhabitants. The proper answer to this threat might not have been to drop a million tons of high explosive with pinpoint accuracy all over the desert, but to send in Cardinal Hume with a bucket of Holy Water, some sprinklers and whatever other kit he may require for a successful exorcism.

## 25th February, 1991

### Icehouse effect

IT IS not often that a sensible idea emerges from the idiotic cacophony in Westminster, but we must all support the proposal by Mr Henry Bellingham, Conservative MP for North West Norfolk, to amend the National Heritage (Scotland) Bill now passing through Parliament so as to reintroduce wolves and wild boars in the Highlands and other parts of Scotland.

The purpose of this amendment, as he cheerfully acknowledges, is to control the numbers of ramblers who, in their brightly coloured anoraks, are now becoming a serious menace and blot on the landscape of rural Britain.

These people are encouraged by their association in the serious error that they own the countryside. In fact the only way to own the countryside is to work hard, save up your money and buy a bit of it. Merely rambling around in an anorak is no substitute.

Unfortunately, most land-owners are too polite to point this out, with the result that their privacy is invaded and their landscape disfigured. Wolves were last seen in Scotland in 1701, and it is high time they were invited back as our country gets colder and colder to receive them.

The new Icehouse Effect, which a few honest scientists are just beginning to notice, is largely attributable to the decline in cigarette smoking and the gases given off by anoraks when heated by exertion.

## 27th February, 1991

### Bonsai classes

CROWN Prince Naruhito of Japan, who was 31 on Saturday, has been unable to find a bride in the whole of Japan, despite a five-year search. One of the qualifications is that she should be shorter than his 5 ft 4 in, but one would not have thought that this would present many difficulties.

Japanese women are not only among the most beautiful and best mannered in the world, they have also, traditionally, always been fairly small. But it occurs to me that on my last visit to Japan, some eight years ago, a change was already taking place before my eyes. Although the women were still slim, cheerful and enchantingly small one saw galumphing great schoolgirls towering over their mothers and threatening to knock down everything in their path.

It occurred to me even then that affluence, and a switch to Western diet, might be having a terrible effect on Japanese women.

What can we do to help poor Prince Naruhito, heir to the 2651-year-old Chrysanthemum Throne of Japan? All we have to offer, really, are the Princesses Beatrice and Eugenie of York, who may be quite small now, but will almost certainly not stay like that for long.

On the other hand, it is always possible that the Japanese have clever ways to stop people growing, as they do with trees.

Perhaps they are deliberately breeding a larger size of Japanese, attributing their comparative lack of success in the last war to this cause.

Far more useful, I would have thought, to teach Westerners how to keep themselves smaller. It would do wonders to environmental pollution in our overcrowded island if we were all half the size.

## Call to duty

WAS IT anything to do with intemperate and disloyal criticism of the Royal Family in the uneducated press which persuaded the Princess of Wales and the Duchess of York to announce simultaneously that they had no intention of bearing further children?

I have forborne to comment until now, hoping that I misread the news, or that they were misreported. What on earth do they think we journalists will find to write about, if there are to be no more young royals? Although I suppose some Britons will be able to take it on the chin that there should be no more young Yorks, the news that the Princess of Wales has decided to stick at two is very sad.

Let us hope they decide to adopt some Romanian babies. This

is a much kinder, less self-indulgent thing to do than buying Filipino servants, which was all the rage a few years ago. Romanian males, as they grow older, often develop interestingly hairy ears. It is the duty of the modern Royal Family to keep us all amused, somehow, and as a family they have seldom neglected their duty in the past.

## 2nd March, 1991

### Brainwave

I THINK I owe an apology to Gen Norman Schwarzkopf, the American commander in the Gulf, whose buffoon-like appearances at the beginning of the campaign led me to wonder whether President Bush might be bluffing. Now it would appear that this Pekingese-like American with the name of a famous German operatic soprano is the greatest strategist and military philosopher since Julius Caesar.

Figures for casualties published on Thursday suggest that he has developed an entirely new concept of warfare, whereby enemy soldiers are invited to leave their tanks so that the Americans could destroy them without hurting the soldiers who would otherwise have been inside.

No other form of warfare could possibly explain how 3,696 Iraqi tanks were destroyed without the loss of a single allied tank, as was claimed on Thursday. Nor is there any other explanation for the claim that the total Iraqi human casualties were consistently smaller than the total number of tanks and guns destroyed.

All this is attributable to Gen Schwarzkopf's brilliant idea of advising Iraqi soldiers to stand well clear of their equipment. Let us thank our lucky stars Saddam Hussein did not think of it first. Now we can return to worrying about the caviar crisis.

## 4th March, 1991

### Meditation

STRONG RUMOURS of a June or 'khaki' election decide me to take a long walk with the dogs to ponder the available choice. I would like to think I am a sufficiently serious person not to be influenced by the thought that a vote for the Hattersley-Kaufman dream ticket would result in a quadrupling of my taxes, the selling of the family silver, confiscation of my few remaining acres, the beggary of my widow, orphans and other dependents, the destruction of my dogs and horses . . .

Hattersley and Kaufman are also committed to banning the hunt, which will cause endless misery in the countryside, and they would give free television licences to pensioners, which strikes me as being both unwise and cruel. Worst of all, they promise to spend even more on the Health Service, which is manifestly insane.

Against this is the choice of an unknown Mr John Major. It is true that our new Prime Minister used the computer viruses hidden in his phantom moustache to very good effect during the recent war in the Middle East. Enemy command and communications headquarters were thrown into complete confusion from the start of the war, and scarcely a single shot seems to have been fired at the advancing allies.

Nevertheless it is an eccentric and possibly rather dangerous thing to vote for someone one has never met – rather like asking a strange man to take one's wife home after a ball. On the other hand, I have never met General Norman Schwarzkopf either, and I can see he is a splendid fellow, despite his slight resemblance to Gazza Gascoigne, the embarrassing footballer.

I think on balance I shall probably vote Conservative. Oddly enough, I nearly always seem to come to this conclusion in the end.

## *6th March, 1991*

### Fire and brimstone

MISGIVINGS have been expressed about the new 'charismatic' form of religion which appears to be the only growth area in contemporary Christianity, and the only one of the slightest interest to our beloved younger generation. No doubt it is psychologically manipulative and hysteria-inducing, but I see no great harm in that.

If there are people around with so little sense of the ridiculous that they wish to sway together, gyrate, talk double-Dutch and utter 'prophecies' in all seriousness without giggling, then it is surely better for them to do it in private among themselves. The alternative is that they cause general embarrassment at cocktail parties.

Perhaps it brings them closer to God. My own feeling is that God may be in rather an Old Testament sort of mood nowadays, ever since He struck York Minster with lightning immediately after the consecration of Dr Jenkins as Bishop of Durham.

We do not like to mention the Aids scourge in this context – to suggest there is any connection between Aids and sodomy is undoubtedly a heresy in the Church of England – but I am made a little bit nervous by all these hurricanes we seem to suffer nowadays. If I lived near Skegness, I would probably feel more than a little bit nervous.

Over the weekend, the Butlins camp at Skegness, called Funcoast World, was filled by 1,200 homosexuals and transvestites celebrating their state. By all accounts they had a wonderful time, and many will wish them luck. But can we be sure that Others agree? One thinks of the Cities of the Plain. It will not be much comfort to people in Skegness when the brimstone and fire come raining down, to explain that it is probably something to do with the greenhouse effect.

## Freedom or licence

PERHAPS the most far-reaching court decision of modern times has passed almost unnoticed in legal circles, no doubt because it was reached in a humble county court, rather than handed down from the Court of Appeal or the House of Lords. By its nature, it was not the sort of case likely to reach a higher court, but now it has been reported, it may come to affect the lives of most people in this country, all those who live in flats, terraced or semi-detached housing.

In Blackpool County Court, Judge Mary Holt issued a court order forbidding Tracey Scott from watching television after 11 pm, after her neighbours had twice complained.

Is this an unacceptable infringement of a basic human right, or is it a necessary limitation of freedom? Should television, perhaps, be forced to close down at 11 pm to allow the nation's 'workers' a good night's sleep? Why should one person's sleep be given greater importance than another person's enjoyment of noise?

These are the great questions which will eventually determine the quality of modern life. I do not see why the debate should confine itself to the question of noise. The close proximity in which many people are forced to live also raises questions of cooking smells. Some people cannot abide the smell of curry, others the smell of boiled cabbage. Is it possible to inhale cigarette smoke, with all its attendant dangers, through walls, floors or ceilings?

## Victory

IN ROMAN times, victory parades were attended by the defeated armies, brought back in chains to make obeisance to the Emperor, before being sold into slavery. I imagine that this will not be possible in London. The Americans will have grabbed all the prisoners for their own celebration, and the servant problem is even worse in the United States than it is in Europe.

Perhaps a good idea would be to recruit all those journalists and broadcasters who seemed to doubt the wisdom of our involvement in the Gulf War and make them pull Mr Major's chariot through the streets of London.

Words cannot describe the loathing and contempt which many of us will feel for those worthless people, especially on the BBC, or the admiration which we quite rightly feel for those journalists who stood up for Our Boys and Girls.

Even if the Army, perhaps sickened by its experiences, declines to take part in the proposed ceremonies, I am sure the country would like to see a Victory Parade of all the brave journalists who were intelligent enough to back the winning side.

## 11th March, 1991

## The real crisis

THE number of people visiting stately homes has fallen for the first time in 20 years, and wine consumption, after years of spectacular growth, has similarly fallen for the first time in 21 years.

The only bright spot in a gloomy world is that, according to Caviar House, the world's biggest caviar company, its British sales have risen almost 50 per cent over the past six months.

'History has shown time and again that caviar is relatively

recession-proof,' says a spokesman. 'There is no other food that boosts the morale in quite the same way.'

Even so, Britons ate their way through only four tons of caviar last year, compared to 35 tons consumed by the French and 25 tons by the Swiss, who are eight and a half times less numerous than we are.

We have a long way to go, and the future is not made more hopeful by the great caviar crisis, which threatens to deprive our kiddies of the caviar they so desperately need. Industrial pollution of the Caspian Sea and the collapse of discipline in Soviet Russia are thought to be the reasons for this desperate state of affairs which is bound to dominate any political debate long after the Gulf crisis has been forgotten.

## A cleaner Britain

TODAY in Weston-super-Mare, scarcely 20 miles away from where I write, history is being made. The first international conference of chimney sweeps ever to be held in Britain opens at Pontins, in Sand Bay, to discuss a new law making it compulsory for all chimneys in western Europe to be swept regularly.

The conference, which will last for six days, is sponsored by the National Association of Chimney Sweeps and by British Coal. It is called Chimtech Euro 91, which seems rather an odd name to give a conference. More than 100 delegates from 15 European countries will discuss the effect of the new law on millions of home-owners whose chimneys have not been swept for years.

Vice-president of the National Association of Chimney Sweeps and project manager, Mr Bill Hughes, reckons that up to 10,000 new jobs could be created when the new law comes into force. It all seems too good to be true. Police helicopters come in useful to ensure that people are obeying the law. Extreme cases of non-compliance can be met with pin-point bombing from helicopter gun ships and Tornado bombers.

## *13th March, 1991*

## Greed

TODAY on National No Smoking Day we might all brood on the great question whether this frenzied quest for long life is something noble, as the BMA would have us believe, or whether it is selfish, unpatriotic and doomed to create nothing but misery.

The Queen herself has recently spoken of the 'alarming growth in the world's population' as a problem created by scientists determined to prolong life at all costs. This was part of her recorded message to the Commonwealth on Sunday, and we should all think hard about what she had to say.

Smokers not only pay huge sums in tobacco duty, subsidising non-smokers and paying for half the entire hospital service, they also die younger, on average, than non-smokers and save the country billions of pounds in pensions and geriatric health care.

While not wishing to discourage or humiliate anyone who decides to refrain from smoking on this day, the more reflective among us might set it aside to honour those who continue to smoke in the face of massive discouragement from a medical profession which grows rich on looking after the old. It is not generally known that the over sixty-fives consume 50 per cent of hospital resources, while accounting for only 16 per cent of the population.

It beggars belief that many hospitals now forbid their elderly patients to smoke. Is there no limit to the greed of these doctors?


# Worry

POPULATION pressures are unlikely to be eased by the new policy of the British Pregnancy Advisory Service to impregnate virgins, for a fee. I do not know whether or not this charity is prepared to impregnate virgins who smoke. My doubts on the score have deterred me from asking Mr Rushton to compose a picture for the embellishment of this column: The Impregnation of the Smoking Virgins. It would not have been a pretty sight.

The offspring of this process will now join the 750,000 children in the country who have no contact whatever with their fathers. Many people are worried by this, just as the Queen and Prince Philip worry about the problems of world overpopulation.

Personally, I do not feel there is much I can do about it. I once knew an Oxford don who went mad worrying about the national debt. Yet it is possible to live a full and happy life in England without worrying about any of these things.

# Poor Ludwig

I HAVE never tackled the philosophical work of Ludwig Wittgenstein, and for many years have been putting it off. If I could live a happy and fulfilled life without studying Wittgenstein, what possible reason was there to try and understand his tortuous anxieties about the use of language?

So it came as something of a relief to learn in Sunday's newspaper that his writings make no sense; they are the products of a deranged mind, showing all the classical symptoms of schizophrenia.

Of course, we must be careful about these attempts to knock down the great figures of the past. Oxford and Cambridge, not to mention the provincial universities, are full of chippy, bearded young dons anxious to announce that Shakespeare was an inferior playwright to Beaumont or Webster or someone called John Ford.

But on balance, I am convinced by the arguments of Dr John Smythie, the neuroscientist, and of Dr John Marshall, the Oxford psychologist, both of whom are convinced that his confusion and incomprehensibility are to be explained by the simple fact that he was a madman. 'This raises as many questions about the pathology of his disciples as about him,' Dr Marshall says.

Among his most ardent disciples was Bertrand Russell. In the 18th century, fashionable Londoners amused themselves laughing at the poor lunatics gibbering in their cages at Bethlehem Hospital. Throughout the first half of this century, the beau monde hailed them as genius philosophers, painters, poets, architects. It is hard to decide which was the crueller treatment.

## 16th March, 1991

### Health notes

WHEN my grandfather, Arthur Waugh, was sent away to school his father, who was a GP in the north Somerset mining village of Midsomer Norton, always produced a large medicine bottle, labelled The Mixture, for him to hand into the school dispensary with instructions to take two teaspoonfuls a day.

It contained cherry brandy, and helped to keep my grandfather happy and healthy through five years at Sherborne. I do not know what superior medical knowledge is claimed by Mrs Peter Bottomley, the health minister, when she refuses to allow doctors to prescribe cherry cake, as well as instant coffee, toothpaste, Crunchie bars, pizza mix and Fairy washing-up liquid on the National Health Service.

These are exactly what many sick people want. They are also cheaper and much less harmful than most of the medicines prescribed. Neither the toothpaste nor the washing-up liquid should be eaten, of course, but both can be therapeutically employed – one for squaring into patterns, the other for blowing bubbles.

When one thinks how much damage has been done by the barbiturates and tranquillisers in recent history, and may even now be being done by the cortico-steroids, there must be a good case for prescribing cherry cake whenever possible.

## *18th March, 1991*

---

### Delicious

LAST Friday's newspapers all carried gigantic photographs of a horse having its throat cut in a Spanish slaughterhouse. Their purpose was to elicit support for the RSPCA and I suppose it may have had that effect on some people. In my own case, its effect was simply to make me feel very hungry.

I have never understood why horsemeat is not eaten in

Britain, or why people show such aversion to the idea. It is just as good as beef and rather healthier, having less fat.

Perhaps it is thought that horses are more intelligent than cattle, making it crueller to kill them. I doubt that this is the case. Horses are unbelievably stupid. For my own part, I hope to celebrate European integration with a horse barbecue under the equestrian statue of the Grand Old Duke of York in Waterloo Place.

If the health authorities forbid it, we can always eat raw horse cut in thin slices with a gingery sauce, in the Japanese manner. Europe must learn to look outwards.

## 25th March, 1991

### Voices in the void

GREAT hurt and great anger have been occasioned among the nation's cellular telephone users by the Chancellor's new tax on their instruments. Although all such machines have been banned on this column since long before their invention, I do not feel I can bring myself to support any new tax, however admirable its purpose. Extra money in the hands of the Government can cause nothing but mischief.

When I come to power I think I will abolish this tax, as, indeed, I will abolish most taxes, but I will pass a new law requiring anyone using a portable telephone in a public place – whether train, restaurant, or in the street – to wear a dunce's cap for the duration of his call.

This may seem oppressive, but my experience from overheard conversations convinces me that 99 per cent of these calls are completely unnecessary, and they are certainly annoying to everyone else on the scene.

That is not the most serious objection, however. I have seen it suggested that they contribute to the sanity of people when they are separated from their offices, but it is my contention that these telephones do exactly the opposite.

When a person is in his office he may or may not be working but when he is at luncheon he is definitely lunching. It is absurd to pretend that there are decisions to be made and instructions to be given which are so important that they cannot be put off until the end of luncheon which requires as much concentration as anything else if serious dyspepsia is to be avoided.

This frenzied desire on the part of the modern executive to be self-importantly making decisions all the time, however fatuous or ill-considered they may be, is part of a larger lunacy. Modern technology has given us greatly improved methods of communication with each other, but it has not given us anything useful to communicate. Much of the destructive, mindless change we see all around us – never worse than in the past 12 years – can be attributed in one way or another to this greater ease of communication between our masters, and between master and servant.

By forcing them to wear dunce's caps on these occasions we might at least impress on them the absurdity of their activity, if not its dangers.

## Greenwatch

EVERYBODY in England seems to be talking about senile degeneration and death – a strange manifestation in the first week of spring. No doubt it all flows from the endless, boring preoccupation with health and long life which kept us going through the winter.

I wonder if I am alone in being slightly alarmed by the proposal for a Natural Death Centre in London, as revealed last week by my colleague Peterborough, who attributed it to Teddy Goldsmith, the eccentric Green philosopher.

'We want to set up a system of death-midwives to ease the transition from life to death, and we are looking into the possibility of re-using coffins to save resources,' said a spokesman for the centre, which plans to open next month.

On the second point, I can assure them that coffins are not re-usable. In one of the first stages of decomposition, corpses release an oily liquid called adipocere or grave-wax, caused by the breakdown of fatty tissue in the body, which is highly offensive and which taints the wood of a coffin, often for 100 years.

On the first point, I am puzzled to know exactly what function is proposed for these midwives of death. We already have a dedicated and admirable hospice service, which every right-minded person should support. The Greens have always had an obsession about human overpopulation of Planet Earth, as they call it, although they are happy to let it swarm with bats and adders and other unpleasant creatures.

So far, they have confined their anxieties about overpopulation to various more or less fatuous and oppressive suggestions for preventing births. As I never tire of pointing out, the Greens need watching.

# 27th March, 1991

## Well held

MANY will sympathise with the Princess Royal and her estranged husband, Captain Phillips, in their reported difficulties over the division of the 1,500 wedding presents which, by convention, are given to couples jointly.

It give me some satisfaction to think that I have not added to their problems. At the time of the Royal wedding, in November 1973, I could not make up my mind between some transparent oven-proof Pyrex dishes and a slightly more ambitious set of Pillavite ramekins for baking eggs, which were decorated by pictures of baby rabbits.

In the end, I more or less decided on the Pyrex dishes. But, having watched the young couple walk down the aisle, I thought I would hold on a bit and see how things worked out. At times they must have wondered at the long delay.

Seventeen and a half years later, I am glad to see that my caution was justified. I have not only saved myself a considerable sum of money, I have also spared the couple any possibility of further friction at this difficult moment in their lives.

## Murderous thoughts

IT WAS alarming to read of a wife who attempted to murder her husband by making it look as if he had driven his lawn-mower into the pond that she had thought of this wicked idea as a result of something she had read in *The Daily Telegraph*. I hope it was nothing she had read in this column.

But I must admit that when I read one of my colleagues' claim that when he walks his dogs in the Buckinghamshire countryside they not infrequently bring down a deer, I could not help wondering.

On my walks in Somerset the pekingeses often bring back a wildebeest or an ostrich and lay it at my feet. Once they even put up a cow elephant. How easy it would be to pretend that they had mistaken one or another of my Enemies for a Rambler . . .

# 1st April, 1991

## Stay at home

THE MOST interesting thing about the response to British Airways' offer of 50,000 free air tickets later this month is not that a million people in this country should have applied for them, but that nearly 56 million did not. They must have decided, as I did, that there is nowhere else on earth we particularly want to go; that Britain, for all its horrible faults, is the best place to be at the moment.

The problem with foreign travel nowadays is that there are too many people involved. All the main sites of the world are swarming with tourists from every other corner of it. Add to this the list of destinations which are too unstable to visit, whether as a result of criminality, disease or political danger – Tripoli, Baghdad, New York, Maputo, Khartoum, Bogota, Phnom Penh – and it is easy to decide there is nowhere left worth the effort.

Even train journeys in England are fraught with horror. Anybody who travels nowadays automatically loses all freedom and self-determination, becoming the slave of any ticket inspector or railway official or airhostess who gives him orders. The great lesson of our times is to stay at home and watch our own backyards.

## The brown look

VISITORS to Butlins Camp at Minehead have been complaining of a face rash which afflicts them within two or three days of arriving in West Somerset, leaving them with bright red cheeks. The symptoms sometimes survive several days after they have left the area. Camp authorities are arranging to collect blood samples to see if they can trace a common cause.

In fact the disease is well known down here, and is probably endemic in the soil. Cases of *facies rufa* or apple-cheeked syndrome have been reported since the early Middle Ages. The only certain cure for it is decapitation, but in former times, before the 'grey look' became fashionable, it was thought rather comely.

John Major might care to spend a few days in Minehead before he next visits the United States, in order to avoid being insulted about his appearance by the President of that curious country. But I doubt if it would work. His red cheeks would be taken as a sign of some infectious disease, and he would not be allowed to meet the President, even if he was allowed off the plane.

Americans, for some reason, cultivate the 'brown look', exposing themselves to artificial radiation for hours on end. I imagine it is something to do with guilty feelings about the Red Indians, whose hunting grounds they appropriated, and the blacks, whom they imported as slaves. The idea is that if they sit in front of an ultra-violet lamp long enough, they will all end up the same colour and nobody will mind.

In any case, I am not sure that Mr Major is quite ready to visit the West Country yet. He might be terribly shocked by some of the things he saw. For his next few visits to the United States, he will have to make do with blanco or shoe polish to hide his attractive grey appearance.

## 3rd April, 1991

### Call to arms

UNLIKE some of my colleagues, I felt the Gulf war was too far away, its objectives too vague and its possible benefits too implausible to engage my strongest emotions. Similarly during the miners' strike, while many of my contemporaries were straining at the leash to be allowed to go out and bash a miner, I felt inhibited by ancestral memories of the miners in Midsomer Norton, Somerset, in the days before Scargill when miners were respected members of the community.

None of these inhibitions applies to the threatened strike of the National Union of Teachers. Militant members of the NUT can surely be identified as the Enemy Within, the very ones who have turned our young people into these abject figures of misery and helplessness, forever moaning about tropical rain forests and cormorants, unemployable by virtue of their ignorance, laziness and indiscipline.

Of course, the teachers have a case. Many of them are too backward to take the new tests for seven year olds themselves, let alone to prepare others for them. To expect them to read a

66-page document explaining the tests may well be thought rather harsh when so many have difficulty with their reading. Even if most can read the instructions, we have no reason to suppose that they will be able to understand them. Many teachers come from disadvantaged homes and received little or no schooling in anything except anti-sexist plasticine modelling.

Even so, I cannot help seeing the struggle against militant teachers as the next great battle for Western civilisation. We defeated the miners, drove the Russians out of Eastern Europe and pulled down the Berlin Wall without a shot being fired. Now let us sort out the teaching profession.

## *10th April, 1991*

### Short order

THE LATEST theory about Peter Sutcliffe, the Yorkshire Ripper, is that he may have turned into a mass murderer because he was forced to wear short trousers as a 12 year old.

His father, John Sutcliffe, appeared on a late night Channel 4 chat show to explain what happened: 'We were very unjust,' he said. 'He was the only kid in short pants, and he was very shy and self-conscious about his thin legs.'

Short trousers are horrible garments on men, I agree, but I doubt whether this really explains Peter Sutcliffe's subsequent behaviour, which was strange even by Yorkshire standards. But it seems to me that this reluctance to wear shorts might be put to some use.

If people convicted of violent crime could be sentenced to wear short trousers for the rest of their lives, this would not only act as a punishment but also enable potential victims to be on their guard before the trouble started.

Other people could continue to wear short trousers if they wished, of course. But perhaps fewer would be tempted.

## 20th April, 1991

### Welcome tosas

DOG LOVERS will be excited to learn that the Japanese tosa has at last been introduced to Britain. With an adult weight of 17 stone, these splendid creatures are the biggest dogs in the world, often mistaken by the short-sighted for a Shetland pony or even a young carthorse.

Not surprisingly, the RSPCA, which specialises in killing stray dogs, has demanded a ban on further imports, describing them as among the most dangerous in the world.

Dr Roger Mugford, the animal psychologist who numbers the Queen's corgis among his clients, is quoted as saying: 'This is, frankly, not something that deserves to be called a dog . . . The idea of any more coming into Britain makes my blood run cold.'

He misses the point. These dogs are desperately needed to deal with all the Dog Wardens, RSPCA officials and animal psychologists now swarming over the canine scene.

My Pekingeses are fleet of foot and do not know the meaning of fear, but their comparatively small size makes them vulnerable to a dog-catcher with a net.

## Retreat

NOTHING much seems to have happened in Britain during my absence in the Great Satan across the herring pond, except that Hackney Borough Council has cancelled its black lesbian bereavement counselling service. The new service was announced with a fanfare of trumpets just as I left for New York, and I very much looked forward to following its subsequent history. It was cancelled, apparently, because not a single grieving black lesbian turned up to any of the four lessons.

Another service which may never see the light of day is the proposed Dolphin Line, for dolphins in Hackney and elsewhere which may wish to make allegations of sexual abuse down the telephone at any hour of the day or night. One by one, all the signposts of a civilised, caring community are being taken down.

# 27th April, 1991

## Lost column

ALL week long, the Way of the World telephone has been ringing. It is an historic object in its own right, being one of only two left in the country with an M15 tap attached to it, put there many years ago when it was suspected that a Jacobite office boy was using it to communicate with sympathisers on the Continent.

Once a year the office is visited by a man who says he is called Carruthers and wishes to check that the tap is still working. He turns it on and draws a brown, sticky liquid which he pronounces to be Madeira. He then invites everybody present, with many nudges and winks, to drink a toast to the King across the Water, and disappears for another year, having collected the evidence for his secret file in Curzon Street.

Or so I have been told. I have been able to visit the new office on the Isle of Dogs only once, travelling on a toy railway through the East End of London and seeing sights such as no Somerset man should be asked to look upon.

The telephone calls, I have been told, were all from readers who were unable to find the column. Inexplicably, it has been moved from the lush valley region it has occupied unmolested for 34 years. Perplexed and terrified, readers have had to be guided through the expanded obituaries section, like tourists through the great necropolis of Cairo, to the narrow strip of frozen, inhospitable ground which is all that is left to the Way of the World.

Perhaps the entire newspaper will be devoted to obituaries before very long. It does not seem an altogether bad idea. There is not so very much to be said about the living.

# 1st May, 1991

## Enemy within

AN ADVERTISEMENT for two new jobs on the Bat Conservation Trust describes it as a fast-growing organisation supporting a national network of 80 local groups. Soon it will be in a position to take over the reins of government.

As I never tire of pointing out, bats are not only frightening and smelly to meet; they also constitute a major potential health risk. They and they alone can foster and transmit the rabies virus without succumbing to the disease. Without bats, it would disappear from the face of the earth in a matter of months.

After 1991, of course, we will be obliged to introduce rabid dogs from the Continent of Europe to all restaurant menus, but it is thought that cooking probably kills the germs.

The greatest danger will be from Continental bats, which are bound to come swarming through Lady Thatcher's tunnel as soon as they learn about our cheese 'n' onion potato crisps, our British bangers and our bat support groups.

Who can blame them? What is needed is plainly a pre-emptive anti-bat coup. It will not be easy to track down all 80 cells of the existing organisation and expose the undercover bat agents who have already infiltrated newspaper offices, universities and the BBC.

When I come to power, something between the UnAmerican Activities Committee and the Holy Inquisition may be required. Suspects will be confronted with a live bat; those who fail to swoon or scream will be sent down the Channel Tunnel with a sack of cheese 'n' onion crisps and never seen again.

## *4th May, 1991*

---

## Save a princess

AS A CHILD, I was constantly faced by the moral dilemma of the Chinese button. Press the button, and a Chinaman drops dead in China. Nobody will ever tell you his name or worry you about the circumstances, but you will receive £1 million in the post next day. Do you press the button?

The correct answer was to say 'no', but even as a very young child, I felt that further and better particulars were required. Was there any causal relationship between my pressing the buttons and the Chinamen dropping dead, or was it merely coincidence? After all, about 35,600 mainland Chinese die every day in the normal course of events, 25 every minute or one every 2½ seconds. Since I started writing this paragraph, with a moment off to refer to population tables, about 500 Chinese in the People's Republic of China have died. It is a distressing thought, but I refuse to take the blame.

I feel rather the same about the Princess Royal's injunction to

Skip Lunch, Save a Life. On Wednesday, at Dover Town Hall, she refused an elaborate buffet lunch of smoked salmon, prawns, roast fowl and strawberries. All 400 guests followed her example. Presumably the food was thrown away. Are we to suppose that 400 African lives were saved?

It may well be an excellent thing to give money to African charities, but I fail to see what missing lunch has to do with it. Many Englishwomen have a perverse desire to be thin, but that has nothing to do with the Africans.

These are not matters to be treated lightly. For many Englishmen, luncheon is one of the most important meals of the day. Another challenge might be to go on eating luncheon, and see what effect it has on the Princess Royal.

## Don't skip lunch

IN THE United States, where practically no one eats luncheon any more, morality has taken an even queerer turn. According to a survey conducted by the J. Walter Thompson advertising agency, 16 per cent of married Americans would murder their spouse for $2 million, while seven per cent (18 million) would murder a perfect stranger for the same sum.

One in five American women say they have been raped, one in five lost their virginity before they were 13, a third would be prepared to pull the switch on the electric chair, one in six say they were physically abused as children, a quarter would be prepared to abandon their families for $10 million. Nearly three quarters of Americans have never spoken to their neighbours, 90 per cent 'truly' believe in God, and 46 per cent expect to go to heaven.

All this is in a book called *The Day America Told the Truth* by James Patterson and Peter Kim. I do not know what to advise except that they might all be happier if they had a cooked meal in the middle of the day.

## *11th May, 1991*

---

### Happy, happy land

BERTRAM WOOSTER would almost certainly have been a member of Lloyds, and would almost certainly have lost all his money in the present debacle. It is sad to think that an entire class which survived a world war and three socialist tyrannies in my own lifetime should come to grief in this way, but I have often noticed that those whose wealth is predominantly inherited, see nothing bizarre or suspicious in the suggestion that they should receive further vast sums without effort or risk on their part.

Those who have had to earn their money are generally less trusting, but I can't help feeling that the middle classes may be being taken for a ride with these direct debits. My local council in London, which is said to have run up astronomical debts in playing the currency markets, solemnly asks me to sign a form allowing it to help itself to any sum of money it may find in my bank account at any time it pleases.

The safeguards are derisory. I suppose I can understand signing one of these documents under torture, just as one might sign a false confession to murder if police were *very* insistent . . . but sensible, middle class people are blithely signing direct debits all over the place. Is this the New Jerusalem, where we all love and trust each other?

Even the so-called working classes seem infected. An

announcement on the front page of Wednesday's *Mirror* urged readers to get their skates on if they wanted to buy Mirror Group Newspaper shares at £1.25 each. It showed Andy Capp, the great working class cartoon hero, who has never worked in his life, skating off to buy his shares. Are we to suppose that Andy Capp has been saving money all this time, and that he will lend it to Captain Robert Maxwell if he has? Alleluia.

## 18th May, 1991

### Good neighbours

WAS I alone in detecting a slight note of panic in the *Sun*'s reaction to the news that a Government Minister had criticised the television soap opera, 'Neighbours'?

Mr Michael Fallon, Minister for Schools, suggested that excessive television viewing dulled the minds of young children and interfered with their homework. The *Sun* immediately hired a number of teachers, child experts and psychologists to tell its readers 'Why Neighbours is Good for you', adding a thought of its own:

'Neighbours has a massive audience. Fourteen million people cannot be wrong. Especially when they have votes.'

Even harder for the *Sun* to swallow was its own announcement that the Prince of Wales has banned satellite dishes from the outside of Kensington Palace because he thinks they are ugly. 'It is not the first time Charles has shown himself out of step with the latest trends,' the newspaper commented darkly.

Of course it is true that these aerials are architecturally intrusive, but that is not the main reason for hating them. The main reason is that they make a public statement about the people who choose to exhibit them – proclaiming themselves to be social and intellectual cripples of no moral or aesthetic discrimination who are content to wallow in their own stupidity and ignorance. Like the bad smell of a slaughterhouse or tannery, they lower the social tone of a neighbourhood and reduce property values.

If any neighbour of mine puts up a satellite dish I will open a pig farm.

# Gossip column

FRANCE's first woman Prime Minister, Mme Edith Cresson, explains that hints about loose sexual morals always trail women who succeed in French politics:

'Not one woman is elected without the explanation being heard that she really got the post because she slept with so-and-so or so-and-so.'

At the time of Mrs Thatcher's appointment as Prime Minister, and throughout her period in office, I kept my ear to the ground. My work took me among the most reckless gossips and vilest traducers in the land, but I never heard the faintest whisper, however implausible, against her sexual morals.

She was regarded with a certain amount of suspicion until recently as the wife of a commoner. She was also suspected, perhaps unfairly, of being on the make. Now she has found her place in English society as the wife of a baronet, we can open our hearts to her unreservedly.

Perhaps it is my imagination, but she seems to have attained an almost ethereal beauty since her elevation – like Ayesha, Rider Haggard's original She-who-must-be-obeyed, after walking through the flame of eternal life. Gossip has it that Lady Thatcher achieves the the same result through herbal baths at an establishment in Shepherds Bush. The results are certainly striking. We must pray that she is never tempted, like Ayesha, to take one eternal remedy too many.

## *22nd May, 1991*

## Clog peril

A NEW public health risk has been brought to my attention through the pages of the magazine of the Royal College of Surgeons of Edinburgh, which recently carried an article on the dangers of spinal dislocation from traditional Zulu dancing.

To many of us, these dangers may seem remote, but a letter from a senior surgeon in the accident and emergency division of Basingstoke District Hospital avers that while working in the north of England, he saw similar injuries on a clog dancer:

'A 60-year-old woman was celebrating her birthday and retirement with family and friends at a public house. During the course of celebrations she was persuaded to perform a clog dance.

'In the north of England, clog dances such as the Lancashire and Liverpoool hornpipes are performed on table tops . . . The unfortunate dancer lost her footing and sustained a fracture dislocation . . . with neurological deficit. Traction was applied but she died some days later of bronchopneumonia.' The writer goes on to urge that the public needs educating in the risks of alcohol ingestion while engaged in physical pursuits requiring any degree of co-ordination.

This seems to me casting the net rather wide. All we need is a simple law restricting the sale of tables to those with a GCSE certificate or better in clog dancing, with compulsory government health warnings on all tables, to emphasise the dangers of dancing on them when drunk.

How many more clog dancers must die before the Government takes action?

### *27th May, 1991*

## A place to have fun

WHEN I mourned the collapse of Lloyd's recently, I attributed it in part to the hideous architecture of the new Lloyd's Building in the City of London but mostly – and primarily – to the fact that it had admitted the terrible generation of 'classless' New Britons, of proven dishonesty and doubtful competence in any field.

Being no expert in business matters, I was unable to be more specific. Now I am informed by Bernard Levin, who certainly knows a thing or two and claims to read *The Sunday Times*, that these incompetents somehow managed to pick up £2½ billion of debts from the $500 billion collapse of the American Savings and Loan Scheme.

Since the whole point of the Savings and Loan Scheme – it was also the reason for the catastrophe – was that losses were guaranteed by the American government, one can only salute the genius of whichever Lloyd's insurers managed to drag their syndicates into it.

Levin also informs me that vast claims for pollution damages have been pouring in from across the Atlantic. In the next 20 years, claims concerning pollution and allied matters may climb as high as $100 billion.

As I say, I am not a businessman, but if these hopeless young people will listen to a word of advice from someone else, here it is: *never, unless you are an American, try to do any business in the United States, or with any of its citizens*. You can't win. If they owe you money, they will not pay it. If you insure them for personal injury, they will claim $120,000 for a stubbed toe. If you insure them against pollution, they will claim $1 million for breathing.

The United States is a delightful country, with low taxes, and an agreeable way of life; several amusing and attractive people live there. Where Europeans are concerned, it provides an unusual and inexpensive holiday location for the more adventurous. Most of the inhabitants are friendly, as well as picturesque. But it is not a place to do business.

## Defence cuts

FURTHER to my suggestion that certain units of the British armed forces should be reserved for homosexuals, I hear proposals for an extension of the ethnic principle in regimental designations from a colonel in the West Country.

As he points out, we already have regiments of Welsh, Irish and Scots Guards. Why not a regiment of Black Guards? This would serve as a worthy focus for pride among our fellow citizens who happen to be black, and would also remove the constant niggling allegations about colour prejudice in the Brigade.

It is an excellent suggestion. I am always pleased to hear from anybody in the armed forces above the rank of major. But when my correspondent suggests that the new regiment should be equipped with white bearskins, made from the pelts of polar bear cubs, I feel he is going over the top. Not only would white bearskins be too conspicuous, they would also be much too expensive.

Those of us who have lived and worked among the Masai in East Africa will remember how Masai warriors frequently spend four days at the hairdressers before an important parade or military engagement.

They achieve an effect which, although by no means similar to the bearskin in shape, is certainly comparable to it in magnificence.

I would suggest that the new regiment dispense with bearskins altogether, thereby achieving an important economy in the new spirit of defence cuts. This may or may not be a logical response to the apparent relaxation of tension in the Cold War.

## *29th May, 1991*

## Media studies

FOR YEARS I have been assuring any journalistic colleague who told me his telephone was tapped that he was suffering from strain, alcoholic poisoning, paranoid delusions. Take an aspirin, I have said.

To tap a telephone is an endlessly cumbersome and expensive operation I told them. Anyone who has ever had a crossed line will know how boring other people's telephone conversations are.

Phone tapping was carried out only behind the Iron Curtain, where vast resources were earmarked to suppress the news that socialism does not work. It is a well-known form of lunacy to suppose that you are under surveillance.

Now Scotland Yard has admitted tapping the telephone of a former BBC journalist who was engaged in investigating police corruption. For years, his complaints met with a blanket denial.

An inquiry was set up by the South Yorkshire police in 1987 which enabled the Assistant Commissioner of Scotland Yard a year later to write that the complaint was unsubstantiated. Sir Peter Imbert repeated the denial to a House of Commons committee in 1989.

Four years later, after this splendid series of denials, Scotland Yard admits it all. I will never again be able to reassure my friends that they are imagining things when they hear crackling noises or heavy breathing.

I fear this action by the police will have an appalling effect on the sobriety of my profession.

## 3rd June, 1991

---

### Loosen the ties

SOUTH KOREA, which has been agitating for reunion with its socialist northern half for the last 46 years, seems to have experienced a change of mind. After a glance at the appalling cost to West Germany of taking on the moribund East German economy and unemployable East German workforce, South Koreans are beginning to wonder whether they can really afford unity.

A gradual, controlled easing of tension and slow expansion of business and other links may be what the doctor ordered, they feel. I confess I feel rather the same about the socialist northern parts of England – the People's Republic of Liverpool, the Nuclear Free Zones of Derbyshire and Sheffield etc. Of course one remains emotionally attached to the inhabitants in various ways, and many southerners admire them for their warmheartedness and the unusual way they sing. But it is tremendously expensive for the rest of us to keep them in the style to which they have become accustomed.

After long thought I decided not to contribute to the appeal launched by David Bookbinder, leader of Derbshire County Council, to help him pay the £120,000 costs of his unsuccessful libel action against Norman Tebbit. He had hoped to receive enormous damages without even bothering to give evidence to explain why he thought he should have the money – a typically northern attitude, if I may say so.

But Bookbinder, who spent vast sums of ratepayers' money advertising Derbyshire as a Nuclear Free Zone, is just the sort of person whom the Government should be talking to about future arrangements. If Derbyshire could become not only nuclear-free but also a development-free, industry-free and technology-free Socialist state along the lines of East Germany it might make an inexpensive holiday location for the rest of us.

# After pindown

WHEN we learnt that victims of pindown, the new method of child-torture allegedly pioneered by the socialists in Staffordshire, were suing for enormous damages, we might have hoped that newspapers and television programmes would leave the subject alone for a while, since all these allegations are now *sub judice*.

It was not to be, but the respite might have allowed us time to reflect on what has been happening. For all the welfare jargon attaching to it, the essence of pindown seems little more than an extension of the ancient cruelty of sending naughty children to their bedrooms, as practised by Saddam Hussein, Stalin and General Pinochet in Chile.

In Staffordshire, we are told, exceptionally violent and disruptive children were sometimes sent to their bedrooms for weeks at a time. This is what gives rise to their claim for punitive damages against Staffordshire's socialist County Council.

It is none of our business to decide what Council workers should do with violent or disruptive children who are out of parental control. As we all know, there is no such thing as a

naughty child. There are only children deprived of the affection which is their birthright. Any child should be able to sue if it is denied affection, or anything else it wants. I was shocked recently to hear a so-called modern mother tell her three-year-old daughter to take her hands off a chintz sofa cover.

'Please take your jammy hands off my sofa, darling,' she said – exactly as if she was talking to a servant. My blood boiled. The child began to cry. When I reported her to the police, they said there was nothing they could do under existing law. The child has got to sue. We must all hope that the mother gets taken to the cleaners.

But I cannot help feeling a long prison sentence would be much better. Then the child could be taken into care and other methods of training applied.

## 5th June, 1991

### Don't know, don't care

MANY years ago I appeared on BBC 'Question Time', and was so appalled by the stupidity and unpleasantness of the audience that I vowed never to appear on it again. They were not people with whom it was possible to have a conversation because they had been dredged out of some fishtank in the dependency culture to represent a particular point of view on a particular subject, and nothing was going to deviate them from that point of view.

Since then, the audiences seem to have got worse. Watching them, it would be easy to decide that Britain is fit only for a socialist government, that we are a nation of half-witted students, Left-wing activists and disgruntled public employees.

One has to keep reminding oneself that these people are not typical Britons, men and women from the street. They are specially chosen for their stupidity and their unpleasant opinions. They are also, it appears, constantly urged to be as rude as possible.

Even so, as one begins to hear the same opinions repeated by people who should know better, in offices, pubs and in the privacy of their homes, a terrible dread is born. Can the British really be so stupid that they are going to elect another socialist government? I don't believe so, myself. I don't think we want a more decisive Prime Minister than nice Mr Major. We certainly don't want a more active or interfering government. Change is the only thing we really resent. As a nation, we are not really interested in politics at all, and give only the answers we think people want to hear. Why does the licensed scepticism of television audiences never reflect this?

## 8th June, 1991

### Beleaguered outposts

REPORTS are coming in from all over the country of public libraries being sacked and burnt down, librarians assaulted by gangs of infuriated youths. Outrages in Buckingham, Birmingham and Cleveland are only the latest to attract attention. In places like Camden, librarians have been living in fear of their lives for as long as many can remember.

So it was with the Christian missions in darkest Africa throughout much of the last century. For no apparent reason, the fury of the young men – half devil and half child – would be aroused, almost as if they resented the arrival of Christian civilisation in their midst.

The difference, of course, is that whereas the missions went out to Africa to teach gentler ways to a savage culture in retreat, these libraries are the last beleaguered outposts of Western bourgeois civilisation in retreat from the new barbarians: Shirley's children, as they swarm out of their vandalised comprehensive schools, jail fodder, equipped only for a life of resentful dependency on the state.

The libraries' mistake, if I dare suggest it, has been to make themselves too accessible. By insisting that they are focal points in the community, rather than quiet places for bookworms, they have aroused unrealistic expectations. Nothing is more likely to enrage the customer for video nasties than the sight of someone reading a book. It can be only a question of time before we hear of librarians being eaten in the north of England.

## 12th June, 1991

### Blessed oblivion

I DO NOT believe that breathing other people's cigarette smoke is 1,500 times more dangerous than working in an environment

103

polluted by asbestos powder. The Association for Non Smokers Rights made this absurd claim recently, and every newspaper has faithfully printed it.

Similarly, I do not believe that the London Underground has been losing £250,000 a year to Londoners who have fraudulently wrapped their florins in silver paper in order to convince the foolish ticket machines that they are really 50p coins. Yet London Underground has used this as an excuse for refusing 50p coins, and nobody has demurred.

When it comes to the new information that potato crisps provide a better, more balanced diet than apples for the growing child, I simply do not know what to believe. I would like to believe what Professor Don Naismith, head of nutrition at King's College, avers, but years of conditioning to the contrary make me uneasy.

So many pressure groups are bombarding us with advocacy statistics that it is a waste of time trying to keep up with them. The sanest approach is to read what everyone has to say, and then forget it all again. Eat apples or potato crisps, according to taste. Nothing seems to make much difference to average life expectancy.

In this context we must all have conflicting feelings about Glaxo's new wonder-drug, which promises to restore our memories and give us the mental agility of someone eight years younger. On the one hand, it is intensely irritating to find oneself forgetting simple, necessary things, like one's own address and telephone number, who one is and where one is going at any given time.

On the other hand, as one gets older, there are so many things which one should forget, which have no business to be crowding into one's memory. It is part of the dignity of growing old not to be able to remember everything.

## *15th June, 1991*

### Here be sex maniacs

NOBODY has yet explained the sudden spurt in solar activity which now threatens global disruption to power supplies. All the scientists can tell us is how a violent magnetic storm, caused by a mass of charged particles, blown on what is known as the solar wind, now threatens to trigger chaos throughout what we are pleased to call our electronic civilisation.

It all sounds rather like the night York Minster was struck by lightning and set on fire after the consecration of the Bishop of Durham. This week, by coincidence, we learn of Britain's first satellite sex channel to be launched into space in October.

Its headquarters will be in Edinburgh, but it will use the existing British Sky Broadcasting machinery to transmit what will presumably be pictures of Scots women without any clothes on. They will be seen in the homes of people all over England. Those who have bought one of Mr Murdoch's dish aerials and are prepared to pay extra for the privilege, will be able to watch naked Scots women all through the night.

I wonder if there is some purpose, some grand design behind it. Is it intended to make sex maniacs of us all, or simply to cater for existing sex maniacs? The presence of a dish aerial on the roof of a private home already advertises the presence of people who are unintelligent, incurious, possibly unemployable, probably part of that social residue which is nowadays called the 'underclass'.

After October, a dish aerial will also act as a warning that there are as likely as not to be sex maniacs there, too. With a bit of luck, they will be the sort of sex maniacs who never leave their homes under normal circumstances. But it needs only another solar flare, or violent magnetic storm, or a temporary power cut . . .

## *19th June, 1991*

### Look, no trousers

ANNOUNCING the welcome scheme for a statue of General de Gaulle in London, my friend and colleague Kenneth Rose of *The Sunday Telegraph* ended on an admonitory note: 'I hope the committee will consider an aesthetic point. Monumental statuary died with the trouser, and can be seen in any work put up this century . . . better stick to a bust.'

This aesthetic point is well taken. It plainly enshrines an important truth which had never occurred to me before. Monumental statuary died with the trouser. It should be set to verse or cast in letters of stone over the entrance to every art college in the country.

Whatever anyone says, trousers look utterly ridiculous on a statue. But it seems rather drastic to restrict all monumental masonry to busts. Perhaps the time is past when we can dress people up in togas and pretend they are Roman senators, but why should de Gaulle not be shown bare legged? There is nothing ridiculous about bare legged statues. One thinks of the Venus de Milo or Michelangelo's David. De Gaulle will be in good company.

I am not suggesting that he should be shown nude. That would be going too far. If he were shown tastefully debagged, it would cover Kenneth Rose's aesthetic point while comforting the anti-French faction in the Conservative party, which might query whether London really wants de Gaulle back, having fought a long and costly world war to the bitter end in order to get rid of him.

My proposal may also reassure Mme Cresson, the Socialist prime minister of France, who believes that one in four Englishmen is homosexual. At least the Borough of Swindon is putting up a statue of its distinguished daughter, Diana Dors, wearing a slinky dress. That should satisfy the majority of Englishmen, but it would be a good joke if the de Gaulle monument became a shrine for London's gay fraternity.

## Black museum

IN A brilliant analysis of the troubles besetting Lloyd's of London, Christopher Fildes does not discuss my theory that the collapse may have been brought about by Sir Richard Roger's hideous and absurd building in the City of London. But he does ask what use may be found for the building after the crash, suggesting either a vertical greenhouse or a giant percolator.

This is a question which should be thrown open to public debate. Personally, I would not like to drink any coffee which came out of such a percolator, and I would be worried to think that tomatoes served in a London restaurant might have come from such a greenhouse.

An obvious use for it would be to house the Arts Council and its chairman, Lord Palumbo. Then it could be turned into a sort of Black Museum of the Modern Movement. Bit by bit, all the 20th-century rubbish which has accumulated in the Tate and in municipal art galleries throughout the country could be bought and dumped here, as in a national refuse tip. In years to come, when intelligent, educated and humane people no longer feel a great anger bursting out of them when brought face to face with the 'art' of the post-war period, we might be able to laugh and laugh and laugh as we walk around the melancholy exhibition in its hideous surroundings.

Unfortunately, the French thought of it first. The equally ludicrous Centre Georges Pompidou in Paris fulfils every purpose to which my own Palumbo Centre could aspire.

What Britain needs more than a new gallery of modern art is more prison space. I would like the Lloyd's building to house only the most violent and intractable prisoners in the country.

When they rioted, as they would be bound to do in protest against the inhuman surroundings in which they were kept, they would be encouraged to go on rioting until the whole monstrosity was demolished. This might help save one or another of our beautiful Victorian prisons. Once the site has been cleared, I would suggest planting a grove of medlar trees.

## 26th June, 1991

### A tangled web

IS IT unpatriotic to disbelieve lies we are told in the national interest? Must we all believe that the Challenger 2 tank was chosen for the British Army because it was thought better than its rivals, rather than for political reasons?

Once you accept the duty of newspapers to tell lies – as well as to suppress the truth – in the national interest, I feel you are on a slippery slope. Perhaps Challenger 2 was thought better than its German and American rivals, but I don't believe it. The Challenger 1 did not distinguish itself, by many accounts, in the Gulf war and Challenger 2 was placed last out of four tanks tested by the British Army.

If we are to be told lies in order to improve the chances of Vickers selling a few more tanks to the Arabs, why should we believe anything we are told?

For the purposes of this war, we were assured that Saddam Hussein ruled by terror and was detested by all his people; furthermore, that defeat had discredited him utterly. Yet we see pictures of him being cheered by huge crowds with every sign of genuine enthusiasm wherever he goes in Iraq. How are we expected to know which are the propaganda dupes, the Iraqis or us? Could we have been on the wrong side all along, backing the odious Sheikh of Kuwait against the benevolent and popular Iraqi leader?

## French opportunities

MME Edith Cresson criticised the Gaullist leader Jacques Chirac for his language when he spoke of the 'noise and smell' of Arab and African immigrants. 'M Chirac has gone a little too far,' said this attractive and articulate Socialist Prime Minister of France.

But what English folk may have missed, in their astonishment over the robust language of French politics, is the context in which Chirac spoke:

'The French worker sees on the landing of his crowded council block a father with four wives and a score of children, making 50,000 Fr (£5,160) a month on welfare, without working, of course.

'Add to that the noise and the smell, and the French worker on the landing goes crazy. It's not racist to say that.'

Racist or not, it will come as news to the poor welfare scroungers of Britain that with a couple of extra wives and a bit of work on the children front they can draw £5,160 a month (nearly £62,000 a year) in France. What are they waiting for?

This should settle the argument between Mr Heath and Lady Thatcher once and for all, enjoyable as it has been while it lasted. Heath is right and Thatcher wrong. We will be much better off inside a Europe with open frontiers and a single currency. The whole concept of national sovereignty, as brandished by our politicians, is a deliberate deception. It covers only a government's right to screw up the economy once every four years in a cynical attempt to be re-elected, and we would be better off without it. Full membership offers an unrepeatable opportunity to solve the problem of Liverpool.

## 1st July, 1991

### Time to balkanise

IF THE Methodists genuinely intend to relax their almost obsessive disapproval of alcohol in any form, we might suppose the world would be a jollier place a result, but I am not sure.

The Methodist prohibition is not derived from an idiosyncratic interpretation of the Scriptures – any such interpretation is pretty well vitiated by events at the Marriage Feast at Cana – but is based on sociological observation. Methodism was designed as a form of Christianity which would be particularly suited to the needs of the poor. It is a sad fact, frequently remarked, that drunkenness does not become the lower orders.

Methodist teaching on drink and gambling is thus something of which we should all approve on the principle 'Don't do what I do but do what I tell you.' It is only when Methodists start exerting pressure in the opposite direction – urging the rest of us to observe their own peculiar abstinences – that friction begins to arise.

Nothing else can explain the extraordinary attitude of the British Government to alcohol. Excise duty on a bottle of table wine is 90p a bottle in Britain against a Common Market target of 9p a bottle. Our Government refuses to countenance EC moves to harmonise excise duties because, it says, Britons need to limit their drinking 'for health reasons'.

Croatia and Slovenia have shown the way. Now that the Methodists have withdrawn objections, it can only be a matter of time before Wales and the West Country, the ancient kingdom of Wessex, secedes from the semi-Islamic State of Britain, with all its Customs and immigration controls, its crippling taxes on alcohol, its huge prison population and its rows and rows of wonderful old Prime Ministers, to join the Federal Super-State of Europe.

# Metaphysical point

THE STAFF of Independent Television News recently voted to impose a £50,000 limit on all salaries. I can see that they derive a certain amount of pleasure from the exercise of spite and envy in this way, but it does not seem to occur to them that we, the viewing public, do not wish to have our news read to us by paupers or slaves. I shall certainly avoid ITV in future.

In the same way we would lose all respect for the monarchy if we thought it paid income tax like the rest of us. It is part of the mystique of monarchy that it should be above such things. The exploitation of newscasters and royals is no different, in principle, from the exploitation of children for prostitution in Liverpool, or the exploitation of chickens in battery systems.

When the RSPCA served battery-reared chicken at its annual luncheon in Queen Elizabeth Hall, London, at the weekend, proceedings were interrupted by Chickens Lib demonstrators waving banners which declared 'Meat is Murder'. This seems an extreme view, but it is equally hard to imagine why anybody should choose to eat battery chickens at all. The system impoverishes man, woman and chicken alike.

So it is with taxation. If meat is murder, taxation is theft. We may not be able to avoid the contamination of it ourselves, but there is no reason to rejoice when others are contaminated. For the Queen to be taxed would not only diminish the monarchy, but diminish us all. It is hard enough to hide the disgust we already feel for each other when we reflect that each and every one of us is a taxpayer. If we had to look at the Queen with the same disdainful eyes as we regard each other, our own loss would be incomparably greater than hers.

## *20th July, 1991*

---

### Queen Edna

THERE must be worse things for us to worry about than the Australian Republican Movement. None of us would ever have heard of this body, let alone had time to worry about it, if various newspapers had not been determined to tell us all.

Thomas Keneally described it best, in Thursday's newspaper, when he revealed that many Australians are beginning to ask themselves a number of banal and pedestrian questions, like retarded teenagers beginning to query the reality of Father Christmas.

'Australians are coming to an awareness, for the first time in their history, that they are on their own. And yet our constitution is still British-dependent. Is it appropriate for a nation which wishes to make its own way in the world to depend on a distant British succession for its Head of State?'

This boring question produces a suitably pompous and irrelevant answer:

'The Australian Republican Movement believes that on January 1, 2001 . . . Australia should become a republic . . . We believe it is time that, for economic reasons and reasons of national pride, we took an oath to Australia and Australian institutions instead of to a – however worthy – distant and differently oriented institution in the Northern Hemisphere.'

Teenage awkwardness soon gives way to teenage

sentimentality in his nightmare vision of the future:

'This inevitable 2001 departure is not seen as a denial . . . We will say goodbye with a kiss, as mature children should, not denying our childhood but justly asserting our maturity. I foresee a great party in the sun, where the Monarch of Great Britain celebrates with us this full maturity . . . '

Alas, I feel that such a grisly occasion would celebrate exactly the opposite. Why do Australians suppose we retain our own monarchy? By advertising to the world that they could no longer see the joke, they would be advertising their immaturity, as well as their humourlessness, their pomposity and their mediocrity.

Who, in any case, could they possibly choose as their Head of State in this great act of maturity? John Pilger, the mature political thinker, or Dame Edna Everidge, the mature Australian hostess and superstar?

Obviously, the better class Australian would vote for Dame Edna. But would she, really, be any more sophisticated, or funnier, in the long run?

112

### Under the iron heel

MY FIRST reaction to the plight of the Western Isles, which have lost at least £23 million entrusted to the Bank of Credit and Commerce International before some of its operations turned out to be crooked, was one of great sympathy. An article in Saturday's newspaper by the City Editor, Neil Collins, was headed: 'There is no magic formula to make your money grow.' It might more accurately have been entitled: 'There is no known way to protect the value of your savings.'

Between the certainty of inflation, a punitive level of capital taxation which survives after 12 years of Conservatism and the frenzied activities of speculators in the money market, our big institutions are increasingly vulnerable and there is nowhere for the ordinary saver to go. In times gone by there were trustworthy people to do these things for us, but as Mr Collins points out, they are no longer easy to find. Anybody who understands finance is in the thick of things trying to get rich quick on his own behalf.

As a London resident of Hammersmith, whose council has lost hundreds of millions of pounds gambling on currency markets, I could sympathise with the poor Western Islanders at the hands of local smart alecs who turned out not to be smart enough.

Now the poor Scottish islanders have applied for a government grant to be treated as an environmentally sensitive area, with the backing of the all-powerful Royal Society for the Protection of Birds, which has ordered the Government to make Orkney, Shetland and some of the inner Hebrides environmentally sensitive areas forthwith.

So it is that another previously free area of the British Isles falls under the iron heel of the RSPB's ever-expanding empire, with its network of informers, its electronic surveillance techniques and its dawn raids on the homes of suspected egg-collectors.

I would not be at all surprised to see the entire country fall to RSPB occupation and control if we cannot keep these financial smart alecs in their place. They should, of course, be exposed and ridiculed before they can wreak their havoc, but they are protected by all the pride and avarice of our legal profession in its abominable libel laws. What chance did the poor Western Islanders ever have?

# Pride and joy

A CORRESPONDENT who has observed how farmers are obliged to dump dead animals in fields and ditches nowadays, since knackers refuse to collect them, suggests that we should introduce vultures into England in order to deal with the problem.

This would not only clear away all the carrion, it would also delight the growing number of bird-lovers. Officials of the Royal Society for the Protection of Birds could have the time of their lives injecting the birds with silicon chips and other delights, listing them in national registers and following their movements on electronic surveillance equipment.

If they could be persuaded to settle on top of the nation's growing number of mosques, they might have the effect of making some of our immigrants feel more at home. In fact, it would be an admirable idea if we could adopt the vulture as our national symbol, rather as Americans have adopted the bald eagle.

This would not only emphasise our multi-racial society, but also our post-Imperial role generally. The trouble with St George is that it seems unlikely he ever existed.

The trouble with the Union Flag is that it has been worn as shorts or underpants and sat upon by too many *Sun* readers. I would like to see these revolting people try to sit on a vulture.

## 3rd August, 1991

## Nothing left to say

LAST week the High Court, in a constitutionally unprecedented case, ruled that government ministers were above the law in their official capacity: they were immune from punishment for contempt of court, so that if a court finds against a minister, neither the minister nor his ministry has to pay any attention.

That was the finding of Mr Justice (Simon) Brown when Treasury counsel put it to him that Mr Kenneth Baker, as a servant of the crown which was the 'fountain of all justice and power', was protected against any prosecution for contempt because it was impossible for one part of the Crown to be prosecuted by another.

I suppose Mr Justice Brown knows what he is talking about, although it sounds like poppycock to me. Then, in the civil court this week, we learned that a party activist who criticises his MP as being vain, deceitful and unconcerned with the good of the party – in a limited-circulation leaflet to other party members – may have to pay £150,000 in 'compensatory' damages and a further £200,000 in costs.

It has been a gloomy week for England, feeding the self-importance of lawyers and politicians alike. In 30 years of writing about the contemporary scene, I do not think I have ever mentioned the name of Mrs Teresa Gorman, MP for Billericay, who has already had successful libel actions against the *Daily Express, Private Eye* and her local newspaper, the *Billericay and Wickford Gazette*. One thing is absolutely certain, that I shall never voluntarily mention her name again.

## *5th August, 1991*

### Kutch as kutch can

I NEVER knew the last Maharajah of Kutch whose death at the age of 81 was reported in last Thursday's newspaper, yet he had been living among us, in a modest cottage in the village of Mayford, near Woking, for many years, spending less and less time in his magificent palace at Kutch.

Although a man of enormous wealth, he despised politics and politicians, confining himself to such patriotic gestures as donating 100 kilograms of gold to the Indian war fund at the time of the Chinese invasion of Assam.

Madansinh Sawai Bahadur was very well born, tracing his acnestry back to the Moon by way of Krishna in a family that had ruled Kutch for more than 1,000 years. How galling it must have been for such a man, in retirement, to find himself frequently asked to lunch at Broadlands by Lord Mountbatten, the European upstart who had tricked him out of his princely inheritance.

Madansinh, whose enjoyment of the *Gadi* (royal couch) of Kutch was so tragically brief, nevertheless became a noted diplomat, as well as tennis player and pig sticker. The Rann of Kutch, we learnt from his obituary, is a desert salt marsh which has traditionally protected his principality from invaders.

It is only from obituaries that we learn such interesting truths nowadays. Those who read modern poetry and criticism will be intensely irritated by the vogue word 'epiphany' and 'epiphanic' to describe any joyous manifestation. But it is surely true that while the plastic and visual, poetic and musical arts have sunk beneath the consideration of intelligent people and vanished from sight, the obituarist's art, drawing on so many strands of shared experience within our culture, is flourishing as never before. It is within our obituaries that our remaining epiphanies are to be found.

## *7th August, 1991*

### Pity them

MANY people measure a nation's social health by the number of single parents, or abortions, or infant deaths, or violent crimes, or road fatalities, but these seem to me rather obvious measurements, like judging the gravity of a patient's fever by taking his temperature.

A subtler measurement might be found in the consumption of China tea, or The Gentleman's Relish, or sherry. Sherry is a quintessentially English drink. Few Spaniards outside Jerez drink it, and many have never heard of it. When the English drink sherry, they assert their belief in moderation, restraint, understatement.

Now we learn that sherry is disappearing fast from the social scene. In 1979, the year of Mrs Thatcher's election, we imported 75 million litres. In 1980, sales were 48.7 million litres, but these had shrunk to about 28 million litres last year.

The Sherry Institute in London blames tax and the recession, but excessive taxation has always been with us, and I do not see how the recession can possibly be blamed for what is plainly a fundamental shift in taste and outlook. Moderation, restraint and understatement are out; strong lager, rum and coke, and vodka fruit jellies are in.

It may seem to be the British character which is changing; the joyless Murdoch elite, or 'yobbocracy' as it wittily calls itself, disguises its social and intellectual inadequacies by making ever louder noises in the land.

But even 28 million litres of good Spanish sherry is not such a bad sale, when one comes to think of it. It will be interesting to

116

see which group will be hit furthest by the recession in the long run: the sherry drinkers or the money-mad, alcohol-starved helots in Murdoch's Black Hole of Wapping.

## 10th August, 1991

### Hello and goodbye

ONE OF the BBC's most popular programmes for the past 14 years has been called 'Follow Me', designed to teach foreigners to speak English. It has been screened in 70 countries, including China, where at peak times it played to 100 million people. Now, in response to world demand, the programme will be scrapped and make way for a new BBC educational programme, 'Hello', designed to teach foreigners to speak American.

This seems rather sad. Many foreigners, in my experience, are highly intelligent people, humorous and well educated. From now on, whenever they try to speak English, nobody will be able to take them seriously.

Many Americans, too, are intelligent and humorous, and some have had the good fortune to be educated in Europe. It is only in the matter of language that they have reason to feel inferior, carrying their colonial intonations and barbaric usages round their necks like so many carthorse ornaments at a gymkhana.

The truth of the matter is that divorced from its roots in European Christendom and liberal Judaism, American culture – like that of all devolved colonial societies – is a culture of rubbish. Must all those patient Indians and earnest Chinese listen politely to Dr Leonard Jeffries, America's leading radical philosopher, while he preaches the new 'Afrocentric' theories of education: how Afro-American development is held back by a conspiracy of Jews and mafiosi aimed at the financial destruction of black people: how black people are genetically superior to whites, handicapped by their lack of skin pigment: how Beethoven was black, and the rest of it?

It would be absurd to suspect foreigners of harbouring these rubbishy opinions just because they talk with an American accent, but it seems a shame, just when we were beginning to convince ourselves that foreigners are not necessarily inferior, that they should choose to take this great step backwards.

117

## Save a Yuppie

I AM not sure that I agree with the policemen who have been urging us not to give money to the innumerable beggars who now swarm the streets of London as in the old souks of Fez and Marrakesh. Many of them, we are told, come from affluent homes, fitted with all modern conveniences, to which they repair every evening after a day's begging. They can reckon to earn about £75 a day which, with social security benefits, might help them to keep a boy at Eton if they had a boy at Eton.

Others have bicycled all the way from distant Merseyside to profit from what Detective Chief Inspector Jackson, head of crime for the Charing Cross division, has called the 'goodheartedness, generosity and charity that abounds in Londoners'. But he urges us to harden our hearts to these 'vicious parasites'.

Yet many of them are probably young merchant bankers, made redundant. All have had the enterprise to get on their bikes and come and beg in London, rather than waste their time applying for phantom 'jobs', applicants for which are expected to be able to spell and understand simple arithmetic.

Of course there are always a few no-hopers in the profession, but as DCI Jackson says, most of the people we are dealing with are young, fit and intelligent. They fly the flag for British initiative and we should support them.

## *2nd September, 1991*

---

## Travel section

'I HAVE loathed fascism and loved freedom all my life but . . . ' wrote the Lyme Regis novelist, John Fowles, complaining about the summer invasion of trippers, or 'grockles' as they are now called, into his Dorset retreat.

A responsible Government, fond of issuing health warnings on every conceivable subject, should not ignore the possibility of a violent rustic uprising against the grockle menace, whether it takes a fascist or a Marxist turn.

But there are other reasons why the Government should try to persuade as many people as possible to stay at home in the summer months. The British Association was warned last week of the perils which await grockles in the countryside: bulls, vipers, infected leeches, horseflies, cancerous bracken, poisonous berries. Hepatitis, dysentery and typhoid lurk under every dandelion leaf. The entire countryside and coastal region should be declared a major health hazard.

Those Britons who find themselves incurably restless, like the great seadogs of yore, might pay a visit to the wondrous new terminal at Stansted Airport, designed by the great Sir Norman Shaw. Almost cathedral-like in its inspired simplicity, this masterpiece resembles nothing so much as a giant hangar, standing empty and expectant, like a Rhine-maiden awaiting violation by a pack of wolves.

If the spectator stands on his head in front of this mighty building, shutting his eyes and blocking his ears, it is possible for him to entertain the illusion that he is being wafted on a magic carpet over the ruins of Angkor Vat in Kampuchea, as Cambodia is now called. It is an experience not to be missed.

The staff, too, are most helpful, as one would only expect in any building designed by Norman Shaw.

## God bless him

A NEW national sport seems to unite the lowest and vilest in the land – readers of the *Sun* and *News of the World* – with the so-called intelligentsia who announce their superior moral outlook by writing letters to the *Independent*. It is to insult the Prince of Wales.

Much as one welcomes anything which unites the country and conciliates its warring factions, I cannot help feeling that on this occasion the new alliance of louts and pseuds may find itself out on a limb.

Any child of nine can see that on architectural matters the Prince of Wales is obviously right, and that all the fine opinions of the 'experts' – the architects who, since the war, have reduced our urban landscapes to a succession of eyesores – are mercenary in their inspiration.

We have the worst architects in the world, also the most conceited and obstreperous. Modernism never took root in Britain; our common sense rejected it even as our soil rejected the hideous concrete and our climate the emphasis on plate glass. Time has discredited Le Corbusier no less than it has discredited Marx, Lenin and Freud, demonstrating that the four of them bring nothing but ugliness, poverty, oppression and brutal stupidity.

The Prince of Wales, by contrast, goes from strength to

strength. When his toast was proposed at the recent presentation of *Literary Review*'s £5,000 Real Poetry prize, awarded to Paul Griffin and sponsored by the *Mail on Sunday*, music and singing spontaneously broke out accompanied by shouts of 'God Bless the Prince of Wales'. He has never, so far as I know, expressed an opinion on the vexed point of whether poems should rhyme, or scan, or try to make sense, but we instinctively felt he was on our side.

# 4th September, 1991

## Beast in view

IT WOULD be hard to think of a more unpleasing consortium than one composed of the World Wide Fund for Nature, the Royal Society for the Protection of Birds and the Ramblers Association. All three, by their public utterances, have convinced me that they are so demented by self-importance as to present an eventual challenge to the constitution and established laws of the country.

Yet it is this consortium which has applied to Mr Heseltine for money to buy the £10 million Mar Lodge Estate in the Cairngorms. It is the most famous deer-stalking estate in Scotland and quite possibly the world.

The consortium, which promises to promote nature conservation (as if nature could not survive in the Cairngorms without the help of nature conservers) 'rambling', cross-country skiing and other improbable pursuits, will also ban deerstalking and grouse shooting.

This is no time to waste valuable newsprint pointing out that the Cairngorms will be completely spoilt if they are tramped and skied over by all the millions of semi-hysterical nature-lovers, bird-spotters and 'ramblers' in our sick urban society, rather than preserved for the contemplation of the well-to-do about their sporting occasions.

There is no need to point out to Mr Heseltine, as *Daily Telegraph* readers well understand, that grouse regard it as a privilege to be shot at by the indigenous gentry, and are proud to serve the nation by offering themselves as targets to Arab and Japanese guests; that deer go into a nervous decline if they think no one is hunting them.

Suffice to say that if Mr Heseltine gives so much as one penny of taxpayers' money to this unspeakable consortium, I shall make it my business to hound him out of public life.

I shall abuse him in *The Spectator*, mock him in Way of the World; if he writes anything I shall ridicule it and tear it to pieces in *Literary Review*. If any newspaper prints a photograph of him I shall threaten the editor with private prosecution for provoking a breach of the peace.

Worse than this, if ever he visits his Exmoor property again, I shall set my highly trained pack of pekingeses on him. He will be a marked man.

## Straight talking

LADY Thatcher, at the beginning of a 10-day tour of Japan for which she is thought to have been paid £1 million, has congratulated the Japanese Prime Minister, Mr Toshiki Kaifu, on his 'delicate diplomatic approach' to the Chinese on the subject of human rights.

While she was undoubtedly right to compliment Mr Kaifu – a large part of Japanese conversation is made up of compliments – I am not sure that human rights was the best subject to choose.

They have never been a matter of tremendous interest in the Far East. Quite possibly Mr Kaifu was too delicate to mention the matter at all to the Chinese. Europeans and Americans are interested in human rights, Japanese and Chinese are interested in flower arrangement and things of that sort.

We do not expect Mr Major and President Mitterrand to discuss flower arrangement when they meet, and it would be a waste of time to congratulate them on the delicacy of their approach to it. I am not sure that my friends in Japan are receiving value for money.

## *7th September, 1991*

## Ordinary bloke

EVER since that night of December 8, 1980 – I was in a taxi in Manila, trying to find the French embassy, when I heard the dreadful news – I have taken a censorious line about Mark Chapman, the man who shot John Lennon.

It was no excuse to say he was reading J. D. Salinger's *Catcher*

*In The Rye* at the time. Many of us may have found Lennon irritating but we managed to contain our irritation. If we all decided to mow down anyone who irritated or displeased us there would be general mayhem and nothing would ever get done. Chapman richly deserved to be put in prison.

That has been my attitude throughout, and that is what it remains. But on studying Paul McCartney's exclusive series of interviews in the *Sun* this week, I can begin to understand some of the pressures young Chapman must have felt.

McCartney, whose obese, grinning face appeared with those of his wife and 'kids', was at pains to make himself as likeable as possible to the vile readers of that odious newspaper:

'I feel I'm an ordinary bloke,' he said. 'Not an ordinary ordinary bloke, because I'm famous, but I'm ordinary in the sense that I was brought up in Liverpool by very ordinary people.'

He also emphasised his high moral attitude: 'For instance, I don't think it's a good thing to go around the home swearing all the time.'

Perhaps it is such strict morality which has persuaded this ordinary, fat millionaire from Liverpool to buy a neighbouring farm in Somerset for no reason but to deny it to the local hunt. I do not suppose McCartney has ever been down to this part of Somerset, with his amusing slogans along the lines that all you need is love. I am afraid he would not be very popular if he did.

In fact, these sick, urban animal sentimentalists are becoming a serious menace as they spread their activities into the countryside. Where Mark Chapman is concerned, the moral theologians teach us that while we should hate the sin, we should love the sinner. When he is released from prison, I shall ask him down to Somerset, give him some Surtees to read and ask his advice about protecting traditional country pastimes.

## Quality of mercy

IF DEREK Bentley was as innocent as he now seems to have been of the small part in the murder of a policeman for which he was hanged in 1953, then we may take comfort that these cases of judicial over-enthusiasm are not a recent development, as people might have feared.

But if Bentley's ghost is to be given a free pardon, as I have always felt it should be, I hope the authorities will take the opportunity to review the free pardon given to the ghost of

Timothy Evans in October 1966 when Roy Jenkins, the then Home Secretary, decided to pardon it for the murder of its daughter.

If we accept the evidence produced by Ludovic Kennedy in his book *10 Rillington Place*, it is apparent that Evans must have been an accomplice to the murder after the event, and it seems much more likely than not that he was an accomplice before the event as well.

I have always been of the opinion that Evans was guilty. On the other hand, one cannot expect the Lord Chief Justice to pass the death sentence on him a second time, since the death penalty has mercifully been abolished; even the present mandatory life sentence seems inappropriate when one reflects that Evans is no longer, as it were, alive.

Perhaps we should concentrate on present-day excesses. It seems to me that the sentence of nine months imprisonment passed by Judge David Miller at Isleworth on a 36-year-old housewife who massaged two male French teenagers in her bedroom, was altogether excessive. Must we wait another 38 years before justice is done?

## *9th September, 1991*

### Ladies of Greenham

THERE is something almost unbearably poignant about Greenham Common's Outdoors Camp for Independent Ladies as it has been visited and described by various intelligent and sympathetic women reporters on its 10th birthday.

The cruise missiles, which provided the original purpose of the settlement, have long since been removed. Yet still these ladies sit over their cooking pots in long floral dresses, casting spells and celebrating the more irrational aspects of their womanliness.

*Swift as the wind my sisters are, strong as the rain*
*Sure as the sun that shines, we'll sing this song again.*

Strong as the rain they may be, but I would be surprised if they were much good at cooking. I have not tasted what is inside their cooking pots, but I rather fear it would be utterly disgusting.

This is because, more than anything else, these ladies seem to be protesting against the traditional role of womanhood – especially, of course, in relation to their menfolk. The reason for this rejection of men is that men, too, have given up their traditional roles of warrior, hunter and protector.

I was never much impressed by their adherence to the anti-nuclear cause, and the survival of the ladies' camp after it has been removed rather proves my point. Brainwashed as they were by Freud, they were originally drawn to Greenham by the brooding, phallic presence of the cruise missiles behind the barbed wire.

It was to embrace these as symbolising their lost lovers that the ladies first started cutting through the barbed wire in maenad packs. Now that the missiles have been removed, the ladies must celebrate their bereavement in a succession of increasingly meaningless rituals, in which police are required to cover the retreat of the fugitive, rejecting male.

No good purpose would be served by telling these ladies that Freud has long since been discredited, along with Marx, Lenin and Le Corbusier. The only solution to this problem, as to so many problems, is the return of National Service.

# 11th September, 1991

## Tweet tweet

IT IS modest of the Royal Society for the Protection of Birds to demand only one place in the Cabinet for a Secretary of State for Wildlife. What we really need is a Secretary for State for Birds, with junior ministers for every known species of bird.

According to the RSPB there is reason for concern over 117 of Britain's native bird species: ploughing of land threatens the corncrake; inappropriate conifer planting threatens the greenshank and the dunlin, while overgrazing by red deer threatens pinewoods, whose disappearance will threaten crested tits and Scottish crossbills. Fluctuating water levels threaten the black-throated diver and the Slavonian grebe, while a rise in sea level threatens avocets, bitterns and garganeys.

Poor management of sandeel fisheries threatens the arctic tern and the kittiwake, poor management of the fishing industry threatens razorbills and guillemots, while Dartford warblers are threatened by what can only be described as a general lack of management in Dorset, Hampshire, Surrey and Berkshire.

Some of these problems are easily solved. One can quite easily tell the sheep and red deer to stop overgrazing. Problems of how to succour the crested tit by planting pine trees which the greenshank and dunlin may find inappropriate must be left to experts.

Farmers can be prevented from ploughing their land by the threat of heavy fines or prison sentences, but the prevention of fluctuating water levels (to save the Slavonian grebe) may be rather more expensive, while the problems of the Dartford warbler seem to require that the RSPB should take over all local government in Dorset, Hampshire, Surrey and Berkshire.

Oddly enough, I should not be at all surprised if all these birds, the crested tit and Dartford warbler alike, managed rather better in the long run without any help from these frenzied busybodies.

It is one thing to enjoy looking at birds, quite another to expect the whole world to accommodate your little hobby. If the RSPB was an occupying army one would understand its readiness to dictate to the Government and to private citizens on every aspect of their lives. Since it is nothing but a collection of sentimental bores, it is surely time someone told it to shut up and leave the birds alone.

## *14th September, 1991*

### A merciless judge

CAR-STEALING, joy-riding and ram-raiding are now the main sports of young people in many parts of the country. In Northumberland and Tyne and Wear alone, 31,000 cars were taken for these purposes in 1990. No wonder there are riots whenever the police try to enforce the law. We shall see the same but probably worse when Hattersley and Kaufman try to enforce their idiotic ban on hunting.

The terrible question of an appropriate punishment for joy-riding has to be faced, and it begins to look as if the legal establishment does not shrink even from such extreme remedies as community service. I am not sure what exactly is involved in this dread penalty, but understand it must be pretty unpleasant. Nearly everything connected with the word 'community' is unpleasant: community charge, community centre, community arts . . . one does not like to think what may be involved in the idea of community punishment.

Last Saturday's newspaper told of the extraordinary case of a North London teenager, Ahmed Helwa, who jumped into the car of a Japanese accountant, 28-year-old Mr Yoshinao Kikuchi, while Mr Kikuchi stopped to use a cash machine. In an attempt to stop the teenager driving off with his car, Mr Kikuchi stood in front of it, but the teenager drove over him and failed to halt. The accountant, whose wife was four months' pregnant, died of multiple injuries.

Arrested four days later, Helwa pleaded guilty to taking a car without consent, but not guilty to the charge of causing death by reckless driving claiming he had not seen his victim. An Old Bailey jury accepted this. Imposing a two-year driving ban, Recorder Anthony Arlidge, QC, said that Mr Kikuchi's death was a tragedy 'for all concerned'. He told Helwa: 'I want to make you appreciate the terrible consequences of what you did. But I don't want to make it seem impossible for you to drive again.'

Even this seems pretty tough. A two-year ban, after all, is what you receive for a really serious offence like drinking a glass of wine over Sunday luncheon in a neighbour's house. Poor Ahmed Helwa will be 21 before he is allowed to drive again.

But Recorder Arlidge was still not satisfied. He sentenced the unfortunate youth to a further 100 hours' community service – just for borrowing a car and accidentally running over its owner! It was not Helwa's fault the owner died, or that his widow was pregnant. Helwa was just exercising every young Briton's right to borrow a car from time to time.

## Rumours of war

TO START another war in the Gulf for no other purpose than to keep foreign tourists out of England may seem a desperate remedy, but before we dismiss it out of hand, there are one or two things which I feel we should be told about the Gulf war.

A person I met recently in a Somerset country house assured me that she knew as a fact that Baghdad had been completely flattened by American bombers. Press and television had agreed to keep it secret, she said.

She refused to be influenced by my assurance that I had been a newspaperman for 30 years, and it simply is not among our vices to keep a secret of that sort.

But something odd was certainly going on out there. This week a Pentagon spokesman claimed that American troops burst through the Iraqi front line using ploughs with which they buried the Iraqis alive in their trenches. There were no US casualties at all.

This virtual absence of casualties on the American side – no figures have been given for Iraqi casualties either – leads me to the suspicion that there was no war in the Gulf, or at any rate no effective contact between the two armies. The trenches so ingeniously filled in were already empty.

What happened was that the Americans simply dropped a couple of million tons of high explosive into the desert and withdrew. The Iraqis set fire to Kuwait's oil fields – in reprisal for Kuwait's flouting its Opec obligations, overproducing and underselling its oil – and also withdrew. Both sides declared a victory.

The chief result of the war has been that American citizens have more or less given up on the idea of foreign holidays. Without wishing to sound inhospitable, I must say it has made it much easier to find a cab in London this year.

Perhaps it would be over-reacting to start a new war every year. Rumours of war might do the trick. But if the British Tourist Authority could forget about Peter Rabbit and adopt Beatrix Potter's Fierce Bad Rabbit as our national emblem, that should manage to frighten them all away.

## Deference due

THE REASON given for the decision of Thames Valley police to abolish saluting was that it was 'outmoded and of no worth in modern policing'. One wonders what it is exactly about modern policing which gives such cause for satisfaction.

Thames Valley police came in for some savage criticism recently when the previous Chief Constable took it into his head to set up roadblocks all around Ascot to ask drivers if they had a drink while at the races.

This behaviour not only created a serious nuisance for motorists in the area, it also wasted police time, wasted public money and, by removing officers from proper policing duties, played into the hands of the criminal classes.

The new Chief Constable of Thames Valley, Mr Charles Pollard, reveals that the decision to abolish saluting was taken after 'discussion workshops' involving all 5,000 police and civilian members of his force.

And just what, might one ask, were the criminals of Oxfordshire, Buckinghamshire and Berkshire doing while the area's 5,000 policemen were engaged in discussion workshops about whether to salute each other or not? The salute is not only a sign of personal deference, it is also an acknowledgment of authority. Of course, there is no need for authority if decisions are going to be taken by a process of discussion workshops.

Thames Valley is the first of 55 police authorities to abolish saluting, and I shall be interested to see what happens if the idea spreads. But I feel the police would be ill-advised if they forgot how to do it. One day, by sheer misfortune, they might bump into a burglar or similar villain as they go about their business of hunting down motorists and masseuses. Then it might be very useful to know how to show respect.

## 5th October, 1991

### Moment of doubt

FOR MORE than 10 years I have been reading about Rod Stewart's marital and amorous adventures in the tabloid press with great interest. This week it suddenly occurred to me that I did not know whether Stewart is a racing car driver, a footballer, a radio comedian or a television soap actor. On Thursday, for reasons which I cannot now remember, I decided to inquire. I was told he is a pop singer.

My question provoked a certain amount of derision. Presumably he sings on television and is also a television star. There seems to be an almost unbridgeable divide in this country between those who watch a lot of television – the young, the old, the poor, the unemployed – and those who do not. Soon the two nations will have no cultural references in common.

It would be nice to think it was the desire to bridge this great divide which persuaded Thames Television to make an hour-long documentary film about me, to be broadcast on Tuesday week, October 15 at 10.40 pm. For more than a year I have been climbing up church towers, pulling funny faces and composing little speeches to camera.

My predecessor, the great Peter Simple, used to warn that

television corrupts not only those who watch it but also those who perform on it. One can see how it softens the skin and empties the mind, producing intellectual and physical effeminacy in men, general vacuity in women. But its true effect is infinitely more pernicious, according to Simple. It is the greatest force for evil in the modern world.

The programme I have made, called 'Waugh Memorial', takes the form of an hour-long paean, a hagiography, a litany of praise offered like incense before the altar of a heathen idol. I had hoped it might momentarily lighten the lives of the television generation – 'lazy, loutish and lawless'. Now, having seen the film, I suspect I might have had other motives. I may have done something very wicked. Perhaps it is time to make a pilgrimage, barefoot, to the ancient shrine of St James in Compostella.

# 7th October, 1991

## Ecclesiastical news

SO MUCH dragging of the feet has gone on over the great European adventure that it now looks as if there will be no station at our end of the Channel Tunnel when this monstrous folly is officially opened in June 1993. The best we can hope for is a cluster of Portakabins and Nissen huts.

I hope that at least some sort of shrine can be put up in time to welcome the Pope when he arrives on the first train to accept the homage of England's bishops and take control of the Church of England.

So uninterested has Britain become in Europe that not many people in this country have even read the Treaty of Rome. It may come as a surprise to some when they learn that the Archbishop of Canterbury will be required to make this simple gesture of submission, involving little more than a short prostration and a token or symbolic kissing of the feet.

The Service, which is called an Act of Reconciliation in the Anglican liturgy, or Pedilingus Normalis in the Roman, is thought to be very beautiful. While the Pope is here, I hope to interest him in a special cause which has been very close to my heart ever since the ecumenical movement got under way in the early Sixties.

This is the canonisation, or at very least beatification, of Titus Oates (1649-1705) the Cambridge theologian whose discovery of

130

the Popish Plot in 1678 must surely qualify him for the post of Patron Saint of journalists. If Dr Carey is prepared to lick Karol Wojtyla's toes this seems a small price to pay.

## *12th October, 1991*

---

### End to criticism

ON TUESDAY, as I have already mentioned, the entire independent television network will be given over to an hour-long documentary extolling my life and work. Cunning television viewers – if such there be – will suspect that the purpose of the operation is to publicise my autobiography and promote its sales, although I am not sure whether there is really much common ground between people who watch television and those who read books.

Others may interpret the documentary, called 'Waugh Memorial', as an act of atonement by its makers, Thames Television, for the distress they caused to Lady Thatcher and to some of her admirers in the Conservative party by the film 'Death on the Rock' a few years ago.

Many people thought the film raised rather tasteless questions about the killing of some suspected terrorists in Gibraltar. It will be remembered that the Government explained quite clearly afterwards that its undercover soldiers were only trying to arrest the three dead Irishmen (one was a woman), but the soldiers wrongly thought they might be armed and connected by wireless to a non-existent pile of explosives in the vicinity.

Whether it was all a ghastly mistake or not, everybody agreed that the Government has a perfect right to shoot suspected terrorists in the street whenever it chooses and television journalists have no business to query this right. There was much talk that Thames Television would be punished for its intrusion into the Government's private law enforcement arrangements by not having its franchise renewed when it came up for renewal.

By odd coincidence, Tuesday October 15 is also the day when the Government's decision is due. If Thames Television has lost its franchise, this might well teach other companies a lesson. Criticism of this or any other government should be made by a specially appointed and properly supervised government ombudsman, if at all.

## *14th October, 1991*

### Englishman's home

MANY people, for a variety of reasons, have observed how confidence in the police has sadly diminished in the last few years. It seems odd that as trust and affection recede, the Government should be concerned to give the police new and draconian powers over the law-abiding private citizen – powers which no thoughtful policeman would possibly want.

The new Explosives Regulations, laid before Parliament as Statutory Instrument 1991 No. 1531, appoints the police to the role of Health and Safety Inspectors. They will be empowered not only to enter places of work, but also any private residence which they believe may contain any explosive – let us say a firework, a cartridge or old war souvenir.

If the Statutory Instrument becomes law, the police will not only be empowered to enter any private residence in the country without a magistrate's warrant. They will also be empowered to search, confiscate property and order the taking of photographs. Perhaps most grisly of all, the occupants will be required to answer questions – silence is not permitted.

I suppose I am as much opposed to the private ownership of explosives as most people, but it is a minority taste and a minority anxiety. To lay every private citizen's home open to instant police inspection is an over-reaction, like Douglas Hurd's hysterical gun-licence law which continues to create so much hatred of the police all over the country. The new Explosives Regulations will pass into law without debate or vote in either House, unless enough Members lay a 'prayer' before the end of the month, requesting a debate.

## Stay at home

PETER Simple was right. Television may or may not be the greatest evil in the modern world, as he maintains – at present I am still in the deluded stage of supposing it might be put to some wholesome purpose – but it is certainly addictive.

On Friday a team of American televisionists from CBS's '60 Minutes' programme came down to Combe Florey to make a film on the subject of tourism. Much as one likes Americans, one had to remember what a wonderful place London has become since the disappearance of the American tourist: plenty of cabs, no difficulty getting into theatres or restaurants, so much less noise . . .

Americans would be mad if they left their own beautiful country, with its exciting amusement parks and catering facilities, to visit Britain, I said. Even if they avoid being shot down by crazed Arab gunmen in the street, blown up by Irish freedom fighters or attacked by American pit bull terriers – nobody in Britain is allowed to carry a weapon in his own defence – they will almost certainly catch a cold in our climate.

They will be robbed by our taxi-drivers and shop-assistants wherever they go. Any kids they bring to Britain will almost certainly be sexually abused by the natives. Worse than any of this, the British diet is not suitable for delicately nurtured Americans. On first contact with our salmonella-infected chickens' eggs, our listeria-ridden dairy products and our beef made from mad cows, many American visitors have found that their stomachs have simply dropped out. Since the collapse of socialism in Britain, there are no medical facilities of any description.

I hope I undid some of the damage done by the British Travel Association with its multi-million pound budget. Those who work in the hotel industry may not agree with me, but I am beginning to see tourism as the greatest evil in the modern world.

## Crock of gold

READING recent wills and bequests, as we all tend to do in times of recession, I was impressed to learn of a man who had amassed his £4.5 million fortune simply by returning discarded soft drinks bottles to the factory. Mr Frank Moody, of north Nottinghamshire, who died at 66 in April, used other people's carelessness over bottles to found an empire based on the Yorkshire Bottle Exchange, later the Yorkshire Bottle Company, handling 250,000 crates of empty bottles a week.

This is the sort of thing we were always encouraged to do as children. Silver paper, as tin foil was called in those days, was thought to be another means of amassing a fortune, although I never heard of anybody actually amassing one from it. But I doubt whether the new generation of youngsters, or 'kids', will be interested. They look for quicker ways of enriching themselves.

In fact, they would almost certainly be unable to count the bottles. A terrifying report by the National Foundation for Educational Research, which took a sample of 3,400 seven year olds tested last summer, revealed that after two years at school nearly half the pupils were unable to add or subtract, fewer than one in seven could multiply five by five, only one in seven could work out the cost of three 50p loaves of bread, only one in three could count up to 100.

Perhaps the only way to get rich quick in the years ahead will be to set up a small table and pack of cards outside the DSS office, the Labour Exchange, Post Office and other places where benefits are paid and challenge them to Spot the Lady, or to draw a higher card than your ace of spades.

Alternatively, of course, one could just knock them down and take away their great wodges of £10 notes. There *must* be ways for young people to make their fortune, even after 11 years of Nanny Thatcher.

## And so farewell

WHEN the *Independent* was founded five years ago I was full of hope. Moulds were being broken and a new spirit was abroad. All the pomposity, self-importance and humourlessness of the old

*Guardian* were to be buried under the collapsing structures of socialism, welfarism and modernism in the arts. News would no longer be controlled by the government press departments, or handed out unattributably to the toadies of the Parliamentary Press Lobby . . .

Sadly, I observe that all these fine aspirations are now one with Nineveh and Tyre. The newspaper caters for the same congregation of embittered female social workers, ineducable teachers, unemployable arts graduates and redundant health administrators as the *Guardian*, with a slightly stronger pitch towards the 'gay community'.

On Friday it launches 'The 1991 Constitutional Convention' in Manchester, when all the bores of the north of England will assemble to be addressed by such thrilling objects of national concern as Beverly Anderson, Patricia Hewitt, Des Wilson, Marina Warner, Alan Bleasdale, Tony Benn and Ben Okri, who will surely be the United Nations' next Secretary-General.

'The 1991 Constitutional Convention promises to be a turning point in British political history,' intoned the *Independent* on Monday. If it believes that, it can believe anything. There is no harm, of course, in all these nice, boring people coming together and exchanging ideas. Marina Warner, the most charming of them all, explains that a chance meeting with Cecil Parkinson in the Garrick Club persuaded her it was time to change the constitution:

'All through the decade's development I have not felt represented either in Parliament or in the law, and if someone such as myself does not feel represented, then how much greater the frustration of others . . . ' she wrote.

Nothing could be lovelier than that Marina Warner should be represented. But for a newspaper to encourage such people to hold meetings and talk, rather than write letters to the editor, is a denial of the newspaper's function, and a sign of despair.

## *2nd November, 1991*

### *Res ipsa loquitur*

IT HAS become a commonplace in Britain to complain bitterly about the state of British Rail – its monstrous expense, its incompetence and its dirt – but an institution which seems to be in every bit as poor a condition is British law.

Almost every day we read of the appalling mistakes it has made – on Wednesday, a man was released after 11 years in prison on a false charge of rape. It now appears that there was evidence which may have proved his innocence on at least one of the charges 11 years ago, but it was not produced.

Lawyers are so dishonest that libraries complain they can no longer stock legal textbooks. They are stolen even faster than theological books. And now we learn of a drive by Anthony Scrivener QC, the chairman of the Bar, to save barristers the trouble of learning Latin: 'We should acknowledge at last that the Romans and their civilisation have gone for ever and their language went with them,' says this firebrand. 'Let the classical scholars argue in Latin or Greek, but let us get on with the language of the people.'

If we despise our lawyers now, how much more will we despise them when they try speaking our langauge? The truth, I suspect, is not only that they are too ignorant to understand the simplest Latin tags and too idle to learn them – *De minimis non curat lex, Volenti non fit injuria* etc – but they also find the commonsense they encapsulate deeply repugnant.

But perhaps the ignorance and intellectual degradation is now worldwide. It was in Ottawa, Canada, that the Princess of Wales had to pretend to be amused by being mistakenly described as the Princess of Whales. Soon, practically nobody in Britain, either, will be able to distinguish between the blubbery, almost inedible marine mammal it is fashionable to admire and the lovely, maniac-haunted Celtic principality which derives its English name from the plural form of Waugh.

## *4th November, 1991*

### Will Jim fix it?

BUDLEIGH Salterton celebrated the 106th birthday of one of its residents, Mr William Cornish, on Thursday, and Mr Cornish celebrated the day by smoking through it like a chimney, as he has for the past 80 years. 'It's never done me any harm,' he said defiantly.

Even while he has been smoking away quietly in Budleigh

Salterton, the mighty resources of the government-funded anti-smoking organisation have been at work to frustrate him. Its latest 32-page *Manifesto for Tobacco Control*, submitted to the Department of Health, demands that the Government should order cigarette companies to produce 'plain and uniform packets'. They would carry the brand name in identical type face, and no other information except health warnings.

I wonder if this is a very sensible way of looking after the health of Mr Cornish, who smokes a pipe in any case. Sir Jimmy Savile, who celebrated his 65th birthday on Thursday, used never to be seen without a cigar, like Winston Churchill, who lived to be 90. We might ask ourselves whether we really need another 25 years of Sir Jimmy – or another 41 years if he takes after Mr Cornish and switches to a pipe – but that is not my point.

My point is that Sir Jimmy, who will be 106 in 41 years' time, used always to wear a fur coat, and he never wears one now. Instead he wears a tracksuit, which is an unappealing garment at the best of times, and most unsuitable for a man of his age. If he wears it in Somerset, he runs the risk of being mistaken for a rambler, in which case he will probably be killed.

Which would be a great shame, but that is not my point, either. My point is that I rather suspect Sir Jimmy has been bullied out of wearing his nice fur coat by these same violent, mad and thoroughly unpleasant animal sentimentalists who have infiltrated the National Trust and threaten to impose themselves on a gigantic slice of what is unquestionably our national heritage. Can Sir Jimmy save us from them?

## The last knight

EVERY day I continue to receive agonised telephone calls from Croats in Britain demanding to know why it is that as President of the British Croatian Society since 1973, I have not been writing more letters to the newspapers or demonstrating against the Serbian occupation of Croatia.

The answer is that I do not think letters to the newspapers or demonstrations would achieve anything. Nearly everybody in Britain who is at all interested in the matter agrees that it is not our squabble. Nobody feels threatened by Serbian imperialism. Perhaps we exhausted our feelings of outrage when Iraq occupied Kuwait – something which, by many standards, it had a reasonable right to do.

The idea that a Serbian army would be able to hold Dubrovnik, or Split, or Zagreb, even if it occupied them, strikes me as an absurdity. What people may not realise is that the frontier between Croatia and Serbia marks one of the great cultural divides of the world. After Croatia was converted to Christianity in the seventh century, it remained attached to Rome and the West, while Serbia went Orthodox in 879 and thereafter looked to Constantinople, later Moscow.

Croatia is a country of the West, like Hungary, to which she belonged for 800 years, while Serbia is unmistakably a country of the East. Relations between East and West have never really been the same since the sacking of Constantinople by the Fourth Crusade under Dandolo and Baldwin in 1203. Perhaps the time has come for Dr Carey to call a final Crusade to save Western Christianity in the Balkans, but I have an uneasy feeling that such a call, coming at such a time, would achieve about the same as a letter to the *Guardian*.

## By jingo if we do

THE *Daily Telegraph* was surely right in Monday's leader to identify the anti-hunting movement in the Labour party as a deliberate extension of the class war. What distresses me about the class war is that it seems so extraordinarily one-sided.

We, the upholders of the older tradition, (whether liberal bourgeois or conservative and feudal) which does not try to stop mankind from hunting animals for sport, may not approve of the class war. We may not wish to be drawn into it at all.

But if we find ourselves drawn into a war, whether we like it or not, by being attacked, then the only sane reaction, apart from instant surrender, is to pursue the war as vigorously as possible to a successful conclusion. The enemy must be engaged, defeated, subdued, generally biffed and jumped on.

Where the anti-hunt fanatics are concerned, it may not be enough to black-ball them from the clubs, cold-shoulder them in the fish queue, remove all support from their businesses and discriminate against them whenever possible. It may also be necessary to disrupt their meetings, picket their homes and release foul smells to put them off the scent in their anti-hunting activities.

There is probably no need to emulate the hooliganism of those hunt saboteurs, who specialise in digging up graves and desecrating tombstones to make whatever debating point they feel may assist them in the class war.

But these people are coming in ever-increasing numbers to live in the countryside, where they do not belong, have nothing to do and threaten to become a nuisance to those already living there, not to say a pollutant of the environment and a health hazard.

I am not suggesting that the pet cats which they bring with them should be disembowelled to see if they have Aids, or that their budgerigars should be plucked for signs of salmonella, and I would hate to see herds of cows 'accidentally' driven through their gardens, or runaway pigs availing themselves of their bird baths. But the war must be fought and won.

### Very like a whale

AFTER the award of £50,000 to the television actor William Roache for being called 'boring' by a writer in the *Sun*, and after Dr Malcolm Smith was awarded £150,000 for being unjustly accused of sexual harassment by his colleague Dr Alanah Houston, it may seem that being libelled or slandered offers the easiest path to riches in our sluggish economy.

I confess that when I first heard of Robert Maxwell's disappearance from his yacht off the Canary Islands, I assumed, like many other journalists, that he had merely gone into hiding, and planned to emerge in a couple of weeks' time to rebuild his shaky fortunes by suing us all over his obituaries.

While it would be good news to learn that he was alive, after all, I resolved to be more circumspect than usual in my assessment of this philanthropist, international statesman and saviour of the *Daily Mirror*.

When it emerged that his body had been found – floating naked, face up in the Atlantic, some 30 miles off course – I supposed it was time to accept the tragedy of his death. But then it occurred to me as most unlikely that they would be able to find a body, however large, in the immensity of the Atlantic Ocean. Far more likely, the helicopter had picked up the body of a smallish white whale, a creature that abounds in those parts possibly as a result of marine pollution, or damage to the ozone layer, or the melting of the polar icecaps.

But the shock of finding a body was made worse by the fact that so few of us thought he was dead. We need not be surprised if those who found the corpse were unable, through their shock and tears, to distinguish the marine from the terrestrial Colossus. This would also explain its absence of clothing since whales seldom wear clothes except in comic strips.

It may not say much for the Spanish pathologists that they do not seem to have noticed anything odd, but perhaps nobody told them what to look out for, or nobody understood their lingo.

There is a certain poignancy in the thought of a smallish white whale being buried tomorrow on Jerusalem's Mount of Olives with all the solemnity due to a Napoleon or a Rhodes.

So long as we are all ready for the return of the Great Man.

## 11th November, 1991

### Sale of the century

AS I FEARED, the time is now approaching when we should all avert our eyes from whatever is happening in the Soviet Union, as it struggles to convert its 'command' or slave economy into the model for a free and dignified society such as the Russians have never known. Riot, murder, rape, starvation and cannibalism are the inevitable consequences.

Rumours that Moscow was preparing to sell the embalmed remains of its favourite mass-murderer, V.I. Lenin, to anyone who would pay $15 million (£8.5 million) for them have turned out to be a hoax, but I bet Mr Yeltsin would sell them for much less if anyone made an offer. I remember urging the Labour government of Harold Wilson to sell the remains of Karl Marx out of Highgate cemetery after the Callaghan devaluation of 1967 – in those days the Russians had plenty of gold to pay for them.

In the event, we proved too sentimental. How much more sensible it would have been to sell these smelly old bones when some people might have wanted to buy them. When all is said and done, I think we should be very much in favour of the Government's idea that public museums and art galleries should be able to sell off their surplus antiquities. If everything old and worthwhile is stored in these places, it means that private citizens must fill their houses with hideous modern rubbish. This produces not only insanity and violence, as the Americans demonstrate, but also, as may well be the case, various forms of horrible illness.

## 16th November, 1991

### Business supplement

THE Maxwell mystery deepens on every side. It has been suggested that the publishing firm he ran from his home near Oxford was being used by the KGB to syphon Soviet funds to approved recipients in the West. There were plans for him to produce a public relations magazine for the KGB, rudely interrupted by his death.

Throughout Eastern Europe there is the problem of these gigantic concrete statues of Lenin which are proving indestructible. Would it not be cheaper and esaier to knock off their beards and, by careful adjustment of the features, convert them to likenesses of Maxwell in one or another of his manifestations, whether as the unknown Hoch, the slender Pte du Maurier, the dapper, pencil-moustached Cpl Jones, or the fuller-figured Capt Robert Maxwell MC we all came to recognise?

I do not understand why he was ever considered a good businessman. His saintly wife, Elizabeth, whom he married in 1945, brought with her a dowry of £150,000, say £2,400,000 at today's values. This may not be a huge fortune, but should have provided a sufficiency for a man of Maxwell's comparatively humble background.

In a lifetime of business activity he managed to convert this modest fortune of £2,400,000 into a debt of $2 billion. Is this the sign of a good businessman?

When I ask why the beautiful and blameless Elizabeth stayed with such a ruffian so long, my ever-practical wife suggests that she was hoping to get her money back.

# 18th November, 1991

## Safety regulations

TIME was when great noblemen fell out the whole country would tremble. Last week, two earls, both of them on the fringes of the Royal Family, appeared to be at each others' throats like a pair of pit bull terriers, to the great sorrow of all Englishmen who revere their betters. But only the *Sun* newspaper appeared to notice.

Perhaps Lord Snowdon was not referring to Lord Spencer when he attacked the latter's refusal to admit people in wheelchairs to Althorp. If not, he should have refrained from quoting the Althorp brochure: 'Wheelchairs would damage the highly polished floors, and the persons pushing the wheelchairs might slip and hurt themselves.'

Snowdon, who later refused to say whether he was referring to the family home of the Princess of Wales, told members of the disabled charity Adapt: 'I find this attitude horrendous and totally unacceptable.'

Which leaves the rest of us in the unenviable position of having to take sides. Snowdon has done well for himself and earned our respect in many ways. He has achieved a hereditary earldom without having to commit a murder, like Macbeth, or even stand for Parliament, like all the poor fools in the House of Commons. Moreover, at the end of the day, he has a beautiful, elegant and sweet-natured wife. He has many things on which to congratulate himself.

But what he has not acquired is a stately home. There are no armies in wheelchairs battering at his gates. As an earl of the first creation without a seat he really has no business to criticise a grander and richer eighth earl.

If ever I am reduced to opening my home to the public, I shall ban not only women in trousers, men without ties and those of either sex who squint or smell or cough offensively, but also anybody under 50, all Americans and anyone who looks as if he might write poetry.

## 23rd November, 1991

### Horror story

'WORKING-HOURS alcohol ban wins growing support,' read an ominous headline in Tuesday's newspaper. Among whom was this support growing? Among a survey of personnel managers, came the answer.

I do not think that in all my 52 years I have ever met a personnel manager. Perhaps I have led a privileged existence, but I have met architects and newspaper designers in my time, I have met smooth-faced and cherubic men in the Languedoc whose trade was that of *hongreur*, or professional castrator. They spend all their working days castrating small animals.

Yet never in my life have I heard anyone (outside such organisations as Alcohol Concern) advance the fatuous opinion that people should be forbidden to drink at luncheon.

A survey of 313 'personnel executives' revealed that 83 per cent were in favour of banning alcohol in 'working' hours. The danger is that with the collapse of trade unions, these 'personnel managers' will start trying to impose their filthy ideas on the British worker. No doubt we will soon read that support is growing for the 72-hour week, for women and children to resume work down the mines, for a smoking ban at *The Daily Telegraph*.

If ever employers are tempted to listen to these lickspittles, they should look to see what has happened to the poor old *Sunday Times*, recently denounced by Mr Norman Lamont, the Chancellor of the Exchequer, as a 'pretty squalid newspaper'.

Seldom, in British politics, does one come across such elegant use of the understatement. Perhaps the Prohibition of alcohol at Mr Murdoch's Wapping headquarters was intended as some sort of Australian practical joke, to humiliate the journalists and make them be seen to crawl for their money. The result is what one discovers in every British Railways waiting room or public lavatory, haunted by the flea-ridden piles of discarded newsprint which are all that are left of a once-great newspaper.

## *27th November, 1991*

### Call of duty

I SUPPOSE that to be a worthy successor of the great Peter Simple I should mourn the arrival of the sexual revolution in India. Simple always takes an unyielding view on these subjects. One has to read his excellent memoirs – *The Missing Will* (1984) and *A Dubious Codicil* – to spot the fun-lover under that grim exterior.

Nevertheless, the news that extra-marital sex and other previously unthinkable practices – semi-nudity and advertisements for condoms – have finally reached the subcontinent must produce a wistful look in the eyes of some old India hands when they think of the armies of beautiful, shy young Indian maidens they left behind.

The new permissiveness, coming about in India 25 years after it swept the West, is a result of the condom advertisements, now encouraged to prevent the spread of Aids (or the American disease, as it is known through large parts of the Far East).

Not all these advertisemens have quite the same tone as their European equivalents. One, which has caused offence to some women's groups, shows a man tugging a woman by the hair with the exhortation: 'Show her who's boss'.

But these advertisements have opened the floodgates, exciting India to a new frenzy of eroticism, with sex surveys, sexy advertisements and endless discussions about what we should

144

all think about it. Even the more staid magazines and newspapers have taken to illustrating articles on these subjects with photographs of young women, to remind their readers what they look like.

And there's the rub, as Hamlet remarked. India's young women are often of a most extraordinary, dumbfounding beauty. It is hard to know what to think. Few things are closer to my heart than the integrity of the Indian family and family life, and I am sure I speak for most other Englishmen when I say that. On the other hand, it never does to get stuck in the mud.

Perhaps I should go to India and spend six months preparing a report for *The Daily Telegraph* on what is happening out there.

## *2nd December, 1991*

### A theory of art

I SOMETIMES wonder whether the whole phenomenon of 'modern art' – as it survives to insult our intelligence and mock our commercial judgment in the post-socialist age – may be explained by a desire to conciliate primitive or aboriginal peoples. In 50,000 years of roaming the great Australian plains, aboriginal society left no history, no records, no buildings or monuments of any description – nothing beyond a vague memory of having used some spots for the purpose of dreaming, and a few painted daubs of a standard which would have been thought unacceptable – before the invention of the 'modern art' market – in an English child of four.

Perhaps it is guilt at the thought of these dispossessed tribesmen which has stultified such large parts of the New World, and persuaded it to swamp us with this ghastly 'art' which we, in deference to the New World's greater wealth, have to pretend to take seriously.

My own feeling is that it is anger at finding themselves with so little history and so little culture which explains the strange behaviour of these former colonial peoples. We can observe how those countries with the least history are always the keenest to debunk what little they have.

Last week Congress ruled that the Custer Battlefield National Monument in Montana (site of Custer's Last Stand, one of the very few memorable incidents in American history) should have

the name Custer removed from it. This initiative arose from a feeling that Lt-Col George Armstrong Custer – one of American history's very few heroes – may not have been politically correct in his attitude to the Red Indians or quasi-autochthonous American Indigenes, as they might also be called.

But none of this explains the new American habit of granny-dumping. All over America, little old ladies are being left sitting outside hospitals and emergency rooms, usually with a note pinned to their handbags – 'She's sick. Please take care of her' – or words to that effect. A survey of 169 emergency rooms across the country reported an average of eight abandonments a week.

One explanation put forward for this worrying new development is that American families are crumbling under the strain of caring for elderly relatives as everyone lives longer and longer and longer in the smoke-free, alcohol-free, saturated fat-free environment. My own theory is that Americans, as they cut themselves off from European culture and history – from everything which has hitherto been identified as civilisation in the Western world – find themselves increasingly appalled to contemplate even their own recent past. These blameless grannies are a reminder of times gone by; for that reason they must be rushed out of sight and out of mind.

## Noise abatement corner

FOR MANY years we kept peacocks at Combe Florey, and nobody ever complained of the fearful shrieks and howls they made during the mating season. Occasionally, guests would announce that they had heard a baby being murdered outside their bedroom window in the middle of the night, but in those days people minded their own businesses.

Now we read of something approaching an insurrection in Cheshire, where two peacock lovers have been served with a noise abatement order and taken to court.

Perhaps what upsets modern country dwellers about a peacock's love call is the suggestion of sexual activity. But I should have thought that the nation's busybodies would be delighted to hear such noises, reminiscent as they are of a baby being murdered.

Every child abuse vigilante in the country should be on the telephone to Miss Rantzen within minutes; the social services could recruit another thousand shock-troops and carry off every child of abusable age for disgusting and inaccurate tests. But the wretched villagers of Bucklow Hill, near Knutsford, complained that the birds' shrieks drowned out the sound of passing jets. No free-born Englishman can be denied the sound of passing jets.

## *4th December, 1991*

## Sensible, thrifty people

IT IS EASY to feel a middle-class distaste for the desperate British shoppers who so overloaded their coaches with beer and wine from the French hypermarkets that one coach was five tons overweight. Kent police, launching another of its endless 'crackdowns' against the respectable, law-abiding civil population, stopped 80 coaches over the weekend and forced nine of them to offload crates of beer and cases of wine.

Such shoppers are easily made to seem greedy. 'We couldn't believe it when we discovered how much booze they were bringing in,' said a police spokesman. Why on earth should a policeman be remotely interested?

Only, I would suggest, because of a residual British insistence that alcoholic refreshment is somehow naughty, even if it isn't illegal. If they had been buying any other commodity in large amounts where it was cheapest, they would simply be thought prudent.

It is this ingrained guilt which accounts for the phenomenon of lager louts. One of the greatest advantages of the Common Market was to have been that our rates of duty on alcohol and tobacco would be harmonised. This would mean about £3 off the price of a bottle of whisky in Britain, £3 on the price of a bottle of whisky in Portugal.

It was Mrs Thatcher (as she then was) in Bruges who said that the harmonisation of our Excise duties with those of the EC would be a 'nightmare'. But we got rid of her. Last week I sat at lunch between the chairman of a famous Scotch whisky firm and a former Chancellor of the Exchequer. The whisky man was moaning on about how badly affected he would be by the increased duty in Portugal. I said surely he would sell more whisky as a result of the reduced duty in Britain than he would fail to sell in Portugal.

Oh no, said the recently retired Chancellor of the Exchequer, there could be no question – there never had been any question – of reducing the duty in Britain. That would cause endless problems with the temperance groups, and campaigners against drunk driving . . .

The temperance lobby is small enough, while those associating themselves with the other hysterical, vindictive groups can be counted in hundreds. Must these unpleasant people rule us simply because they are the only ones prepared to waste their time talking to politicians?

## Stop this brutality

HAVING said which, I must confess to an icy moment when I read of vegetarians demonstrating outside the Royal Smithfield Show on Sunday, chanting 'meat means murder' and presenting the organisers with wreaths to represent all the animals eaten in Britain this year.

Vegetarians always struck me as the gentlest and most harmless of people. So long as they ask for no more than cabbage

148

and potatoes, I am happy to take the extra meat and gravy when they come to lunch. But I worry, sometimes, about their health, having seen too many idealistic literary young women waste away and go mad.

This is particularly worrying since scientists have discovered that many vegetables are poisonous. Some projections say that 50 per cent of female vegetarians now in their late twenties or early thirties will be dead in 60 years.

The Government, perhaps sensibly, has no plan to do anything about this. However, now we learn that militant vegetarians are agitating to prevent the rest of us from eating meat, the time has surely come to counter-attack and start agitating for a total ban on all forms of vegetable.

As I see it, the issue is a moral one. We can sit quiet and do nothing, if we wish, while so many impressionable young people eat vegetables and prepare themselves, ineluctably, for the grave. That is their decision. But what harm have the vegetables done in order to deserve this fate?

Have any of us thought what it would be like to be planted where somebody else decided to plant us, to spend our entire lives in rows being fattened on the soil until we were judged fat enough or ripe enough to eat? Then to be harvested like so many turkeys at Christmas time? Torn to pieces and mashed up by the sharp white teeth of a young secretary or deputy editor of a literary magazine? The whole process degrades the human race.

## 9th December, 1991

### Pekes to the rescue

LAUNCHING this year's Christmas Police Terror, the Chief Constable of Warwickshire, Mr Peter Joslin, gave notice of road checks as well as speed checks to celebrate our Saviour's birth, adding on a slightly grimmer note:

'Drivers who choose not to take our advice over Christmas must be prepared to find themselves in police custody.'

I had not heard of this new offence, whereby anybody rejecting unsolicited advice from a policeman can be taken into police custody, but it occurs to me that the Treasury might look into Mr Joslin's proposal, since the average cost of keeping someone in police custody is now £200 a night, or something like that.

149

It is odd that although we often read of public corruption in Africa and South America I have never heard anyone query, let alone explain, the extraordinary cost of police custody.

A correspondent who will be visiting Warwickshire over Christmas in order to see his 95-year-old mother asks if it will be safe to take her for a drive after her annual glass of Wincarnis. The answer is that until recently it would have been quite safe, even during our national season of Abstinence and Immobility or annual Police Terror.

But in Bristol recently an Avon councillor (and member of the police authority) was fined £300 with £106 costs for refusing to produce a breath test while in occupation of a passenger seat. He also had his licence endorsed with 10 points despite the fact that, not being a driver, he had no licence to endorse.

We must expect that one of these days the police will wish to breathalyse our dogs if they are travelling with us in the back of the car. I hope they put up more resistance than the present abject, cowed race of Britons who are too terrified to complain about whatever the authorities do to them.

## 14th December, 1991

### A bad joke

LETTERS continue to pour in by every post from *Telegraph* readers all over the country agreeing that they had never heard of Freddie Mercury, the alleged singer, before his widely reported death from the American disease a few weeks ago. Some of them are beginning to query whether he in fact existed.

The theory seems to be that he may have been a practical joke played on us all by *The Daily Telegraph*'s learned but skittish Obituaries Manager, Hugh Montgomery-Massingberd – possibly in protest against the constant pressure on all newspapers to print material which might be of interest to the present empty-headed generation of teenagers.

This pressure is misguided, as I never tire of pointing out, because few members of this smelly generation can read, and none has any money. People with serious money to spend are found only in the 50-65 age bracket, by which age people do not wish to read a teenage newspaper. But we are slaves to the lustful fantasies of our incompetent, half-witted advertising industry, stuck in the Sixties, which interests itself only in hip-hugging jeans rather than comfortable tweeds for the fuller figure.

No sooner had other newspapers seen Mr Montgomery-Massingberd's joke in the early editions of the *Telegraph* than they decided they were missing out on youth appeal and started printing ever more extravagant obituaries of this non-existent pop singer, saying that he was born in Zanzibar of Iranian parents, that he had landed in a flying saucer from the planet Mercury . . .

The most frightening aspect of the whole phenomenon is that if you see a British teenager sitting vacantly on a wall with its mouth hanging open and ask it if it knows about Freddie Mercury, the chances are that it will nod its head and say 'yeah'. With their small memory span and almost infinite suggestibility, our teenagers have convinced themselves that there was indeed a singer called Freddie Mercury to whom they once grooved, who was tragically struck down by Aids and died the next day.

Which is all very well, but many teenagers are now so heartbroken by news of Freddie's death that they are refusing to eat or speak or wash themselves. I hope Mr Montgomery-Massingberd is feeling ashamed of himself.

*His jest will savour of but shallow wit*
*When thousands weep, more than did laugh at it.*

# 1st January, 1992

## Too modest

PERHAPS the Duke of Norfolk thought he was being delightfully modest when he hazarded the opinion that hereditary peers should not be allowed to influence legislation, but he caused great distress in Lucerne and Berne where I discussed his revolutionary ideas over steaming cups of hot chocolate with resident intellectuals and political philosophers.

Government by common people may work in countries like Switzerland, where there is very little central government of any sort, everyone is well educated and clever and friendly and gets on together like a family of Pekingeses. But I wonder if the Duke of Norfolk has ever walked a few paces down the corridor to the

House of Commons and seen the sort of people to be met there.

Six long years I spent as a political correspondent in the House of Commons and in the course of that time I saw sights such as no human being should be required to look upon. It is not that the one party is any better or worse than any other, although I must admit to having been seriously worried by a recent feature in this newspaper on the Tory young pretenders. Anyone in England who puts himself forward to be elected to a position of political power is almost bound to be socially or emotionally insecure, or criminally motivated, or mad.

You hear it in the animal noises which rise from the floor of the House at question time. You see it in the grimacing faces and depraved gestures of hatred and rejection. In my six years' experience of the House of Commons, I have never before seen such low grade human material, particularly among its younger members. I should be surprised if it has ever been so bad in Parliament's long history.

This means that the role of the hereditary peers has never been so important. The Duke of Norfolk enjoys enormous privileges, receiving the deference and hero worship of most sensible Britons. For my own part, I feel he richly deserves them. But the least he can do in exchange is to govern the country for us. Nice Mr Major is all very well in a decorative and reassuring role. But there is serious work to be done. It is the Duke's job to lead us, cheering, into the European future while nice Mr Major reassures the more timid among us, holding our hands and making compassionate faces at those who fall behind.

## *4th January, 1992*

## Thoughts after Christmas

IS IT safe on January 4 to suppose that the great Christmas festival of immobility and abstinence is finally over? As the new theology develops, we see the feast through new eyes. Christ was not made incarnate in order to promote a general sentimentality about children, as we were taught at school and as some old-fashioned Christians still believe.

His purpose, as we can now see, was to promote temperance and MAKE THE ROADS SAFE for kiddies, which is not the same thing at all. The chief rite of the religious ceremony is no longer the giving of presents to children. All ritual nowadays centres around the breath test, and it is significant that those appointed to conduct the rite (or administer the sacrament as one prefers) are no longer priests or parents but policemen.

Christmas has become a public affirmation of the power and benignity of the state, to which we all make obeisance in the symbolism of the breath test ceremony.

Good citizens spend this Period of Reflection at home, listening attentively to whatever television and radio choose to tell them. Those who can still read may look at the newspapers, which will be full of the same wholesome instructions.

Many will know the familiar words of the much-loved litany by heart: how drinking invariably impairs the vision, slurs the speech, detracts from sexual performance, destroys the sense of balance, produces incontinence, obesity, a staggering gait and often ends in murder. Only one claim this year struck me as new. Professor Paul Brain, of University College, Swansea, revealed the existence of something called a 'battered alcoholic syndrome':

'The link between alcohol and violence is terribly mixed up. It is not just that people become more aggressive. They are more likely to be attacked. Whether people become easy targets, or more easily give offence, we're not sure.'

I can think of several possible explanations for this syndrome, whereby harmless drunks find themselves viciously attacked by sober passers-by. Can anyone else?

## *13th January, 1992*

### Crème de la crème

IT IS within the context of our ignorant and unemployable young that we should refrain from laughing too loudly at the police entrance exam, details of which were released last week. Of course we may find it funny that grown men and women should be asked to ring one of five possible answers to the question: 'If a shift begins at 14.15 hours and lasts six hours, when will it finish?'

If candidates fail, they are allowed to take exactly the same test six months later, which might seem to make it funnier. We may laugh even louder to reflect that these brilliantly tested officers are the very people for whom chief constables demand unfettered discretion to stop us about our lawful occupations, boss us around and make as much nuisance of themselves as they choose.

But on this occasion I do not think we should blame the police. They can recruit only from what is available, and the sad truth is that a very large part of the available labour force is unemployable. Police spokesmen have made valiant attempts to pretend that the abysmally low standard of test is designed to attract ethnic candidates – 'ethnic' in this context being another of those slightly insulting codewords, like 'inner city' and 'disadvantaged', meaning 'black'.

'The old test was devised for white, middle-class people and did not reflect the type of recruit who is now coming forward to join the police,' said a West Midlands police spokesman. But it is simply not true that the blacks are any worse than the whites. Of eight applicants who took the exam in the West Midlands last week, four failed: two black and two white.

Nor is the problem confined to the police. Candidates for the priesthood at one time were expected to be fluent in Latin and reasonably well grounded in Greek, to be familiar with Aquinas and have some knowledge of the early Councils of the Church. Nowadays they are required only to be able to clap their hands together without missing. Even this qualification may be waived, on the grounds that it is unfair to those who can't co-ordinate their movements, or whose eyesight is defective.

## *18th January, 1992*

### A terrible risk

MANY patriots will have been alarmed to see photographs in the vulgar newspapers of the Princess of Wales queuing with Prince William, unnoticed, in a crowded hamburger bar in Kensington High Street. We are told that Her Royal Highness ordered a £4.76 takeaway meal of two hamburgers, six chicken McNuggets, regular French fries, a cola and apple pie.

Our alarm did not concern itself so much with the evidence of penury which the incident affords. Many Princes of Wales have gone through patches of poverty, and it is always the wives and children who suffer. If there was no food at Kensington Palace, or no one there to serve it, then it was perfectly reasonable for the

Princess and her son to seek nourishment in a neighbouring restaurant.

What is disturbing is the food she bought. Of course there is no reason to associate hamburgers, chicken McNuggets and cola with the dreaded American disease which threatens all human life in five continents, but I refuse to believe that diet is not a factor in what one can only call the American phenomenon.

Anti-Europeans who rail against German dominance in Europe do not take cognisance of the only alternative, which is political, economic, cultural and intellectual absorption by the United States. The German influence is at least diluted by French, Italian, Spanish and other influences, as well as being reduced by linguistic incomprehension. The American takeover is more total, and more deleterious.

Few people would take such a strict view as to say it was high treason to be caught feeding American food to the heir to the throne. But I am sure there is a decent pizza bar somewhere in the neighbourhood.

## 20th January, 1992

### Hail the dawn

THE more I read about scenes in Strangeways prison during the riot of April 1990, the more they seem to resemble my own projection of what Britain would be like after a Labour victory later this year.

According to one witness, who was a prison officer, the alleged leader of the riot came up to him: 'He had set of keys. As he come round the top, he looked me straight in the face. He said "Right you bastard, I'm the boss now. I've got the keys". He was like some wild animal, high as a kite, stripped to the waist, and screaming abuse.'

Is this not exactly how we can expect Messrs Hattersley, Kaufman and Kinnock to behave as soon as they are told they have won the election? At the first hint of freedom, Manchester Crown Court was told, the inmates ran from the chapel shouting 'Get the beasts', allegedly meaning that they intended to attack, mutilate and possibly kill those of their fellow prisoners who were held for sexual offences.

Never mind that it was the right-wing gutter press which

taught them to think, talk and act in this way. The sad truth is that when the lower classes take control of their own destiny, they invariably succeed in creating a version of hell on earth – for themselves, as well as for everyone else.

The rest of the world has seen this all too clearly. The present agonies of Russia testify to the difficulty of returning to sanity after a prolonged period of self-deception. At present, Messrs Hattersley and Kaufman promise only a small 'pickpocket tax', or second tier of income tax to oppress the industrious and feed the sullen envy of the poor.

But as soon as they are in power, we may be sure a great howl of triumph will go up from the rat holes in Tower Hamlets: the welfare departments, the teacher training colleges, the probation officers' messes, the institutes of public hygiene, the child abuse and bottom inspection centres. They will have the keys, they will be the bosses once again.

## *27th January, 1992*

### Travel section

I THOUGHT that nothing in the press could ever shock me after the hysteria over Freddie Mercury's death, but I must admit to being shocked as well as disgusted by Saturday's holiday supplement in the *Guardian* which was trailed as revealing 'parts of Spain where sun worshippers can avoid *Sun* readers'.

It was not the social divisiveness or even the naked snobbery of this claim that took the breath away, although one would like to think that holidays might present a good opportunity for *Guardian* and *Sun* readers to get together and discover whatever they have in common – an interest in jazz, or football, or modern art or whatever. They should both do their best to promote nice Mr Major's classless society, should they not?

What shocked was the arrogant assumption that *Guardian* readers were any less objectionable than *Sun* readers to meet on holiday. For my own part, I always study the travel pages of both the *Sun* and the *Guardian* in anguished search for any corner of the globe where I might meet neither faction.

While the *Guardian* urges its readers to visit little-known parts of Spain this year, the *Sun* suggests its readers might tour theme parks and other tourist delights around Orlando, Florida.

I suppose the editor knows what he is doing, but I feel he should warn his readers about the health risks in America, the perils of bonking, etc.

All these travel writers seem to ignore the fact that we are in the grip of a major recession. If we are really to get *Guardian* and *Sun* readers together, I suggest that *Guardian* readers stay at home this year and *Sun* readers take their holidays in sunny Hampstead.

A McDonald's hamburger place is to be built there specially for them. They will find plenty of room on Hampstead Heath for picnicking, spreading litter and bonking. The perfect holiday, really.

## 3rd February, 1992

### No excuses

IT WAS to be expected that British womanhood's self-appointed spokesmen would take a pretty dim view of events in the Old Bailey last week when a London businessman was released who admitted to having killed his nagging wife in the sight of their three children, who cheered him on.

Clare Short, Labour MP for Ladywood, pointed out: 'The woman cannot answer for herself. Even if she was domineering, that does not justify killing her.' Mrs Gorman, Billericay's Conservative Member, accused the judge of double standards.

'Nagging is nothing compared to what some women have to suffer,' she said.

Neither spokesperson commented on a much stranger story which appeared, inconspicuously, in the same day's newspaper. A Romanian mortuary attendant was committing necrophilia with the corpse of an 18-year-old woman on a Bucharest mortuary slab when the corpse came to life.

Police arrested the shocked necrophile for rape, but the parents refused to press charges because, by his actions, he had restored their daughter to life. What is the modern women's politically correct or 'right-on' reaction to this story? Rape and necrophilia are quite separate offences. Is it possible to commit rape by accident? Should the fact that the mortuary attendant had saved a women's life be admissible in mitigation?

Neither Ms Short nor Mrs Gorman, great jurists as they both are, has volunteered any advice. I fear the right answer may be that when in doubt, you send the man to prison – any man, anywhere.

## 5th February, 1992

### The enemy within

IF I read a news report in this week's *Sunday Telegraph* correctly, half the degree-awarding authorities in Britain are now prepared to award a degree in English literature to candidates who have never read a word of Shakespeare.

This emerged from a survey conducted by Dr Tim Cook, of Kingston Polytechnic, who commented:

'Students are learning a cultural language and coming from schools which don't give them the background or mental equipment to interpret the difficult texts from the past.'

While Milton's *Paradise Lost* appeared in only 15 of the 31 institutions surveyed, feminist writers such as the Canadian Margaret Atwood, and the black Americans Toni Morrison and Alice Walker were studied in two thirds of them.

If these figures are true, they seem to call for something more than a fogeyish splutter. They call for a scream of outrage and hate. It is not true that our beautiful, humane, bourgeois culture is committing suicide. It is being deliberately murdered by these teachers who are too ignorant or too idle to learn the subject they claim to teach.

What sort of a cultural language does Dr Cook suppose these miserable students are learning, and who is teaching it to them? Shakespeare is our great gift to the world. Britain has never excelled in painting or music or sculpture. It has its great literary tradition to offer. Those who would deny us that comfort and substitute the work of Alice Walker should not be complained about in whingeing tones in the correspondence columns of the better newspapers. Such people should be hung upside down in the Tower of London and shown to tourists beside the Crown Jewels as representing yet another side of the British character.

## 10th February, 1992

### A touch of drama

'I HAVE to say that as the Secretary of State for the Environment, perhaps the single most dramatic thing I will have done is to knock down this building,' said Mr Heseltine, announcing his intention to demolish the hideous DoE headquarters in Marsham Street which has been defiling the Westminster skyline for the past 21 years.

Now there is keen interest, most especially among the nation's architects, in where the 3,000 displaced civil servants will be rehoused, and what will happen to the huge site.

If Mr Heseltine wishes to do something really dramatic, he should announce that the displaced civil servants are not going to be rehoused – least of all in some wonderful new building. The only function of these gigantic buildings is to provide offices for civil servants to fill. Once inside them, they occupy themselves in creating work for one another, with reports, memos, surveys, studies and regulations flying back and forth between themselves.

Neither the DoE nor the Department of Transport conducts any useful business which could not be conducted just as well from two medium-sized gentlemen's residences in the countryside. All the rest is work-creation.

Public opinion in the Suffolk health farm where I have taken up residence seems to be swinging behind the idea that the buildings should be knocked down with the 3,000 civil servants still inside them, but this strikes me as a shade too dramatic, even for Mr Heseltine.

When the site has been cleared, it should be planted with

medlar trees – perhaps the occasional mulberry and quince for variety. Its 3,000 occupants will realise that once they have no office to go to they are well and truly redundant. They must be told to go home and do something productive, like growing mushrooms.

## 12th February, 1992

### Cut her in half

AT A TIME when nearly everybody in England was brooding about the monarchy, a thought occurred to me through contemplating the pages and pages of unpleasant propaganda which have been pouring out of the *Sunday Times*, trying to stir up envy about the Queen's alleged wealth.

Among the titillating illustrations supplied was a picture of Gatcombe Park, the Princess Royal's seat in Gloucestershire, set immediately beside Sunninghill, the Duke of York's hideous dude ranch near Windsor. Gatcombe, by any standards I can think of, is a beautiful, dignified, reasonably modest country houses such as any civilised Englishman would be happy to live in, if he had the means. At the same time, I must accept that a substantial number of New Britons – not all of them readers of the *Sun* – would much prefer the £5 million dude ranch.

Writing for *The Daily Telegraph* I need address myself, thank God, only to the first group of Englishmen. But the monarchy has to address itself to both. The two nations in Britain are not nowadays composed of the rich and the poor, as they were in Disraeli's day, but of the educated and uneducated, civilised and uncivilised, as I would put it, or of the outdated and modern, as the new barbarians would prefer.

To reign over two such different nations, and be a beloved monarch to both, must produce severe strain. I wonder if there might not be some way of splitting the two personae. Recently the Berkshire County Council invited guests to celebrate HM Queen Elizabath [sic] II's accession.

Just as various African Commonwealth countries chose to embrace Independance rather than Independence in the Sixties – I believe Independance remains the official spelling in certain London schools – so perhaps the New Brits would like to revere Queen Elizabath II rather than Elizabeth II. Special press officers to Elizabath could keep the *Sun* and *Sunday Times* informed about whether the Royal corgis were bonking satisfactorily or not, how much the Queen's teapot is worth, while the dear Queen went about fulfilling her vital role of patting good people on the back and telling former Prime Ministers they are expendable.

# 22nd February, 1992

## House of horror

IN THE Turkish part of Nicosia, on my last visit, I was taken to something called the Barbaric Museum which celebrated all the outrages committed by Greek Cypriots – and, to a lesser extent, by British forces in Cyprus – during the Cyprus emergency of the late 1950s.

As a member of the British armed forces in Cyprus at the time I was quite interested to see this monument to my past exertions, rather as the Bridge on the River Kwai, now a tourist attraction in God's own kingdom of Thailand, is a favourite haunt of Japanese tourists, who are also to be found swarming over the American military cemetery outside Manila and other war sites.

I imagine that it is in the same sort of spirit that the National Trust now appeals for £500,000 to preserve numbers 1-3 Willow Road, Hampstead, the three 'modernist' houses designed by Erno Goldfinger for himself and two others in 1937. Perhaps 55 years ago they were thought daring. Now they look like the sort of junk architecture any provincial developer would put up if he thought he could get away with it.

Goldfinger, whose name was immortalised by Ian Fleming in his eponymous film, is chiefly remembered as the architect of Alexander Fleming House, the Ministry of Health headquarters in Elephant and Castle, soon, mercifully, to be demolished.

The idea is to fill Goldfinger's home with all the repulsive 'modern art' he himself collected: works by Max Ernst, Marcel Duchamp, Henry Moore, Roland Penrose, Robert Delaunay, Man Ray – as a sort of Chamber of Horrors to remind us all of the futility of the Modern Movement, still limping along in America with the help of billions of dollars of trust money from dead, trusting American philistines.

That is good enough reason to support this crazy scheme. Another reason might be to punish Hampstead for its arrogance and wrongheadedness over the years. In 1937 the old Hampstead Protection Society quite rightly described Goldfinger's wretched designs as 'disastrously out of keeping'. It was overruled by the New Hampstead Progressives. Now I feel we should rub Hampstead's nose in everything it has championed over these 55 years.

### Beetroot will save us all

ONE does not need to have an exceptionally raw social conscience, perhaps, to feel a twinge of anxiety over proposals to turn the European Community's 32-million ton grain mountain into motor fuel. So long as there are people starving as the result of drought or wars, it seems a little bit wicked to use this heavily subsidised food material to drive motor cars.

But the principle of growing our own petrol-substitute must be better than buying petroleum from Arabia and fuelling the Islamic world revolution. Corn will always be a sensitive crop for this purpose, but beetroot is much more efficient than corn for conversion into ethanol. It grows readily in our climate, has limited nutritional value, very little appeal to the Third World, can be alternated with cereal crops to avoid the need for nitrate fertilisers, and produces no carbon dioxide when burned. Alcohol from beetroot would cost less than a penny for 20 litres, before marketing and distribution costs – at the full, unsubsidised cost of beetroot.

It might seem that most of our current anxieties can be solved by beetroot. After the war, it was normal to see vans and cars in France driven by a strange charcoal-burning contrivance on the roof. What a happy nation we shall be when we can drive from Land's End to John o' Groats on a suitcase-full of beetroot.

## *24th February, 1992*

### Two halves continued

MR John Martin, Editor of the Church of England newspaper, wrote a dignified letter in Friday's *Daily Telegraph*, defending the Archbishop of Canterbury against an unnamed bishop who had attacked him publicly. The burden of the attack claimed that the Archbishop was inexperienced and unsure: 'Dr Carey's inexperience shows. The Church, unless the man at the helm does better than this, could be saddled with an unsure leader well into the next century.'

In the course of his letter to this newspaper, Mr Martin urged that Dr Carey be given time to grow into the job, and quoted the results of a survey which were favourable to the archbishop: 'Based on these figures, it is the unnamed bishop who could be criticised for lack of sureness of touch,' wrote Mr Martin.

Apart from the hint of a *nominativus pendens* or hanging participle in that sentence, Mr Martin seems to be putting his case well; the implied rebuke to the unnamed bishop is delivered with dignity and moderation.

Then I turned to the *Sun* newspaper of the same day, where Mr Martin was quoted as saying: 'This bishop sounds like a cowardly clot who's had one pint too many.'

The difference in tone between the two statements illustrates well the difference between the two nations of modern Britain which I write about from time to time: on the one hand you have the gentle, educated, well mannered folk such as one might expect to read *The Daily Telegraph*; on the other hand the rough, uneducated and increasingly rude folk who tend to buy the *Sun*.

The Church, like the Queen, must address itself to both halves. So entrenched have attitudes and antipathies become, that I find myself less disposed to associate even with those few remaining institutions like the Monarchy, the church, and Parliament which try to cater for both halves of the country, rather than just for my own half. I wonder if those in the other half feel the same.

## The shame of rosy cheeks

WE COULD not help chuckling in Somerset over a news story taken from an article in the *British Medical Journal* where a number of campers at a West Country holiday camp had developed the rosy cheeks for which we have always been famous down here. They rushed in terror to the doctor, fearing an outbreak of scarlet fever, or the American disease, or worse.

A learned doctor explains that this example of the 'slapped cheek syndrome' was probably caused by bed linen in the camp. The reason we laughed in Somerset was because we know perfectly well that the cause of our rosy cheeks is that we do, indeed, spend much of the time slapping each other's faces.

It has been a closely guarded secret until now. I don't know why we do it, nor do I know exactly how the Somerset tradition began. It is quite fun, once you get a taste for it, and there is not much else to do down here, especially since they closed down all the cinemas. Now the Lord Chief Justice has invented a new law, making it an imprisonable offence to hurt each other for fun. Goodness knows why he wants to invent new reasons for sending people to prison, but I suppose judges must have their satisfactions, like everyone else; it can only be because they like sending people to prison.

And why shouldn't they? We all have our different ideas of fun. Problems arise only when they conflict. Now any rosy cheeked couple which dares set foot out of doors is liable to be clapped in irons by the nearest policeman or environmental health officer, and Somerset folk will revert to being as whey-faced as everyone else.

## *26th February, 1992*

### Spirit of the free

FURTHER to my note about Berkshire County Council's decision to celebrate the 40th anniversary of Queen Elizabath II, rather than that of Queen Elizabeth II whom most of us know and love, I have now been sent the photocopy of a High Court writ on which she is referred to as Her Majasty.

It seems that this usurper Elizabath is increasing her kingdom daily at the expense of Elizabeth. Australians who complain at the £750,000 cost of this week's Royal visit should be told quite firmly that they are paying for two monarchs, not one: Her Majesty Queen Elizabeth II, who concerns herself with educated, well-disposed, loyal subjects, and Her Majasty Queen Elizabath II, who addresses herself to those less adept at reading and writing – out-of-door types, perhaps, and swagmen.

Even so, the republicans can point out that no less a person than Michael Jackson, the singer, was able to visit Britain for four days last week at a cost of only £56,000. Michael Jackson may not be officially recognised as the uncrowned King of the United States of America, but nobody can deny he represents the spirit of that extraordinary country, rather as Marianne, the lady seen on French coins, represents the Spirit of France.

Neither black nor white, of an appearance which might indicate questionable gender, living cocooned in a sterile bubble, stupendously rich, earning a reputed £100,000 a day, and buying only children's toys, videos and occasional comics, he represents the *beau ideal* of Mickey Mouse capitalism, more like a god than a monarch in the society which produced him, the great teacher and avatar of the West.

Perhaps the Australians should be given a choice between the Queen and Michael Jackson for their constitutional head of state. It may be too confusing for those simple souls to accept that we have two Queens, one for them, one for us.

## *29th February, 1992*

### Gunge-ho for oldies

THE MORE one learns of what has happened to Oxford University since it started appointing militantly proletarian professors of English, the more one wonders if there might not be a good case for closing it down and turning the colleges into retirement homes for gentlefolk.

The latest practice among the new-style undergraduates, or 'students' as they laughingly prefer, is called 'gungeing', and involves emptying dustbins over one another. After exams they spend their government grants on bottles of champagne – for spraying over each other, as the *Sun* newspaper has taught them to do, rather than for drinking.

Quite possibly these activities represent no more than the 'students'' understandable dislike for each other, but now something called the university's 'rules committee' (does this mean the proctors?) has suggested that every college sets aside a 'gungeing area' where its members can gunge each other to their hearts' content, leaving the rest of the university gunge-free.

This seems an impractical suggestion. The essence of gungeing is surely to express your dislike by gungeing someone else, not to be gunged yourself. Nobody would go to these gungeing areas for the purpose of being gunged, or on the off-chance of finding an enemy there to gunge.

It would be much more sensible to declare the whole of central Oxford a national gungeing area, where we could all take our dustbins and empty them over any 'student' or proletarian professor of English we found.

In this way we would eventually succeed in driving out the 'students' and their wretched mentors, leaving all those beautiful quads to be cleaned up and repopulated by gentle, rich, pleasant-mannered oldies like ourselves.

# *4th March, 1992*

## The saving of America

THIS column sees no reason to waver in its support of Pat Buchanan for the Republican nomination and Presidency just because he draws attention to the problems caused by an epidemic of sodomy in the United States

His advertisement showing a film of homosexual men in leather straps and chains dancing in the street while President Bush appears in a corner of the screen is not, of course, intended to implicate the President in these activities, merely to rebuke him for his complacency. It is an unarguable fact that the American disease, now killing several hundreds of America's brightest and best every day, is very largely caused by sodomy.

There is no need for us to feel censorious about this, but I would have thought it incumbent on the government medical authorities to point out the true cause of this disease. For some reason which I do not understand, but which may be related to 'political correctness' (the new American euphemism covering both brain paralysis and congenital imbecility) the government has refused to make this point.

If one had to identify a reason for this outbreak of sodomy, I suppose the most likely explanation is ignorance. Education is more or less non-existent in the United States, reduced for the most part to putting ticks and crosses in squares, and many Americans have the greatest difficulty in communicating verbally with each other. They have the same procreative urges as everyone else, but, like camels, only the haziest idea of what to do about them. On the other hand, I do not see that it is the President's job to instruct them.

In a memorable article in this newspaper recently Claudia FitzHerbert described how she and her classmates received sex instruction from a heroic nun at St Mary's Convent, Shaftesbury, called Sister Daniel.

What the United States needs is a missionary army of Sister Daniels to instruct them in the facts of life, using simple sign language and videos if absolutely necessary.

## 9th March, 1992

### Parturient montes

IT IS no accident that the central boulevard in Europe's Disneyland, to be opened outside Paris on April 12, is called Main Street USA. The whole enterprise is a celebration of the victory of American mass culture over the educated, humane liberal civilisations of Europe.

I suppose they decided to build it in France rather than in Britain because they were frightened our lager louts would smash it up over here. For the first time one begins to see the point of our lager louts. It would be nice to think that young Anglo-Saxon males have an inbuilt resistance to the Disney philosophy, but I see little enough sign of it.

My heart bleeds for the younger generation in France, so much politer and better behaved than our own.

If Mickey Mouse were human, they might be able to convert him to the superiority of the French culture, to produce a Gallic Mickey from all the mess of sentimentality, self-deception and inaccuracy of observation which the Americans have put into his invention.

But of course Mickey isn't human at all, even less than Tammy Wynette or Jimmy Carter. Let us just hope that in this splendid recession – long may it last – the whole enterprise will flop, and Mickey Mouse will have to go back to Florida with his dear little tail between his cute little legs.

## 11th March, 1992

### Ecclesiastical news

WE SHOULD not be too distressed at pictures of Dr Peter Carnley, described as 'Archbishop of Perth', laying his hands on 10 Australian women, or 'Sheilas' as they are known locally, with a view to turning them, miraculously, into priests. Now he has 10

Reverend Sheilas he can try a little harder if he wants, and consecrate 10 Bishop Sheilas, but I don't see that it will make any difference to anything at all.

In Western Australia, around the St Margaret River, they make some of the best white wine from the chardonnay grape in the whole continent, but I have never heard it suggested that Western Australians were gifted at ordination. The whole idea of Australians ordaining each other is faintly comical, but none of us who used to play at doctors when we were children should be alarmed.

The sacrament of Holy Orders is not conferred merely by some quasi-magicial gift derived from the Apostolic Succession. It is also a question of intention. One day it might occur to me as an amusing thing to ordain my three Pekingeses. As the Rev Leo, the Rev Hyacinth and the Rev Quince, they would have more gravitas and carry greater conviction than many bomber-jacketed clergymen around today. They are all male and one, I am happy to say, is black (Quincy). But those are really the only qualifications they have. My action would not be invalid just because I am not a consecrated bishop, but because my beloved Pekingeses lack various essential properties of an ordained priest.

In the same way, Dr Carnley can perfectly well go through the motions of ordaining a kangaroo, if that is what he feels like doing. In fact I would be pleased if he did, as it would make the point better than he has already made it. Such an initiative would not hurt the kangaroo, nor would it do any harm to the rest of us, but neither would it have created a new priest to help meet the church's desperate shortage.

## Play up, play up

LAST week found me on a visit to Clifton College, housed in what must be the most beautiful collection of 19th-century school buildings in the country. The boys and girls were polite, intelligent and seemed happy, the masters were relaxed, friendly and amazingly normal. It was a corner of an England which has largely vanished, and I could not help wondering what happens to all these pleasant young people when they go out into the world. Do they become architects and help make the country uglier and tawdrier every year, or clergymen, and drip around in bomber jackets trying to ingratiate themselves with young people, or poets, and bore us with their irritating, insignificant conceits?

Probably most of them go to Saudi Arabia, poor things, to make money so that they can live in rose-clad rectories in Surrey when they retire. It was of the Close, at Clifton, that Sir Henry Newbolt, an old Cliftonian, wrote his admirable poem 'Vitai Lampada':

*'There's a breathless hush in the Close tonight*
*Ten to make and the match to win*
*A bumping pitch and a blinding light*
*An hour to play and the last man in . . . '*

The College Close looks almost exactly as it must have done in Newbolt's day – a small church in classical style, some pretty, medium-sized houses of various dates and styles – a delightful prospect in every way except for one monstrosity which towers over everything else. This is Clifton's Roman Catholic Cathedral, dumped there at some depraved moment in recent history, of an ugliness and brutality which can only make one gasp. Its hideous concrete 'wings' on the roof, added at who knows what extra cost as a gesture towards the idea of decoration, might almost have been calculated as an insult to man's intelligence.

It occurred to me that this disgusting object might have some function apart from its role as a standing insult to man and God. This is to warn the generations of Cliftonians – at any rate until it falls down – never to heed the subtle blandishments of architects, always to be ready, when introduced to one at a party, to say nothing, keep a stiff upper lip and punch him in the face.

*'The voice of the schoolboy rallies the ranks*
*Play up, play up and play the game.'*

# 16th March, 1992

## No more wages

A NEW survey of the so-called 'underclass' – defined as those who are out of work and living in families where nobody else is in work – reveals they will soon form a majority of voters.

Its members are revealed as faceless and work-shy, often characterised by dishonesty and a degree of incompetence which make them virtually unemployable even if they had sufficient organisation and discipline to get themselves to work. Many feel themselves to be so much disadvantaged that they have difficulty in getting out of bed to perform the ordinary morning ablutions.

This may explain an apparently irrelevant aside in the report which seems to suggest these people are smelly as well as dirty. The report recommends compulsory scrubbing, a return to traditional teaching methods in schools, two years' military service after schooling and penological reform to include the reintroduction of hard labour . . .

It is at this point that I wake up from my daydream. The report from the Policy Studies Institute, called *Understanding the Underclass*, says none of these things, except that the underclass is growing. In fact, it says that its members are absolutely splendid people: their trouble is caused by mistaken government policies. It recommends 'a change in the social and economic structure so that paid employment is no longer the source of everything that society counts as valuable.'

What simpler solution than to abolish wages? This would remove not only the stigma from those who, for whatever reason, do not actually seem to do much work, but also the cruel disparities of wealth which are a source of such unhappiness to many people in the world today. The boost to their morale would be incalculable. It is not that people in this country object to other people working. They merely object to other people getting paid for it.

## Not in their socks

I TRY to believe everything I read in the newspapers, but I had difficulty with last week's account of the London vagrant who was found, after death, to be carrying £1,500 in small change in his socks.

My reason for doubting the story is that I, too, like to carry small change in my socks, but I have found that with more than £15 or £20-worth it becomes impossible to walk.

The English have tended to assure each other that it is wrong to give money to beggars because most beggars are tremendously rich, and only pretending to be poor, but I would like to think that the origins of this false rumour are more metaphysical.

It used to be believed that every toad carried a precious jewel in its head. Many millions of toads were killed by ignorant people searching for this jewel. I myself have never much liked toads, but I have the greatest respect for those like Peter Simple's Julian Birdbath who do like them. They are said to make excellent companions.

The jewel rumour was intended to be taken symbolically, suggesting that an ugly exterior may hide a beautiful nature, or brilliant intellect. Again, I am not sure that this is universally true. Ugly people, in my experience, are no less likely to be stupid, and possibly more likely to be unpleasant, than attractive ones. Perhaps the message was intended to be that we should not close our minds to the possibilities of paradox.

No doubt the story of the London vagrant with £1,500 in his socks was also intended to be taken symbolically.

It would be a sad thing if the new wave of street-dwellers from unhappy homes in the north of England took it literally, and started cutting the feet off older London vagrants in a vain search for their hidden treasure.

## 23rd March, 1992

### Home sweet home

TOWER Hamlets, traditionally among the looniest of Left-wing London boroughs, is also succumbing to the fashion for selling its public lavatories which has made London such a dangerous place for out-of-towners to visit. They may be brilliant at supplying evening courses in Red Indian War Dances for lesbians in Tower Hamlets, but they cannot any longer provide the simplest amenity of all.

The most encouraging aspect is the price. On a traffic island in Bow Road, east London, you can buy a 19th-century underground public lavatory comprising ladies' and gentlemen's compartments, each with their own front door.

The entrance to the gents is under a statue of Gladstone, and the ladies' entrance is in the grounds of nearby Bow Church. And the price is only £15,000 – about a quarter of what a one-car garage is liable to cost in the West End.

Further West, these abandoned public lavatories are being converted into desperately needed fashion boutiques, and changing hands at £150,000 each. With a little imagination and effort, the Bow Road public lavatory could easily be turned into a young couple's first home.

The good news must be that where the market is allowed to find its own level – without housing associations or banks intervening to maintain an artificial price – the true value of housing in central London is beginning to emerge.

People talk of a slight dip in housing values, but the truth is that in relation to wages it is grotesquely over-valued – by a factor of some 40 or 50 per cent. No wonder nobody is buying, and house-hunters are being forced to scour the public lavatories of London.

Distress caused by the absence of lavatories must be balanced by happiness that our young people have found somewhere to live.

## *25th March 1992*

### Threatened beavers

FURTHER to my note on Monday about rumours of a great drought, I observe that the *Sun* newspaper carried a '*Sun* news special' on the same day, boldly headlined:

'WE'RE IN GRIP OF WORST DROUGHT SINCE 1745: Trees parched and animals dying.'

Millions of families face drastic water shortages in 'the worst drought for nearly 250 years'. I read: 'Thousands of oak and beech trees are starting to die in an area stretching from South Devon to Sherwood Forest. Wildlife such as geese, waterfowl, beavers, otters, frogs and toads are badly hit as streams and rivers turn to trickles.'

I can't speak for the otters, because I have not been looking out for them recently, but my own ducks – mallard and teal for the most part – are in fine shape, and have just been joined by a handsome pair of Canada geese. There is plenty of water and they are all having the time of their lives.

As for the beavers, it's a funny thing, y'know, but I have been around the woods, rivers and hedgerows of England this past half century, or so, and I can't rightly recall ever seeing a beaver. In fact I don't think there are any beavers in this country. Whichever 'expert' informed the poor *Sun* reporter that the nation's beavers were being badly hit by this non-existent drought was relying on that newspaper's regrettable ignorance about the natural world and its indiscriminate sentimentality towards animals.

The 'experts' may have been helped by the fact that the newspaper is written in windowless concrete bunkers. Journalists enter them in the dark and leave them in the dark. They never have a chance to glimpse the green fields, the sparkling rivers and streams, the frogs and toads cavorting in the spring sunshine. They will believe whatever the 'experts' tell them. I still have an open mind about this alleged drought, but I can't help asking myself what sort of drought it is which requires its supporters to tell such whopping fibs to convince us of its seriousness.

## Election fun

GOOD news that the Islamic Party of Britain launched its first general election campaign on Sunday, fielding five candidates on a programme of pardoning Salman Rushdie, or at any rate lifting the death sentence imposed by a dead Persian mullah all those years ago.

The reason for this clemency is explained by Mr Daud Musa Pidcock, the party leader – that, having studied Rushdie's unreadable *Satanic Verses*, he reached the conclusion that the author must have been suffering from a spell of madness or breakdown.

This seems the most charitable interpretation to me. I wish I had thought of it when the rubbish first appeared. I am glad that a proper and responsible Islamic party is to take up the task of representing Muslims in this country. They have often struck me as being much nicer people than their religious spokesmen would have us believe.

On the other hand, I wonder what effect the move will have on BBC plans to broadcast the Koran in the daily 15-minute Radio 4 slot at present occupied by the Bible. This scheme was announced at the same time as the BBC's plans to screen a version of Lawrence's *Lady Chatterley's Lover*, directed by Ken Russell.

The great danger is that readings from the Koran will be taken as a party political broadcast on behalf of the Islamic Party of Britain. At least the Lawrence filth is unlikely to be mistaken for a party political broadcast – unless, I suppose, for the ludicrous 'Paddy' Pantsdown and his fun-loving Liberal Democrats.

### Imitation of Kanga

THE ARCHDEACON of York, the Venerable George Austin, has a point when, in protesting against the BBC's proposal for a television version of the Gospels in which Jesus is played by two women, he said: 'They wouldn't dream of causing offence to Muslims.'

Of course, if they did, there would be immediate *fatwahs* against John Birt and all the other BBC grandees whose names for the moment escape me. But the remarkable thing is not the BBC's reluctance to cause offence to Muslims – why on earth should it wish to do so? – but its determination to offend ordinary, conventional Christians. I can think of no other explanation for their decision to screen these trans-sexual Christs during Holy Week.

Perhaps the purpose of the operation is to convince more impressionable viewers that Jesus Christ really was a woman, or

at least a transvestite. Perhaps the more extreme feminists in the corporation believe it. A few weeks ago, when the Anglican Archbishop of Perth announced that he had 'ordained' 10 women in western Australia, I jocularly suggested that he should try 'ordaining' some kangaroos, too.

Nobody in Perth has been in touch to tell me whether or not the Archbishop took me up on that suggestion.

But it can be only a matter of time before animal rights groups in Perth start demanding that kangaroos should be given the parts of Mary and Jesus in the play. From there it will be a short step to convincing the more simple-minded animal enthusiasts that Jesus and Mary really were kangaroos. Animal rights extremists will go round all the churches and galleries of Europe altering portraits of the Madonna and Child to the new perception.

The masterpieces of Henry Moore are probably as well designed to represent Mother Kangaroo with Young as Mother and Child, but I fear that some of the older paintings will not be improved by this *aggiornamento*. Mr Rushton has kindly agreed to see what he can do for us, to illustrate the point.

## *8th April, 1992*

### Cleopatra was not American

MR KINNOCK has announced that when he becomes Prime Minister he will give the Elgin Marbles to Greece. Never mind that Prime Ministers do not actually own the Elgin Marbles. They belong to the British Museum, which bought them in 1816 from Lord Elgin, as every schoolboy knows. I wonder what other pieces of our national heritage this Welsh oaf proposed to give away. The Egyptians are asking for Cleopatra's Needle, the great granite obelisk of 1500BC which stands on the Thames embankment just a few yards from the Savoy.

Where the Elgin Marbles are concerned, I am surprised that the present inhabitants of the Greek mainland want anything to do with them. Anybody with a tape measure could see in a matter of minutes that the figures on these marbles have nothing whatever in common with the Greeks of today who, short-legged and stocky with lowslung, hairy bottoms, blunt noses and crossed eyebrows, are plainly a race of Turkic origin. The idea that these people could have designed the Parthenon or carved the sculptures of Praxiteles is laughable.

Cleopatra's Needle is slightly different. It is one of many ancient Egyptian obelisks to be found all over the civilised world: in Paris and Istanbul as well as London – Rome has a dozen of them – although there are still plenty on the banks of the Nile. Many were taken away by the Romans, others by Napoleon, but ours was a present from the Egyptian government in the last century – a jolly nice present, too, if I may say so. There can be no doubt that in the 112 years it has been standing on the embankment it has become a part of the London scene. The people who live in Egypt now have little relationship to the ancient Egyptians, being (apart from the Copts) Arab invaders from the seventh century AD. They must learn what every child knows that you can't ask for a present back.

But all is not lost. The twin to our own Cleopatra's Needle stands, neglected and absurd, in the middle of New York's sex maniac-haunted Central Park. If New Yorkers notice it at all, few have any idea that it is 1,500 years old, and many would be deeply shocked if they knew, reckoning that anything over 20 years old must be dirty and out of date.

Most New Yorkers probably feel that Egypt is part of Europe, and won't want a dirty old European stone cluttering their favourite wilding ground; others, the more politically correct, will feel that Egyptians have the greater moral claim because Arabs are slightly blacker than they are.

## 11th April, 1992

### Keep them moving

A DESPATCH from Rome in Thursday's newspaper seemed to tell us that the Pope has been urging sex education for priests. We can only hope that the message was garbled in transmission, or possibly in translation from the Italian – a much more difficult language than many seem prepared to believe.

The message is apparently contained in a 220-page apostolic exhortation to the clergy, most of which is uncontentious: priests must be ascetic and chaste as well as celibate, taking a keen and benevolent interest in the poor and in sinners who are the poor in spirit.

But is it really a good idea that students should be taught

about sex in seminaries? The idea seems to be that if priests are given a 'properly informed sexual education' this will prevent their 'love of chastity' being displaced by the temptations of the flesh, but I see no reason why it should have this effect.

The Pope's theory is that priests should be specially educated to arm themselves with 'more than supernatural means' against possible temptation. What can he mean?

Many doctors in the post-Freudian age believe that nothing but harm can come from sex education. One has only to look at the United States, where they take sex education very seriously but seem to have got everything wrong, with the most appalling results to the nation's health.

It can be argued that American children are not always very intelligent or easy to teach, with catastrophically short attention spans, but one can see the beginnings of a sad muddle even in England, with the publication of a homosexual prayer book giving instructions for a 'coming out' liturgy next door to prayers for those who already suffer from the American disease.

I feel the Pope should draw his clergy's attention instead to these new things called Buzzboards – motorised two-wheel scooters on which the driver travels upright at a dignified speed of 20 mph. There can be no question of indulging in sexual impropriety while driving a Buzzboard. An enthusiast points out that its real attraction is that it is fun: 'When you ride it you have a permanent smile on your face.' Exactly what a celibate clergy needs.

## 15th April, 1992

### Merrie England

I DID NOT see the London Marathon this weekend, and so cannot complain about it too loudly, but my heartfelt sympathy goes out to those who found themselves confronted by 25,000 runners, all anxious to show how goodhearted they were and what fun they were having.

From photographs I see that some were dressed as chickens, some as rabbits, some as Indian statesmen. Many men wore cushions under their shirts or put on grass skirts and false breasts, whether in emulation or mockery of the gentler sex.

There are those who will argue there is no harm to this, it is all for charity; my objection is not moral but aesthetic. It is not true to say that anything is justified in a good cause: vulgarity, exhibitionism and ugliness are things to be avoided. There is no excuse for inflicting them on your fellow-citizens by saying it is done in a good cause.

The pains of living in an overcrowded island are apparent enough for those who have to travel inside it. But if the torture is to be compounded by organised mass merrymaking, life will soon become unendurable.

When Disney's Euro park was first mooted I, too, saw it as a cultural Chernobyl and prayed that some mad French intellectual would blow it up. It certainly sounds my idea of Hell on Earth, with no alcohol being sold (as in Fortress Wapping) because as the American organiser explained: 'We want to keep the Magic Kingdom magic.'

Now I feel that the French intellectuals are wrong. There was a time when we might have hoped to educate our Disney-fodder to something better. That time has now passed. The theme for the future is not education but segregation. If hundreds of thousands of Mickey Mouse fans choose to celebrate their preference together in a small area set aside for them in the north of France, then the rest of the country can breathe a sigh of relief and head somewhere else.

By the same token, if the London Marathon can be persuaded to run round and round Wembley Stadium, then the rest of us can happily offer to sponsor it.

## *18th April, 1992*

---

### Song of songs

IT WAS civil of Lord McAlpine to attribute the Conservative victory to support from the Press, and it will be good for Tory MPs to reflect on this, as they jostle and climb over one another like so many iguanas in a pit. But McAlpine stressed the role of the tabloid editors, at the expense of weightier sheets. I would like to think we did our bit on Way of the World.

Over the years I have seen many journalistic colleagues fall in love with the Prime Minister of the day – first with Harold Wilson, then with Mrs Thatcher – and I have always been the first to mock them, denouncing them as toadies and sycophants.

But what are these strange stirrings I feel when I contemplate the blameless countenance of our nice new Mr Major, with his miraculous phantom moustache, his hair like a flock of goats, teeth like sheep that are newly shorn, temples like a piece of pomegranate within his locks.

'My beloved is white and ruddy, the chiefest among ten thousand . . . his hands are gold rings set with beryl: his belly is as bright ivory overlaid with sapphires. His legs are as pillars of marble . . . His mouth is most sweet: yea, he is altogether lovely. This is my beloved, and this is my friend, O daughters of Jerusalem.'

Perhaps it would be premature to describe Mr Major as my friend, as I have not yet had the pleasure of meeting him, but if the daughters of Jerusalem will just wait around . . .

All the editors named by Lord McAlpine have denied their part in the victory, but it would convince nobody if I put in such a modest claim for my own role. There can be little doubt it was the Way of the World column which dragged the nation back from the precipice, and saved the Elgin Marbles for the nation.

Those who suffer aggravation and annoyance from the crowds of their fellow citizens over the Easter break should reflect how much worse things would be if the idiotic Mr Kinnock were Prime Minister.

## *22nd April, 1992*

### Tea break

SOME years ago, while on a visit to Cuba, I had the good fortune to be given crocodile to eat. It was perfectly acceptable, tasting like a cross between lobster and pork, and it set me off on a quest for unusual foods which has led me to eat snake in Thailand, raw horse in Fukuoka Province (Japan), dog in Manila, monkey's brain in Senegal, etc, although I was unable to secure any giant panda in China and was once asked to leave a restaurant in Adelaide after asking for koala.

So it was with some excitement that I read how the island of Lewis, in the Outer Hebrides, is the only place where young gannets (or guga) can legally be seized, split, boiled and pickled to make a delicacy which is said to taste half-way between steak and kipper. Or so Susannah Herbert claimed in Monday's newspaper.

I do not suppose it will be a very enjoyable experience since I have always thought gannets rather unpleasant birds – the guga will vomit a vile-smelling oil when it feels frightened or spiteful – and its numbers have grown abominably in recent years, with no fewer than 100,000 pairs nesting in Britain, 40,000 of them on the tiny, defenceless island of St Kilda, which they have turned into a hell on earth with their various excrements.

It will be good to think I am doing my bit to keep the numbers down. If all goes well, I shall return with Mr Rushton to Way of the World in 10 days' time.

## 6th May, 1992

### Children's hour

ONE could easily become indignant about proposals to make it a criminal offence for parents to smack their children, but only if one supposed that anyone would pay the slightest bit of attention to such a law. But apart from its fatuousness, it is a thoroughly bad and oppressive idea.

I can quite accept that corporal punishment does not always prevent children from becoming delinquents, but that is only part of its appeal. Another part is to relieve parents' feelings. Personally, I derive no pleasure from smacking children, but that is no good reason for me to put a stop to other people's pleasures. It is like the hunting issue, which almost certainly lost Labour its fourth general election in a row.

Many parents may have children only to smack them, in much the same way that people keep dogs only to shout at them in a gruff, peremptory way. There are few enough incentives for young couples to have children in our ageing society; we should do nothing to discourage them.

Perhaps anti-corporal punishment fanatics can think of other things to do with small children than smack them. I have heard that babies can be used for netball or American basketball, and this (unlike being smacked) is something they enjoy. But even then the bossy fanatics will probably insist on passing a lot of fatuous laws controlling the height of the goal, etc.

180

# Obvious situation

WHEN the United Nations Population Fund produced its report in Rio last week, to the effect that the world's population will more than double in the next 60 years, this alarming news was presented in a vacuum, as if it was somehow complete in itself. The lesson was that we should put our hands in our pockets and send shiploads of condoms to the Third World.

But of course there are countless other United Nations reports arguing that people are starving in east Africa and being drowned in Bangladesh, there is a plague of locusts in the Sudan, living standards are slipping in Russia. We must rush money to all these places. No sooner do they receive the money than they start breeding again.

Possibly many of the world's problems are insoluble, but I feel there should be some sort of clearing house for them where they can be related to each other and see if they can cancel each other out.

For instance, it seems to me that the greatest single cause of unhappiness in Britain today is caused by the modern British woman's hatred of housework. About once a year I remind the Chancellor of the Exchequer that if he wishes to remove the problems of unemployment and homelessness at a stroke, he has only to make resident domestic help tax-allowable, thereby restoring what was, before the Second World War, the biggest single employer of labour in the country.

Over the years I have come to doubt the wisdom of this advice. The modern British woman hates housework not only because it demeans her intelligence (or her husband's manhood), she is also no good at it. Nor are all the young 'homeless' Brits we see begging on London stations the sort of people one would necessarily want in one's home. Apart from anything else, there is the problem of what to do with their dogs.

But the Third World, bursting at the seams with humanity which it cannot accommodate or support, surely offers the perfect solution to housewives' blues. There is scarcely a home in the country so small that a broom cupboard could not be found to hold a small Asian maid or houseboy. In exchange for board and a modest wage – say £12 a week – everybody's problems would be solved. Is it just some notion of political correctness which prevents our adopting this obvious solution?

# 11th May, 1992

## Bishop's move

IDLE to pretend there could be any conversation this weekend except about the poor Irish bishop who had an affair 18 years ago with an American woman; she appears to have been receiving money from him ever since. Despite a large financial settlement two years ago, Mrs Annie Murphy and her acne-faced teenage son decided to shop the Bishop of Galway, Dr Casey, last week.

Master Peter Murphy, the 17-year-old product of this unfortunate liaison, describes his motives thus:

'What I want from my father right now is for him to come right over to me, take my hand and call me son. He has no right to be a bishop, while I live here with nothing. I don't want his money, but I want his acknowledgement and his love.'

Now the Bishop has had to resign, I can think of several things he might choose to call this spotty youth as well as 'son'. But the oddest result of Mrs Murphy's decision was a leading article in Saturday's *Independent* which should be set to music and sung to the strains of computerised bongo drums in every Anglican church. It was entitled *Pastores dabo vobis* ('I will give you herdsmen'):

'Whether this story is interpreted primarily as a human tragedy or as an example of the hypocrisy of the Catholic Church, it is bound to revive the debate about the celibacy of the Catholic priesthood . . . Dr Casey's fall is like a parable on the internal contradictions of the Catholic Church, at the centre of which lies the celibacy issue. Unless those within it join the debate, its authority as well as its manpower will be seriously eroded.'

These dirty-vicar stories used to be left to the *News of the World* which could be relied upon to take a pretty high line, but seldom quite as high as this. One does not know whether to interpret this high-minded newspaper's interest in the matter as a human tragedy or as an example of traditional newshounds' hypocrisy.

It may be hard luck on Dr Casey to be publicly denounced 18 years after the event, but it is scarcely a tragedy; bishops have been fathering children ever since the first Council of Nicaea, meeting in 325, determined that they shouldn't. I should guess that the incident will prove helpful, rather than unhelpful, in recruiting young men for the priesthood.

## 13th May, 1992

### Historic breakthrough

THE EARTH SUMMIT in Rio de Janeiro, where representatives of 160 nations, including 60 heads of state, will meet to discuss Global Warming, promises a historic breakthrough in opportunities available for world leaders to waste their own time and everybody else's money.

We have had Commonwealth Conferences, which gave the Queen an opportunity to be photographed with rows of grinning Africans. We have had municipal 'goodwill' delegations which eat and drink themselves into a stupor in all the best hotels in Europe. But nothing has ever been so fatuous or wasteful as this global celebration of a phenomenon which does not, in fact, exist.

It goes without saying that all the world's leaders are tremendously keen to establish global warming as a threat to life on the planet, let alone civilisation as we know it. This gigantic imposture enables them to strike important attitudes, and raise and spend vast sums of taxpayers' money. Soon it will be an offence punishable by fine or imprisonment to point out that the world has not, in fact, got any warmer since 1864, when people started measuring these things.

Normally, one would wish the world's leaders a pleasant break. No doubt they can find occupations to amuse them. They shoot children in Rio de Janeiro, I believe. Our delegates could lend them a hand in helping to clear some of these pestilential rain forests which clog the whole area. But there is a terrible danger that if the world's leaders make a habit of meeting in such exotic locations – another group is off to Nairobi to draw up a global wildlife treaty – one day they will all end up being eaten.

## 18th May, 1992

### Our secret smile

TUESDAY of last week may well go down in history as the day 32 people climbed Everest, but I am afraid that the new record may not hold very long. It can be only a matter of time before 50 or 100 climbers will arrive simultaneously. Then the Japanese will install a lift, and we will have a karaoke bar on the summit.

Sir Edmund Hillary's lack of enthusiasm is understandable enough. He hoped that the 32 climbers would carry down all the rubbish they had carried up. Apparently the whole mountain is now littered with camping and picnic debris, worse than Brighton beach after a Bank Holiday.

Mount Everest's fate is not particular. It is a sad fact that all the chief sites of the world are now crowded out with visitors from all over the world. Nowhere is a pleasure to visit any more. There is nothing to be done about it except to stay at home and cultivate our own gardens. This was a discovery I made when I finally reached the Great Wall of China three years ago and found it swarming with Germans, Americans and Swedes, all wearing shorts and all shouting at each other.

I do not think I would even advise Britons to explore the beauties of their own land too closely. Apart from the driving rain which looks as if it will be a permanent feature in the West Country this summer – many visitors have already drowned; others are upset by the bloated carcasses of cows and horses floating in every ditch – they have discovered something called radon gas which haunts many of the buildings and kills people in their thousands every year from lung cancer. Radon gas is measured in becquerels per cubic metre. Devon, Cornwall and Somerset are swarming with these becquerels which nobody can see, and only West Country men can sense. That is why we sometimes smile rather strangely at visitors from other parts of the country.

## *20th May, 1992*

### Great global joke

ENGLAND, despite the leadership of its national church , has one of the highest population densities in the world. There are 941 of us crammed into every square mile. By contrast, Latin America, which is the one big area over which the Roman Church holds some sway, is virtually unpopulated. No major country has more than 65 inhabitants to the square mile.

In England, where it is scarcely possible to find a house whose tranquillity is not spoiled by the roar of traffic, even in the depths of the country, we can easily imagine that if there were half as many of us we would be twice as happy, but I am not sure that is true. What may be needed is not population control,

184

which would be oppressive to enforce, so much as some form of prosperity control. This would be quite easy to achieve, by bank rate, or whatever.

It is a sad but easily observed phenomenon that as people become richer they make more noise, occupy more space, put up more and uglier buildings, move around more, leave more litter, and generally make life less pleasant for everyone else. In this respect, I feel Dr Carey is making a helpful contribution when he urges the world's 80 million Anglicans to lead simpler lives. 'We have really got to consume less,' he says. 'One of the models can be a very simple life-style which is almost Franciscan.'

In the modern context, this means staying at home and not making too much noise. In exchange for this helpful suggestion, I will let him into the Great Global Warming Joke, although he must promise not to tell anyone until after the Earth Summit in Rio next month.

This is the joke. In the first place, there has been no global warming – certainly none to compare with that in the 10th century, when Vikings farmed in Greenland. The cooling which wiped out their colonies has never been explained, nor the warm periods in pre-history, but they were certainly not caused by cars or power stations.

I remember a BBC documentary, in the mid-Seventies, threatening us with a new ice age unless we curbed our use of fossil fuels. This suggestion was prompted by the *fall* in world temperatures during the 1960s, a time of profligate use of fuel. Its tendency, however, was the same: to discourage people from using cars.

The final twist of the joke is that even if global temperature increased to what it was in the 10th century, it would make virtually no difference to sea levels. This is because floating ice displaces its own mass. If the whole Arctic Ocean were to melt there would be no rise in sea levels. It is something every schoolboy used to know. Modern education has a lot to answer for.

## A natural solution

AS MENTIONED in my first item, I do not believe that the Roman Catholic position on birth control is of great environmental importance. However, since Dr Carey has been decent enough to urge his Anglicans to make as little noise as possible, I will tell him how to treat the matter when he pays his first call on the Vatican next week.

The Church's position is that since the prime purpose of sexual intercourse is, by definition, procreative, any sexual intercourse which has no such purpose or possibility must, by natural law, be wrong. This doctrine was put together from the story of Onan and various biblical imprecations against sodomy. It was also influenced by the fact that in biblical times all heterosexual intercourse was thought to carry the possibility of conception, and so this activity had to be strictly controlled in order to provide for the resulting offspring.

The last consideration no longer applies, and it would be a development, not a repudiation, of Catholic doctrine on natural law to say that since a procreative intention is, by definition, necessary to sexual intercourse, ergo any form of congress between the sexes which precludes procreation is not sexual intercourse. Where there is no sexual intercourse, there can be no fornication. In its place, there is merely a recreational activity of no great moral significance.

I have demonstrated elsewhere how this development might affect the rule on clerical celibacy. Dr Carey is not concerned with that. Let him take this article, suitably translated into Latin, with him when he goes to see the Pope next week. It may not work this time around, but it will achieve more than any amount of babbling about global population or over-population in Latin America.

## 23rd May, 1992

### Hail the millennium

WE SHOULD be nervous of proposals for a new Festival of Britain to celebrate the year 2001, it being 150 years after Prince Albert's Great Exhibition of 1851 in the Crystal Palace, and 50 years after Hugh Casson's socialist fiasco of 1951.

In the first place, everybody else will be quite exhausted from celebrating the 2000th year of Our Lord's birth, not to mention the 22nd Olympic Games (to be held, I hope, in Berlin rather than Manchester – the Germans are better at this sort of thing than we are, as they demonstrated in 1936). How can we be certain we will have anything to celebrate in 2001?

Lord Palumbo, the property developer whom Mrs Thatcher

put in charge of the Arts Council, appears to have barnstormed his way into a position of influence over the scheme. He proposes, among other things, a rash of new public buildings such as community centres and arts centres to celebrate the millennium.

I would have thought one construction would do the trick. Our modern age is not much good at building, and is rotten at architecture, but it can sometimes achieve reasonably good effects with cubes in black reflecting glass.

I would suggest, on the original site of the Crystal Palace in Hyde Park, a gigantic black glass doss-house with rubbery composition floors which would be hosed down and disinfected every morning.

Anybody could sleep there who was destitute, or came from the north of England, or from overseas, or did not fancy paying the exorbitant sums demanded by London hoteliers for bed and breakfast.

## More medical notes

IT WAS kind of the King of Saudi Arabia to give £150,000 towards the £350,000 cost of four-year-old Laura Davies's combined bowel and lung transplant in America. Even people as rich as he must be rather worried by the cost of medicine nowadays.

A new cure for migraine, to replace the old aspirin, has been developed by Glaxo. The only snag is that it costs £20 a shot, and it will cost the National Health Service an extra £1 billion a year.

Other painkillers which doctors welcomed as being more expensive than aspirin, like paracetamol, turned out to be potentially dangerous. No doubt the new medicine is totally safe, but £20 a time still seems rather steep.

When I was a young man, hypodermic syringes in public hospitals were sterilised after use, their needles re-sharpened and used again and again. Bandages were boiled and used again. There was probably no more cross-infection then than there is now, when everything is used only once and then thrown away.

But the latest refinement is best of all. Medicine spoons for young children are to be withdrawn and replaced by disposable syringes. The advantages are that this method may avoid tooth decay in children who take so much medicine it rots their teeth; and smaller quantities of more concentrated drugs may be given.

So now the NHS is to send out more than a million syringes every year, backed by a gigantic advertising campaign to teach mothers how to use them.

I hope the King of Saudi Arabia can be persuaded to take an interest in paying for this.

## 25th May, 1992

### Time to change sides

EVER since the start of the US Presidential campaign, this column has loyally supported Mr Pat Buchanan as the best person to lead America where it wants to go, away from further involvement with the rest of the world, in an orderly and dignified manner, back up its own, ahmm, umbilical cord.

I now see that Buchanan is not going to win because he does not have enough money. Accordingly, the entire column has swung behind the new third candidate, called Ross Perot, who appears to be standing on an independent platform.

This is not just because Perot is extremely rich, apparently worth £1.42 billion. Nor is it because of anything in particular which he stands for. He is reluctant to commit himself to specific policies, and on the one issue where he has made a proposal – for solving the drug problem – his solution is puerile. He proposes a once-for-all search and arrest operation on the inner-city ghettos, using the National Guard.

My reason for preferring Perot – he is an extraordinarily unattractive man of 61, with jug ears, brutal crew cut and redneck Texan twang, as well as being incomprehensible and largely moronic – is that when he is President of the USA he will confront smart-aleck 'Eurosceptics' in this country with the reality of the American alternative to Europe. So long as they gaze at mild-mannered President Bush and idealistic Governor Clinton, they are living in a fools' paradise.

The Americans themselves are interested only in the abortion issue, but I do not know where Mr Perot stands in the great Old Glory Condom debate. Last week the US Patent Office refused to sanction condoms of Stars and Stripes design, sold under the slogan Worn with Pride, Countrywide as part of that country's courageous struggle against the national disease – on grounds of scandal.

Our own flag has no such protection. Having read about the American idea, British condom makers will even now be planning a Union Jack condom, to be sold in London and Belfast, if not Glasgow, under some embarrassing slogan about Jacks and sexual union. The further Britain and the United States can distance themselves, the happier both will be.

## Greatest Englishwoman

WHILE we are all pondering a suitable honour for Lady Thatcher – should we make her a Countess, or Duchess in her own right, or Deputy Queen of England, or will Life Baroness do the trick? – we might spare a thought for Elizabeth David, who died last week at 78.

She achieved more for her fellow countrymen, in terms of improving their standards of comfort, well-being and general happiness, than any woman in my own lifetime, and I dare say in the history of England. She not only revolutionised our approach to food, teaching us how it can easily become one of the principal pleasures of life, she also opened the gates of Europe, teaching a timid and sceptical English middle class the delights which awaited them there. I wonder whether Britain would ever have voted 2-1 in favour of Europe in the historic Referendum of June 5, 1975 if it had not been for Mrs David.

It is against this tide of olive oil, garlic and wine that the Thatcherite lower-middle class backlash is now trying to shut the gates once again. Only those who remember how disgusting most English food used to be before *French Provincial Cooking* (1960) – let alone before *A Book of Mediterranean Food* (1950) – will appreciate quite what these people are trying to do.

In a recent article on reforming the honours system, W. F. Deedes urged politicians to observe the rule 'family hold back' and not grab all the top honours for themselves and their relations. By doing so, they devalue the honours they award themselves.

Mrs David, who saved her country from gloom and despair, received the OBE in 1976 and the CBE, when well over 70, in 1986. This is just a step or two ahead of the award Lady Thatcher chose for her cleaning woman in Downing Street, the admirable Mrs Booker. Yet if any woman has ever deserved a peerage, the Garter or the OM, it was surely Elizabeth David.

I feel Lady Thatcher should wait, like Mr Heath, until she is 75, before being offered further honours. Heath's award is thought to be by way of an apology from the Queen for having called him 'dispensable' on television. I wonder what the Queen will choose to call Lady Thatcher. Between now and October 13, 2000.

## *27th May, 1992*

### Lessons of tennis

JUNE of this year marks the 15th anniversary of the Grunwick riots, when gangs of extremely unpleasant 'workers' from the north of England, led by Mrs Shirley Williams, descended on a London suburb to try to stop some pretty Asian women from working in a photographic processing plant.

They coincided with the Wimbledon tournament, and I remember switching television channels between pretty Sue Barker playing tennis at Wimbledon and the hideous, grimacing faces of Mrs Williams's 'workers' on the news. What a distressing illustration they provided of the Two Nations, I thought. If only Mrs Williams's 'workers' could be persuaded to watch Wimbledon . . .

I do not think we should be too distressed that Mr Murdoch plans to buy exclusive rights to Wimbledon for his own lower-class television channel, now called BSkyB. There can be no question for most of us of having BSkyB in the house. Apart from anything else, it damages property values in the neighbourhood if you stick a 'Rupert's ear' on your roof, and it cannot be long before posses of neighbourhood vigilantes start burning down the houses which display them.

So there will be no more Wimbledon on television, but in truth it has got much duller. Powerful new carbon-fibre racquets mean that the ball moves so fast you can seldom see it, while fewer and fewer services are successfully returned.

Most of us have more important things to do than watch such tedium. What we must all hope is that when Mr Murdoch's 'workers' watch, however, incomprehendingly, on their BSkyB machines, something of the gentle spirit of English tennis enters their poor, muddled minds and sweetens their sour temperaments.

### Northern Princess

IS IT true, as the popular papers keep telling us, that the Princess Royal is about to announce her engagement to a naval officer, Commander Tim Laurence? It has also been mooted – and not in any sensational or irresponsible way – that the wedding will take place in Scotland, probably at the Balmoral parish church, according to the rites of the Church of Scotland.

The Church of England, of which the Queen is Supreme Head, has very strict rules about the remarriage of divorced persons – considerably stricter, in fact, than the Church of Rome, which will declare an annulment on many grounds which are not available to Anglicans. The Presbyterian Church of Scotland has always been more easy-going than either of them.

At least Commander Laurence is not a Roman Catholic priest. That would really have set the cat among the pigeons. As it is, there has as yet been little or no outcry from the High Church. Perhaps it is another step in the great lesson of our time, that the Royal Family is human, just like us, rather than semi-divine, as we would prefer to believe.

I suppose this is correct, but it occurs to me that the Royal Family must be semi-divine in some respects. If its members are not divinely appointed, at very least, why should they expect to receive large sums of money from the rest of us simply for existing, or gracing us with their presence at the opening of things?

And if they are divinely appointed above us, by the fact of their birth, have we not the right to expect higher standards of behaviour from them in acknowledgement of their exalted status? Perhaps to say all this is to be spiteful as well as pompous, but the current behaviour of some of them makes it harder (where we can feel no affection), to feel much respect. No doubt it will all be perfectly acceptable if the couple agrees to remain north of the Border. None of us can be so pompous or so spiteful as to mind what goes on in Scotland.

## *30th May, 1992*

### Continuous assessment

EVERY day the newspapers are full of miraculous developments in the world of medicine. Tests on unborn babies can reveal whether they are likely to be homosexual or not, so that those who feel strongly about such things can have them killed before they are born. I suppose the same might be true of babies likely to be heterosexual, or just male, but nobody has pointed that out yet.

Head teachers at their conference in Bournemouth this week called for an end to testing of seven-year-olds, on the grounds that they might be better tested by 'continuous teacher assessment'. This is plainly wrong. The nation's generation of seven-year-olds may be gravely flawed, but as nothing compared to its generation of teachers, who are not only uneducated, but in many cases deliberately perverse. Their idea of continuous assessment is to denigrate anyone from a happy or prosperous home and praise anyone from a disadvantaged or criminal background.

No doubt tests on the foetus could establish whether it was likely to pass its CSE or become a criminal. If the former, it could be killed, thereby sparing the need for continuous assessment.

On the other hand, it seems to me that we rely rather a lot on the omniscience of medical scientists. I was not terribly impressed by the story of the man who was taken into one of London's proudest hospitals – the Royal Free, in Hampstead – suffering from haemorrhoids, or piles. While making a telephone call in the corridor he was shot in the head four times and died on the spot, but nobody noticed the shooting and it took hospital staff five-and-a-half hours to diagnose what was the matter with him. Perhaps every NHS hospital should be equipped with a £3.5 million machine able to detect bullet wounds in haemorrhoid patients on the basis of a 24-hour continuous assessment.

# 1st June, 1992

## Twitchers' itch

IT IS not altogether bad news that after the collapse of the ramshackle and implausible Yugoslav federation, the Balkans should revert once again to a battleground of war lords, robber barons and mountain bandits.

I often complain that all the main beauty spots in the world have been ruined by mass tourism but, in fact, every year that passes adds to the list of countries which are no longer safe for any but the most intrepid traveller. Perhaps Prague, Warsaw and Budapest are about to be spoiled by mass tourism, but large areas of the former Soviet Union have already dropped off the tourist map. Parts of Kenya are now almost as dangerous as New

York or Los Angeles.

By the same token, it can only be a matter of time before such sites as Angkor Wat, in Cambodia, and Persepolis, in Persia, become visitable again. The great thing will be to get there before the crowds.

Meanwhile, the perils of travel in our native land are growing. A plague of hairy caterpillars has been reported stretching along the south coast from the Thames estuary to the Isles of Scilly. They cause a terrible rash and many visitors who come south to sunbathe develop such a violent itch that they shed their skins entirely, like lizards, on the beach, returning home in a very sorry state.

But the best news on the environmental front is that a breed of sheep which eats birds has been identified in the Shetlands. I have nothing in particular against birds, in fact I quite like them, although I suppose that as Enoch used to say about Commonwealth immigration, it is a question of numbers. But wherever you get birds you get bird-fanciers or 'twitchers'. These dreadful people think they have a right to trample over anyone's property, usually wearing absurd clothes and staring through binoculars, sometimes jabbering into a wireless set.

Where there are no birds there can be no bird fanciers. Any day now the Somerset hills will echo to the merry bleating of Foula lambs, and the indignant yelps of birds being eaten – at any rate until they decide to go back to Upper Egypt, or Pakistan, or wherever they came from.

## 8th June, 1992

## Path of salvation

IT IS slightly depressing for those of my generation who grew up with the idea that membership of a European Community might save us from another European war – not to mention from the worse excesses of British revenge-socialism – to learn the results of last week's *Sun* poll on this subject.

An odd aspect was that *Sun* readers should have had any particular opinions. If that newspaper is to be believed, more than 20,000 of them took the trouble to answer a 10-point questionnaire, starting with: Would you like to see Britain part of a united Europe? (Yes eight per cent, no 92 per cent) and ending with: Should Britain quit the Common Market? (Yes 80 per cent, no 20 per cent).

In June 1975, when we last held a referendum on the subject, nearly 26 million votes were cast and the result was over two to one in favour of staying in (the exact figure was 67.2 per cent in favour, 32.8 per cent against).

Tremendous efforts were made at that time to persuade the British public one way or other, while no effort at all has been made this time round apart from a few impassioned squeaks from the anti-Marketeers. There is always a chance, I suppose, that once the debate has started, people will take it seriously once again but I have my doubts.

This is not so much because the country has become stupider since 1975 – although it may well have done – as that the humane liberal bourgeois ascendancy has lost its hold. In a society where long distance lorry drivers have been earning more than university professors for nearly 20 years, humane education has lost whatever appeal it once had.

The stupid and unpleasant opinions which once confined

themselves to retributive punishment and immigration policy must now be heard in every area of life, from television programming to field sports and the Common Market debate, where public policy is easily reduced to a handful of sound bites, endlessly repeated: 'national sovereignty', 'bureaucracy'; 'up yours Delors'.

It seems to me that a little effort may be required if we are not to be ruled by these louts. A good start might be for the Waleses to get together with the legal profession, ignoring Lady Thatcher and the Conservative rump, and get rid of Murdoch.

## 10th June, 1992

### Gourmet notes

AS WE giggle and point at the absurd figures attending the United Nations Earth Summit in Rio de Janeiro, reckoning it a capital joke to see so many solemn fools assembled together in the same place, it may not occur to us that these frivolities could produce yet another stream of hysterical instructions regulating what we should eat, drink and wear, think, say and see.

Already, I hear, we are going to be forbidden to eat mongoose or monitor lizard in Hong Kong, as well as the Hong Kong newt, Cascade frog or the thumbnail-sized Romer's tree frog. The instruction has gone out: thou shalt not touch them nor cook them.

To be absolutely honest, I had never heard of these last three. Now that I learn I am not allowed to touch or cook, let alone eat them, I am burning with a desire to do all these things.

All my life I have dreamt of eating a giant panda. In the course of five weeks travelling around China a few years ago, I never found anyone prepared to cook one for me. China, for all its disgusting regime, is quite liberal in its dietary laws, but I was told that cooking a giant panda carried the death penalty.

'Is life not cheap in the Far East?' I inquired.

Possibly so, they replied, but giant pandas are very expensive – about £30,000 each.

Then I remembered that Edward Heath had been presented with a giant panda by the Chinese government, many years ago. Being active in politics at the time, he did not eat it, but presented it on loan to London Zoo.

195

If the British people demand another referendum and vote themselves out of Europe, they will also have voted themselves out of the affection or benevolence of the civilised gourmet. It is not yet illegal to eat giant pandas in England. Every cloud, as they say, has a silver lining.

# 13th June, 1992

## Save lives discreetly

'WE TREAT all motorists equally, whatever their social background,' said Mr Peter Joslin, Chief Constable of Warwickshire, in the chippy tones we might expect from a former Essex policeman. 'The enforcement of the traffic laws is not some perverted wish on behalf of the police to persecute motorists, but is intended to save lives.'

He was speaking in answer to a speech by the Home Secretary, Mr Kenneth Clark – surely one of the milder and more intelligent members of the Conservative team – who had urged the police not to antagonise their natural supporters – the middle-aged, middle class, law-abiding, solid citizenry – by rudeness and excessive zeal in persecuting motorists.

In fact, it is not true that the law treats all motorists equally, regardless of their social background. By instructions which went out to all magistrates this week, higher earners and higher tax-payers will be required to pay heavier fines.

This unjust and regressive measure, which might have emanated from some demented Wedgwood Benn in a Barnsley bunker, uses the 1991 Criminal Justice Act to introduce socialism by the back door, rather as Keith Joseph once tried to make higher tax-payers pay more for their children's education. The idea is to punish people not only for their traffic offence but also for working too hard, or too efficiently. Such measures are wonderfully popular with the lower classes and their running dogs in the newspapers.

It seems perfectly reasonable to me that if higher wage earners are to pay higher fines, they should be treated more politely by policemen, but that is probably not the point the Home Secretary was trying to make. Mr Joslin's anxiety to save lives is commendable, but we all know perfectly well that deaths from drunken driving account for less than one sixth of one per

196

cent of all deaths, and that in their zeal to reduce this miniscule proportion still further, the police are casting a blight over the whole country, as well as turning us into a nation of police haters. It is not as if there are not plenty of other things for them to attend to.

All that is required from the Association of Chief Police Officers is a firm commitment to the law of the land, which requires the police to have a reasonable suspicion before stopping and terrorising motorists.

Mr Joslin lists among his recreations the pleasures of good wine and after-dinner speaking. As a chief constable, he has a chauffeur-driven limousine to take him everywhere. Does he never spare a thought for his unfortunate audiences?

## Wonderful people

MANY years ago my cousin Claud Cockburn invented the archetypal boring *Times* headline:

SMALL EARTHQUAKE

IN CHILE

NOT MANY DEAD

On Wednesday I bought a copy of the *Guardian* – something in the newsagent's face appealed to me – and found what must be the archetypal boring *Guardian* headline of our time:

Advancing Sahara

threatens Europe

Tragedy in the making

for 1.2bn

This massive yawn, needless to say, originated at the Earth Summit in Rio, where the Gambia's Sonko Bolong, demanding large sums of money to reduce deserts, and Nigeria's Dr Bukar Shaib, complaining that the desert's advance has broken into a gallop, were joined by a group of European bores, announcing that the Sahara was about to jump the Mediterranean and move up through Spain.

They were headed by a wonderful new bore, Dr Reidulf Molvaer, of the Norwegian Peace Research Institute, who claimed that by 2025 there 'could be' 400 million environmental refugees in the Horn of Africa (where the present human population is about 49 million), all planning to flood richer parts of the world like Norway.

Perhaps there 'could be' 400 million refugees in the Horn of

Africa, but it is hard to know how they would get there, or where from, or why they should choose to go there.

All these bores are hoping to cash in on the great western appetite for things to worry about. Perhaps we should be proud of our nice John Major banging the drum for birth control ('Major Rubber Johnnie', as he is affectionately known on the smart Rio cocktail circuit) and Baroness Chalker . . . but no, I cannot repeat what they are saying about our Lynda.

Oh yes, and Labour's Ann Clwyd is out there, complaining that the Government is not spending nearly enough money on all this sort of thing.

## 15th June, 1992

### All honourable women

AMID all the honours being thrown around, the only one which seems to have caused some unhappiness was the honorary doctorate awarded to Jacques Derrida, the French philosopher, by Cambridge University, and that was not the result of arbitrary political decision but careful deliberation by some of the finest minds in the land.

Derrida's great message to the world is that language is an imperfect vehicle for the communication of ideas because accretions of meaning on words can cause ambiguity and undermine the intention; but even the intention is seldom unambiguous, in any case. So all you are left with is the text, which might be worth a bob or two for an idle academic to take to pieces.

All of which might seem too obvious and too unimportant to be worth saying, but by saying it incoherently enough, Derrida has allowed huge numbers of semi-literate academics to squabble over it. The award should be seen as being in recognition of efforts in the field of academic job-creation.

The only recent honour about which I had some doubts was Lady Thatcher's parting award of the British Empire Medal to her cleaning woman, Mrs Booker. I am not saying for a moment that Mrs Booker did not deserve the BEM. I am sure she did, but then so did many hundreds of thousands of others. One of the cleaning ladies at Combe Florey recently retired after 21 years' service – a good friend, who is sorely missed – and all I was able to give her was a rotten old book. No medal, no ribands.

Why is it thought more meritorious to clean up Lady Thatcher's mess than that of ordinary private citizens? Where is the sense, where the justice, in this?

## 20th June, 1992

### Use for the zoo

LONDON Zoo's closure is proof of the trend which I have often remarked: a growing indifference to animals which amounts to downright hostility among many intelligent and independent-minded people who feel battered by sentimental and mendacious propaganda from the various green lobbies.

Some may be surprised by this in the light of all the evidence to the contrary. At the Rio Earth summit, it is true, the heads of nearly every country in the world gathered together at enormous expense to discuss African monkeys and suchlike, but their interest may be what finally killed popular enthusiasm.

It is also said that young people care more about cruelty to animals than anything else on earth, but the young are always behind the times in any ideas which eventually settle in their poor heads, and the truth is they care very little about anything.

Proof of this growing indifference to animals is to be found in dramatically falling attendances at London Zoo. Present plans

are to move all the 13,000 animals to other zoos, like Whipsnade, but this merely spreads the problem and prolongs it.

A more sensible scheme would be to turn London Zoo into a huge restaurant, catering for every taste and every pocket. Even as interest in animals has declined, so interest in gastronomy has grown.

This would provide the opportunity for all those who have dreamt of eating a giant panda to indulge their little whim. Those animals which proved best to eat could be bred selectively for future generations of gourmets. After the collapse of Lloyd's, London can find a new role as the world centre of exotic gastronomy.

## 24th June, 1992

### The lies they tell

FOR connoisseurs of the newspaper apology, I commend the following, which appeared on page seven of Monday's *Daily Mirror*:

Redborne School

'A REPORT on May 5 stated that a girl at Redborne Upper School in Ampthill, Beds, had been told by a teacher, Mr Ralph Raynor, to strangle a chicken during a science lesson. We reported that she refused to do so and fled in tears.

'We now know that the girl's story was completely untrue. We wish to apologise to Mr Raynor and to the headmaster and staff and regret any embarrassment or distress our report may have caused.'

It was an ingenious accusation for a schoolgirl to make against a teacher, that he had ordered her to strangle a chicken during a science lesson, and we may be tempted to take our hats off to the unnamed heroine who managed to convince a national newspaper it was true, despite our sympathy for Mr Raynor and his colleagues.

When we think how much mischief has been caused by the unsupported evidence of children to credulous labourers in the ritual abuse vineyard – the families and marriages broken up, reputations destroyed – we must accept that social workers, who are not trained to disbelieve anyone, are possibly the worst people to deal with the problem. Much less damage is caused by untrue stories in newspapers, which few believe in any case.

Perhaps the British Press Awards should include an annual Titus Oates prize for the informant who has most successfully led a newspaper up the garden path. This might take pressure off the hard-pressed social services.

# 4th July, 1992

## In praise of France

A WEEK spent in Bordeaux among the unsung beauties of that remarkable city, its friendly, honest, clever inhabitants, its splendid restaurants and magnificent wines, revives my flagging enthusiasm for the Common Market and increases my irritation with those who cannot see that our cultural survival depends on keeping the United States at a distance.

French democracy is in a much healthier state than our own, largely through the refusal of French citizens to allow themselves to be pushed around by animal sentimentalists, safety fanatics, health fascists and the rest of them.

In reply to an EC directive against the shooting of turtle doves, sportsmen who have shot these irritating birds for centuries blocked all the roads of the Gironde and put up candidates at the local election who secured 37 per cent of the votes. Needless to say, the Maastricht clause which concerns itself with animal rights was put there by a British minister responding to approaches from our own bestially self-important animal lobbyists.

In the same way, stiffer penalties for motorists in France have been met by a blockade of all motorways. When we compare this to the British motorist's cringing acceptance of every oppressive ordinance, it becomes plain that the only terror which Maastricht need hold is terror of our own cowardice.

I was shocked to read that Lord Ferrers, a Home Office minister, when booked for speeding and presented with a £40 fixed penalty with three penalty points, then wrote to the Suffolk police to thank them for catching him. There is a sickness in England. If his lordship appreciates punishment so much, it was unkind just to fine him. He should have been caned, with his trousers down, by the side of the road. Let us hope the French will save us from ourselves.

## Aggiornamento

A CORRESPONDENT in Kent has been kind enough to send me his weekly parish news-sheet, which includes six 'prayer points'. Here they are:

(a) Praying round the Parish; residents of Whetstead Road, and the commercial properties there.

(b) For the family and friends of Mrs Madge Moon in their bereavement.

(c) For the European Community and the Maastricht Agreement.

(d) For the continuing situation in Yugoslavia.

(e) For dental-health care in view of the proposed cuts in payments to dentists.

(f) For the situation in South Africa.

The most exciting suggestion is that religion should concern itself with dental health, as well as spiritual health. This could be part of the campaign to win converts which was launched in November by Dr George Carey under the name of Spearhead. When members of the Jewish and Muslim communities (already nervous at the prospect of being converted), complained that Spearhead was the name of a well-known Fascist magazine, Dr Carey obligingly changed the name of his great crusade to Springboard.

A springboard is quite a useful thing to have in a swimming-pool, I must agree, although it has few uses anywhere else and it is by no means essential even there. I am not sure that these luxurious swimming pool accessories really reflect the right image for the Church in the modern world. Perhaps he should change the name of his mighty religious movement once again, this time to Spearmint, after the well-known toothpaste flavour.

Salvation through Dental Hygiene can be its anthem. Many young people today relate to the smell of toothpaste more readily than to the smell of incense. And the old are nearly all concerned about their teeth.

## Today's kids in class war

IT WOULD be affected to pretend that I am heartbroken by the news that Lord Snooty and his pals are to disappear from *Beano*, the weekly comic, since I have not seen a copy of *Beano* for more than 10 years and am mildly surprised to learn that it still exists. The strip was an amusing chronicle of the class war, as fought in earlier times before the advent of nice Mr Major's classless society. But the reason given by *Beano*'s editor strikes me as odd.

'Our readership can't relate to him,' said Mr Euan Kerr, 41. 'His top hat and Eton collar must baffle today's kids. At the time he was created in 1938, it was a more divided society and children at that time would have liked to be like him and live in a castle.'

There seems to be two misunderstandings here. The first is that children of any decade ever related to Lord Snooty in his top hat and Eton collar, rather than treating him as an agreeable fantasy. The second is to suppose that 'today's kids' read *Beano* or anything else. They are scarcely in a position to do so, poor things, being for the most part unable to read.

Until recently, *Beano* was the favourite reading among undergraduates at Oxford and students at the better redbrick universities, but the days are long past when university students read for pleasure. *Beano*'s chief readership nowadays, I would guess, would be in the senior common rooms, among professors and senior members of staff in the English Literature departments.

Even if no one else in Britain is interested in the class war nowadays, these people certain are. Witness John Carey, Merton Professor of English at Oxford University, who has just written a book explaining that there are no such things as 'high' or 'low' culture, that Mickey Mouse is as valid a literary hero as Hamlet, or the Marxist 'Terry' Eagleton, Warton Professor of English at the same university. If *Beano* drops the class war from its agenda, I should guess it will lose half its circulation.

## Lost leader

A FORTNIGHT after the Road Traffic Act 1992 came into effect, fixing a maximum sentence of five years for motorists who cause death by dangerous driving, or by driving while under the influence of drink, Mr Kenneth Clarke, the Home Secretary, has announced that he proposed to double this sentence to 10 years.

His motive, apparently, is to reflect public concern on the matter, but public opinion feels that everyone whose driving 'has resulted in the tragic waste of another human life deserves to be punished accordingly'. I wonder what he really hopes to achieve, except possibly a pat on the back from the embittered, alcohol-deprived oafs who write leaders in the tabloid press. Does he suppose that s single drunk will be deterred from driving by the prospect of a 10-year sentence who would not have been deterred by a five-year one?

Does he suppose that any grieving friend or relative will be justly comforted by the thought of these once-off offenders cluttering up our prisons for 10 years, rather than five?

It is easy enough to find moronic and unpleasant people prepared to demand a life sentence or even capital punishment under these circumstances, but such people are seldom, if ever, chosen to be Home Secretary. What has happened to Kenneth Clarke, whom we used to think of as one of the pleasanter, more intelligent and civilised members of a largely barbarian Cabinet? He knows perfectly well how crowded our prisons already are. He also knows that drink-driving deaths have fallen by 60 per cent since 1979; 12 per cent last year alone.

It is well known that the permanent staff of some major government departments – especially the Home Office, Transport and Health – include various dangerous madmen. As often as not they are Scottish temperance fanatics. It is possible he has been nobbled by one of these, but it seems more likely he is making up to everything that is stupidest and vilest in modern Britain. In neither case does he deserve to remain as Home Secretary. Let him be Chairman of the Party, if this is the best he can do.

# 25th July, 1992

## Sparing the rod

IN A thoughtful leader on Tuesday *The Daily Telegraph* gave qualified approval to the Japanese experiment in treating recalcitrant schoolchildren with electric shocks, suggesting that the principle of corporal punishment had been cleverly adapted to the electronic age.

One is bound to admire the ingenuity of the idea, and I can well believe that Japanese children respond well to electric shocks. The great question remains whether or not the electric shock treatment would work in England.

For many hundreds of years it was educational orthodoxy that young Anglo-Saxon males responded only to beating. No other country beats its children. No other country needs to.

The young Anglo-Saxon male, by nature defiant of authority; prone to acts of great daring; unruly and resistant to most forms of education, repines if he is not beaten, just as deer repine if they are not hunted, growing into abject, waddling things like Belgian hares.

It might be said that this is what has started to happen to our young people since we stopped beating them. The Americans, who have never beaten their children, use electrocution only to finish them off at the end of the day.

Obviously they were attracted to the idea of electrocution, as against hanging or decapitation, because they thought it more modern, but the sad truth appears to be that it hardly works at all. They nearly always need three shots at it, and still the heart goes on beating. Perhaps this is one occasion where we can give technological innovation a miss.


# 27th July, 1992

## Doing their job

THE SUMMER police campaign against motorists continues to gather strength. Police in Cambridgeshire, where all the sub-post offices have agreed to help to support the campaign, point to a survey in the county which claims to show that people give higher priority to police action against drink-drivers than to police action against assault, burglary, drugs and serious crime.

The same point was made even more forcefully in Henley-on-Thames, where the *Henley Standard* reported how ram-raiders ploughed a car through a shop window before escaping with goods worth £25,000. The ram raid was the second at the store in 12 months, and the latest of several in Henley recently: 'Police admit they have little information about this week's break-in. They are asking the public to come forward if they saw anyone acting suspiciously during the evening.'

In another part of the same newspaper, reporters follow two Henley policemen, PCs Craig Buchanan and Rob Hoppé, about their business. The two officers stopped 'dozens' of drivers, we are told.

'Though the team failed to net any drink-drivers, they succeeded in spreading the message that they mean business,' said the reporter approvingly. They breathalysed one unfortunate woman whose test proved negative, but PC Buchanan said he believed she had learned her lesson after being stopped. 'People seem to have this idea it will be all right if they consume a certain amount,' said PC Buchanan. 'It has to be the zero option.'

'The majority of people can see the point of us doing it,' said PC Hoppé. 'This campaign is all about us being seen doing our job.'

## 29th July, 1992

### Worse than rabbits

TEN or twenty thousand hooligans – call them Hippies or New Age Travellers – who descended on a Welsh farmer's 80-acre field, ripping up his fences for firewood while their dogs killed 20 of his sheep – were supplied with water tankers, mobile lavatories and rubbish skips by the county council, while the farm was surrounded by 900 policemen, apparently concerned that the hooligans might be smoking illegal substances.

When the first 800 vehicles arrived on his farm, the farmer, 60-year-old Stanley Pugh, was told they were planning to hold a music festival, but he took a dim view of it all: 'They are terrible people, I spoke to the first arrivals . . . they said they had come because it was a special place. It is special to the cows and sheep that graze there, and it is special to me because I have to make a living.' A neighbouring farmer described how the invaders had been 'chopping down trees, pulling up fences, trampling hay and using the fields, streams and rivers as one big toilet. The pollution is terrible.'

The 'Hippies' ' point of view was put by a spokesperson called Leila, 24, from Birmingham:

'We are just like anyone else but our homes are on the move . . . people are scared of us because of the bad pictures they see on the telly, but we love the countryside and the freedom. We don't want trouble but all we get is confrontation from angry landowners or the police.' Perhaps this love of the countryside is what the president of the Country Landowners' Association meant when he talked of people loving the countryside to death, but I wonder what Leila, 24, from Birmingham, thinks she means by freedom. The right to private property is the greatest guarantee of freedom which civil society affords. It is enshrined in the Declaration of the Rights of Man as 'inviolable and sacred', as well as in the American Constitution. Leo XIII, in his Rerum Novarum (1891), describes the right of private property as 'one of the chief points of distinction between men and the lower animals'.

The freedom to which these 'Hippies' aspire is not the freedom of mankind in civilised society. It is the freedom of bandits or wild animals. A society which protects the right of such people to usurp the property of others is a society on the verge of disintegration. Eventually, these New Age Travellers are bound to be seen as marauding vermin.

Conversation in the pubs down my way revolves around the best way of treating them. Something clandestine and biological seems recommended. The general feeling is that myxomatosis might be too good for them, but a variation of bovine spongiform encephalopathy might hold the key.

## 5th August, 1992

### Is it a walrus?

A PECULIARLY disgusting photograph in this week's *Sunday Times* showed Paul McCartney, the popular singer who now claims to have been a Scottish farmer for the past 30 years, feeding a strange pie-bald animal through a bottle.

I showed the picture to my staff on *Literary Review*. The Deputy Editor, Miss Lola Bubbosh, who is the office animal lover, identified it as a cross between a sheep and a goat. Miss Nancy Sladek, Chief Editorial Assistant and Production Manager, said it was a sheep with the tail of a dog. Mr Sam Leith, editorial assistant, said it was a baby llama. Mr Dennis Sewell, a visiting contributor, said it was a dog.

Nobody was impressed by the *Sunday Times*'s claim that it was a stag which McCartney had rescued from a roof where it had been chased by the Exmoor Hunt. Perhaps it is unfair to expect a poor Liverpool boy to tell the difference between a stag and a Jacob's sheep. But he should have known that a stag, being an adult male deer, was unlikely to take milk from a bottle. And he might have taken the trouble to learn that the Exmoor are a foxhunt.

McCartney has bought a wood at Upton, in Somerset, only a few thousand yards from my own birthplace outside Dulverton. His purpose in buying it was apparently to annoy his neighbours by excluding the local hunts. Now he preaches to them from Sussex in that endearing Liverpool accent.

'Some people assume that deer are just burglars taking man's rightful crop. I don't believe that. We are leading ourselves into the terrible holocaust of a world where nothing lives wild. Mankind will be in control but control of what?'

I suppose it depends what he means by living wild. If there were no hunting, there would be no deer on Exmoor. How many deer are there in his native Liverpool, among all those panting animal lovers?

If by living wild he means being bottle-fed by a sentimental pop star from Liverpool, I think the countryside would be well rid of such creatures. Perhaps one day McCartney will realise how happy it would make his neighbours if he gave Exmoor back to the Exmoor people.

## *19th August, 1992*

### And did those feet . . . ?

EVER since leaving the Army I have been searching for people whom I could pay to polish my shoes. There seems no point at all in joining the mad scramble for money if, at the end of the day, with your pot of gold, you are still left polishing your own shoes.

As a recent report from the Monopolies and Mergers Commission confirms, fewer and fewer people are polishing their shoes nowadays. Many of those in the 30-50 age group have never learnt how to do it, while those under 30 have never so much as heard of its being done.

Instead they wear sneakers, trainers and other forms of tennis shoe all day. These are always rubber soled and often with a top of some synthetic material which makes the feet sweat and smell and grow various forms of fungus.

When one thinks how strict the health fanatics are about every form of food, drink and cigar, pipe or cigarette, you would think they would show some concern about these pools of sickness and infection at the bottom of everyone's legs. It may take a year or two for the baneful effects of this footwear to be noticed – nearly four centuries elapsed between the introduction of tobacco by Sir Walter Raleigh and the setting up of ASH, the organisation of anti-smoking hysterics – but I would not be surprised if most of those smelly feet eventually had to come off.

It is a sad thought to see these jogging enthusiasts out every morning and reflect what they are doing to their feet. But if you gave them a proper pair of shoes, they probably would not know what to do with them.

If our politicians do not wish to preside over a more or less footless nation, they must immediately introduce degree courses in shoe polishing throughout the university system. Hairdressing is not enough.

It also seems utterly wrong that unemployment figures should be mounting inexorably just because our young have never been taught how to polish shoes. A golden future awaits any of those bright lads on Merseyside who can take the trouble to learn.

## *24th August, 1992*

### Saving the world

MY EYE was caught by an interview with Lady Antonia Fraser which appeared in *The Times* on Friday. The interviewer, Valerie Grove, quoted her as saying that she wished every woman could be called Lady:

'It establishes femininity without divulging married state. It is pretty. And it is so friendly to be called by one's Christian name. It could even become classless, if everyone used it.'

Might not men also be permitted to call themselves 'Lady' in the post-sexual dawn? The Roman Catholic Church would be delighted by this development. It already has a group of scholars at work to produce the first 'non-sexist' Mass, leaving God's gender ambiguous and no doubt referring to His single parent as Our Person. In Rome, they are prepared to countenance any degree of trendiness except, thank heaven, the ordination of women. That is seen as the ultimate denial of religion, the final abomination.

It is a shame that the Church should choose to take this principled stand just at the moment when it must also announce a catastrophic shortage of priests. The last time I discussed this matter – in relation to the Church of England in Australia, which had started 'ordaining' women (or Sheilas, as they are known in ecclesiastical circles) – I suggested they might try ordaining kangaroos instead.

Now we learn of a great kangaroo explosion in Australia – at more than 20 million, they outnumber humans by about three million. Conservationists are anxious they should not be culled, and I would have thought the obvious thing was to ship them to Britain for training in the ministry.

Then there will be no shortage of priests and England will be merrie again. Male and female kangaroos are distressingly easy to tell apart under ordinary circumstances, but dressed in clerical attire, they might easily be confused.

## Light still shines

I ALWAYS dreamt that somewhere in the world there might be the opposite of an Aladdin's Cave, where all the bad art which had ever been praised by silly intellectuals and empty-headed aesthetes could be stored – a museum of human folly. Richard Rogers's ugly and half-witted Lloyd's building has been proposed for such a use, once the last defaulting underwriter has been ejected.

Now we learn that such a museum already exists, in Holland. In a suburb of the Hague can be found the largest 'art' mountain in the history of the world – the product of 37 years of arts patronage by the Dutch government which not even the Americans are prepared to buy. This immense pile of rubbish is thought to include 205,000 canvases and *objets d'art*.

I wish a similar warehouse could be found to store all the intellectual rubbish which our government has been subsidising through the universities, the BBC, the Arts Council and Poetry Society in the name of the Modern Movement. Unfortunately, it is still in circulation, used to clutter the poor, muddled minds of schoolchildren.

A small flame still burns at the shrine of Truth and Beauty. On Wednesday, at the Café Royal, the winner of the *Literary Review*'s annual £5,000 Grand Poetry Prize, sponsored by the *Mail on Sunday*, will be announced before a small gathering. The contest is restricted to poems that rhyme, scan and make sense on a different set subject each month. No modern poet will be present. They will all be celebrating their own little epiphanies elsewhere, no doubt at the taxpayer's expense.

## 29th August, 1992

### Crusade against bats

IT WOULD be too much to expect that the Church of England would make a squeak of protest against proposals by the Bat Conservation Trust to turn 8,000 English churches into bat sanctuaries. The Bishop of Portsmouth has already launched a campaign to warn clergymen of their duty to bats, and bat conservation seems set to become another of those good causes to which all *bien pensants* subscribe.

At long last, however, a vicar's wife has arisen, like Don John of Austria, to lead her people into battle. Mrs Catherine Ward, whose husband has five parishes around Fakenham, in Norfolk, has written to the *Church Times* to object to the use of her husband's churches as bat lavatories. The endangered species is not bats but congregations, she argues, and they are mutually incompatible, one driving away the other.

On a tour of 75 Norfolk churches, her husband found that more than half were fouled by bat mess. The problem is that, whereas bats are regarded as sacred animals and their habitats protected as shrines by the law of the land, no such protection is afforded to Christian congregations or Christian shrines. Once bats have moved into a building, human beings frighten or disturb them at their peril.

The real injustice of it all is not so much that bats are ugly, dirty, disease-ridden and frightening animals. We can all see that for ourselves, and if others choose to develop a slightly perverted taste for them, even keep them as pets, we must decide that the world is big enough to accommodate bat fanciers as well as bat haters. Bat lovers, it appears, are not prepared to allow those of the contrary persuasion any rights whatever.

But the true monstrosity of it all is that bats are simply not in peril, either in this country or anywhere else. Any so called 'bat expert' can announce that they are, and everybody defers to him without ever asking when or how they were counted or pointing out on which side the bat expert's bread is buttered.

Within three hundred yards of my home in Somerset there are at least four bat settlements, three of them on my property. Nobody has ever been to count them, or show the slightest interest in them. Even if some years their numbers seem reduced, they always come swarming back into my cellars the next, just as ladybirds, having become few and far between, nearly took over the whole country in 1976. It is time for a religious crusade to drive the bats out of our churches.

## *31st August, 1992*

### But life goes on

LAST week we learnt that the most beautiful house in Somerset – what Christopher Hussey described as the most beautiful sight in the world – has been sold. Brympton d'Evercy has gone to an unnamed English family who seem unlikely to open it to the public when redecoration is finished in a year's time.

All of which strikes me as very good news. It is sad, of course, for the family which has owned it for the best part of 300 years, the Clive-Ponsonby-Fanes, who made a valiant effort to keep it going. But the even sadder truth was that it did not succeed as a showpiece: they had run out of money, the internal decorations were dreadful and they lacked the proper kit to make it look like anything more than a prep school on open day.

So now the most beautiful house in England will be a private family home once again. The historian A. L. Rowse once remarked to me that in the entire history of human civilisation, the most perfect form of existence was that of the English country house in the earlier years of this century.

Without its full supporting cast of indoor and outdoor servants it may be a shadow of its former self, but from my own observation I would guess that even this shadow provides the most agreeable form of life available on this planet.

Others may prefer lying on a Miami beach or watching satellite television on top of a skyscraper in Manhattan, but I would be surprised if there is any greater happiness than that provided by a game of croquet played on an English lawn through a summer's afternoon, after a good luncheon and with the reasonable prospect of a good dinner ahead. There are not all that many things which the English do better than anyone else. It is encouraging to think we are still holding on to a few of them.

## 2nd September, 1992

### Not strange at all

HOME Office immigration officials nearly always get a bad press whenever they exclude someone who has no right to be here, but I feel they may have had a point when they decided to deport a Swedish teenage boy who came to work as an *au pair* to a Leicester family.

'Today everybody is supposed to be equal, men are supposed to be more caring and I really find it all very strange that I am not allowed to do this job because I am a man,' said 19-year-old Johan Egelstedt.

Unfortunately for Egelstedt, and others like him, English law says an *au pair* must be an unmarried girl, aged 17 to 27, without dependants. Immigration officers wanted to send him back to Sweden as he arrived. They searched his baggage, emptied his pockets and conducted a body search – no doubt looking to see if he had any dependants. 'Fortunately, I did not have to take my clothes off,' he said.

This seems an odd statement from a Swedish teenager. I thought the Swedes were so far removed from original sin that they no longer noticed whether they were clothed or not. Perhaps the immigration officers should have made him take his clothes off, to ensure he was a genuine Swedish male teenager and not an East German nun in disguise.

If Johan Egelstedt is really what he claims to be, one can only suggest he has grievously misunderstood the sexual revolution. The idea is that women should take over men's jobs, not that men should take over theirs.

Four thousand years or so after the expulsion from Eden, men have grown tired of tilling the fields and eating bread in the sweat of their faces. They seek a more restful, more contemplative life. It is time for women to take over the work.

So it was in no neo-Nazi spirit of England for the English that we asked Johan Egelstedt to go back to Sweden with all his fine ideas about everybody being equal and keeping their clothes on. We just didn't want him here until he had changed sex, like everyone else. Now he has been allowed to stay. Perhaps I shall become a nun.

## 12th September, 1992

### Disappearing species

THE DUKE of Westminster, no longer, at 40, so distressingly young as he used to be, is surely rich enough to be heard with respect whenever he decides to make a public pronouncement. The poor can make public pronouncements whenever they choose, but the rich have better things to do with their time, and generally need a good reason for making one.

Westminster's pronouncement was called The Problems in Rural Areas, which is as good a title as any, although Some Rural Problems might have been shorter. Among the problems he mentioned was the outflow of young people, which is not really a problem at all, as young people have very little to do in the countryside and generally get in the way.

Another was poor public transport, which is largely overcome by the general availability of private transport. Another, the closure of public houses. Country pubs have been pretty ghastly for as long as I can remember, but the reason they are closing is the Police Terror. Nobody dares go to them for fear of being reported and molested by the police when they leave. It has nothing to do with poverty.

When the Duke demanded a relaxation of the 'planning stranglehold' which prevents landowners turning the whole countryside into a housing estate, we pretended not to notice; and when he demanded huge government grants for landowners we blocked out ears. That was no public pronouncement so much as a clearing of the throat. Whenever landowners speak, they always demand huge government grants, whether for farming or for not farming, but I see no reason why people should be given public money just because they own some land, any more than that they should be given it because they don't.

But we must all agree with him when he says that the countryside needs protecting from the environmentalists. The bat conservationists meeting at Stirling University last weekend threatened to turn the whole of Europe into a gigantic bat conservation area. This is even worse than the RSPB, which demands a mere 30 per cent of the countryside for the purpose of bird conservation.

Personally, I don't believe a word of it when these conservationists claim that birds and bats are disappearing. Even if it is true, it will make life more exciting for enthusiasts if, when they spot their corncrakes, red-shanks, lapwings and bats, there are only a few of them left. Nobody else cares how many there are. Dukes are much rarer than any of these creatures. I believe there are only about 24 left, not counting the Royal Dukes, and they are dying out at the rate of one every three years.

## Luxury whirlpool

A PECULIARLY odious and whingeing letter appeared in the *Daily Mirror* this week, from a woman in Barnsley:

'The Royals simply ask for criticism when Princess Diana is allowed £3,000 of taxpayers' money for a luxury whirlpool bath.

'We have three children and we cannot afford even bubblebaths.

'But we make do by putting some washing-up liquid in the water to make a few bubbles.

'It would do the Royal Family a lot of good to try going without for a while. They would then realise what it is like for most of us all of the time.'

I have never been to Barnsley, and have no wish to go. I imagine that anyone of the slightest intelligence who had the misfortune to be born there would spend much of his active life trying to get away – like Arthur Scargill, who moved the whole National Union of Mineworkers to the bright lights of Sheffield.

But I am surprised at the feebleness of Barnsley's response to the challenge of poverty. In the South of England, poor people often put their babies in the washing machine to give them the illusion of a £3,000 luxury whirlpool bath.

Perhaps there are those in Barnsley who will claim that they cannot afford a washing machine. I don't believe it, but Northerners traditionally expect all the good things in life to be supplied by the Government, and many of them may be prepared to do without a washing machine until the Government gives them one.

The best advice for these people is to put their children in a metal tub with some washing-up liquid, then lift up the tub and run round in circles to give the illusion of a whirlpool. Without some such initiative on their part, the children may grow up as underprivileged and inadequate as they are themselves.

## 14th September, 1992

### Welcome reminder

I WONDER if I am alone in detecting a note of *accidie* – sloth, torpor or spiritual exhaustion – in the tabloids' continued persecution of the Royal Family. It is almost as if, having grown weary of freedom, they are begging to be gagged. Listen to the *Sun* on Saturday: *'They Won't Silence Us . . . They Can Pass Any Law They Like. Fine Us. Jail Us. String Us Up By Our Thumbs. Nothing Will Stop Us Printing What We Believe You Have the Right to Know . . . '*

This may be seen as a desperate cry for help, especially when taken with the two examples given that day of the sort of thing the *Sun* thought we had a right to know: the 'exclusive' news that the Princess of Wales was visiting a masseur for back pains caused by stress, and the announcement of a new 'exclusive' series, Downfall of a Duchess, explaining why the Duchess of York has enrolled in a group therapy centre.

My main reason for hoping that the tabloids are not gagged or made to behave better is that we shall thereby have lost our last reminder of how extraordinarily cruel and unpleasant the lower classes are.

In England it is normal to assure ourselves that these people are the salt of the earth, and so they are, no doubt, until they take control. Until recently we had the oppressive and incompetent regimes of eastern Europe to remind us what happens when the 'workers'' leaders have their way. Before that, we could contemplate our own trade union leaders as they created misery and poverty around them. Now we have only the tabloid newspapers to remind us how nasty life would be in a proletarian society.

Mr David ('Dave') Mellor, the Heritage Secretary, has complained of being dragged into a circulation war between the *Sun* and the *Daily Mirror*. One remembers how, in ancient times, if the plebeians wanted a treat, they were shown prisoners being pulled apart by horses.

It would be hard to imagine a more suitable candidate for this treatment than Mr Mellor, who, by his populist and vulgarian approach, has encouraged the very people who are now pulling him apart. Others in the Cabinet may not be pulling their weight but it seems to me that Dave is doing a grand job reminding us all of what we need to be reminded about.

## 16th September, 1992

### They can laugh now

I SUPPOSE we should welcome the news that Marlborough College has appointed a girl as its new head boy – a pretty 18-year-old called Bronte Flecker. It all depends on whether head boys at Marlborough are still allowed to cane their fellow pupils.

Many people believe that public schools, with their strange practice of beating boys on their bottoms, give pupils a taste for being beaten which never leaves them. It was not true in my own case, but who can say what would have happened if the punishment had been administered by an attractive young woman of one's own age?

Marlborough's initiative may yet provide employment for Soho's Miss Whiplashes of the future, not to mention generations yet unborn of *Sunday Mirror* hacks waiting to sneak on them

However, I cannot rejoice with Mr Kenneth Rose of The *Sunday Telegraph* that the headmaster of Uppingham, Mr Stephen Winckley, has decided to replace the black ties worn by the school ever since Queen Victoria's death with a blue and white stripe. For those of us who have been mourning the great Queen all these years, nothing has happened recently which might persuade us to mourn her the less.

At Downside, the Benedictine abbey school which I attended, we always wore black ties in the winter, with stiff white collars, black coats and waistcoats and hair stripe trousers, but I do not suppose this was out of any feeling of bereavement for Queen Victoria, or even for Good Queen Mary Tudor.

I think we were simply in mourning for our lives, as they say in Russian plays. A former headmaster, on hearing it said at the Headmasters' Conference that the purpose of public school education was to prepare young lads for life, mournfully replied that the purpose of a Downside education was to prepare them for death.

Revisiting the place last year, I was surprised to discover the boys dressed in garish grey suits and striped ties. Perhaps they have forgotten what inevitably awaits them.

## 19th September, 1992

### Our daily hamburger

SOME years ago, I suggested that one of the few useful things any of us could do with our money was to contribute towards the restoration of Salisbury Cathedral's magnificent steeple, visible for miles around in the Wiltshire countryside just as it was first seen in the 13th century, and later by Constable and by Turner.

Recently, we learnt that the Dean and Chapter had decided to use the cathedral in an advertising stunt for McDonald's hamburgers. The idea was that every visitor to the cathedral would receive a bogus medieval scroll which, when presented at the Salisbury branch of McDonald's would entitle the bearer to a discount on Big Macs and McChicken sandwiches.

From this it would have been but a small step towards substituting Big Macs and McChicken sandwiches for communion wafers, Coca-Cola for altar wine. Luckily the Bishop of Salisbury came home from his holidays in time to put a stop to this nonsense. But the Bishop of Salisbury is now 64 years old. We can have no guarantee that his place will not be taken by some sort of Eurosceptic, who will wish to turn the close into a baseball park and use the 404ft spire to advertise Colonel Sander's Kentucky Fried Chicken.

Our only refuge from this sort of degradation must be in Europe. Just as the Britons of 45 years ago were no longer up to sustaining an empire, so we are not up to the task of keeping America at bay. Anglican clergy are no more to be trusted with the Church of England than English politicians are to be trusted with the currency.

## 23rd September, 1992

### Whither the Left?

AS CONSERVATIVES cast their arms abroad for agony and loss, with no idea of where they wish to lead us next, we may ask ourselves what salvation is to be found elsewhere. At a time when even Sweden is cutting down on its welfare programme, what has happened to all those Left-wing thinkers in the universities, the BBC and journalism, now that everything they ever thought has been proved wrong? How do they spend their time nowadays in Hampstead?

Glenda Jackson, the actress and Labour MP for Hampstead and Highgate, has thrown herself into a charity called Community Hygiene Concern, involved in a campaign against head lice in schoolchildren. The charity issues warnings of a head lice epidemic. In order to heighten head louse awareness, it is to hold a National Head Louse Day at the end of next month. Its critics point out that incidents of head louse infection are in rapid decline; that the country now suffers only about 60,000 cases a year, whereas head louse awareness is so high that three million bottles of louse medicine are sold every year at a cost of £8 million. This suggests that only one in 50 bottles of louse medicine is ever poured on the head of a British child with lice on it.

Dr John Maunder, director of Cambridge's Medical Entomology Centre, goes further, and says that this medicine contains dangerous pesticides which can do nothing but harm when applied unnecessarily. 'It's not a case of louse epidemic, but an epidemic of louse hysteria,' he says.

Glenda Jackson, who was widely credited with launching the Mohican hairstyle with her performance as Tchaikovsky's girlfriend in 'The Music Lovers' (1971), may yet launch a new fashion for totally bald primary school children. No doubt she will have her critics, but I think it is quite an amusing idea – certainly less harmful than Socialism.

## 26th September, 1992

### Recessional

THE MOST poignant comment on the state of the country may

be in the letter sent by the Duchess of York to those who wrote commiserating with her on the turn things have taken:

'As you can imagine, it has not been easy but receiveing (sic) your letter has been a great comfort'.

No doubt Nell Gwyn would have made the same spelling mistake, but she was never married in Westminster Abbey nor accepted as a member of the Royal Family.

The miracle is that our coinage does not yet bear witness to the national decline in literacy.

Throughout Roman times coins were struck to commemorate great public events.

How suitable it would if the new 10p coin, to replace the old florin at the end of the month as our last link with a sound currency, could be designed to celebrate the retirement of Fergusson, Dutchess of Yawk.

## 30th September, 1992

### Principles and pastimes

IT WILL come as no surprise to readers of this column that the Bush campaign for re-election based on 'Family Values' has grievously backfired. As I never tire of pointing out, there is virtually no such thing as family life in the United States. Family Values are a euphemism for the recreational activity of queer-bashing, which is a minor leisure pursuit and certainly not a voting issue in a country where so many other leisure pursuits are on offer.

More thoughtful Americans are eschewing it already. The reason is simply that as the evil doctrines of feminism tighten their hold on America's womanhood, more and more men are driven together for mutual comfort and support. This is happening not only in New York and San Francisco, but all over America, even in Kentucky, where queer-bashing is as traditional a pastime as foxhunting in Virginia.

American women used to be among the most beautiful, bravest and most agreeable in the world. We must see it as a triple tragedy for America's manhood when we reflect on the splendour of what they have lost, the risk of Aids they run from consorting together, and the ghastliness and boredom of their fellow American males, into whose company they are now driven. If Bush wants a vote-winning platform, he should not mock American men who have been forced into homosexuality; he should promise them their women back.

## *10th October, 1992*

### A better way

'NO WAY' were the last words uttered on this earth by Mr Keith Thompson, the popular Essex postman gunned down in Orlando, Florida, after he had refused to hand over his wallet to two muggers in the home of Disneyland, where much of Essex now goes on its holidays. Poignantly enough, 'no way' was also the rallying cry of Essex Tories as they paraded themselves, bearded and loutish in their repulsive T-shirts, at the Conservative Party conference at Brighton.

The Foreign Office is adamant that all Britons visiting the United States should hand over their wallets immediately whenever requested to do so by a native American. Perhaps it would set a good example if the next Criminal Justice Amendment Act made it an imprisonable offence not to hand over money on demand.

At present, we have comparatively few armed muggers and are seriously lagging behind the Americans in that respect. For my own part, when I am in the United States, I never take any money but carry all my credit cards in my mouth so that I can swallow them if a stranger approaches.

Something will have to be done about these Essex Tories, or they really will succeed in pulling the country down to their own disgusting level. Mr David Amess, the unattractive anti-hunting Member for Basildon, spoke to the *Times* on Thursday: 'Let the intellectuals think what they like. Essex man has had the last laugh, and he is here to stay.'

I do not know why Amess should suppose he has had the last laugh. With the general collapse of businesses which will follow whatever economic policy is pursued – and permanent collapse if the anti-European faction prevails – we may yet see his stinking county return to the plough and to the sporting pursuits of happier times.

At present, Essex Man appears concerned to establish a new bank holiday in October, to be called Trafalgar Day in order to annoy the French. Perhaps, if they decide to hold it in August, they will call it Hiroshima Day. Neither strikes me as very polite. When I come to power, I will institute a national holiday on August 16 in honour of Peterloo, the famous victory of 1819 against domestic malcontents.

## Shades of the prison house

ONE of the problems with this new voice of the Tory Party, according to Michael Heseltine, is that one cannot understand a word it says. Oddly enough, that was one of the complaints made by Baroness de Stempel about her fellow-inmates in the various prisons where she has been spending the past four and a half years.

I am always fascinated to read people's accounts of life in prison because it seems to me that with the crazy laws pouring out of Parliament, any of us might end up in prison at any moment – whether for frightening a burglar in our home, picking a lettuce without wearing rubber gloves, or docking the tail of a puppy (this is a brand new offence since the nation's vets have secured a monopoly of the practice and have announced they will not do it).

I was delighted to hear Mr Howard Hellig, president of the British Veterinary Association, complain that the European Community was holding back on animal welfare legislation. 'Because of this, we cannot move at the pace we would wish,' he says. The more I learn about the European Community, the more I see it as our only protection against our own monopolies.

Baroness de Stempel complained of constant piped music in prison – I hope there is some European convention against cruel and unnatural punishment of this sort – and makes the very intelligent suggestion that the prison service would attract a better type of warder if it paid them much less money. I am sure that it is true. Where are all the people who once worked as railway porters? With low basic wages and a certain reliance on tips, the prison service would present a human face once again.

## *19th October, 1992*

## Land of great dates

ABOUT 15 years ago I remember proposing, in the light of growing anxiety about rape, that couples should keep a pile of consent forms by the side of their beds which both partners should sign before any act of sexual intimacy, let alone union, was contemplated.

In an ideal world, these acts of consent would be witnessed by a solicitor, a magistrate, a psychiatric counsellor, a clergyman, a woman etc., but this would not always be practicable. In time, I guessed, these legal formalities would be welcomed as a type of courtship ritual or foreplay.

In America, the idea has just caught on. The National Centre for Men, believing there has been an epidemic of false rape accusations, is urging men to persuade women to sign 'consensual sex contracts' before they get down to the nitty gritty. However, the Centre for Women Policy Studies has rejected the idea angrily.

It may seem exorbitant to ask a woman to sign such a contract before she is taken out to dinner, but poor, bungling American men are nearly always accused of rape at the end of the day, and one can sympathise with them. Nobody is going to believe their protestations of innocence unless they can produce some sort of documentary proof.

But I suppose they could still be accused of using improper blandishments to persuade their partner to sign the form. Nothing will ever be allowed to interfere with the American woman's right to accuse her partner of rape.

## *4th November, 1992*

### Gathering storm

NEW Zealand, surely one of the most interesting as well as one of the most beautiful countries on earth with its shuffling, earth-bound parrots and handsome, tattooed women, proved perfect refuge from a London full of people whingeing about the Maastricht and striking sentimental attitudes about the miners. It is a trip which all Englishmen wishing to preserve their sanity should make as often as possible, if it were not for eight hours spent hanging around American airports at Denver, Colorado, and Honolulu, Hawaii.

The only thing to do in America is to watch television, which was all about the elections. In Hawaii I learnt that the Republican challenger, Ric Reed, had accused the incumbent senator, an elderly Polynesian called Daniel Inouye, of having

223

groped his former hairdresser, called Lenore Kwock, in 1975

'If the people of Hawaii re-elect Inouye in spite of what we've learnt . . . Hawaii will become known as a place where sexual molestation by men in positions of authority is considered acceptable,' said Reed. We were then treated to an interview with Reed's former wife, who testified that she had been abused as a child and later assaulted, but Reed had been most understanding about it.

In Denver I saw Clinton hug a mother of two children who had died of Aids and continue hugging her for what seemed like 20 minutes. I was told that 92 per cent of America's nine million homosexuals proposed to vote for Clinton, who promised an Aids supremo to promote knowledge and acceptance of the disease wherever possible. In addition he expected to attract the votes of America's dreaded young people.

I admit I was terrified. Clinton may or may not have planned to take over his country with armies of shouting, baggy-clothed young people, but what of the rest of the world? Would nice Mr Major be able to introduce the long-awaited quarantine regulations in good time?

## *7th November, 1992*

### Punishment notes

MEANWHILE, the state thinks of ever more ingenious ways to humiliate its citizens. A 25-year-old driver who was put on 18 months' probation by Andover magistrates after he smacked his two-year-old son for playing around at mealtimes has been ordered to attend an 'anger control clinic'.

This is obviously a refinement of the counselling torture, by which offenders have to listen to ignorant young women with flat, whining voices, often for hours on end. Some have to submit to being touched by these women in an especially caring, non-judgemental way.

In time we must hope the European Community will forbid such cruel and unnatural punishments, releasing thousands of female counsellors to earn an honest living in massage parlours or kissogram delivery services. But while these sadists in the social services are allowed full rein, one can't help wondering who tipped them off about this Andover man's crime.

Was it an embittered neighbour, perhaps, or could the boy have telephoned Esther Rantzen on her notorious Childline, which invites children to denounce their parents whenever the mood takes them? The British need no encouragement to denounce one another to the authorities nowadays, as testified by the success of the various Crimewatch schemes, but even some Britons are appalled by the scramble for the telephones whenever someone leaves a country pub.

Is it really such a good idea to train children as young as this to denounce their parents? I think of myself as an equable man, and the only thing guaranteed to produce a fit of homicidal rage would be compulsory attendance at an anger control clinic. Is the idea to galvanise us out of our apathy until we rise up as a nation, and kill all the social workers?

## *9th November, 1992*

### Lady for burning?

DR CAREY, who will be 57 on Friday, looks as if he will be around a long time to remind us of the terrible last years of Mrs Thatcher. Another such relic is Lord Palumbo, 57, at the Arts Council, whose plans to destroy the beautiful Mappin & Webb building in the City have hitherto been valiantly opposed by English Heritage.

Now the scene has been joined by another Thatcher `discovery in Jocelyn Stevens, 60, the former women's magazine editor, who, since being appointed chairman of English Heritage, has let it be known that he warmly supports the efforts of his friend, Lord Palumbo, to despoil the Poultry site.

It can be little more than bravado which urges these men to further orgies of destruction, since the demand for new office buildings in the City is now precisely nil, and looks like remaining so as far ahead as anyone can see. Contemplating these outposts of Thatcherism, as they fight their last battles over the ruins of London, one is reminded of the German army in retreat setting about the systematic destruction of Warsaw in front of the invading Russians in 1944.

Warsaw was miraculously rebuilt in all its former glory, but I cannot see that ever happening to London whose architects are the worst in the world. The sad truth is that Britain will never be herself again until we have finally exorcised the ghost of Mrs Thatcher, now lying like a great succubus in the nation's bed, encouraging the hopeless fantasies of every fool in the country and many who should know better.

It would be an appalling shame if this ghostly presence succeeded in excluding us from the company of our fellow-Europeans and reduced us to a cultural and financial dependency on the United States comparable to that of Puerto Rico.

The French, I believe, have never forgiven us for burning their national saviour, Joan of Arc, in 1431. The time may be approaching when we are called upon to make a comparable sacrifice by way of atonement.

## 11th November, 1992

### The secret people

WHEN I was in New Zealand last week I was profoundly touched by their concern about the royal marriage, and on reflection I see that they were right to take it seriously and I was wrong to adopt a flippant attitude. The single-minded determination of the Murdoch press to destroy the marriage of the Prince and Princess of Wales is now in crescendo, with the *Mirror* close behind. But the monarchy is more important, as a symbol of historical continuity, than anything represented by this sadistic Australo-American gambler, and his socially disadvantaged imitators.

In this week's *Sun* (flagship of Murdoch's English fleet) we read a continuation of the revolting book about the marriage originally launched by the *Sunday Times*. Monday's headlines ran 'The Final Chapter' and 'Time to end the big charade'. Richard Littlejohn, the *Sun*'s equivalent to Way of the World, or to Mr Booker's column in *The Sunday Telegraph*, suggested that the Princess would be better attached to an American negro basketball player than to the heir to the throne.

'Why do they persist with this farcical marriage?' he asks. 'I have always preferred Sarah to Diana. She never made any bones about being a gold-digging bimbo . . . Diana has come to believe her own publicity, she really does think she is a cross between Jerry Hall and Mother Theresa . . . I couldn't care less what happens to her marriage. But I can live without the brave little martyr act . . . She is not doing anyone any favours by hanging on in there. Least of all herself.'

Perhaps Murdoch's influence will succeed in destroying the marriage and ending the monarchy, but I feel that Murdoch, like many foreign anglophobes, may have an imperfect understanding of what he has taken on. There are certain aspects of our national character which even I contemplate with a shudder, among them the English taste for cruel punishment.

We are a secret people, but Murdoch might learn a little more about us if he read his own disgusting newspapers. In Monday's *Sun* there was an account of how 15 inebriated private soldiers ('drunk squaddies') in the 5th Airborne Brigade had befriended a 30-year-old civilian in an Aldershot bar, then frogmarched him back to their barracks for a homosexual gang rape.

The victim is still in hospital. Of course we do not know whether this story is true, but it might well be. Nor do we know what was the victim's offence. I hope it was not that he spoke disparagingly of the Royal Family.

## Historic occasion

TODAY'S vote by the General Synod of the Church of England on the vexed question of whether women can usefully be ordained as clergymen has been hailed as the most important thing which has happened to religion in England since the Reformation. This week 11 life peeresses wrote to *The Times* demanding that women be ordained forthwith.

Personally, I do not see why the handful of eager women wanting to be ordained should not receive their heart's desire. But neither do I see why they should. There is nothing wrong with the gratification of personal desires, so long as they do not annoy other people, and this one obviously does. Where two desires are opposed to each other, all human wisdom points to the preservation of the status quo.

If these women wish to become clergymen, there is no earthly reason why they should not found their own religion and be clergymen in it. They should not force themselves on the C of E, whose rules specifically exclude women from the priesthood. The idea of a women-only religion, possibly worshipping a female God – Mother, Daughter and Female Essence – is much more in line with contemporary ideas than that women should compete on equal terms in a man's world. Perhaps the Queen might be persuaded to take the new church under her wing also, or at any rate the Princess Royal or Princess Michael of Kent.

Alternatively, if innovation is what everyone wants, we could do worse than ordain some giant pandas. Nearly everyone thinks they are sweet and I have been told it is hard to tell the sex of a giant panda, so this solution should please traditionalists and feminists alike. Now that it is forbidden to eat pandas, or to use their skins for rugs, they have no useful purpose, and might as well become clergymen.

## *14th November, 1992*

### How very sad

THE SIGHT of women embracing each other is normally calculated to inspire elevated and sanguine feelings in the male sex. Why, then, do we feel shame and embarrassment at photographs of women kissing and hugging outside Church House, Westminster, on news that the House of Laity had followed the Bishops and Clergy in accepting the idea of women as clergymen?

It is a great cliché of the feminist movement – by definition composed of women who are unhappy in the feminine role – that men who oppose it are misogynists or woman-haters. The truth, of course, is that it is men who love women who are distressed to see them making such fools of themselves.

Men are suited to the role of clergymen – preaching what is good and pure and noble – because men are by nature absurd creatures: bad, impure and ignoble. It is all part of the essential joke of the human condition that men should be chosen for this role. By no means all clergymen appreciate the point, but enough of them do so to keep the show on the road.

Women by contrast, are by nature nobler and more prone to self-sacrifice. The cult of the selfish woman, however strong in the United States, has not yet established itself in this country to the extent of influencing the ordination debate. Women in religion, lacking any real sense of what it is all about, can only attract the sniggers of the women-haters who put them there.

## He embodies the law

NORMALLY, when I read of large sums of money paid to plaintiffs in libel actions, I am filled with gloom. They seldom deserve so much money – in many cases they deserve none at all – and the survival of the libel laws after Maxwell must be seen as a monument to the cynicism of our lawyers. He used these laws to rob his employees of hundreds of millions of pounds – about 60 'gagging' writs were extant at the time of his death. Yet no suggestion for reforming the libel law has yet been made, more than a year after an object purporting to be Maxwell's carcass was fished out of the Atlantic.

Mr Rupert Allason's victory over the *Daily Mirror* is a cause for rejoicing. Allason, the young Conservative MP for Torbay, was made the subject of a series of violent attacks in the *Mirror* after he drew attention to Maxwell's link with Mossad, the Israeli secret intelligence and terrorist organisation. After Maxwell had issued a writ against him (it was the last writ the old crook ever issued) Allason felt he had no alternative but to counterclaim.

I remember, some years ago, describing to some French friends an entirely different libel case, brought by a millionaire. When I reached the judge's summing up, they said: 'But of course the judge was bribed.' It was with some irritation that I explained to them how in England we did not bribe High Court judges. They are pillars of integrity. Even if they weren't, there are the Appeal judges over them – of such integrity as Frenchmen can only dream about; over the Appeal Court are the Law Lords – in the history of England, there has never been the whisper of corruption against a Law Lord. Over the House of Lords, in charge of the entire judiciary, stands the Lord High Chancellor of England, embodying all the integrity that has ever existed in the history of the world.

And when Lord Havers retires as the Lord High Chancellor of England, he takes a lucrative job advising Robert Maxwell on how to issue gagging writs. Perhaps our self-serving legal system will be reformed one day, but I do not think it is fair to expect the lawyers to do it.

## 28th November, 1992

### Those were the days

ONE of the cruellest jokes you can play is to take a cockroach in a matchbox into a restaurant which has displeased you, release it from captivity and then telephone the local environmental health officer as you leave.

I hope this is not the explanation for events in the Harrods kitchens on Monday. Inspectors were crawling about for hours on end on their knees with a torch and a knife until the cockroach was discovered and carried away in a matchbox. The anonymous tip-off was never explained.

Environmental health has taken over from the Black Death as a chief terror of urban life. When I was a boy, in Gloucestershire, the kitchens, larders and sculleries all swarmed with cockroaches. If you turned on the light, the whole ceiling and floor began heaving. There was much less illness connected with food then.

But anything to do with the production, preparation or sale of food is nowadays supervised so heavily that we are lucky if we can get anything into our mouths, at the end of the day. A friend with whom I was having dinner in a Soho restaurant this week suddenly remembered that it used to serve *crêpes suzette*, a dish much fancied in the Fifties. She was told that they had been forbidden to serve *crêpes suzette* by the Health Inspectors, ever since the night of the King's Cross fire.

## 30th November, 1992

### News from the front

ON SATURDAY I warned that what remained of civilised Britain – the liberal humane bourgeois culture which miraculously survived the war and 17 intermittent years of socialist government after it – shows fewer and fewer signs of having survived the Thatcher-Murdochian Proletarian Revolution of 1979-1990.

Wherever I go in Somerset I hear voices of sorrow and shame that the Queen should be publicly humiliated after 40 years of honourable service by a handful of guttersnipes posing as public opinion. But there is also an uneasy feeling that the rest of England may not be like Somerset.

Perhaps it is true that 62,475 telephoned the *Sun* to demand the Queen be made to pay for repairing Windsor Castle. A mere thousand such unpleasant calls would be enough evidence of mean, envious people at large waiting an opportunity to inflict their cruelty on the rest of us. More than 10,000 should convince us all that the new Peasants Revolt has got out of hand. The last one, in 1381, was effectively ended by the heroic actions of the Lord Mayor of London, William Walworth. Is it not perhaps time the present Lord Mayor, whoever he may be, came forward?

At least we can identify the beginnings of a movement against the new philistines. No sooner had Lady Thatcher settled in Chester Square, Belgravia, than she wanted to disfigure the pretty late Victorian façade with one of the disgusting satellite aerials being promoted by her friend and hero Mr Murdoch.

The point about these aerials is not only that they lower the tone of the neighbourhood, announcing the wrong sort of neighbour, and reducing property values, but they also create their own little area of ugliness.

The Grosvenor estate, owners of Chester Square, have told her firmly that if she wants to do that sort of thing she must go back to Finchley, or Dulwich, or wherever it was she came from before she met the Marlboro cigarettes man. Nor will she be permitted to stick up photographs of herself, nor build a car port nor Portakabin waiting room. Only a small victory, perhaps, but I judged it worth a bottle of champagne in Somerset.

## *2nd December, 1992*

### Duke of Soho

NOTHING could be more suitable than that the richest man in Britain, Mr Paul Raymond, should have built his fortune on a high-class striptease theatre in Soho, followed by a string of soft porn magazines.

Now he is said to own £1.4 billion worth of property in Soho, including much of Berwick and Frith Streets, most of Romilly Street and a big slice of Wardour Street, all acquired through thrift and careful management.

If *Business Age* magazine is to be believed, he has overtaken the Duke of Westminster, who inherited 200 acres in Mayfair, Belgravia and Pimlico, but who has never staged so much as a risqué Christmas pantomime to stay ahead in life's struggle.

Raymond should be held up as a model citizen. The Brits are not much good at manufacturing industry, and some are unemployable in most occupations by virtue of a temperamental disinclination to take orders. It is not easy to make money in this country, even by pushing vast, imaginary sums of bogus money – junk bonds, unsecured promissory notes, bad debts, Eurodollars – across the oceans on video display units.

This is because English operators soon lose interest in this fatuous occupation, develop Repetitive Strain Injury and have to be compensated by large sums of real money. Nevertheless, it is a curious fact about the English which only Mr Raymond appears to have observed, that many of our women are very happy to take their clothes off in front of a crowd of men.

It is high time a new duke was created. The last I think – not counting royal dukes – was the Duke of Westminster in 1874. Politicians are capable of honouring only one another, which does nothing for the credit of the nobility, but Paul Raymond, whose perception may yet save the country economically and give it a new role in the world, deserves to be created a duke by popular acclamation.

## *5th December, 1992*

### Legoverland entertainments

I NEVER visited the Windsor Safari Park, but it did not seem particularly incongruous that imported giraffes and antelope should roam over the land which was once Windsor Forest, haunted by Herne the Hunter, the spectral figure of medieval legend brought to life for generations of English school-children in Harrison Ainsworth's memorable *Windsor Castle* (1843).

Will Herne the Hunter still blow his horn through the Legoland Educational Theme Park now planned to replace Mr Smart's wild animals? How will they keep him out? They can pass laws against hunting, those Tory stinkers up from Essex, those socialists and those grunting relics of the industrial working class, but they can't pass laws against ghosts.

Of the 28 Tory Stinkers who voted to ban hunting on St

Valentine's Day, only 19 survive in the House of Commons – largely, I imagine, as a result of the curse put upon them by this column – but most of the hideous new intake of Tory MPs have yet to declare themselves on this crucial issue, and I fear there will be a couple of dozen dedicated to destroying the only sport at which England has ever excelled.

I imagine that when confronted by the £60 million Legoland theme park, Herne the Hunter will hang up his horn and retreat, snarling, into the roots of the ancient oak which bears his name in Windsor Great Park. But I cannot believe the English will wish to contemplate these plastic Danish bricks for very long. Eventually, the national spirit will reassert itself even in a country where citizens are not allowed to hunt, or smoke, or drink, or handle any food which has not been sterilised, reduced to powder and impenetrably wrapped in plastic.

Whatever may happen in the meantime, I think we may be sure that the site will end up as a gigantic striptease complex, giving useful employment to many hundreds of English women who will display themselves by polite Japanese visitors where once tame giraffes and antelopes waddled around.

## Privatise the rain

TAUNTON under water makes a strangely encouraging sight. It must have been quite a pretty county town once, but ever since I have known it, greedy shopkeepers have been permitted to cast their blight. Although there are several good buildings left for those prepared to search, the overall effect of the town is dingy and commercial. On balance, it is better submerged. Let laughing Neptune reassume the land.

How the 'privatised' water boards must be grinding their teeth at this development. Having fed us with preposterous stories about there being a national water shortage – as an excuse, one imagines, for having metered water in every home and eventually charging an extortionate price for every bath we take – they now find themselves unable to charge us money for all this rain.

One or two water companies are doing their best, however. A pub near Ambleside, in the Lake District, uses only the water from its own well – rainwater, collected on its own land. Before Mrs Pat Yates, the publican, is permitted to do this, she has to pay North West Water £900 a year to have the water tested.

Now the National Rivers Authority has decided to charge her for using it, too. Mrs Yates said: 'It is God's rain. I cannot see how they can have the nerve to try to charge me for it. They do nothing for the money. They don't even provide me with a bucket.'

A spokesman for the NRA said: 'We are guardians of water. We cannot allow anyone to take which water they choose. Rainwater ends up in streams, rivers and reservoirs. Every little bit helps, you know.'

Perhaps the simplest and fairest thing would be for the water companies to charge every time it rains. This would spare them the effort of making up a lot of nonsense about our underlying state of drought, and also the expense of installing water meters in every home. If, having paid for our rain, we were then left to enjoy it, the water companies' employees could go away and live in luxury hotels somewhere in the Third World, and never worry about anything ever again.

## 14th December, 1992

### Swing, swing together

IT COMES as no surprise to learn that Aids counsellors now outnumber Aids and known HIV victims in the British Isles. In Orkney, where there are no Aids or HIV cases at all, they have only three counsellors being paid £65,000 a year between them to give advice on the disease, but in places like Edinburgh, where the disease is rife, there are two and a half Aids and HIV counsellors per victim.

There are those who argue that the £700 million being spent annually fighting Aids would be better spent elsewhere, but those already inside the Aids industry reply they will have to invent a better disease first. It may be true that the Aids epidemic has failed to materialise – rather than there being 7,000 new cases a year, as estimated, there have been fewer than 6,500 new cases in 10 years – but the epidemic of Aids counselling shows no sign of going away.

We should not talk about cost so much as about jobs. If word got around that in the whole of Britain there are only nine women and eight male sufferers whose condition cannot be traced to one of the high risk groups, then the jobs would disappear. As an expert at the London Polytechnic put it: 'If the threat to the heterosexual population evaporates, so do the jobs.'

Jobs are the most important thing in Britain today. If there are not enough Aids victims to provide employment for all the people who wish to counsel them, the government must recruit a new generation of counsellors specially trained to counsel frustrated Aids counsellors.

## Balm of hurt minds

ANOTHER serious problem in modern Britain is insomnia. According to a new survey, more than five million people are unable to sleep at night. This leaves them tired and irritable next day; they quarrel with their partners and under-perform at work.

It would be hard to imagine a more obvious use for counsellors. These people are specially trained to ask fatuous questions in flat, whiny voices.

Some feel they are wasted in law enforcement, as an auxiliary to the various punishment systems still permitted by law. Others are surprised that a compassionate society like ours which has abandoned the rope, the scourge and the rod can still inflict such cruel and unnatural punishment on offenders, most of whom come from broken homes.

But if we see counselling as medicine, rather than as punishment, everything falls into place. Medicine is nearly always unpleasant. The nastier it is, the better it works. All we have to do is to recruit another five million counsellors, and the problem of the five million insomniacs solves itself overnight. Half a dozen idiotic questions about their childhood, or their relationship with their parents, and they will all drop into a dreamless sleep.

At present many insomniacs watch television. A rival scheme proposed by Michael Grade, revolting New Brit-style chief executive of Channel 4 television, threatens a £49 million winter season of programmes almost entirely built around sex.

It will include a nude chat show, with naked guests as well as naked performers, a new Dennis Potter series, 'Lipstick on Your Collar', and an educational programme, called 'Get a Grip on Sex', explaining to Channel 4 viewers how these things are done.

Agreeing that sex is nowadays a minority taste, Grade explains that the purpose of the sex season is to attract advertisers. It is thought that viewers in the eighth level of narcolepsy are even more receptive to advertisements than those who are wide awake and trying to make head or tail of the moronic American noises on ITV.

## Old and new

AMONG the programmes planned by Grade to send us to sleep over Christmas is a repetition of last year's damp squib called 'Pallas', devoted to vulgar, unfunny jokes about the Royal Family – except that this year, we are told, the programme will venture into areas of serious bad taste, with an actress representing the Queen naked in a shower.

Sir John Junor, the Sunday commentator, reckons that so soon after the Queen's plea for mercy, delivered at the Guildhall lunch to honour her 40 spotless years on the throne, a majority of viewers would welcome at least a temporary halt to cheap, sneering attacks on her. Sir John puts it even more strongly, suggesting that 'a vast majority' would prefer to see such a halt.

I wonder if he is right, or whether, at his venerable age, he has missed the extraordinary new division among Britons which has little to do with money or politics or jobs or education or age, as the old divisions did. It would be hard to say exactly what the split between Ancient and New Brits is all about, except that it is more total, more bitter and more irreconcilable than the former class divisions ever were.

Perhaps the best way to describe it is that New Brits wish to expunge everything that reminds them of the past, while Ancient Brits tend to revere a certain sense of continuity in human affairs.

I am impartial, but I can't help noticing that new Brits also have the manners of pigs and frequently smell of sewage, while

236

Ancient Brits have beautiful manners and smell of mown grass.

On the question of numbers, which Sir John raised, the *Sun* reports that 60 per cent of its unpleasant, Murdoch-fed readership wish to scrap the monarchy. On a private poll of my own Murdoch-free, non-*Sun* reading acquaintances, I found that 95 per cent wished to retain it.

I do not think we want any more polls or referenda. I think it may be time we had a civil war. The Army is solid, but the police wobble somewhat from area to area, depending on whether their Chief Constable reads the *Sun* or not.

Perhaps one way to settle the matter would be if we all went out and slit the throats of anyone we found carrying the *Sun* or the *Sunday Times*. I don't know. What do you think?

## *19th December, 1992*

---

### A brave woman

AMID all the sad and irritating news from every part of the globe, it was immensely heartening to read of the 45-year-old South African woman who, attacked by a male ostrich outside Harrismith, in the Orange Free State, engaged it in a fight to the death with her bare hands and eventually managed to strangle it.

Ostriches are unpleasant and dangerous animals, as well as being ugly and stupid. Their kick is stronger than a mule's, and their toe-nails sharper than a serpent's tooth. Knocked to the ground several times, with a couple of broken ribs and a punctured lung, Mrs Annalie Pieterse, a leading marathon runner in her country – but no human can run as fast as an ostrich – stood up to the brute and throttled it. The whole of the human race should celebrate this brave woman's victory.

In Britain she would probably have been prosecuted under some clause of the Wildlife and Countryside Act giving blanket protection to all animals not listed as vermin or game. The law takes a very dim view of anyone acting in self-defence and nearly always prosecutes them, even when there is not the faintest chance of a conviction.

One of the saddest speeches made in Britain must have been that of Norman Waller, the Newcastle businessman accused of murder after he was attacked by a gang of thugs he found wrecking his neighbour's car for the 12th time in a matter of months. 'They were like a pack converging on me and I was terrified,' he told the court. 'They were swarming all over me. I was panic-stricken, just trying to get away. I am sorry for the injuries. I regret it intensely. I wish I had gone to bed and let them wreck the cars.'

At least, on this occasion, Newcastle's fearless constabulary turned up in time to arrest Mr Waller and his neighbour for the crime of defending their lives and their property. Now let us stop thinking about Mrs Thatcher's New Model Police and marvel anew at the bravery of Mrs Annalie Pieterse when confronted by a savage ostrich.

## Spirit of the Blitz

DIETING has emerged as public health enemy number one for 1993; worse than eggs, milk, cheese, saturated fats, tobacco, alcohol, sex, meat, vegetables, potatoes, unsaturated fats, soft drinks, fast food, botulinus toxin and any known form of nerve gas yet developed.

It destroys the brain cells and permanently impairs mental performance. It distorts moral perceptions and tends toward unsafe driving, removing all libido while making the dieter more prone to HIV and its concomitant scourge, Aids. It adversely affects foetuses and is linked with an increase in cot deaths.

It makes those who fall victim stupid, mad, ugly and boring. Death is seldom long delayed. In time, no doubt, it will be forbidden to drive while dieting or to diet on the London Underground; special carriages for dieters will be supplied by British Rail, with improved ventilation and nurses, morticians, etc in attendance. But until society wakes up to the dangers, our only hope lies in education.

Its risks are certainly greater than those of being blown up by an IRA bomb. I spent two and a half hours in a train stuck in a field outside Taunton station yesterday, while police and bomb experts examined a suspicious suitcase in the station. Perhaps it is too much to expect everyone to share in the spirit of the Blitz – to ignore bomb scares, merely clear up the blood and broken glass afterwards and keep things moving – but I can't help feeling it might be a better idea *not* to report suspicious packets or parcels to the authorities.

## Wallowing in gloom

ABOUT 10 years ago I stopped reading the *Economist* magazine, reckoning that it had nothing to tell me about Britain's relentless economic decline which I could not see perfectly well for myself. The subject was not something any of us would wish to gloat over. If the magazine ever has anything of interest in it, *The Daily Telegraph* will tell us.

By this means I learn of a survey in the current issue which looks at the present occupants of what are called the 100 top jobs: head of state; Speaker of the House of Commons, Director of Public Prosecutions, head of MI5, etc. All four of these posts are now held by women, it reports gloomily, only one of whom went to public school.

As if that is not bad enough, the number of public-school folk in these 100 top jobs has suffered an overall decline in the past 20 years, from 67 in 1972 to 66 in 1992, at a time of catastrophic decline in public education. No wonder the country is going down the drain.

There might be some comfort in the news that the 'Oxbridge' element has increased, from 52 per cent to 54 per cent, if we did not know the sad truth behind this figure, which is that for the past 20 years Oxford, at any rate, has embarked on a policy of deliberately choosing the weakest, most 'disadvantaged' candidates in accordance with some mad, egalitarian theory or other. So an increase in the number of Oxbridge appointments to the top jobs probably signifies an overall decline in their quality.

Yet it is the bald, unadorned figure of a one per cent decline in public-school participation which strikes the greatest chill. If we continue at this rate, there will be no public-school people at all in any of the 100 top jobs by the year 3313. One does not wish to be alarmist about this. Some of those who did not go to public school are among the nicest people in the world and quite intelligent, like Mr Major. But who on earth will tell them what to do, or inform them where difficult places like Ulan Bator and Helsinki are? I do not think I will be ordering the *Economist* again for a while.

## Back to the Class War

WILL education become a luxury for the rich? asks Nigella Lawson in the *Standard*, reacting in dismay to the announcement by Enfield's Tory council that it can no longer guarantee full-time education to pupils in the borough. What frightened her even more than the denial of education in a country where it has been taken for granted for so long, was the fact that nobody seemed to mind.

I think it would be true to say that Mr and Mrs Joe Public are pretty well fed up with education. It never did them any good, and in a society where professors are paid less than long-distance lorry drivers, there seems no point to it. Education is a divisive force in the modern world, shoring up the class system, an obstacle in the path of the proletarian society to which we all aspire.

'It's about time the upper-class snobs knew their place,' shouted my opposite number, Mr Richard Littlejohn, in Thursday's *Sun,* complaining about David Frost's knighthood: 'What has the Royal Family done to earn our respect? They have been exposed as a bunch of deceitful freeloaders.'

On the first matter, I feel he may have a point. It is indeed time that the upper classes – inevitably described as 'snobs' by their turbulent inferiors – remembered their place. By the same token, it may well be time that the lower-class yobs – so brilliantly catered for by Mr Littlejohn's newspaper – were reminded of theirs.

What have Mr Littlejohn's people done to deserve our respect in the past few years? They have not even succeeded in making Mr Murdoch rich, since his companies' debts are legendary.

All that Murdoch and Littlejohn have succeeded in doing is to bring the scum to the surface. Just as our market-led television programmes get stupider and more American by the month, our dominant voices grow nastier, more vindictive and more envious. Before long, I dare say, we shall be executing people on television. Perhaps it is time we snobs stopped worrying so much about protecting ourselves from these people, cowering in our little private corners. Perhaps it is time we went out and trapped them in their holes in the ground and gassed them like badgers. I do not know. What do you think?

## Dogs before babies

AN OPPOSITION amendment to the Housing Bill, soon to be debated, will allow the surviving homosexual partner of a deceased council tenant to inherit the tenancy, in line with existing provision for spouses, common-law partners and members of the family.

This is agreeable to current views on Gay Rights, although councils emphasise the problem of deciding whether a homosexual relationship is genuine. The people concerned might just have been friends. In the words of Matthew Warburton, of Labour's Association of Metropolitan Authorities, 'It may prove difficult to define a gay and lesbian relationship. Any test of whether a partnership is genuine is a bit of a blunt instrument, and there will always be some cases which fall down. But the problems are not insuperable.'

No doubt these blunt instruments are available from the Child Welfare Department, which uses them constantly in cases of suspected child abuse. They will already have come in useful with the new adoption rules, which allow single people and homosexual couples to be considered as candidates for adopting babies.

However, this enlightened policy may come into conflict with the new tendency among social service officials banning couples from adopting a child if either partner smokes or owns a dog. Dogs not only present the dangers of savage attacks and disease but, according to Mr John Jevons, social services director of Clwyd: 'This also raised the question of whether owners' interest in dogs may be to the exclusion of their interest in children.'

I can see some agonising choices ahead. Take the ideal adoptive parent – homosexual, single, vegetarian, teetotal, reads the *Guardian*, votes Labour – and then you discover he owns a pipe-smoking Airedale. At such moments, I thank my lucky stars I am not in a position of authority, trying to lead Britain into a joyous and socially responsible 21st century.

### Bart's before 'Arts'

IT IS good news if Mrs Bottomley has decided to save Bart's Hospital in Smithfield, as was reported on Sunday – and not just because it is the most ancient hospital in London and one of the most highly regarded in the world.

The hospital has occupied its present site since 1123 and has recently been re-equipped with the most up-to-date (and expensive) operating theatre complex in Europe. It is now the only hospital in the City of London, where half a million people go to work every day, keeping its casualty wards endlessly occupied. But these considerations are only part of it.

Another part is that Bart's occupies the most valuable site of any National Health building. In a neighbouring village to mine in Somerset a badly needed mental hospital is being closed down, which is sad enough, and the health authority has applied to build 600 houses on the site, which is catastrophic.

If you have heard a strange noise around Great Peter Street, Westminster, recently, it may have been Lord Palumbo licking his lips. Dedicated as he is to the rebuilding of London in the ghastly, 20th-century idiom he favours, he would see this as the golden opportunity which has been eluding him for so long.

No doubt the Arts Council, which he heads, is full of sincere and amiable people, but I cannot help seeing it as one of the forces of destruction in our culture and our society. At the Arts Council's insistence, composers are now graded according to how much their concerts may be subsidised. For a Strauss concert (Grade D) you will receive no subsidy. For a Beethoven concert (Grade C) you will receive the minimum grant of £450. For Mahler (Grade B) you will be given £1,000, but if you want the full £2,000 (Grade A) you have to play Harrison Birtwistle or Peter Maxwell Davies.

Kenneth Baird, music director of the Arts Council, explains: 'It is our duty to support the new and most adventurous, given that it is the least likely to appeal to audiences and sponsors.'

In other words, it is not the Arts Council's function to promote enjoyment of the arts, so much as to encourage a lot of modern rubbish which no one wants to hear. This can only discredit our higher culture among the very people who have yet to learn about it. If I were Peter Brooke, I should close down the Arts Council. I think it does more harm than good.

# Sit this one out

THIS evening the new President of the United States, Mr 'Bill' Clinton, holds his Grand Inaugural Ball at the White House. I shall not be attending it. This is only partly because I have not been invited, in common with Robert de Niro, Geena Davis, Kim Basinger, Richard Gere, Cindy Crawford and half of Hollywood. The President has indicated that it will be a celebration for 'ordinary' people – factory workers, nurses and such-like – as a symbolic demonstration that he is on the side of the people.

But it would not have been for class or snobbish reasons that I would have refused to attend if I had been asked. In fact, I have always had a soft spot for nurses, and assume that American nurses, too, must be healthier, cleaner, sweeter-natured people than their sisters who work in magazine offices and university departments of women's studies.

My reason for avoiding the occasion is no more creditable, however. You could call it cowardice, but I have seldom felt such terror and dread as when I saw the photographs of Chelsea Clinton, the new President's 12-year-old daughter, as they appeared in Monday's newspapers. Presumably she will be at the ball, slipped in among all those unsuspecting ordinary people.

Anybody who has made a study of the hamburger gases which are even now destroying Rome's historic centre, or of the new 'electronic smog' given off by television sets, mobile telephones and other gadgets, which is credited with stopping mighty juggernauts by mysteriously applying their automatic brakes, will recognise the symptoms. I do not know how many American children are affected, but I suspect it depends on how much they watch television, how many hamburgers they eat.

How will this affect inhabitants of the Royal Borough of Chelsea? It is too late for them to change its name. My sympathy goes out to them, but we must try to look on the bright side. Chelsea's humiliation may easily increase property values in Hammersmith, where I have my London abode.

# 23rd January, 1993

## Times have changed

DAY after day after day the *Sun* continues its sadistic attack on the Royal Family and all associated with them. One would have thought that even *Sun* readers would grow bored, but there are signs that the constant drip of poison is beginning to have effect. A cab-driver told me that the Queen should be required to pay for restoration of the Albert Memorial. 'It's her ancestor, and let's face it, she's the richest woman in the world,' he said.

This week the *Sun* picked on Prince Philip's proposed official visits to the Commonwealth islands of the Caribbean: Dominica, Montserrat, St Kitts and Nevis, Antigua, British Virgin Islands, the Turks and Caicos Islands – to complain about the expense:

'Philip's £5m junket to sun: MP's fury over cruise' it blazoned the news, concluding, in a leader, that the proposal was 'A BLOODY INSULT . . . Why can't he charter a yacht at his own expense? The Royal Family must realise that times have changed.'

They found a Tory back-bencher called David Evans to aver: 'He must need his head examining.' Labour's Tony Banks said: 'Britannia is a luxury the nation simply cannot afford'; and Charles Kennedy, the Liberal Democrat, said it was 'inept'. At the same time, the *Sun* offers money to any reader who telephones a 'hot-line' to report a sighting of Mrs Parker Bowles.

Do the New Brits, whose chief motive in life would appear to be a psychotic determination to show deference to no one, really need a Royal Family? The *Sun*, on Wednesday, announced that it was looking for a new Royal Family, one 'we could all look up to'. Readers are invited to send in photographs of themselves, and the winners will tour London in a horse-drawn coach, wearing crowns and waving to the crowds, open a Murdoch printing factory near the Tower of London, and dine at Claridges, 'the posh restaurant where only the best people go'.

It occurs to me that whoever the *Sun* chooses as its ideal Royal Family may not be to everyone's liking. This could be an opportunity for some of us to show what we think. It would be in a grand tradition if the *Sun*'s Royals were pelted with bad eggs and cabbages wherever they went. Then they could be taken out of their coach, dubbined or blacked up, and thrown into the Tower of London, where they would be left to rot for the rest of their lives, according to the best *Sun* formula, with the key being thrown away.

## *30th January, 1993*

### Hear no evil

EVERY day, from every direction, we are being bombarded with information, some of it true, some slanted, some false, or invented, or drawn out of a hat. According to the Institute of Alcohol Studies, 1,200,000 men and 200,000 women in Britain drink at harmful levels. Let's raise our glasses to the Institute of Alcohol Studies.

According to Dr Brian Mawhinney, Health Minister, 50 children under five are admitted to hospital every day suffering from the effects of passive smoking. If he is telling the truth, there are 18,250 such admissions every year and have been some 951,737 in my lifetime. Yet I have never heard of one.

Even *The Daily Telegraph*, extrapolating from *Social Trends*, informed us on Thursday that although our roads were among the safest in the world, there were 9.4 deaths on the road per 1,000 people in Britain. If this were true, there would have been some 526,400 deaths on the roads last year, which not even Dr Mawhinney has claimed. We all know there were fewer than 5,000.

The great thing to do is to let this great tide of information, alleged information and misinformation, wash over us. The Prime Minister is ill advised to take note of unsubstantiated allegations concerning his relationship with a catering manageress. He should ignore them. If Paddy Pantsdown's experience is anything to go by, such rumours would have done him no end of good among those simple enough to believe them. We will be able to remain sane in this great communications explosion only if everyone is allowed to say anything he wants, and nobody pays any attention to it.

## *1st February, 1993*

### Hikers' tales

ANIMAL lovers are strange people, prey to inexplicable fears and hallucinations which do not visit ordinary folk. At the time of the Braer tanker disaster we were confidently told that the otter would disappear permanently from the Shetland area. A massive operation was launched to save them, but only four dead otters were found: two had already from gastric ulcers, one was run over by a Norwegian television crew and the fourth was very, very old and had almost certainly died from old age, which was nothing to do with the spill. I was as excited as anyone to learn that three hikers in New Zealand's icy South Island had spotted and identified a moa, the large flightless bird halfway between an emu and an ostrich last seen 500 years ago. Photographs were taken, but when examined by experts they turned out to show a deer.

Deer are very common in New Zealand. On my visit there recently I saw several deer farms where they are bred – not for hunting, as one might expect, nor even for the meat, which is only quite good, but for the velvet fur which grows on their new antlers. They sell it for large sums to Japan, where it is thought to have rejuvenating properties.

But I should have thought that even an animal lover would be able to tell the difference between a moa, which, like most birds, has only two legs, and a deer, which has four. It was the absence of feathers, apparently, which finally convinced the experts.

This reminds me of the time a few years ago when a writer on *The Sunday Telegraph* mistook a fairly common moth in his garden in north Somerset for a humming-bird, and wrote in the newspaper to warn that global warming was upon us. I hope he never meets a moa bird in the country lanes.

## *6th February, 1993*

### Statesman of our time

WHENEVER I see the name Terry Dicks in print I am overcome by gloom. No doubt the Member for Hayes and Harlington has private virtues, but when he opens his mouth in public it is to say something stupid, unpleasant and obviously wrong. No doubt this is why the gutter press always approaches him for a comment on the issues of the day.

On Wednesday we read: 'How I sneaked shotgun through Customs, By MP Terry Dicks: "I bought a shotgun in France and smuggled it back into Britain without any questions being asked ... I went to France to buy the gun to expose the peril to Britain caused by the dismantling of Customs controls." '

He later reveals that this story is not quite true. He did not actually bring a gun into Britain. His point is that he could easily have done so if he had wanted.

For as long as I can remember, travellers from France have been more likely than not to be waved through. Is Mr Dicks suggesting that every single car should be stopped and searched

247

in case it is carrying an unlicensed shotgun? His message seems to be more menacing than that: 'If we are going to be integrated with Europe, the French and the Belgians have got to stop selling these weapons over the counter to anyone.'

Why? Because the English are so much more unreliable that they cannot be trusted to own shotguns? Or our criminal classes are so helpless they will be prevented by this means from acquiring one? What Dicks says is so stupid, so unpleasant and so obviously wrong that I despair of any dialogue between us.

## 8th February, 1993

### Workers of the world

READERS of this newspaper were made aware that the Government was heading for a £50 billion deficit on current account some three or four months ago, when the City Editor, called Mr Collins, informed us of this. Now the Treasury appears to have woken up to it, and this week's news is all about plans to cut expenditure.

Well, I will withdraw my demand that the Government should give £1,000 to anyone who will promise never to watch television again if the Army withdraws its demand for armoured helicopters, which are a complete waste of time and money. But, even if we persuade everybody to stop demanding more money, we still have the problem that the Government is over-spending by £50 billion a year. We must look for radical ways of cutting down on this.

More money is wasted on health than on anything else, reflecting the anxieties of the times, but is there any reason why the government should continue to take the burden of these anxieties on its shoulders? The time when there were votes to be won by promising a free health service is long since past. Nobody believes it any more. Is there any reason why the National Health Service should involve itself in anything except infectious diseases? Anything else is a personal matter which can be covered by private health insurance or not, as the case may be. We nearly all live much too long. Within eight years, we will have 6,750,000 over-65s and 2,500,000 over-80 year olds.

Similarly, education as it has evolved, is not only a tremendous waste of time and money, but also deeply unpopular. It is all very well for the Secretary of State to issue edicts that every child shall be taught the English language, to speak it and write it properly. Very few of the post-1975 teachers have the faintest idea of how English should be written or spoken – nor, as they have made abundantly clear, would they be prepared to teach it if they did. For reasons which are too complicated and too fatuous to discuss, they do not approve of people being taught things.

If between a third and a half of public employees were put on the dole, we would all be better off – it is infinitely cheaper than keeping people in public employment. A wonderful new culture of unmoneyed leisure would emerge, with whistling competitions, rat fights, bridge and whist tournaments, Morris dancing, boar hunts, jousting, pebble collecting, budgerigar breeding and a thousand other hobbies contending with each other. When the books returned to balance and the economy picked up, we would then be in a position to offer people £1,000 each not to watch television.

## 15th February, 1993

### Question of numbers

'RAMBLERS demand new legal rights' read a headline in Friday's newspaper. It appears that the Ramblers Association, which claims 91,000 members in a country of some 56 million inhabitants, has demanded that the laws of private property should be suspended to allow its members to ramble wherever they wish without being accused of trespassing.

Those who have studied the subject will be aware that the most significant feature of the English law on trespass is that there isn't one. An attempt was made to introduce one through the House of Lords a few years ago, but it failed in the Commons. So long as you do not use or threaten violence to gain entry, or carry an offensive weapon, or damage property, you have nothing to fear when walking across anybody's land.

Why, then, does the Ramblers Association bother to demand a change in the law? Is it simply in order to intimidate landowners who already have no rights worth speaking of? Fewer than one in 625 Britons belongs to this unpleasant organisation. What right does such a tiny minority have to 'demand' a change in the law affecting the rights of 56 million citizens to private property?

249

The difference between Ramblers and other people is that whereas ordinary walkers are often happy to go walking alone, or with one or two or even three companions, Ramblers insist on travelling in packs, sometimes as many as 25 or 30 strong. Many of them are bearded, and all wear disgusting clothes. They are a sinister and rather terrifying sight, like a medieval band of robbers, or the ferocious gangs of deserters, former camp inmates, escaped prisoners and brigands who roamed Germany after the collapse of 1945.

From the way they demand government obedience you would think these 91,000 people were victorious Bolshevik revolutionaries. Politicians, who love passing laws and will listen to anyone prepared to talk to them, are probably drawing up the new laws even now. I am not saying there is any need to legislate against joggers, irritating as they undoubtedly are. But buckshot must surely be seen as the best answer to ramblers who travel in gangs of more than eight.

## *17th February, 1993*

### Be daring, Mr Lamont

ANOTHER committee of seven experts or 'wise men' has emerged in the Treasury's new panel of economic advisers. A coloured photograph of the wise seven – squeezed, grinning, around a hideous, narrow table in the modern style without an ashtray in sight – should have done much to unsettle confidence in sterling.

These seven 'wise' men have applauded the Chancellor's policy of lower interest rates. They certainly look like borrowers themselves rather than savers, with their strange, whiskery faces and mad, fixed grins.

As a saver, I am not sure I would be in a hurry to lend them any money. But whatever these seven 'experts' said, the *Sun*'s instructions to Mr Lamont are quite specific:

'We need a climate where overdrafts no longer cripple business. Where men with nerve can afford to borrow to expand. We need lower interest rates. Much lower. Down to three per cent if that's what it takes. Be daring Mr Lamont. If this is your last Budget, at least go out with a bang.'

I think we can all guess the identity of one 'man with nerve' whom has borrowed billions in the past and will perhaps need to borrow more in the future in order to keep his newspaper, publishing and television empire together. Personally, I would not lend Mr Murdoch a farthing on any terms, nor would I stay with a bank which had done so.

But happily enough, Mr Lamont himself will soon be trying to raise £50 billion – if he is still Chancellor – to cover his Budget deficit for the year.

On behalf of the nation's savers, I should like to be as specific as the *Sun* has been. If he offers us his £50 billion in £100 units at 3.5 per cent, we will buy them at £40 so long as they are redeemable at £100 in 10 years. Otherwise, he can keep his debts. It is high time we joined a common European currency.

I have already told Lamont how to save the country's economy. He should sack 35 to 45 per cent of all public employees and put them on the dole. They do nothing useful, and the saving would be prodigious. If he is not prepared to accept good advice, honestly given, he must fend for himself.

## Not kind or useful

NOT long ago I mentioned various of the enduring nasty smells left behind by Mrs Thatcher in government. It will be a great shame if that admirable woman, who did so much for the country when it needed it most, is remembered only by these nasty smells. One of the nastiest of them, enshrined in the War Crimes Act 1991, would also be one of the easiest to dispel.

The Government has set aside the sum of £11.4 million for investigating and possibly prosecuting 93 elderly and infirm immigrants for crimes they might or might not have committed about 40 years ago, outside the jurisdiction of the British courts and in time of war.

Nobody, with the possible exception of Richard Littlejohn and his fellow punishment freaks, really wants to see our prisons cluttered up with these confused old men. Now it appears that the Act was badly drafted and will have to be rewritten.

I wonder what it costs to put a basin and a lavatory in a prison cell. Even if it costs £2,500 a time, we could still equip 4,560 cells in this way for the price of prosecuting these alleged war criminals. Would this not be a more fragrant monument to the Thatcher years than leaving our prisons in their present disgraceful state and trying to squeeze in a few extra septuagenarians and octogenarians? What do the Friends of Mrs Thatcher feel?

## *20th February, 1993*

---

### Wake up, Bottomley

ASKED how she felt about reducing St Bartholomew's Hospital, London's oldest and proudest institution for the care of the sick, to a poor shadow of its historic grandeur, Mrs Bottomley, who is Secretary of State for Health, replied: 'It is not my job to be an arm of the Department of Heritage.'

In that single flip, ill-considered remark, she sums up a very large part of what is wrong with the way this country is governed, regardless of which party is theoretically in power. *Of course* it is her job to be an arm of the Department of Heritage. It is the job of every single man, woman and child in the country to be an arm of the Department of Heritage.

Not only should we protect our national birthright against those who wish to take it away – whether they are developers or vandals or chief constables or punishment freaks or hunt saboteurs or reorganisers or ramblers or rapists – but we should be permanently conscious, day by day, that everything we do has among its intended consequences that our heritage is protected and our environment improved.

It is this moronic division of responsibilities whereby the Department of Health is concerned only with health, the Department of Transport only with transport, the grocer only with his grocery shop, that explains the aesthetic mess of our urban landscape and hideous depredations into the countryside.

Mrs Bottomley should wake up to the fact that we are all sentient human beings capable of taking in more than one thing at a time. The Department of Health is not a country at war, its interests to be defended against all other departments. It would be easy for us to decide that Mrs Bottomley's dismal preoccupation with health is exaggerated, but even so she must see that there are other things than health to be taken into account, such as beauty, pride, seemliness, tradition, order and degree. Illness is a temporary phenomenon, but ugly buildings torment us the whole time.

## On the pendulum

AGREEING that a six-month prison sentence 'probably was too extreme' on a man accused of rape by his fiancée who changed her mind half-way through their love-making, the *Observer* concluded that it might be a good idea, nevertheless. Too many men in recent history had got off too lightly.

'Just law is not established in one fell swoop, it is arrived at by pendulum swings . . . It [the judgement] may yet help to right the balance, and cast even greater doubt on the view that women mean 'yes' when they say 'no'.'

It seems to me that the good people of the *Observer* have missed a pendulum swing or two. The problem is no longer the woman who means 'yes' when she says 'no'. The problem is the woman who means 'no' when she says 'yes'. Perhaps it will never be solved until it is made an imprisonable offence to doubt the word of any woman who claims to have been raped. Then we will accept that any woman can send any man to prison at any time. But the question still remains: *for how long?*

It is made pertinent by the new outbreak of female mugging in south London: a woman approaches a lone driver for help, forces her way into his car and threatens to scream 'rape' unless he pays her £50.

If these random accusations resulted in only a week's

imprisonment, there might be some who would prefer the prison sentence, although I cannot see myself falling into that category. The good people on the *Observer* will point out that these payments are doing no more than correcting a historic imbalance, by which many women were paid too little for too much work in the past. But I feel the best course of action is to drive with all car doors locked and windows closed.

# Taste of honey

A WEEK in the French West Indies – parts of France basking in the sun off Central America where people talk French, eat French good, drink French wine and read *Le Figaro* in blissful disregard of the Great Satan struggling with all its horrendous problems across the water – reminds you that there is more to the European Community than physical proximity or economic self-interest. It is a question of culture.

For my own part, I look to the European Community partly as a defence of the bourgeois civilisation (in which we all grew up) against further encroachment of a proletarian mass market-led culture from across the Atlantic; partly as a refuge from British politicians and administrators, whose frenetic activities have created more than 3,560 new offences in the past 20 years.

On the aeroplane back, they showed us an American film called 'Honey, I Blew up the Kid', or something of the sort, about a two-year-old American boy, the size of the Empire State Building, who wanders through a city picking things up and dropping them. I did not listen to the sound track, which was virtually incomprehensible, but watched the film as Swiftian satire in mime.

The monstrous American kid plainly represented American kiddiehood in all its terrifying ghastliness, holding America to ransom. In the event, I was told by someone who had listened to the sound track that the film was intended as a celebration of American parenthood, sentimentality, kiddiehood etc.

The sad truth is that Europe and America no longer understand each other at all. Mr and Mrs Clinton have proposed spending another $1 billion on a 'Manhattan project' to cure the American disease, but I fear it is too late. Even without the American disease, our European administrators would have to think of some reason for the proposed quarantine regulations on American travellers. This could be even more hurtful for our good friends across the Atlantic who stood up for freedom so nobly until they let their women come out on top.

Returning to an icy England, past rows and rows of grim-faced Customs officers, apparently looking for drugs and terrorists but actually wasting their own time and our money to flatter the self-importance of our politicians, I cursed the British Government for exposing us to all this. Our place is inside a Greater Europe, possibly under Mr Yeltsin's leadership, but preferably under none, its main purpose to keep out American television, American ideas of political correctness, and American kiddies.

## 6th March, 1993

### New perils of travel

EUROPEANS should not mock Mr and Mrs Clinton for their decision to continue trying to drop food parcels over eastern Bosnia, despite having missed it first time. American food parcels were a major feature of English life after the last war, and will be gratefully remembered by all those old enough, and lucky enough, to have received them.

In those days, American food consisted of delicious things like chocolate bars, crystallised pineapple rings, chewing gum and peanut butter. It tended to arrive by post. I do not know exactly what food they are trying to drop on Bosnia, but American food has different connotations nowadays.

My wife claims to have found mysterious packages of food lying on a road outside Taunton. People should be advised to approach them with the greatest caution. This is for fear of the dreaded hamburger gases which can destroy ancient buildings, as well as drive people mad. The whole of Europe must expect to be bombarded with these dangerous projectiles while Mr and Mrs Clinton's boys valiantly try to work out where eastern Bosnia might be. If they succeed in landing them among the Serbs again, they might be accused of waging biological warfare, and up before their own War Crimes Tribunal.

American tourists should think twice before visiting Europe while this bombardment continues. They might find the idea of being squashed by American food parcels dropped by their Own Boys less scary than being hit by Saddam Hussein's Scud missiles, or blown up by the IRA, but it can be just as painful.

More than three million American visitors came to Britain last year. The British Tourist Authority does not tell us how many returned safely to the Land of the Free.

## *8th March, 1993*

### The way ahead

THE GOOD news comes from a research study group at Manchester University which has revealed that Britons do not regard killing burglars as a serious offence – in fact it comes 31st out of 47 crimes, less serious than shoplifting, next to stealing a radio, and far less serious than drink-driving.

Further encouragement came from Luton Crown Court, where a jeweller who bravely shot two armed burglars was awarded £300 by the judge, despite the fact that he faces police charges for allegedly possessing an illegal firearm. 'It is not my business to comment on the rights and wrongs of that,' said Judge Daniel Rodwell, QC.

No doubt this brave man will also face further charges of frightening some bats in the area, if the police get round to it. Never mind. Mr Major's neo-Bolshevik Criminal Justice Act of 1991, demanding that middle-class offenders be punished 25 times more severely than professional criminals for any crime they commit, has tended to put the whole legal system into contempt, where respectable members of society are concerned. Now there seems to be some hope.

The Police Federation points out, reasonably enough, that of the 5,100 most common offences, 3,560 have been created by Parliament in the past 20 years. While the police worry themselves about the 361 ways car headlights can break the law, illegal possession of ivory toothbrushes and improper use of fresh eggs in mayonnaise, we cannot expect them to concern themselves with such mundane matters as murder, rape, knifing or burglary.

The way ahead is surely to leave the police to get on with their paper work – or even disband them, as an economy measure – and establish a system of reward whereby private citizens will be given £300 for shooting an armed burglar, £200 for shooting a drink driver, £50 for a shoplifter, £25 for a parking offender, £5 for a tax evader, £2.50 for shooting someone who uses fresh eggs in mayonnaise etc. etc.

## Australia's choice

IT IS none of our business to advise the Australians how they should vote in Saturday's election, but I shall be very unhappy if they return the uncouth Irishman whose Labour government has been making them all so miserable for the past 10 years.

The only reason they might vote for Mr Keating, rather than his Liberal opponent, Dr Hewson, is that Dr Hewson has proposed a new form of taxation, like Value Added Tax, to replace Mr Keating's payroll tax. This was foolish of Dr Hewson. Nobody wants to hear about new taxes at election time.

But Mr Keating is so consumed with hatred of the British – and, indeed, of Europe – that he threatens to put his country into permanent trading partnership with the Asians. I do not blame him so much for this, having a certain weakness for orientals myself, except that I am particularly fond of Australia and the Australians, and the Asians will make mincemeat of them.

Already the Japanese are threatening to buy up Australia's better golf courses, and rival gangs of Vietnamese divide up Sydney between them. The Australians, despite an influx of Greek immigrants, and despite a strong Anglophobic element in the Irish and German populations, are still far more like the English than the English have ever been, at any rate since the 1930s.

They are essentially a nation of artists and pleasure lovers. They perform any work they are given conscientiously and well, taking pride in it, but they are equally happy to spend all their time on the beach.

They simply do not have the same dedication to work and profit that you see in Taiwan, Japan, South Korea, Hong Kong and, increasingly, in southern China.

Their proper place is inside the European Community, where, along with New Zealand, they could provide Europe with better, cheaper wine and food than we had ever seen before.

If Mr Keating wins, Australia's commercial future may be seen as an endless rerun of the film 'Bridge on the River Kwai'. But of course, if that is what Australians want, it is none of our business to stand in their way.

# Up the tubes

CARDINAL Basil Hume, Roman Catholic Archbishop of Westminster, has called upon the Government to set up a Royal Commission to investigate the break-up of the family in society. The Chief Rabbi supports him, and the Archbishop of Canterbury comments, perhaps a little mysteriously, 'We are open to a range of options.'

Perhaps it should be recognised as a function of religion in our secular age to urge the setting up of a Royal Commission, wherever thought appropriate. To others it might seem a dereliction of duty, but Cardinal Hume at least has the excuse that he is not married, and so has less experience of modern family life than most people. This has not inhibited his church from advising its members about about married life in the past, of course.

In any case, I hope he tells the Royal Commission to investigate the possible influence of a new type of toothpaste tube on the break-up of the family.

When the new type came in, with a flap instead of screw-top, I welcomed it as relieving friction between spouses on the point of which had last used the top, which had lost it etc.

Now, after long and hard thought, I realise that the new flap-top tubes are much worse, since it is seldom possible to get any toothpaste out of them. Whereas someone like Cardinal Hume, finding himself without toothpaste, will probably confine his annoyance to a little exclamation of *miserere mei* ('silly old me') before toddling off to his lonely bed, many married couples use it as the occasion for an almighty row.

It is by pursuing this sort of inquiry that a Royal Commission would prove useful.

## 15th March, 1993

### Albert forgotten

THE SCANDAL of the Albert Memorial, to which I draw attention on average once every 12 weeks, enters a new phase with the decision by English Heritage to put it on an 'at risk' list, after more than two years of rotting away under the largest free-standing pile of scaffolding in Europe.

I suspect a Smartiboots Conspiracy to deprive us of one of London's best loved monuments. Among those born in the first half of the dreadful decade of the 1930s, it is still considered clever to despise the achievements of the 19th century – intellectually, scientifically and artistically the most exciting century in the history of the world.

So far Heritage has succeeded in spending £1.4 million on a two-year 'investigation' to discover what needs to be done to repair the memorial. Now it announces that no funds are available from the Government to meet the £9-£13 million required, and no work will start until at least 1996. The truth, I suspect, is that nobody has the slightest intention of doing anything.

Will Londoners rise up to pull down the scaffolding and hang the director of English Heritage before stone cancer, cement rot, iron rust and frost destroy the whole structure? In 1861, when Good Prince Albert died, public expenditure was only four per cent of the Gross Domestic Product.

Today, when the Government asks us to believe it cannot afford to maintain the structure, it takes 40 per cent of every penny earned by Britons, spending it for the most part on the wages of unnecessary public employees.

Ah well. Let us at any rate congratulate Barbara Bennet on her appointment as her county's Smoking Cessation Facilitator by Herefordshire Health Authority and FHSA.

## *17th March, 1993*

### A wife's revenge

ONE of this column's duties is to keep a wary eye on what is happening in California. Nearly every novelty which arrives on these shores seems to have started life there. To be fore-warned is to be fore-armed.

The case of 24-year-old Mrs William Nelson, of Santa Ana, California, seems particularly worrying. Mrs Nelson, like so many young women nowadays, was employed as a counsellor for rape victims. I sometimes worry that there will not be enough rape victims to go round. Whether or not this is what happened in the Nelson household, it occurred to Mrs Nelson one day to bludgeon her husband to death (he was 32 years older than she), chop him up, cook him and eat him.

Many will decide this is a perfectly normal reaction from a 24-year-old rape counsellor to the irritating presence of an older man in the house when there is no one to be counselled. But when she had skinned William's body and cooked his head and hands she was taken away by unsympathetic policemen and jailed for life.

No doubt there will be an outcry among feminists against this sentence. We will have to wait and see whether they succeed in winning her release. But I think I can spot a progression between counselling women victims of rape and deciding to bludgeon a husband to death and eat him. Let us hope that the rapists of Britain never drive our womenfolk to such desperate measures. In California, they were said to be losing the appetite for anything except counselling and being counselled.

## 20th March, 1993

### An erotic dream

THE Defence Department's decision to celebrate President Reagan's defeat of communism and removal of the Soviet threat by closing down nearly half our military bands is so obviously wrong, so crass, that we might easily decide that ordinary human intelligence has deserted the country.

Instead, it proposed to buy regiments of armoured assault helicopters – of limited use against the most unsophisticated adversary, as the Soviets discovered in Afghanistan, and no use at all against a modern army, which will soon be able to shoot them out of the sky like pheasants at Sandringham.

The main function of the Army in time of peace (outside the Ulster emergency) is to give civilian morale a boost and preserve the military ethos. Military bands are ideal for both purposes.

However, since nearly every decision taken in any direction nowadays is the wrong one, perhaps we should conclude that democracy, like the jury system, no longer really works in Britain. Silly to waste time on recriminations. We must simply decide what to do about it. If we can't get the Maastricht Bill through this poor addled Parliament, enabling sensible foreigners to make all the important decisions for us, we shall have to find some sort of chap or fellow among our own number to tell us what to do.

By coincidence I was in the House of Commons on Wednesday evening, on my way to a reception in the Speaker's House for the 125th birthday of the Howard League for Penal Reform. One forgets what a truly magnificent building the Palace of Westminster is, and the Speaker's quarters are one of the handsomest parts of it.

Madam Speaker, as Betty Boothroyd is now called, very sportingly showed us the huge state bed she keeps in her dining room. It occurred to me that Speaker's House would make a very suitable residence for whoever is the nation's saviour, just as Benito Mussolini settled himself into Rome's Palazzo Venezia. I wonder how all this can be set in motion? Perhaps a useful first step would be to marry Madam Speaker.

When I come to power, the Army will be almost entirely given over to military bands. Once a year there will be a massed parade on Horseguards, to put a spring in my step as I waddle down Whitehall into each of the ministries in turn, giving them firm instructions for the year ahead. Then back to Madam Speaker's state dining room.

## *24th March, 1993*

### Bill the Conqueror

'CALL no man happy until he is dead, he is at best but fortunate,' said Solon the Wise, dictator of Athens in the seventh century BC, according to Herodotus. In the same way, I have always thought it rash, not to say impertinent, to describe a man as happily married simply because he is married. Yet this is the polite, journalistic convention. I was particularly concerned about W. F. Deedes's description of the Clinton marriage in Monday's newspapers.

'What makes Hillary Clinton worth studying is that she is the most prominent example of a wife who is manifestly cleverer than her partner . . . Mrs Clinton is advertising that a woman can publicly display an intellect superior to her husband's and remain happily married. That is a landmark.'

This is a possible reading of the situation, of course. My own suspicion is that if Mrs Clinton were really clever, she would hide the fact that she thinks herself cleverer than her partner. Clinton, it seems to me, may be cleverer than any of us realise.

Americans often confuse superior intellect with espousal of Left-wing, feminist or politically correct views. By that reckoning, of course, Mrs Clinton is an intellectual giant. Even that posture is not universally admired in America, and the President is allowing her to build herself up as the most hated woman in the country.

It seems quite likely that his main reason for seeking the presidency was to dump his wife publicly, and in the most humiliating manner, in deference to popular demand. For all his goofy appearance, I think he may be a very shrewd operator in the war between the sexes which is tearing his country apart. It will be the first time the American presidency has been used as a ploy to get rid of a difficult wife.

In this country, I feel we should mourn the passing of *Spare Rib*. After 21 years as the voice of all the miserable mad women in our midst, it is no more. While it existed, we husbands and fathers could point it out to our wives and daughters as a terrible example of where liberal or feministic ideas are likely to lead, a monument to the wretchedness of unaccompanied woman. Now that *Spare Rib* has gone the way of all flesh, they can only imagine the horror of it.

## Uses for the land

THE BEST news is that the small majority among a tiny proportion of the National Trust's two million members who voted to ban staghunting on Trust land will not bind its council to obedience.

In an age of increased leisure, when new uses other than farming must be found for the countryside, it would have been a very backward step.

Another use for farmland has emerged, and another occupation for farmers. When a light plane crashed over the weekend on a farm near Sevenhampton, Wiltshire, killing all three occupants, the farmer revealed that if it had crashed any closer it would have landed among a crowd of 250 people who had turned up to watch the lambing. This crowd, which included many children, was on a Mothering Sunday outing, he said.

In an age of sentimentality about animals, when the spectre of vegetarianism is haunting Europe and many honest farmers face the loss of their livelihood, perhaps there is something to be said for the idea of agriculture as a participatory leisure pursuit.

Lambs could be specially bred for their cuddliness, cows for their quaint expressions.

Children from the towns could pay £5 to watch a lamb being born, £25 to assist. Adults could pay £5 to watch a cock with a hen, £10 to watch a ram serving a ewe, £25 to watch a bull covering a cow or a stallion a mare.

This is much healthier than watching videos of humans doing the same sort of thing, I would have thought.

## 27th March, 1993

### Spare our blushes

BRITISH audiences may well be more sensitive than most to the horrors of pornography and violence, and there is a particular horror in the thought that we might be invaded by foreign pornography over which we – or at any rate the controlling echelons – have no control. Hence the stern tone of this newspaper's editorial on Thursday: Let Red Hot Stay Dutch, which dealt with the threat of Dutch pornography being sent to our children and more impressionable citizens by satellite all the way from Denmark.

It would be nice if the controllers could think they had public opinion behind them in banning sexually explicit programmes, but this does not seem to be the case. Research by the Independent Television Commission was disconcertingly summed up in the *Sun* by two headlines: WE LOVE OUR PORN: PUBLIC WANT SEX ON TV.

But they don't want it in Germany. There is a scheme to transmit a sex channel into Germany by satellite from Britain, starting on April 2. Mr Rudolph Seiters, the German Interior Minister, said German diplomats had been asked to lodge complaints. I do not think I am easily embarrassed, but I must admit that I find myself blushing at the thought of Germans watching Englishwomen without any clothes on.

## 29th March, 1993

### Gaseous emissions

NO SOONER had I written last week that there is a spectre haunting Europe, and identified it as the spectre of vegetarianism, than we all read of a Gallup survey revealing that more than 2,000 people a week are giving up meat in this country alone. Most of them say they are fearful of mad cow disease and other illnesses, but I do not see why we should concern ourselves with their motives.

This phenomenon is more worrying than the claim by Nicholas Coleridge in yesterday's *Sunday Telegraph* that the institution of Sunday lunch is endangered. In places such as America they have no meals of any sort on any day of the week; instead people feed themselves out of the fridge between television programmes. In this way, American parents never hold a conversation with their children, but we cannot blame them for that, and there are plenty of psychoanalysts who will pretend to listen to them talking about themselves for a suitable fee.

It may be the case that some people in Britain have decided to forgo their Sunday luncheons, but that is no reason for the rest of us to worry. Vegetarians give more cause for anxiety because many scientists now believe that gaseous emissions given off by these people are responsible in large part for the perceivable fact of global warming, or damage to the ozone layer, or possibly both.

But even vegetarians, for all the danger they represent to the survival of planet Earth, do not try to bully or coerce people into their way of behaving.

Anti-smokers remain the greatest menace. Much excitement was caused last week by the news that adoption agencies have been instructed to refuse babies to foster parents who smoke, but in fact this rule has been applied for ages – I was writing about it in the *Spectator* many years before the dangers of 'passive smoking' were invented.

The reason this policy is made public now must be to soften us up for the next move by the anti-smokists – to demand that children of smoking parents be taken into care and put in local authority homes where they can be subjected to daily anal dilation tests by demented lesbians for the rest of their childhood.

## 31st March, 1993

### Paisley old boys net

'ARMY's snobbish élite wins the war against a classless society,' runs the headline across five columns at the top of one of *The Sunday Times*'s news pages. I am thrilled. Where was the battle fought, and why was I not invited to join in?

I had reckoned without the relentlessness of *The Sunday Times*'s class-war agenda. All it had discovered was a former major in the Royal Ordnance Corps, with the improbable name of Reggie von Zugbach, who has produced a 'study' at Paisley University claiming that the preponderance of senior Army appointments from crack regiments must mean that there is prejudice against those from less-good regiments and support corps.

Major Reggie, who has retired from the Army to take up an academic post in management at Paisley (glittering birthplace of *The Sunday Times*'s brilliant young editor), seems to be making exactly the same mistake as Oxford University when it discovered a high proportion of successful candidates coming from the better schools, and decided this must mean that the system discriminated against less-good candidates from bad schools.

'The old boy network,' claims Professor-Major Reggie von Zugbach, 'is thwarting John Major's plans for a classless society.' Does Mr Major seriously have any such plans, apart from one careless remark?

The *Sunday Times* agenda for a 'classless' society, when examined, means supporting the power urges of the New Brits, the nastiest class in Britain – the same incompetent, ignorant and conceited gang which, by wheedling its way into positions of power for the past 15 years, has brought nearly every aspect of British life to its knees: government, administration, health service, nationalised industries, banking and insurance . . . only the armed forces have managed to keep up their standards. No wonder *The Sunday Times* hates the Army, and seeks to impose its own ghastly standards of mediocrity on it.

Nice Mr Major would be well advised to distance himself from the Murdoch agenda, especially now that the American gambler has gone public and distributed four million copies of his Maastricht petition among the British electorate. A sensible way for the Prime Minister to demonstrate that he is not Murdoch's puppet would be to wear a top hat and morning coat on weekdays as long as he remains in office. This would inspire admiration and affection in equal measure.

## 3rd April, 1993

### Lost its sting

TO A board meeting of *Oldie* magazine, where I find my fellow-directors in a mood of swinish self-satisfaction. The magazine was founded slightly more than a year ago to cater for over-50 year olds who find their interests and concerns ignored by the youth-obsessed modern media, and above all by demented Peter Pans in the advertising industry.

At the time of its launch, people said nobody would buy a magazine called *Oldie*. Those who had the misfortune to be over 50 did not wish to be reminded of the fact, while those of even more mature years might be prepared to consider a magazine called *Afternoon Sunshine*, or *Golden Age*, but would certainly not identify with anything called *Oldie*.

However, people under-estimated the great hatred for young people which is such a refreshing development on the modern scene, and these whingeing crypto-Americans have been proved wrong. But I am afraid that the success of his initiative may have gone to the head of its editor, 86-year-old Richard Ingrams.

The latest edition carries a new slogan on its mast-head: 'Buy

It Before You Snuff It' – which I am convinced will have the effect of alienating not only the morons of the advertising industry, who honestly still believe that teenagers and young adults are the people with money to spend, but also the sensible, prosperous middle-aged and retired people who might be expected to enjoy the magazine.

However, when I raise the matter before the board, I am contemptuously over-ruled. The slogan will stay. Perhaps there is a new spirit abroad among the country's maturer citizens whereby they no longer fear meeting their Maker, are half in love with easeful death, if only as a means of getting away from our half-witted teenage society.

## *14th April, 1993*

### Resistance

WHEN one writes about teachers, one must constantly bear in mind that many – possibly most – of them are among the finest people in the country: conscientious, high-principled, sensible, fair, benevolent and placed in the front line against all the horrors and deformities of modernism. Few teachers are communist agents, few have a sinister social agenda, although a fair number of the weaker minded may have accepted parts of this agenda in a goofy sort of way.

Resistance to Mr Patten's attainment test comes under three headings. The first is indeed on ideological grounds, against any tests, and indeed any education, as being elitist and opposed to the great tide of history, which is towards total equality, total ignorance, total incompetence, leaving us all to be patronised in flat, south London and Midlands accents, by unattractive young women posing as teachers, counsellors and social workers. Although seldom expressed quite like that, this approach has a certain appeal to those whose real objection is less idealistic, but who know perfectly well that the results of any tests applied to their pupils will be lamentable.

These people, in the second group, are inspired by laziness – they do not wish to have to change the idle methods they were taught at their teacher training colleges – but they are also inspired by terror. They know they have nothing to teach: no English grammar, no poetry, no history to speak of and very little science . . .

267

Finally, you have the conscientious, high-principled, sensible etc element which sees Mr Baker's curriculum as hastily and sloppily put together, the tests as inapplicable. Between the three, Mr Patten has something of a battle on his hands, but I think he is making a mistake when he tries to bring the parents into it. They might easily prove to be the worst of the lot.

## 17th April, 1993

### Leave the Yeti alone

IF THE BBC is planning an epic televised expedition to hunt down the Yeti, or Abominable Snowman of Tibet, we may be sure that a dozen television companies from other countries have exactly the same plan.

Like the summit of Mount Everest, now littered with crisp packets and empty Coca-Cola tins, not to mention open latrines, used tissues, contraceptive sheaths and copies of the *Sun* newspaper, so this poor animal will now be gawped at in a billion uncomprehending homes around the world.

What useful purpose is served by disturbing it? They cannot bring back a specimen to put in London Zoo because, as we all know, London Zoo has run out of money and will soon be reduced to exhibiting a pair of white mice and a goldfish.

The only possible justification would be if Yetis could adapt themselves to the role of household pets. It would be a change from the new craze for Fancy Rats, available from Harrods at £8 a time in pleasing shades of silver white, champagne and beige.

For my own part, I find that desire for animal companionship and all curiosity about the animal kingdom are satisfied by contemplation of the pekingese, in all its strange beauty, its complexity and eccentricity of character, its mysterious bursts of frankness and reticence, the lovely noises it makes when asleep . . .

But there may be those who would be happy to keep a Yeti as a pet. We should not discourage them, although I feel sure some pipsqueak politician will immediately pass a law requiring Yetis to be registered, muzzled, castrated and subject to hours of counselling by unemployable Liverpudlians posing as animal psychotherapists.

## 21st April, 1993

### Painful but nice

ALTHOUGH not tempted to join Sunday's NutraSweet Marathon, I cannot help wondering about the motives of the 25,500 men and women who chose to spend their Sunday running 26 miles through one of the ugliest landscapes in Europe.

A curious leader in *The Times* quoted the winner as suggesting that even the last few miles were enjoyable 'if you can enjoy pain'. Under the heading 'Agony and Ecstasy', the newspaper then proceeded to develop the point:

'What makes the marathon both so different from, and so much more democratic than, other world-class sporting occasions is . . . this extraordinary pursuit of the conquest of pain, which is ultimately democratic because the competitor who spends four or five hours completing the course suffers just as much, or perhaps more, than the winner. Even world-breakers are not immune to the pain . . . '

I do not know what the editor of *The Times* thinks the word 'democratic' means, but I presume he thinks it means egalitarian, anti-élitist, not discriminating between classes. In this great pain, a new classlessness is born, if we are to accept his strange perception of the event.

So it emerges that the marathon is a festival of pain and classlessness. No wonder I have never felt tempted to join, but I cannot honestly believe that many of those 25,500 seriously thought they were establishing their classlessness in this way. Some weeks ago I wrote about a curious streak of sadism which seems to run through the Murdoch press. I have never seen the two goals of pain and classlessness so clearly identified before. At least we can learn where this friend of Lady Thatcher is leading us.

## 24th April, 1993

### The cat that barked

TEN years ago the dead body of a Burmese cat belonging to Princess Michael of Kent was found squashed in mysterious circumstances. People claimed that the animal, called Kitty, had been run over by a car.

But I had my doubts about the story at the time, writing darkly about the Australian aboriginal tradition for using cats as cushions to protect themselves against cactus and rough stones in the Outback.

Of course Princess Michael is not a native Australian, but came to us from the beautiful town of Sydney, New South Wales, where her mother worked as a hairdresser. I feared that in some careless or absentminded moment she might have sat on the cat.

Now, we learn from Peterborough that another of her cats has been found in mysterious circumstances. This time it is said that Blue, a seal-point Siamese, was killed by a Hyde Park squirrel in the garden at Kensington Palace. This seems even less likely. In all my life I have never seen a squirrel attack a cat.

Mr Hawke's Labour government made strenuous efforts to educate or counsel native Australians out of this habit of sitting on cats, but to no avail. The new Prime Minister, uncouth Mr Keating, does not seem to care about the problem. At any rate, he has not shown the least interest or concern to date.

My only hope is that it does not blow up into another great Royal scandal. Pat Morris, zoology lecturer at Royal Holloway College, cannot accept the squirrel theory. I feel we should all keep quiet. The Royal Family has suffered enough.

## *26th April, 1993*

### A delicate matter

OVER the weekend, nearly all the homosexuals in America descended on Washington to demand that President and Mrs Clinton honour their election pledges by taking them into the armed forces. At a time when they were trying to cut down on defence expenditure, after President Reagan's defeat of the Evil Empire, this must have been rather worrying for the Clintons.

But it turns out there are rather fewer homosexuals in America than anyone had thought. Ever since Dr Kinsey's 1948 Report on the American Male, people have imagined there were at least 10 million male homosexuals crowding the sidewalks and roaming the prairies of that magnificent country. Now, after the most comprehensive sex survey ever undertaken, the theory is that there may be only a million of them.

Where have the missing nine million gone, asks an anguished

Alexander Chancellor, the celebrated New York *boulevardier*, finding himself virtually alone in that dreadful city over the weekend?

A terrible silence is liable to follow questions of that sort, but of course it is simply not true, or anything like the truth, to say they have all succumbed, one by one, to the terrible American Disease.

A more likely explanation for the missing nine million is that they have all come to live in Britain, or moved to other countries (Czechoslovakia is the latest example) which, like Britain, have no screening or quarantine barriers. In fact, Americans are permitted to enter most European countries without the simplest hygiene inspection.

Of course, it is simply not true or anything like the truth that all American males one meets in Europe are homosexual, but one does not wish to cause offence by saying anything inappropriate, and it might be safer to act in the assumption that most of them are.

## 28th April, 1993

### Aux armes, citoyens

THE MOST worrying development of recent years has been the arrival of Lady Thatcher's Food Police under the Food Safety Act 1990. These environmental health officers, as the stormtroopers are called, some of them scarcely out of their teens, now stride the land like so many standard bearers of an occupying army, spreading bankruptcy and desolation wherever they go.

As I never tire of pointing out, only 100 people die of food poisoning in this country every year, out of a total of some 650,000 deaths. To all intents and purposes food-poisoning is non-existent as a cause of death, and this army of food police is as much a waste of public money as it is a threat to our freedom.

Every journalist worth his or her salt in the country has been inveighing against this gratuitous extension of the fascist nanny state, and it would be churlish not to pay tribute to the sterling efforts in this field of Christopher Booker, *The Sunday Telegraph*'s bird expert. But it occurs to me that the scandal needs a Cabinet minister's involvement, like Crichel Down, or some token victim, like the Winslow Boy, before it can get off the ground.

One of the most sinister aspects of the Health and Safety

stormtroopers is that no one knows which minister controls them. Is it Bottomley at Health, Howard at Environment, Soames at Food, or his boss Gummer?

All deny any responsibility, and it begins to look as if these environmental health officers are a law to themselves, like Rohm's Brown Shirts but without a Rohm in sight. I feel it is time our conventional police, Customs and armed forces organised themselves for another Night of the Long Knives.

Meanwhile, a hero of Winslow Boy proportions has come forward in the person of 67-year-old Ian Macaulay, landlord of the Bell Inn, Aldworth, Berks, and a pipe smoker for 50 years. He has been threatened with a £500 fine and three months in prison if he continues to smoke his pipe behind the bar. Beer counts as food, the local EHO has explained, and even if he does not smoke while serving, the law says: 'If someone is engaged as a food handler they must not use tobacco. The law does not require them to be doing it simultaneously.'

In the quarrel between Mr Macaulay and his local EHO, Mr Grant Courteney, I see the great battle for civilisation in our times.

### *3rd May, 1993*

---

### Spinning wheels

SO MANY people have had so many kind things to say about the Queen's decision to open Buckingham Palace to the public to help pay for the repairs to Windsor Castle that it may be judged deliberately curmudgeonly to say I have no desire to see the interior of Buckingham Palace under these circumstances; that such a dispensation will destroy the mystique of the monarchy more than any number of television programmes called 'It's a Knockout!'

In a fascinating interview which appears in the current issue of the *Oldie* magazine, the Duke of Devonshire debates the point whether the decline of the British aristocracy had any influence on the decline of Britain, which seems to have been happening simultaneously. If I had to choose a moment when the aristocracy started its steepest decline, it would be when the magnates and grandees started opening their palaces as a means of supporting themselves.

I would much prefer to fantasise about the splendours inside Buckingham Palace. When I am 80 years old, and the Queen summons me to receive the OM, or MBE, or whatever, it will be part of the reward to be admitted, however briefly, to those splendours. The idea that the public has a right to inspect them just because it helps to pay for them is absurd. We might as well demand to be awarded the VC.

There was no need for the Queen to pay a farthing towards the restoration of Windsor Castle. It is not her property but a national monument, belonging to the government, which she is required to use for various public occasions.

In agreeing to help pay for the Windsor fire, the Queen was heeding the voices of envy and rancour, not listening to the true voice of her subjects. It was not our decision that she should pay income tax, it was the decision of Mr Rupert Murdoch. Nobody else could give a peppermint either way.

I was puzzled to read a curious article in Saturday's Weekend section to the effect that Mr Murdoch 'has a new spring in his step'; 'his wheels are spinning'; 'he is nicely poised to profit'; 'Murdoch's stock is literally on the up'. Oddly enough, I saw a photograph of him the other day and thought he looked rather old and ill. How sad, I thought, just when he is about to undertake the task of 'refloating' his £4.6 billion of debts by February of next year. Perhaps the strain of running this country as well as his own empire is beginning to tell . . . If I were the Queen, I should announce that on second thoughts I had decided not to pay income tax after all.

## 5th May, 1993

### *Cui bono?*

'WHAT benefit does the Home Secretary think will come to the public from sending the merely negligent or incompetent to prison?' asks Sir Frederick Lawton, the 81-year-old former Lord Justice of Appeal, drawing attention to Mr Kenneth Clarke's plan to increase to 10 years the maximum penalty for the offence by causing death by dangerous driving.

As he points out, the charge is unnecessary. Where an element of recklessness is involved, the proper charge should be manslaughter. There is no sense in sending to prison a driver who has killed someone as a result of momentary inattention or misjudgement.

I do not think Mr Clarke hopes to benefit the public by this fatuous and unpleasant measure. He merely hopes to appease the moronic, vindictive voices of the tabloid press, which demand that every road accident victim should be avenged.

He may think that these raucous demands are the voice of public opinion. They are not, and even if they were, it would be his duty to ignore them.

He may think he will make himself more popular, as when, in the aftermath of the Bishopsgate outrage, he promises to give police power to stop and search anyone they choose, with or without any reason for doing so. He will not make himself more popular. He will make himself loathsome and ridiculous, in equal measure.

## 8th May, 1993

### Remember Ethelburga

IT WAS hard not to admire Asil Nadir, the former philanthropist and founder of Polly Peck, for having the courage to face the world with such a terrible surname. Now that I learn he has a sister called Bilge, my admiration for the entire family grows.

Erconwald, Bishop of London in the second half of the seventh century, also had a sister with a ridiculous name. She was called Ethelburga the Virgin. Erconwald founded an abbey in Barking and made her abbess of it. In time, she became known as St Ethelburga of Barking, and it was her church in Bishopsgate

274

that was blown up by the IRA.

The cost of rebuilding the church has been put at less than £2 million, and we must agree that compared to the cost of rehabilitating the NatWest tower, this would money well spent. The site of St Ethelburga's (15ft by 30ft) is too small to be of great interest to developers, but there is a certain reluctance to invest even £2 million in building another redundant City church.

In any case, so long as the NatWest stands, it will present an open invitation to bombers, and if St Ethelburga's is to be flattened on every occasion, it seems rather a waste of time to restore it.

Many will decide that the saint would be best commemorated by a vegetarian hamburger bar serving Ethelburgas to the new style of City worker. A small tobacconist's shop might be even more useful.

## Safety first

IT WOULD be one for the books if the Queen was prevented from opening Buckingham Palace because of its denunciation by the British Safety Council as 'a potential death trap' from which the public must be protected. Any day now, I feel, the various Health and Safety Executives will close down the Palace of Westminster and assume direct rule of th country.

Mr James Tye director general of the British Safety Council since 1968, later agreed that no member of his council had actually visited Buckingham Palace before describing it as a death trap, but he claimed that his statement was based on examining a tender for work there.

It is perfectly all right for our beloved monarch, her consort and their youngest son to live in this death trap, but if the public are to be allowed in, fire escapes must be available at 10-yard intervals and all the courtiers will be required to wear asbestos underpants.

This is obviously the age of directors general – people responsible to nobody but themselves, unelected, under the control of no minister, able to overrule the Queen of England and close down the monarchy and the courts if they think considerations of health or safety or national security indicate such a course of action.

Our chief terror, in the event of a major fire at Buckingham Palace, must be that Prince Philip will decide to rebuild it in the modern style. At 71 he is too old to learn new tricks, and he still thinks there is something vaguely brave and go-ahead about being modern. It is bad news indeed that he is to sit on the committee supervising the restoration of Windsor Castle. While most of us avoid modern architects, and punch them in the face if we are introduced to them at a cocktail party, this old-fashioned gentleman still asks them to tea.

## *12th May, 1993*

### Health hazard

AS I write, Britons seem to be scaling Mount Everest like monkeys in an Indian temple. Since I described the appalling state of the mountain a few weeks ago – rather like Brighton beach after a bank holiday – further reports suggest that the situation is even worse than I thought.

Within a few thousand feet of the summit, a plateau the size of a football ground is strewn with about 20 ton of the sort of rubbish I have mentioned, but also with the dead bodies of climbers and their Sherpas. There are five of them in the immediate area, but many others are thought to be scattered around out of sight.

Soon the main risk of climbing the mountain will not be from the cold, the exhaustion or the lack of oxygen, but the ever-present danger of infection from these health hazards. It is an appalling reflection on the sort of people climbing Everest these days that they are prepared to leave their Sherpas lying around like so many empty tin cans.

If the Nepalese government is not prepared to do anything about this national disgrace, the very least we can do is to send an army of environmental health officers to inspect the site and issue directives. In fact I think it would be a good idea if all environmental health officers were required to climb Everest – preferably by the North Face, and without oxygen – before being issued with a licence to make a nuisance of themselves in the pubs, clubs and restaurants of England.

Those who complain it might be an expensive form of training should reflect on how much money we will save if the trainees fail to return.

## 15th May, 1993

### Serious women

LIKE the Tories with their internal class war, Labour seems determined to destroy itself by introducing its own internal sex war, now probably called a gender war. Its women's committee is demanding that only women candidates should be chosen for safe or winnable seats until such time as they have an equal number of male and female MPs – possibly by the year 2000.

Perhaps there will be two Labour MPs of each sex left in the Commons by then. The idea that poor old Labour voters will vote for a strange woman just because the women's committee has ordered them to do so, seems to hark back to happier, more deferential times.

But it is not so strange as the idea that the *Observer* should appoint a female editor just because she is a woman. Is this even permitted nowadays, under the recent social control acts? Putting herself forward for this job, the dreaded Polly Toynbee, BBC social affairs editor, gives two reasons why she feels she should be chosen.

The first – 'It is the job in journalism I would most like to have' – is simple enough. However, she proceeds: 'But the reason I am applying is also that there ought to be a serious newspaper by now that is edited by a woman.'

She does not advance the suggestion that she is a *serious* woman, merely that she is a woman. I do not feel that is sufficient qualification. However, when I cancel my order for the *Observer* after she is appointed editor, this will not be because she is a woman, but because she is so serious. I hate to see Englishwomen making fools of themselves.

## 17th May, 1993

### All hands to work

WESTMINSTER City Council has once again shown its officious and obstructive side by ordering a clampdown on bucket-and-sponge gangs – people who take advantage of the endless traffic jams in Westminster to clean your car windscreen while you wait.

This seems to me an entirely benign service – you don't have to accept their help or even pay for it if you do – but the council has decided to prosecute them where it can for illegal trading.

This probably explains why there are virtually no shoe cleaners in Westminster either. In many civilised capitals, you have only to sit down at a café table or stand for a moment at a street corner for some kind person to throw himself at your feet and start cleaning your shoes.

I have often thought how pleasant it would be – and how helpful to the problem of unemployment – if unemployed school and university leavers could volunteer to clean one's spectacles for one, if ever one found oneself stuck at a zebra crossing, waiting for the lights to change.

But Westminster seems to resent any form of personal service. For years it conducted a furious campaign against the massage parlours which offered such a pleasant and harmless relaxation to stressed Londoners. Now they have almost disappeared.

It seems unlikely that we will see unemployment fall much below the two million mark in our lifetimes. Westminster City Council is not only being cruel in preventing the unemployed from making the effort to help themselves, it is also being stupid. If they can't clean our windscreens, or spectacles, or shoes, or massage us, they will certainly take to robbery and violent crime.

### A brave man

A MEMO sent out to its civil servants in the North East by the Ministry of Agriculture warns them against helping farmers with their enormous and incomprehensible new census forms, even if the farmer cannot read or write. I suppose it is the ministry's way of facing up the problem of illiterate civil servants.

In Denmark, where they have a higher standard of literacy than in this country, two-thirds of the workforce is employed by the state and they have a civil servant in the Agricultural Ministry for every farmer. This seems the best way of dealing with agricultural subsidies, which nobody really wants.

I hope the National Farmers Union is planning a memo to farmers who find themselves meeting these civil servants face to face. Apart from the standard advice to be attentive and patient, try to smile, try to solve the civil servants' problems, escort them to a seat, they should never leave a civil servant alone in a lavatory (for fear he falls into it) or a kitchen (for fear he accidentally cooks himself). Above all, they should remember that these inspectors have tremendous powers, and they must not be annoyed.

In this context, I tremble for the outcome of a recent visit to Badminton House by an RSPCA inspector who said he was looking into allegations that the Beaufort Hunt had tampered with a badger sett. After the Duke of Beaufort had politely said he was unable to help because he knew nothing about it, the inspector started taking notes and demanded to know the Duke's address.

The Duke glanced around the palace in which the interview was being conducted and said: 'Guess.'

He is a very brave man, of course, the Duke of Beaufort. I just hope all his goldfish have been receiving their statutory two hours conversation and playtime every day.

### Put to the test

THE TROUBLE with Liberal Democrats, who have swept the Shires in this month's local elections, is that you never know what you are going to get. Some of them, like Paddy Pantsdown, seem perfectly reasonable, or, at any rate, recognisable types of English person – the sort you might meet, dressed in a blazer, in any Home Counties pub.

Others turn out to be militant vegetarians, sex maniacs or save-the-green-caterpillar fanatics, not to be trusted with small children for fear they take their clothes away and tell them about fairies. If the new complexion of the County Councils really poses a threat to some of our best and most historic hunts, from the Quantock Staghounds in Somerset to the Belvoir, Cottesmore, Fernie and Quorn in Leicestershire, then the government must act fast, or forfeit the loyalty of the countryside for ever.

The threat arises because many County Councils own large tracts of agricultural and sporting land. The reason for this land ownership may be lost in antiquity, but it certainly does not apply in the age of privatisation, when government is selling anything it can lay its hands on to pay its gigantic army of public employees.

If even the national police records are up for sale (like the KGB's in Russia), there can be no excuse for councils to own great estates which have nothing to do with their function.

Mr Howard must instruct councils to sell all their land immediately, with an easement requiring the purchaser to keep it open for traditional sporting activities – under pain of cutting off equivalent funds from central government funding.

If the secretary of state neglects to issue these instructions forthwith, we will know what sort of a Conservative he is.

## 22nd May, 1993

### A new role

LABOUR MP Diane Abbott may have been right when she warned the House of Commons that prostitution has become an epidemic in parts of London. She was referring particularly to her own constituency of Hackney North and Stoke Newington, about which I know little, having had few occasions to visit it.

'Ms' Abbott, as she is affectionately known in the House, is probably too young to remember London before the Street Offences Act of 1959, when prostitutes lined Piccadilly at five-yard intervals and stood two-deep in Park Lane. I am surprised by how little evidence of prostitution breaks the surface nowadays. One would expect it to be a boom area as our economy declines in relation to the rest of Europe and north America.

In Africa, prostitution has always been a major part of the scene at every level, and the former socialist countries of eastern Europe have taken to it like so many ducks to water, as the easiest and quickest way to reconcile the huge discrepancies in spending power between themselves and visiting tourists.

I suppose that prostitution can take forms other than the provision of sexual services, at which the English have never excelled. Some clues towards our own future direction may be given by scenes at the opening of a new hamburger bar in London this week, called Planet Hollywood.

It was attended by jet-loads of American film stars flown in for the occasion, rather as people used to fly in soft-shelled crabs from Maryland. Only tabloid press journalists were admitted, and American security guards refused admission to a member of the Royal Family until a journalist on the *Sun* said he would personally vouch for Lord Linley.

A country with any pride left would not have allowed these people inside its borders, at any rate without the most rigorous medical tests. Instead, they are welcomed as conquering heroes. Classless New Britain lies at their feet.

## *24th May, 1993*

### Great leap forward

THE INFORMATION that Britain's latest mother of sextuplets, Mrs Jean Vince, is not married to the babies' father, and in fact lives with him only some of the time even though she already has a six-year-old son by him, says much for the generosity of a free health service which is prepared to put a single mother on a course of fertility drugs.

As we taxpayers joyously take up the burden of paying for Gregory, Rebecca, Jessica, Stephanie, Katie and Valerie, as well as their six-year-old brother, Garry, we may reflect that state benefits, which will total £78.5 billion this year, cost the average worker a mere £10 a day. For £10 a day you can no longer park your car in many parts of central London.

Many public employees, worried for their jobs in the light of this year's proposed £50 billion deficit, are busy proposing ways in which benefits to the public can be cut. They point to the £3 billion expenditure on drugs. You could pay for nearly 230,000 health workers with that £3 billion if you stopped giving people medicines.

The trouble is that many people become attached to their medicines and think them perfectly delicious. They would make a fuss. So the new scheme is to launch a gigantic inquiry into lifestyles. From July 1 all doctors will be required to question all patients about their lifestyle. Vast amounts of extra money will be made available for this purpose, and vast amounts of information will be collected. Then doctors will be able to order patients to change their lifestyle under pain of being 'deprioritised' for medical services.

Smokers are obviously top of the list for being cut off from medical services. In many practices, smokers are already given minimum priority when they develop lung cancer, which means effectively they are condemned to death. Before non-smokers clap their mean little hands over this, they should reflect that the new multi-billion-pound Health Promotion Scheme is going to take account of far more than smoking: diet, drinking habits, exercise and every other aspect of healthy living will come under scrutiny, including sexual activity and leisure pursuits.

Any patient who neglects to attend a Health Promotion Scheme investigation, or refuses to change his lifestyle when ordered to do so, will automatically be 'deprioritised' for medical attention. A huge army of health workers, health informers and health police will have to be enlisted to ensure that patients are telling the truth. It only needs one report of being caught with a cigarette, drinking a second glass of beer, putting sugar in your tea or missing your morning jog and you will be 'deprioritised' on the spot.

Eventually we will have the ideal health service which employs one in three of the population, holds every detail of our private lives in its information banks and, having closed all the wards in all the hospitals and deprioritised all the patients, provides no medical services of any description whatever.

## *29th May, 1993*

---

## Nothing in excess

ON THURSDAY Nigel Burke confirmed what I have often claimed, that any householder who takes a rolled-up newspaper to a burglar is committing a criminal offence. If the householder is still alive when the police come on the scene – and if they ever do – they will be forced to arrest him or her on the spot. Similarly, any 90-year-old lady who goes out after dark with a rolled-up newspaper – let alone an umbrella – intending to use it in her defence, must expect severe punishment in an age when there is public concern about law and order.

Our rulers are so terrified of us that they will not allow the most respectable citizen in the land to take any steps to protect his property or his loved ones. Since our rulers now lack the means to protect us, we can only hope that harmonisation of laws within the European Community will take the matter out of their hands.

But it is no good pretending that this column's campaign to allow householders to shoot has been much helped by events in Baton Rouge, Louisiana, where a young Japanese teenager dressed as John Travolta for a fancy dress party, mistook the address and was shot dead by an enraged householder, who complained that the teenager just kept grinning every time he shouted 'Freeze'.

The householder was acquitted to cheers when his lawyer announced: 'You have the absolute right in this country to answer your door with a gun.'

It would be most disagreeable if one felt one could not knock on any door in the land without being shot by an enraged householder with a .44 Magnum revolver. In the same way,

although I feel that landowners' rights against deliberate and malicious trespass need strengthening, it would probably not be advisable to allow them to shoot at ramblers unless they were in groups of 10 or more. A sense of proportion is the main thing.

## 2nd June, 1993

### New stalking horse

'IT IS NOW as probable that Mr Major will have to go as it was nine months ago that Mr Lamont would have to go. Why wait? Mr Major himself has lost any enthusiastic area of support . . . '

So writes the great William Rees-Mogg, perhaps brushed with the faintest touch of saintly euphoria that the former Chancellor of the Exchequer could be removed so easily. It only took every journalist in the country to write it every day for nine months, and suddenly, WHAM! – Lamont was gone.

William is wrong when he says that Major has no enthusiastic support. I find I am growing fonder of him with every day that passes. But the greatest mistake is to suppose that Prime Ministers are as easy to change as Chancellors. It was on March 6, 1988 – the day of the Gibraltar shootings – that I decided Margaret Thatcher was no longer a fit person to be Prime Minister. Thatcher, I announced, should go.

It is easy to say that sort of thing, of course, but getting rid of a Prime Minister is a major operation. First you have to find a stalking horse. An amiable, elderly baronet volunteered for that thankless role. Next you have to find a desperado like Heseltine to issue a madcap challenge. Then the serious candidates join in. It is unlikely to take less than two years, and by then even the most dedicated journalists have found other things to write about.

The least Rees-Mogg can do is to propose himself as a stalking horse. It will be a poignant touch that, on this occasion, the challenge will come from the Upper House.

Only a few political commentators have seats in the House of Lords, but just occasionally they must be expected to put their hooves where their mouths are.

## On Twitty and Gunn

WHATEVER we may feel about their policies, I would like to think there is room in our hearts to commiserate with Mr and Mrs Clinton on their country's loss of Conway Twitty, the gifted country and western musician. If I were the Queen, I would send them a telegram.

Twitty, who was born Harold Jenkins, did not succumb to the dread American Disease which has claimed so many talented young people in his country's entertainments industry. A blocked abdominal artery is thought to be the reason that he died. Mr and Mrs Clinton may well feel that a bright light has gone out in their world, and in the world of all culturally-aware Americans.

Our point of condolence must be to suggest that in a country as big as the United States of America, with a population of over 231 million, some 7,600 people die every day. The news is bound to be full of unpleasant shocks.

By the same token, it is hard to understand the paroxysms of grief and terror which have followed the murder of Dr David Gunn, a Florida abortionist, in March. A BBC1 programme on Sunday suggested it might justify Mr and Mrs Clinton in banning the anti-abortion movement entirely.

Of course it is a disgraceful thing, but I scarcely think the murder of one abortionist justifies Mr and Mrs Clinton in declaring a state of emergency and suspending citizens' right of peaceful assembly.

In a country where (I think I have read) some 42 murders are committed every day, how many greengrocers have been murdered in the three-month period? How many car-park attendants and clerical outfitters? The presidential couple must try to keep its head through all the news which comes pouring in.

## New threat to health

HUGH 'Bulldog' Drummond used to talk of putting water in someone's beer as the ultimate social sanction and gesture of distaste. What would he – and what will the rest of the country – make of a government which waters the country's beer?

Perhaps it is not quite fair to accuse nice Mr Major or his

pleasant former Chancellor of watering our beer. It is the brewers who have watered it in response to tax changes introduced by Mr Lamont.

Exactly the same thing happened with gin when the brand I had been drinking for 35 years suddenly reduced its alcohol content without any explanation or apology, and without reducing the price. I thought of bringing down the Government on that occasion, but reflected that gin drinkers were not as numerous as beer drinkers. In any case, I found another brand which remains at 40 per cent, costs the same, and tastes no different, so far as I can tell.

But the Government's behaviour is particularly questionable in light of new evidence that alcohol is an important element in the development of strong bones. By watering our beer and gin, the Government is threatening our health. It goes to prove my point that, for all its grotesque expenditure on health and safety, the Government is not really interested in either. Modern society is dominated by armies of ignorant, semi-educated juveniles interested only in exercising power over everyone else. Parliament – especially the House of Lords – should keep these people in their place, but Parliament is not up to the job, preferring to strike twerpish, ineffectual attitudes about Maastricht.

Now, as I read in my *Liverpool Echo*, social service chiefs in the Wirral have issued an edict that all children should be fed on 'ethnic' food – vindaloo curries and chapatis – in order to combat racism. They say they are implementing the Children Act, but Wirral Childminders Association is up in arms.

I don't suppose it will do these Merseyside toddlers any harm to vary their diet of fish fingers and ice cream, but in many ancient and civilised cultures children have been expected to eat the corpses of their parents as a gesture of respect.

I foresee nothing but trouble in trying to persuade Merseyside children to respect their parents at this late stage.

## 14th June, 1993

### Smoking encouraged

IT WAS odd to read the new code for visitors to Antarctica, drawn up by the International Association of Antarctica Tour

Operators. The Guidelines of Conduct include such instructions as these:

• Do not walk on or otherwise damage the fragile plants such as lichens, mosses and grasses.

• Do not smoke during shore excursions.

One tries to be reasonable about requests not to smoke indoors, but Antarctica covers about 5.5 million square miles with a population density of about one person per thousand square miles. Similarly, it seems strange that 'Keep Off the Grass' notices should arrive even before there are any humans there to walk on it.

The only interesting thing about Antarctica is how horribly inhospitable it is. Nobody could possibly wish to live there, and under those circumstances I don't see that it matters very much how its lichen, mosses and grasses fare.

The best possible use for it is as a gigantic tip to receive all the world's rubbish. Developed countries produce more rubbish than they can accommodate. Soon we shall start dumping it on each other, which is bound to cause trouble. Let the whole world decide to dump it on the South Pole.

And if those who visit the world's rubbish dump wish to smoke, for heaven's sake let them do so.

## *16th June, 1993*

### *Sola virtus invicta*

ALL the best part of England will have breathed a sigh of relief to learn that the Jockey Club has cleared Lady Herries of any alleged impropriety after one of her horses which won a race at Brighton on April 8 reacted positively to a dope test.

Lady Herries, married to Sir Colin Cowdrey, is the eldest daughter of the great Duke of Norfolk whose death in 1975 deprived the English nobility of its greatest adornment. At a time when the monarchy is under fire from demented Australians, and in a week when we saw the next head of the Churchill family, heir to the Duke of Marlborough, carried kicking and screaming into a police van, it is good that nothing has yet occurred to taint the Ducal and Illustrious Howards, described by Burke as standing next to the Blood Royal at the head of the Peerage of England.

Lady Herries explains that she was doping one of her spaniels, called Kandy, and assumes that the dog must inadvertently have urinated on a patch of grass which was later eaten by the racehorse.

My only hesitation concerns the dog Kandy, presumably called after the ancient Sinhalese kingdom destroyed by the British in 1818. As Patron of the Canine Defence League, I do not feel that his guilt should be assumed.

Was Kandy legally represented at the hearing? Perhaps the standard of proof required to find an animal guilty may not be so high as it is for a human: 'balance of probability' may be enough to convict a spaniel where a human conviction would require proof 'beyond reasonable doubt'.

Even so, I am not sure a jury would conclude that the balance of probability favours the theory that Kandy urinated on a patch of grass, and the racehorse chose that patch of grass to eat just before the race.

The mystery of who doped the racehorse remains unsolved: was it an animal rights zealot, many of whom disapprove of horse racing, or was it the IRA, whose cruel hatred of horses has been seen in outrage after outrage, from the slaughter in Hyde Park to the kidnap and murder of Shergar?

## 19th June, 1993

### Price of coincidence

BEING neither a businessman nor a candidate for honours, I nevertheless find myself brooding about the list of 'Honours awarded to Conservative Donors' collated by the Labour Research Department and printed in Thursday's newspaper.

The list records voluntary donations of various public-spirited firms to the Conservative Party in order to celebrate the coincidence of honours awarded to their directors at about the same time. The oddest thing about the list is the varying cost of these coincidences.

Thus for a down-payment of only £20,000 the MacFarlane group was able to secure the coincidence of a knighthood for Mr Norman MacFarlane in 1983, followed by the much bigger coincidence of a peerage for Sir Norman MacFarlane in 1991. Against this, Lazards paid £286,100 to the Conservative Party in order to enjoy the coincidence of a mere knighthood for one of its directors in 1986.

In 1989 UEI paid only £1,600 for the coincidence of a knighthood, while four years later, United Biscuits paid £1,004,500 for the same benefit.

What worries me is how we poor members of the public are supposed to tell the difference. Obviously, we would be prepared to show much greater deference towards a knight who had had £1,004,500 paid to the Conservative Party for the coincidence than we would towards some pip-squeak whose coincidence cost only £1,600. But how are we supposed to tell them apart?

## 21st June, 1993

### Causes of crime

MANY senior executives and field officers in the health enforcement industry will be seriously annoyed by the claim of Dr Tony Postle, a researcher, that alcohol consumption by women in the early stages of pregnancy could account for a large proportion of murders, mental illness and violence in our society. Dr Postle, of Southampton University, has received a £100,000 grant to study the subject.

What will annoy people is the implicit denial that all murder, mental illness or violence is caused by smoking – whether by mothers smoking in pregnancy, or infants smoking in their first three months, children on their way to school or the general miasma of nicotine given off by some old burial grounds.

Others will be annoyed by the implicit denial that all murder, mental illness or violence is caused by Nintendo toys, or saturated fat. These people need not worry. It only requires another researcher at another university funded by another £100,000 of taxpayers' money to say that all murder etc. is caused by smoking, Nintendo toys, or saturated fat and every newspaper will print it uncritically without reference to Dr Postle's researches, as if they were all somehow derived from the great bible of science.

My own theory is that many evils in contemporary society may be caused by hamburgers – by the smell almost as much as by the eating of them. Readers of *The Sunday Telegraph* will have been following the case history of the great Sir Peregrine Worsthorne with some alarm since he revealed he had eaten a hamburger in a charabanc to celebrate a friend's birthday.

He was immediately taken ill with an unknown sickness. Mercifully recovered from that, he now breaks wind violently on public transport, he tells us. Worse than this, he welcomes these demonstrations as adding force to an argument conducted in his head with some people sitting near him.

When the evil man responsible for these serial homosexual murders in London is eventually apprehended, I shall follow his recent dietary history with great interest.

## 23rd June, 1993

### Terrible droning

BRITAIN's biggest wind farm, designed to produce electricity in an environmentally friendly way, has turned into an environmental nightmare.

Not only are the 103 turbines, standing 100 feet high (and about to be joined by another 90) an eyesore. They also make a most disagreeable noise, a constant loud droning, like an aircraft engine.

This is odd. I never have any difficulty with electricity. Most rooms, I have discovered, have electrical sockets in them, usually at the bottom of the walls. Put a plug into one of them, check the switches are on, and you almost always have electricity, in my experience. Those who seek more elaborate, environmentally friendly, ways of producing electricity may have good intentions, but they are also likely to be the most terrible bores. This, I feel sure, explains the terrible droning noise which has been keeping Welsh villagers awake for miles around.

It is the droning of a million bores explaining to each other how much more meritorious it is to put up these absurd and hideous towers all over the countryside than simply to put your plug in a socket and turn on the switch like everyone else.

## 26th June, 1993

### Modern life

A FRIEND of mine is being persecuted by something called BC Marketing in Edinburgh, which sends her pages and pages and pages of 'Private Circuit Commentary', labelled 'In Confidence', detailing the performance of all its products, with names like Speechline/Keyline, AccessLine, Kilostream and MegaStream.

Is anybody else being persecuted in this way? Would anyone like to borrow or buy the confidential accounts of BC Marketing, whatever that might be?

Modern life is full of hazards. On Tuesday evening, I had rather a disconcerting experience. Leaving my club in Irving Street after dinner, at about 10.30, I decided that as the night was still young I might walk to my other club – the Academy in Beak Street – for some serious literary discussion before bed. On the way, in Charing Cross Road, I passed a bank with its cashpoint glowing.

Although I did not particularly want any money, I decided this might be an opportunity to have an agreeable conversation with the machine about my wealth, so I put my card into it and tapped out a number which I later recognised as my secret code for the burglar alarm in Somerset.

It told me to try again, but I soon realised that this was not one of those evenings when I was going to remember my number. In the dark, I could not remember where the 'cancel' button was situated, and pressed several buttons at random, hoping to get my card back. Suddenly, a new message appeared on the screen: DO YOU WANT MORE TIME?

Has anybody else had a similar experience? The meaning seemed clear. The machine was suggesting, however politely, that I had had a glass of Croft's 1970 too many after dinner.

After I had firmly pressed the button indicating 'No', grabbed my card and climbed into a cab to go home to bed, the doubts began to form. Did the question have an eschatological edge? Do we want more time on earth or not? Next month and the month after, I think I will be retiring to a health farm in Suffolk to ponder these questions.

## Time for inaction

THE Lime Street Action Group sounds like a vigilante organisation formed by householders and shopkeepers against the local teenagers or Lime Street kids. As such, its days would be numbered. But, in fact, it is an association of 500 Lloyd's Names who face a combined loss of nearly £1.2 billion, or £2.4 million each. As such, it will probably be with us for a long time.

Various explanations have been offered for 1990's record loss of £2.91 billion, but the simplest message from it all is to stop insuring other people. As in so many matters, we should look to America for insight into the likely pattern of the future.

In the United States, where there are now 800,000 lawyers, it is calculated that litigation imposes an annual tax of $117 billion (£75.5 billion) on business. Ambrose Evans-Pritchard, writing about this phenomenon on Sunday, described how American juries almost invariably take pity on a fellow citizen who has suffered hardship and will award extravagant compensation, regardless of liability, assuming that insurance will pay. Civil litigation (with 40 per cent of awards going to lawyers) takes the place of a welfare state in America.

Which is all very well, except that many of the bills end up in London. Never mind the family silver and ancestral acres, Britain's entire savings over the years are now being paid out to finance an inefficient welfare system across the Atlantic.

As Mr Lilley has pointed out, we can no longer afford our own £80 billion annual social security budget. We certainly cannot afford our own litigation system on top. For those of us who are not involved in Lloyd's, the main lesson must be to ensure that we do not go down the American path. Various schemes are afoot to 'reform' our civil law, including the introduction of contingency fees, the extension of legal aid, and an end to the vital principle that an unsuccessful litigant pays the cost of both sides.

Any of these would be disastrous. Just because our legal system stinks to high heaven and is long overdue for reform, it does not mean we should regard would-be 'reformers' with any less suspicion than we regard those who wish to keep things as they are.

## Problem of dirty vicars

THE POPE's tirade against sexual laxity among the clergy undoubtedly struck a deep chord among my colleagues in the tabloid press. There is a feeling that, however tolerant, or even broadminded, we might be among ourselves, we do not want the clergy joining in. The great question remains: what is to be done?

I wonder if the Pope has studied the habits of the emu. This delicate bird, whose females emit a loud booming sound, is both monogamous and chaste in its habits – to such an extent that, in

Western Australia, where it is farmed for meat, all efforts at scientific breeding have failed. The pairs stick together through thick and thin, just as good Christians are expected to do.

Somewhere, the rot has to be stopped. Pope John Paul decided to attack the clergy, threatening them all with hell. I am not sure enough of them believe in it to make this a useful threat. Instead, he might adopt the emu, as the ibis was adopted in ancient Egypt, as a sacred bird and best example to the human family. Every priest should be required to eat an emu's egg every day. It might not work, but is certainly worth a try.

## *30th June, 1993*

### Time to try again

AS ONE who missed all the dirty bits in Ken Russell's BBC1 version of *Lady Chatterley's Lover* I might not have the right to an opinion of the whole, but I caught the last episode on Sunday and was amazed by its ineptitude. Much of the fault may have been D. H. Lawrence's for his humourlessness and defective sense of the ridiculous but I have never before seen him so badly acted or hamfistedly produced.

On the subject of the bogus happy ending stitched on the narrative by Russell, Mr Michael Haggiag, the producer, explained: 'We couldn't end on a downbeat note after four hours of showing two lovers fighting the class system. If we hadn't changed it, everything would have been left hanging.'

I don't suppose that Russell's ending was much worse than Lawrence's, but Russell, like all his generation, is stuck in the 1960s. The class struggle has long since been resolved. The proletarian mass culture finally triumphed in about 1979.

It now spreads its muck and filth over almost every aspect of British life, from *The Times* and *Sunday Times* to the Conservative Party and the Church of England. There is nothing 'upbeat' about celebrating its victory at this late stage.

Under its new Charter, we must hope the BBC will emerge as a bastion of the old humane, bourgeois liberal culture and fight the good fight against the tide of proletarian stupidity and slime. Next time it screens Lawrence's irritating book, I would suggest an entirely new ending.

Lady Chatterley catches a virulent form of herpes from her gamekeeper lover. Covered with spots all over her body, she renounces men and embraces lesbianism. This should recommend my version to the women's movement. As for Mellors, he chokes to death when a shot pheasant falls into his mouth, which he had left hanging open in the manner of his kind. This should recommend my version to opponents of blood sports.

## *5th July, 1993*

### Crimewatch

THERE is a poignancy in the story of Lester Baker who, heartbroken by his wife's infidelity, took her and her lover hostage in an attempt to commit suicide by persuading police in Heathfield, Sussex, to shoot him. They did their best but missed him with four out of five bullets and succeeded only in wounding him with the fifth.

Sentencing Baker to three years in prison at Hove Crown Court, Judge John Gower QC said: 'You caused police their most unpleasant duty, to shoot another human.'

Maybe so, but where police in many areas are pursuing a deliberate long-term policy to allow nobody but themselves access to firearms, they are likely to be called out on this sort of job more often in the future. Under the circumstances, I am not sure whether to recommend that they should take steps to improve their marksmanship or not.

In their anxiety to prevent citizens from defending themselves, police in Bristol took away the truncheon with which 71-year-old Mrs Florence Bascombe had put to flight three robbers, one of them armed. The police said she had no business to own such an instrument.

This is what we must call the rule of law. Now, when the robbers return to Mrs Bascombe's charity shop in Dean Lane, Bedminster, they know she will be unable to prevent them from helping themselves to the till. It will be a terrible day for the nation's burglars and muggers if the police go on strike against Sir Pat Sheehy's reforms. There will be nobody left to look after them. Many will close down shop and take a foreign holiday for the duration.

## *12th July, 1993*

### New adoption plan

THE PROPOSAL that couples wishing to adopt a child should pay a fee of up to £1,500 for local authority inspection is the most glaring example yet of the robber baron style of government which has developed since the wave of demented legislation in 1989 and 1990, imposing government regulation on every aspect of our lives.

The Government is now desperate for the money to pay its swollen army of public employees. As well as finding new ways to harass and annoy us, they must now be given powers to extort huge sums of money in fees for their unrequested and unwanted services. Building inspectors and environmental health officers can already charge for annoying householders and harassing shopkeepers, publicans and restaurateurs.

The idea that the nation's social workers will also be able to charge for imposing their own unpleasant, obstructive and half-witted prejudices is a new refinement. We all understand that the Government is in a desperate situation, but the only way out of it, as I never tire of explaining, is to sack one in three public employees. It is no good relying on the elimination of welfare scroungers, popular as that course might be. You won't eliminate them and you will probably provoke riots in all the inner cities. There isn't enough money in the adoption racket to make any difference. Social workers often manage to spend £8-10,000 on each adoption.

Even if there is no reason for adoptive parents to pay social workers for making a nuisance of themselves, there might be a case for paying the real mothers. This is not a fashionable notion, and the idea of penurious mothers being forced to sell their beloved children, or breeding babies for sale, is a sad one. But I doubt it would work out like that, and the present practice, by which the government bribes single women to have babies and keep them, is certainly more expensive and probably more harmful socially. It is a question of how we see ourselves.

Third World countries may be sensitive and touchy about baby-sales, but since pensioners in the north of England will now be receiving food aid from the peasant farmers of Pakistan, we are plainly Fourth World. I do not see why hard-up British mums should not be allowed to sell their dreadful, whingeing kids if they do not want to keep them. Car boot sales might offer a good opportunity.

## 14th July, 1993

### Never again

HOW many of us were aware that this week, among its many other claims to attention, has been chosen as Women into Politics Week? It started with Betty Boothroyd, the lovely, long-legged Speaker, opening an exhibition in the House of Commons. Then Mrs Shephard, Minister of Agriculture, laid flowers at the statue of Emmeline Pankhurst.

Today Lady Thatcher will unveil a plaque to Emily Davison (1872-1913), the feminist militant who nearly murdered a Baptist minister whom she mistook for Lloyd George and died under the King's horse at the Derby. Next there will be a lecture on 'Why Women Should Be in Politics' and another by Mrs Bottomley on 'Women in Power'. Finally, Lady (Shirley) Williams will ask: 'Women in Europe. Where Are We Today?'

It may well be among the great questions of the hour: 'Where am I? Why am I here? Where am I going?' but of all the causes in the world, this seems among the least worthy of support. Women almost invariably lead their countries into war or civil war, even if they do not launch a male vasectomy campaign. We must tremble for the male populations of Canada and Turkey, and even for American men under Mrs Clinton.

Valiant attempts are being made to pretend that premenstrual tension does not exist. Let us all agree with this, but let us also agree that in Britain we will never, never again entertain the thought of having another woman Prime Minister.

## 17th July, 1993

### Don't trust them either

STRONG language has been used and violent emotions stirred up by the acquittal of Joseph Elliott, accused of murdering a man who remonstrated with him for slashing car tyres in the street. This newspaper even went so far as to suggest that the Old Bailey verdict reinforces the case for plea bargaining.

If it does so, it can only be because jury verdicts are considered to be increasingly unstable, the risk of perverse decisions is growing. To encourage plea bargaining in those circumstances is to encourage blackmail. What is needed is an end to the jury system.

As I never tire of pointing out, Britons generally and Londoners in particular are no longer up to the job. When I read my colleagues in the gutter press railing against the young criminal and against the jury I am reminded yet again of Caliban scowling and grimacing at his own reflection in the mirror. The *Sun* even urges its half-witted readers to try to remember Joseph Elliott's name: 'In case you're on the jury next time he's up in court.' How can any country hope to have a fair jury system when that is the understanding of fairness?

On Wednesday I met a peer who had travelled many thousands of miles to register his vote for a Maastricht referendum in the House of Lords that evening. I remonstrated

with him, citing the Old Bailey jury as evidence, and saying that the opinion of these people had no value, whether it was on Maastricht or anything else.

He replied that if the decision was not offered to the British people it would be settled by the House of Commons. 'Have you seen the new Members? They are just the same scum, only worse,' he said. I think I lost that argument.

## 19th July, 1993

### A use for donkeys

SOMEONE has kindly sent me a copy of the annual accounts of the Donkey Sanctuary at Sidford in Devon. People who have visited the spot describe it as one of the saddest sights in Europe, after the War Graves in the north of France and Euro Disney at Marne-la-Vallée. More than 5,000 donkeys hang around in forlorn groups looking useless, with nothing to do. My correspondent assures me that none of these donkeys is permitted to be ridden or carry anything. They are like steel workers on the dole.

One might ask why they should be any more fortunate in these difficult times, but they are much better endowed than redundant British workers. The Sanctuary has net assets of £8,294,548. Its income, mostly from donations and legacies, was £5,653,393 last year, an increase of more than £700,000 on its income from the year before.

At a time of world recession, sentimentality about donkeys would appear to be one of the great boom areas in Britain. It is a pity we cannot find some use for them. Donkeys are intractable and obdurate animals by nature. It is often necessary to beat them severely before they will be persuaded to perform the simplest tasks.

Perhaps this is why they have never been very popular in this country. But if the Government is serious in its plans to allow education to occur once again in schools, it might be a good idea to put donkeys into all the teacher training colleges for trainee teachers to practise on.

## *24th July, 1993*

### Donkeys to the rescue

MY LETTER box has been filled for several days with letters from donkey-lovers complaining about my recent piece on the Donkey Sanctuary at Sidmouth. An interesting discovery is that donkey fanciers, with one or two exceptions, are rather nice people, unlike Thatcher-fanciers, anti-smokers or militant relatives of road victims.

The sanctuary's administrator, Dr E. D. Svendsen, points out that far from standing around with nothing to do all day, as my correspondent complained, her donkeys are regularly visited and ridden by disabled children. At Devon County Show, they give exhibitions of jumping with deaf riders, a thoroughly admirable thing to do.

My own experience with donkeys has not been happy, but I recognise in the enthusiasm and exuberance of these donkey-fanciers something of my own feeling for pekingese: donkeys are not only beautiful, brave, kind, loyal and brilliantly clever, they are also industrious, articulate, honest, thrifty and endowed with a keen sense of moral priorities.

Many took exception to my suggestion that obdurate and intractable donkeys should be supplied to teacher training colleges so that the trainees could practice chastising them.

Under these circumstances, perhaps I should amend my recommendation, with appropriate apologies to the donkeys of the world and their admirers. Donkeys should be sent to teacher training colleges, but not as whipping posts, to help trainee teachers learn how to deal with obdurate and intractable pupils. Rather they should go as professors to teach the elements of good manners, reading, writing, arithmetic, English, history, French and Latin, from the store of their wisdom, to the almost totally ignorant generation which seeks to educate our children now.

## Opportunity knocks

AT LAST I begin to have intimations that the Kenneth Clarke economic miracle may be just round the corner. In my copy of the *Liverpool Echo* I find no fewer than 10 jobs on offer in the 'General Vacancies' corner of classified advertisements. Among the usual situations vacant for owner-drivers and telephone canvassers there is one for an archimandrite of the Russian Orthodox Church. I give the advertisement in full:

'Archimandrite required for Russian Orthodox Monastery near Dolgellau. Fluent old Church Slavonic essential. Tel: Schedrin 034 141247.'

Perhaps I should explain to any Liverpudlians interested that old Church Slavonic is the liturgical language introduced by Saints Cyril and Methodius to the liturgy of the eastern rite in the 9th century; Dolgellau is a small town in Gwynedd, graced by the presence of Cymer Abbey; an archimandrite is the Orthodox equivalent of an abbot, or head of a monastery.

Nobody with a grounding in Greek and Russian should have much difficulty with old Church Slavonic. No doubt evening classes are available. I am not sure what are the exact qualifications for an archimandrite, but I rather think you have to grow a beard and wear your hair in a bun.

Many of the young men of Liverpool are already more than half way there. Come on, lads. On yer bikes. The light breaks through.

## 28th July, 1993

### Much crueller

THOSE who hold the Army in affection and respect will have been ashamed to read about the former private in the Royal Regiment of Wales, Mr Anthony Evans, who received £8,500 in compensation after being driven out of the Army by a campaign of racial harassment.

A board of inquiry heard how this descendant of a black American GI was called names like 'Sambo' and subjected to a mock trial by a kangaroo court, at which he was charged with 'being black'.

I had heard of similar atrocities committed against African cadets at Sandhurst in the old days – contributing in no small way to our loss of Empire after the last war. At the time, I attributed it to ignorance. Anyone brought up on Heinrich Hoffman's *Stuwwelpeter* will remember the words of the Great Agrippa:

*For if he try with all his might*
*He cannot change from black to white.*

Attempts to alter the skin colour of Africans by scrubbing them are not only cruel and impertinent, but also doomed to failure. One would have thought that with all the scientific education which has been going on in recent years, and with the special emphasis on racial awareness and similar topics, this message would have got through. I had no scientific education at all, but before I left school I knew perfectly well that this was no way to tackle what we used to call the colour problem.

The oddest and most frightening aspect of this case is that in all the photographs published, Mr Evans shows no trace whatever of his African origins. He looks like a perfectly ordinary Welshman. Perhaps scrubbing does work, after all.

If so, it is much worse. Mr Evans should receive twice as much compensation for the impertinence and cruelty he has suffered.

## 4th August, 1993

### The British dream

I WAS sad on Monday when *The Daily Telegraph* announced the end of the European dream and the death of hopes for a single European currency. I always thought that the idea of a single currency – removing all economic decisions from our own crooks, incompetents and social inadequacies in Westminster – was a trifle ambitious. The important thing was that duties on drink and tobacco should be brought down to the continental level. When Mrs Thatcher sabotaged that – and Mr Major was too wet to unscramble her mischief – Europe rather lost its point.

From the viewpoint of Mr Average Briton – in his early fifties, shall we say, with children grown up, no mortgage to worry about, wine cellars nearly full, only about three pekingese (one, perhaps, black) to look after – it no longer matters so much about the Government's iniquitous duties on drink and tobacco. These are matters for poor, idealistic, greedy young people to worry about. What matters for Mr Average Briton is that the Government should do something about interest rates.

One of the most sinister things that has happened in recent years has been the way we have all been brainwashed into accepting that low interest rates are good for the country. Of course they are good for spenders and borrowers, but they are disastrous for savers, as the voters of Christchurch demonstrated. Interest rates are now far too low. But I am full of hope. One swallow does not make a summer, but it is wonderful news that porters have reappeared at King's Cross station.

## Historic decision

ALL my friends are urging me to apply for the headmastership of Eton, which has become vacant after Eric Anderson's decision to move to Lincoln College, Oxford, next year. It is true there is much work to be done to prepare Etonians for the New Britain of Michael Grade, Paul 'Gazza' Gascoigne and Andrew Neil. Their knives must be sharp, their arms strong and their aim straight. My only problem is that I don't like boys. If I asked them to turn it into a girls' school, I fear I would be asking too much.

However, there is no reason why a woman should not be appointed headmaster of Eton. I don't think they want anybody very academic. Education is rather a handicap in our new multicultural, anti-elitist age, and Eton parents are not paying to have their children handicapped in life.

All the Etonian needs in the modern world is a thick skin and firm idea of where he is going. I wonder if anyone has thought of offering the job to the Duchess of York. She is looking for a job. This one does not require any elaborate command of languages or singing ability or great degree of physical beauty. Even a talent for performing conjuring tricks on stage is not absolutely essential, although the headmaster of my prep school had such a talent and we all found it very useful. Fergie seems to me just the person for the job.

A great comfort of the present age is that all our contemporary history, which is stored on computers instead of in documents, will probably have disappeared into a black hole within a few years. Even if they are interested, future generations will never know what we did, so it does not really matter what we do.

## 23rd August, 1993

### Question of numbers

THE NEW diphtheria epidemic in Russia which has led to the cancellation of tours by British holiday firms may seem to add weight to my suggestion that the rest of the world will have to avert its eyes while the former Soviet Union tries to build a free market system on the ruins of a collapsed socialist economy. There is nothing to be gained by pretending we have any role to play in these painful adjustments.

Already the Russian republic shows a negative birthrate, with 200,000 more deaths than births in 1992. Its murder rate is one of the highest in the world, nearly two and a half times the American rate which is itself 10 times our own.

Russia's fall in population is made all the more dramatic by its existing low population density: 22 people per square mile, against 940, for instance, in England. With a certain drift into the towns (where the birth rate is lowest) there are now thought to be 51,000 villages left empty in Russia with many others inhabited by pensioners, mostly old women.

This last phenomenon is not so different from our own countryside, and it makes one wonder if there may not be something useful for us to learn from the Russian experience. If we Britons have a fault, it may be that there are already too many of us for the space available, we are living too long and still having too many children.

A conference of demographers at Trinity College, Cambridge

earlier this month urged that Britain's population should be halved by a judicious mixture of 'public education', better contraception, and tax advantages for small families. It is all nonsense, of course. The sort of people having surplus babies nowadays don't pay tax. A correspondent in Exeter informs me that anyone on DHS/Income Support can claim £1 a day per dog. This explains why so many of London's homeless, New Age Travellers etc, have dogs, she says. If true, I suppose it would be a humane way to tackle the problem if we upped the rates for dogs, reduced them for babies and encouraged single women to have Pekingese instead.

How otherwise can we hope to halve the population? It would be very wicked to spread bubonic plague, as the Japanese hoped to do in America during the war. A despondent letter reaches me from an 80-year-old reader of *Oldie* magazine in Bradford-on-Avon:

'In this country it is possible, by paying for it, to obtain almost any service, from toenail cutting or hair washing to a hip replaced . . . Why, therefore, is it not possible, for a fee, to have oneself "put down" . . . This service would be a benefit to all concerned, and should appeal particularly to a cost-saving government.' Some would have religious objections to this service, but many wouldn't. Another possibility would be to vote Liberal and let the Socialists in. I don't know. What do other people think?

## Republican diversions

ONE of the few advantages of being King or Queen of England, I would have thought, might have been that one would not be persecuted by environmental health officers, building inspectors and the rest. Unfortunately, this is no longer true. Like anyone else trying to set up in business, the Queen has been persecuted by every nuisance on the pubic pay roll. Following a tip off from some members of the public, Buckingham Palace has been declared in breach of Sunday trading laws by council inspectors.

Before that was the firetrap scare. Before that, the Queen was ordered to install a huge number of lavatories to accommodate visitors, and when she did so, the council complained that it had not approved the design of them. Insults will continue to be heaped on the head of our monarch by the unpleasant new breed of Murdoch-fed republicans until we can declare a civil war and kill them all. But perhaps the most pointless of these insults is to require the Queen to open the doors of her home at Balmoral to Paul Keating, the uncouth Irishman who hopes to lead Australia into some hellish Japanese future.

Keating does not fish, shot, ride or play golf. What on earth does he think he is doing as a guest in a private country house? Presumably he will spend much of his time in the lavatory, or 'dunny'. Visitors to Australia have to be sprayed with chemicals before they are allowed to set foot on Australian soil. I hope they keep him well disinfected during his stay here, but must the Queen have the entire castle replumbed to accommodate this man's horrible habits?

## *25th August, 1993*

### Backbench noises

'WE SHOULD make life as uncomfortable as possible in jail,' said the Conservative MP for Luton North, Mr John Carlisle, when asked to comment on rumours that Mr Howard, the Home Secretary, was planning to make our prisons even nastier than they already are. 'Prison is supposed to be a punishment – not Butlin's.'

No doubt a hearty cheer went up from all those places where readers of the *Sun* newspaper meet when they are not themselves in prison. 'At last we have a Home Secretary who knows whose side he's on. OURS,' gloated the *Sun* on Monday.

It is not that the British working class is exceptionally cruel or sadistic by nature. In fact, I think it is rather kind when compared to the working class of other nations. It is just that, in certain places and at certain times, the sadists in any group seem to get the upper hand and make the loudest noise. After 23 years of Rupert Murdoch's disgusting newspapers, it is not surprising if the occasional backbench MP becomes confused.

A Home Secretary is a different matter. He is actually responsible for what happens. The *Sun* seems to hope he will deliberately make prison food nastier. 'Gourmet meals will be a thing of the past,' it claims.

If Mr Howard listens to these unpleasant, alien voices posing as the voice of the working class, he will find himself consigned to the instant oblivion which awaits all politicians who think they can appeal over the heads of decent, educated, humane, middle-class Britain to the brutish masses beyond.

As I say, the brutish masses are not really there. They have no presence, only a voice.

# 28th August, 1993

## Lesson from Rothbury

COUNTRY dwellers would not mind the withdrawal of policing from the countryside nearly so much it if were not also deliberate police policy to leave households unarmed and defenceless against criminals.

The small town of Rothbury, in Northumberland, which was terrorised for the best part of three hours this week by five ruffians armed with crowbars, may feel annoyed that its police station is open only from nine to five on weekdays. This would not matter if lawbreakers were like the rest of us, but criminals are so disrespectful of British habits that they are prepared to commit their burglaries out of office hours and without charging overtime.

The villains spent two hours removing a post office safe while residents watched in terror. In America, of course, there would have been a short fusillade and all five thieves would be riddled with bullets as every window in town bristled with sophisticated automatic weapons, not to mention the occasional bazooka.

We do not wish to be too slavish in our imitation of this fine American culture, but it would be foolish to suppose we have nothing to learn from it. As we get poorer and less able to pay the huge demands of a police force which appears to have the country over a gun barrel, the least the Government can do is allow us to defend ourselves.

## We thought of it first

I WAS touched by the story of two 12-year-old boys from the republican Ardoyne district of Belfast who were sent by an American charity for a holiday in New England to escape from the violence in Ulster. Unfortunately a gunman broke into the house where they were staying and shot their American host dead by his swimming pool.

President and Mrs Clinton have proposed a crackdown on violent crime. They were probably moved to action by the shooting of second abortionist – this time in Kansas, and only in the legs – making it the second gun attack on an abortionist in six months. In March, it will be remembered, an abortionist poignantly called Dr Gunn was gunned down in Florida, very nearly causing the Clintons to declare a state of national emergency, and suspend all rights of free assembly.

If only two abortionists have been shot in the past six months, it must be the safest occupation in the United States. I wonder how many accountants, pharmacists and clerical outfitters have bitten the dust in the same period. But now the Clintons are so worried about violent crime that they are considering the creation of 50 new capital offences, as well as reducing the right of appeal on the grounds that Americans have abused this right in the past. I wonder what these offences will be. Obviously disparaging references to anybody's colour, class, creed, physical appearance, gender, sexual orientation or other deformities will be on the list, and quite rightly so. More controversially, they make make it a capital offence to sneeze or make any other loud noise within half a mile of an abortion clinic. But what we all really want to know is whether they will seize the bull by the horns and make it a capital offence to be caught smoking – as it already is in Manchester's Wythenshawe Hospital, and elsewhere in our pioneering National Health Service.

If the Clintons decide to start executing smokers, it will be sad for those of us who still have friends over there. On the other hand, it will do something for our national self-respect that at least, on this occasion, we thought of it first.

## Why save them?

NOTHING but boredom can result from trying to join the current Tory debate about whether to raise taxes or not as a way of reducing the Government's grotesque over-spending. It may seem obvious that raising taxes will do nothing but encourage over-spending, but if we mention this truth, we will be aligning ourselves with some of the most unattractive people in the country, whose only real interest in supporting the Conservative Party is to torture people in prison.

I told Kenneth Clarke's nice Italian predecessor exactly what he should do if he wanted to save the economy. Unfortunately, he lost his job before he could implement my proposals. Now I have forgotten what they were.

The latest smart thing to say is that the Government has no choice but to raise taxes. All those redundant Customs officers, environmental health officers, council building inspectors, social workers, overpaid and idle policemen, all those tons and tons of unnecessary and harmful drugs handed out by the Health service, one in three public employees, all that idiotic subsidy to farmers and wind farmers and 'poets' must be kept going because it does us good, spiritually, to pay high taxes.

My only contribution to the debate is that if the Government decides to raise taxes instead of sacking public employees and closing down most of the bodies set up to annoy, regulate and ruin Conservative voters, the only possible reason left for voting Conservative is on the hunting issue.

Since, like the majority of traditional Conservative voters, I do not myself hunt, this seems rather a tall order, particularly as there is no Conservative policy on hunting, and a small but growing number of 'Tory' stinkers seems prepared to throw in its lot with the socialists to ban hunting.

If only nice Mr Major would accept Gerald Kaufman's advice and promise to do absolutely nothing ever again.

## *30th August, 1993*

### Caring times

WHEREVER we look we see evidence of the Government's frantic search for new ways to spend taxpayers' and ratepayers' money – most of them, of course, very praiseworthy. West Sussex health authority is advertising the new, full-time post of 'audit facilitator', whose responsibilities will include being Secretary to the Public Health Medicine Medical Audit Committee and the Regional Communicable Disease Control Audit Committee. Well done, West Sussex!

Hammersmith and Fulham is advertising for a Safer Cities Tennis Development Project Worker, to organise tennis matches between the borough's problem teenagers. 'The main objective is to divert young people at risk of offending away from possible involvement in crime.' Good thinking, Hammersmith and Fulham!

South Wales police must deserve some sort of medal for having spent more than £100,000 investigating the claim of a 33-year-old female hairdresser to have been abducted in Cardiff and sexually assaulted in her car. Helicopters were used to trace the alleged route of the car and five police forces were involved before the young woman confessed it was a hoax. Meanwhile, the Metropolitan force has bought a third helicopter for £1.65 million, designed as an 'eye in the sky' to keep us under surveillance and photograph us in the dark.

A Lewisham reader queries my suggestion that those on income support can claim £1 a day for a dependent dog. If this benefit exists, it should be better known – although, if one judges by the number of New Age Travellers and London 'homeless' with dogs, it would seem to be fairly well known already. My point, as a taxpayer, was that it would be cheaper to encourage single women to keep Pekingese than encourage them to have more babies.

The Humberside council which gave a single mother fertility treatment until she produced sextuplets now has to pay £2,150 a week to keep them – £51.19 per baby per day. This is more expensive than paying £1 a day each for six Pekingese. On the other hand, a correspondent reminds me that Pekingese are very fastidious dogs, and might not be happy in the sort of environment provided by many single mothers. The idea of 'home alone' Pekingese, left to fend for themselves while their owners go away on holiday, is too poignant to contemplate.

## A good riddance

I FEEL a twinge of guilt to learn that the Houses of Parliament have been overrun by a plague of mice in the long summer recess. A thousand traps are being set each day, but the palace's maintenance manager, Mr Coombes, has been quoted as saying he does not think he will ever get rid of them. 'They breed very quickly,' he explains.

So we reckoned when a small company of patriots introduced the mice about four years ago. Our plan was to save the country from Mrs Thatcher, who was preparing to hand over power to the socialists with her disastrous poll tax, as well as proposing a mass of insanely bossy legislation, mostly concerned with health and safety, which would transform a happy, easy-going country into something more like an international hygiene exhibition in Stockholm.

Our plan was to arrange for mice to run across the floor of the

House of Commons between her legs and even up her skirt. If she interrupted Prime Minister's Question Time with a piercing shriek and climbed, trembling, on the Treasury Bench, then the Conservative Party would come to its senses and realise that women prime ministers had their limitations. In the event, our plan was not necessary.

Our latest scheme is to introduce bats into the Palace of Westminster. Since making it a criminal offence to annoy or frighten a bat, let alone to kill it, the House of Commons has seen half the churches of England made unusable by bat infestation. Perhaps when its own benches are covered with bat urine and bat droppings, the Commons will think again about 15 years of irresponsible and interfering legislation. If it doesn't, as we now know, it will be siting on a timebomb. As the methane gas from the bat droppings begins to collect, the MPs' own obstinacy will finish the job begun by Guy Fawkes in 1605.

## Yet another Jerusalem

THERE is a silver lining even to the sad news that the Republic of South Africa is now the most dangerous country in the world, with 40,000 people dying of unnatural causes every year in a population of less than 32.4 million.

A more cheerful way to look at this tragedy is to see that Russia, by comparison, is not so bad. Since my note a week ago, it occurred to me that Russia is the obvious place for the English landowning class to take its skills.

In England, the urban proletariat, encouraged by a weak and unprincipled government, regards the land as its own leisure resource. All that remains to be settled is how it should be divided between the ramblers, the mountain bikers, the motorbike scramblers, the four-wheel drivers, the hunt saboteurs, the bird watchers or the beetle worshippers. Between them they will create a wilderness, but the idea of private property does not come into it, having been as much rejected by the modern, urban mind as it was by the deeply gifted Aborigines who roamed Australia for 50,000 years.

In Russia, land is plentiful and cheap. Labour may be a bit of a problem, but between the knout and a bottle of vodka it should be possible to train up some reasonable gamekeepers. Everybody has firearms, but there is no reason to suppose that the Russians are much good at using them. I see a new England arising up on the steppes, while the world averts its eyes from what has been left behind.

# 1st September, 1993

## Why they hate us

PEOPLE in this country who would tend to be worried by reports of a new wave of hatred for Britain among America's chattering classes should comfort themselves that it is all in a good cause. The *Sunday Times* attributes this new hatred to jealousy over what little remains of our beautiful class system, once the envy and wonder of the world. But the *Sunday Times* would obviously make this foolish point, being obsessed with class and owned by a former Australian with a gigantic chip on his shoulder.

The real reason for this hatred is that America is fast disappearing down a philosophical plughole and cannot bear to be confronted by a more stable society in a more decorous and leisurely decline.

The immediate cause of the friction appears to be a disagreement over the civil war in Bosnia. Americans, impatient to see justice prevail, are quite prepared to throw huge amounts of American food at the problem, and even high explosives, from a safe distance, but they feel that Europeans in general and British troops in particular should be in there on the ground, fighting in the civil war for the Bosnian Muslims against the Bosnian Serbs and the Bosnian Croats, or possibly for the Bosnian Croats against the Bosnian Serbs.

Serious damage has been done to the Anglo-American partnership by Britain's reluctance to provide American television-watchers with the action they crave. Never mind. We must comfort ourselves that the American demand is based on a degree of military, historical and geographical ignorance which is, in itself, rather beautiful, too.

## A long spoon

THE MORE I see of Michael Howard, the Home Secretary, the more I feel he will be the man who loses the next election for the Conservatives and hands the country over to the swarm of dangerous socialist insects hiding under Mr Smith's shirt tails.

What was Mr Howard doing in the Banqueting House on Wednesday night, listening to Rupert Murdoch, when he should have been cleaning up the police? Why does he waste time telling the *Sun* about his proposed 'crackdown on rapists' and all the disgusting things he hopes to do to sex offenders when he catches them? He should have been telling the police to fight criminals, instead of organising themselves to rob the taxpayer and harass respectable private citizens.

The great overtime scandal, whereby constables in Manchester have to receive special counselling when their incomes drop below £50,000, should not be seen as an example of slack management but of officially condoned blackmail. To this must be added the withdrawal of policing from most country areas, police refusal to prosecute for even quite serious crimes, because they cannot organise the paperwork efficiently and the abominable harassment of sober citizens like Mr Henry Porter, former Editor of the *Illustrated London News*.

It will be for what the Government has failed to do about the police that it will be blamed. But I think Mr Howard would be foolish to ignore another element in our disillusionment. This is disgust at the vulgarity of a political leader prepared to make 'tougher punishment' noises for the benefit of the gutter press when we all know he cannot do anything about it. Any Conservative who wishes to dine with Mr Murdoch needs a very long spoon.

## Breathtaking

BRITISH Rail confirms what I have often suspected – that it has the nastiest management in the country, as well as the stupidest – with its new proposal to breathalyse typists and ticket clerks in case they might have had a glass of wine at luncheon. It was accepted by the Transport Salaried Staffs Association who advised staff to 'leave a gap of eight hours before your last drink and going to work'.

To think that the English have come to this . . . In my own profession, a similarly disgusting American-style practice was introduced in Wapping, with the tragic results we all see. I imagine that such treatment of employees – which is as shortsighted as it is inhumane – results from putting corporals in charge. Not many people can now remember when *The Times* was an interesting and enjoyable newspaper, part of the intelligent life of this country. Now it is reduced to printing page after page of the 'global vision' ravings of its debt-ridden chairman:

'We are on the edge of a new technological revolution. It is confusing, frightening and breathtakingly exciting . . . Time does actually fly . . . Five of the world's biggest industries . . . are converging into one dynamic whole . . . with a reach of more than two-thirds of the entire planet. But if it has enormous potential, it also carries with it enormous responsibilities . . . With our partners, we will aim to create and cover global events, such as the search for the world's best young opera singer.'

It is sometimes difficult to believe, with other Wapping newspapers, that they are produced by human beings, or intended for human consumption. I was interested to learn that *Sun* readers voted 16-1 that there was nothing wrong with Michael Jackson. Although I am not a doctor, I would say there is obviously much that is wrong with him.

If my opinion is asked, I will suggest that it might be something

to do with diet. I believe he drinks vast quantities of Pepsi-Cola. That is exactly the sort of thing which Mr Murdoch, with his global vision, wants us all to do, in order to create a classless, nationless world. Nobody can say we have not been warned.

# *6th September, 1993*

---

## Kiss of death

SOME will be dismayed that the Arts Council has started paying out money to jobless disc jockeys on the 'rave' scene, as well as to graffiti artists and 'alternative' publications with amusing names like Skunk Comix of Sheffield.

'I was shocked at first that the Arts Council were offering us money to do our thing,' explained Mr Iain Oliver, 25, the Salisbury disc jockey. 'They sent out these really well-worded forms which said something like "Do you want £2,000 for nothing?" and we thought, yeah, we want £2,000 for nothing . . . it's brilliant.'

Let Ruth Jones, project co-ordinator of the Arts Council, explain: 'These are the art forms of the future . . . Who are we to judge what is good and what is bad? The important thing is that there are young people who are doing things.'

I feel that Mr Oliver's first reaction was the right one. For the Arts Council to have heard of anything means that it is about 10 years out of date. For the Arts Council to offer money means that it, the recipient, is moribund or dead, has lost all creative vitality and is reduced to a tired repetition of attitudes once thought daring.

It is wonderful to learn that the graffiti, the comix and the 'rave' music are all now things of the past to be preserved at public expense in the great mausoleum of Modern Studies. When Ruth Jones comes round offering money to the Way of the World column (who are we to judge what is good or bad?) I will know it is time to swim out to sea.

## No recriminations

THE EPISTLE appointed to be read in Anglican churches last Sunday, the 13th after Trinity, taken from Galatians 3: 16-22, is completely incomprehensible in the Authorised Version: 'Now to Abraham and his seed were the promises made. He saith not, and to seeds, as of many, but as of one, and to thy seed, which is Christ. And this I say that the covenant that was confirmed before of God in Christ, the law which was four hundred and thirty years after, cannot disannul, that it should make the promise of none effect . . . '

Subsequent translations (most notably the Revised Standard Version of 1973, the 'Common Bible') strive to explain what these words mean, but so far as most people are concerned, they must be meaningless. Anglicans listen reverently, deferring to the beauty of the language, but without much idea of what it is all about.

Preservation of the English language is one of the noblest causes of our age, never nobler than in the struggle to keep the old Prayer Book. It is only when we are confronted by the present church leadership that doubts begin to creep in. Might not our efforts be better directed towards supporting the Prince of Wales's campaign to teach Shakespeare in the schools, or towards saving the *Literary Review*, whose magnificent £5,000 prize for Proper Poetry (sponsored by the *Mail on Sunday*) will be presented by Clive Anderson today?

Many Britons were proud when a senior Anglican clergyman announced there need be nothing wrong with sex outside marriage, and another that he does not believe in God. But what are we to make of an Archbishop of Canterbury who, commenting on £800 million missing from the safe, said that the Church 'is not in the business of recriminations'?

Dr George Carey plans a goodwill visit to Sudan in January. An Anglican bishop out there has just received a judicial flogging for the alleged crime of adultery. Is this the time for him to announce he is not in the business of recriminations? Muslim fundamentalists cannot, apparently, accept what we all know, that there need be nothing wrong with adultery provided it is part of an ongoing or meaningful relationship. Their leaders will scarcely wish to meet a fellow clergyman who cannot even recriminate.

Instead of making goodwill visits, Dr Carey should declare a new crusade to sack Khartoum as our ancestors in the Fourth Crusade once sacked Constantinople. For Englishmen with a memory, there will be the further satisfaction of avenging once again the murder of General Gordon by the fuzzy-wuzzies in 1885.

## National emergency

ON JULY 15 of this year a distinguished journalist who happens to be a friend of mine had a severe attack of dizziness as he was crossing the road after a working lunch with a colleague. It was the first sign that he was suffering from what his friends subsequently diagnosed as BSE, or 'mad cow disease', now claiming an ever growing number of victims.

When my friend listed the symptoms of BSE – tiredness, excitability, memory impairment, headaches, diarrhoea, distorted vision – I immediately recognised them as precisely the symptoms reported by the many victims of Hamburger Gas (HG) poisoning who have written to me since I first reported damage to ancient buildings in the centre of Rome. It was caused by the gaseous emissions of a new hamburger bar on the Spanish Steps.

Evidence is now flooding in that the ramifications of the HG disaster may extend much farther than previously imagined. It may be responsible not only for BSE but also ME (the 'yuppies' disease'), DTs and certain forms of bovine TB.

It may also be causing damage not only to those who frequent hamburger bars but among ever increasing numbers in the population at large. I am receiving alarming evidence of just how easily this can happen. Lactating cows are treated to hamburgers, so HGs may get into milk. Kangaroos and reindeer are easily drawn into the dangerously attractive world of hamburger bars. We may have a total ecological catastrophe on our hands.

I have hitherto written about this disaster as if it was primarily a matter for the Minister of Food, Mr Nicholas Soames, to resolve. It now seems clear that the scale is potentially so enormous that it can be properly addressed only from the very top.

## Last chance

IT IS hard to know how much credence to attach to anything one reads in the *Sunday Times*, with its inexplicable admiration for

Mr Howard. But an item tucked away in a corner under the heading 'Cautions to be tougher' this Sunday must need expanding:

'Michael Howard, the Home Secretary, is to announce new measures to toughen up cautioning, widely used by police as an alternative to prosecution. Offenders will not just be given a ticking off by a senior policeman, but could also be forced to carry out community service and pay damages.

'The scheme, called Cautioning Plus, will introduce a punishment regime to be decided by committees of social workers, probation officers, teachers, youth workers and the police.'

If I read this correctly, police will be able to turn suspects over to the committees for sentencing without the trouble of prosecuting them, let alone securing a conviction. This will save an enormous amount of police time, freeing officers for vital birdwatching and other environmental activities.

## 13th September, 1993

### Under-represented

PLYMOUTH and Torbay Health Authority is looking for Outreach workers for its Sea, Sand and Safe Sex project. If you feel you have 'a mature and non-judgmental outlook and any appropriate counselling skills' you may be hired as a male Outreach worker to work alongside the Gay and Bisexual Community, but the pay is only £9,985-£12,149 a year for a 25-hour week.

Nottingham, by contrast, is offering £22,596-£23,169 for an 18-hour week as Service Manager in Play Development: 'An exciting opportunity has arisen within the Department for a dynamic and creative person to join and develop the rapidly expanding play section. We are looking for someone with:

• A broad visionary approach to the development of children's play.

• A commitment to equality of opportunity in service delivery . . .

'Applications are particularly welcome from women, Asians, Africo-Caribbeans and disabled people, as they are currently under-represented among our employees.'

There is no suggestion that applications are particularly welcome from women, disabled people etc suffering from body odour and bad breath. Researchers at St Mary's Hospital Medical School have established that it is an inherited gene which causes people to stink of rotting fish. As a study in the *British Medical Journal* points out, sufferers from this faulty gene find their social and career prospects unfairly blighted.

This may be the most important discovery of our age. That intelligence depends on genes and is therefore to a large extent inherited is easy to accept. I have often suspected that other qualities are also inherited – benevolence of outlook and amiability of temperament, as well as malignity, sourness of nature and self-pity.

Shakespeare may have spotted this when he described Caliban as having 'a very ancient, fish-like smell'. If we met Caliban today we would not denounce him as a moon-calf, a monster, a deboshed fish. So long as he had a broad, visionary approach to the development of children's play, I hope we would offer him the post of Service Manager in Play Development in the city of Nottingham.

## Not to be trusted

THERE is a terrible sermon for our times in the story of the religious education master in a Bristol secondary school who was always cadging sweets from his pupils.

To teach the scrounger a lesson, they arranged for a 16-year-old girl to give him a fruit pastille spiked with LSD. The bearded, 46-year-old teacher began hallucinating, dropping books, clinging to walls and asking for help. He was taken to hospital and made to eat charcoal, which is apparently the best cure for LSD poisoning.

With the huge amounts of pocket money they are given nowadays, school-children can easily afford to keep their teachers in fruit pastilles if they wish, but that is not the point. They can also afford to poison them. In modern Britain, middle-aged men must learn not to accept sweets from schoolgirls. It is as simple as that.

# 15th September, 1993

## *Dulce et decorum*

EVERY time a building by Sir Basil Spence is taken down, my heart lifts up. Many of us, I imagine, if we had been in Glasgow on Sunday for the demolition of Spence's two hideous 28-year-old tower blocks in the Gorbals, would have rushed round in fancy dress to witness the historic event, blowing paper trumpets and dancing in the streets.

Mrs Helen Tinney, 61, who was among the 10,000 people who turned up to see Queen Elizabeth Square demolished, died when thousands of tons of dust and debris crashed among spectators. Obviously, her death was a tragic accident but she should be seen as a martyr in the struggle for a cleaner, prettier Britain.

The flats – opened by the Queen in 1965 – were so riddled with damp and other forms of rot within 25 years that they were judged unfit for human habitation. Now, no doubt, people will wish to put up some equally hideous, equally uninhabitable modern buildings in their place, using the same concrete and plate glass materials.

If they do, I feel the citizens of Glasgow should organise themselves into a Modern Architecture Retribution Squad in Mrs Tinney's memory, scrawling rude messages on every post-war building that is ugly or graceless or built in concrete or uses metal-frame windows.

Where Basil Spence's buildings are concerned, 28 years is far too long. In London, we continue to be mocked by Knightsbridge Barracks, destroying the prospect of Hyde Park from every direction. In Coventry, God and Man are mocked by Spence's monstrous cathedral, proposed as an anti-religious joke in 1951.

*His jest will savour of but shallow wit*
*When thousands weep, more than did laugh at it.*

The problem with these concrete monstrosities is that, however much they rot and stink, they are almost impossible to knock down. Many will die in the attempt. The worst of all his eyesores is the British Embassy in Rome. Just as we must be prepared to die in the struggle, so must the Romans. It is hard to think of a nobler cause or one more likely to unite our two countries.

# Knock on the door

IT TOOK the inquest on a boy killed sabotaging the Cambridgeshire Foxhounds last May to reveal who exactly these young people are who rush around trying to stop country folk from engaging in the traditional sports of the countryside.

In the West Country, it is widely thought they are students from modern universities, paid by the day from the huge funds available; however, at the Huntingdon inquest, it transpired that most were teenagers rounded up by an activist from a Milton Keynes home for children with behavioural difficulties.

The boy's death (he was run over by a horse box) has been taken as a signal to revive the Hunt Retribution Squad, with its assassination list which includes members of the Royal Family, Lord Whitelaw, Jane Seymour and Jimmy Hill – all of them suspected of incorrect views on the hunting issue.

So far, the saboteurs' greatest coup was to fail to dig up the old Duke of Beaufort's body 10 months after his death, but, now they have started putting incendiary bombs in publishers' offices, I fear they will do themselves no end of harm. The list of saboteurs burned and blown up will grow so long that everybody will forget about the foxes and other fauna they were supposed to be liberating.

If I were a child with behavioural difficulties, a Somerset Liberal or anyone in what we might call the 'at risk' group, I would live in terror of the knock on the door telling me my presence was required in a retribution squad.

## 20th September, 1993

## Help needed

IF I HAD a vote on Thursday to choose a site for the millennial Olympics, I do not think I would cast it for Manchester, rather than for Istanbul, Berlin, Sydney or Peking. An Olympic City outside Manchester would only create another blot on the landscape. Britain attracted 18.5 million tourists last year, and the figure seems quite big enough.

No country really wants tourists, despite the money they bring. The Turks have an unusual way of discouraging them, according to complaints received by the tour firm Cosmos. They hold ritual circumcisions of up to 18 Muslim boys in hotel dining rooms at dinner time. 'It turned my stomach,' said Maria Weedon, 44, of Wickford, Essex, while Philip Battye, of Huddersfield, said: 'I couldn't eat in the restaurant for the rest of my holiday.'

German tourists are made so unwelcome wherever they go that last year 300,000 complaints were received by German tourist agencies, and about 30,000 travellers sued them. I have no doubt that the rumoured Nazi revival in Germany is really against the idea of a Berlin Olympics. It also crosses my mind that the massacre of Tiananmen Square might have been intended to discourage foreign tourists from China in general, and the Peking Olympics in particular.

Sydney might be the best place – and not just because it is the site furthest away from England. My real reason is that Australians are rather isolated from the rest of the world, and I think it would do them good to study some foreigners before deciding to cut themselves off from their British roots in the year 2001.

Intelligent Australians who insist that the time has come for Australia to stand on her own feet are not showing their maturity. They are behaving like adolescent girls who plaster their faces with make-up to prove they are grown-up. What many Australians share with Britons is a highly developed sense of the absurd. Mr Keating, by contrast seems not to have the faintest trace of one.

## *22nd September, 1993*

### Keep asking

WHEN Mr Major flies to Monte Carlo tomorrow to beg the International Olympic Committee to choose Manchester as the site for its boring and unpleasant activities in the year 2000, I hope he also puts in a plea for the categories of competition to be extended so as to give Britain a fairer chance.

It is painfully obvious that Britons are not much good at anything which requires greater strength, such as lifting weights or putting shot; or great agility – tennis, skiing, gymnastics; or even great intelligence, such as chess. But in one field, we are supreme, and that is in the art of whingeing.

No other country in the industrialised world could have

extracted four jumbo-loads of free vegetables for its old age pensioners from the poor peasant farmers of the Punjab. When the Punjabis heard the terrible noises coming out of Stockport, they even paid for transport.

As I write, Mr Major is asking the new Japanese government in Tokyo whether it will pay some more money to all the elderly Britons who were mistreated by the Japanese 48 years ago. Nice Mr Hosokawa, who was seven years old at the time, has said he will apologise to Mr Major, who was two years old, but he doesn't really see why he should pay any more money.

That was before he confronted a nation of grievance bearers in full whinge. 'What is an apology unless you back it up with something?' demands Mr Martyn Day, lawyer to the Japanese Labour Camps Survivors' Association, which threatens to sue.

When I read of the Prime Minister's trip, I imagined that his brilliantly successful press office, Mr Gus O'Donnell, had fixed it all in advance, and we would welcome Mr Major back, laden with Japanese gold, as a Wizard of Oz. Now I'm not so sure.

Let us hope at least that when he turns up at Monte Carlo tomorrow Mr O'Donnell will have arranged for the International Olympic Committee to institute a special Gold Medal which will be awarded to Britain every year until further notice. The citation will read that it has been won by the country which showed the most outstanding pluck in asking for things.

## Squeak, squeak

IN LAST Friday's *Sun* I read that 'passionate Jane Nottage told last night how she reached "new peaks of ecstasy" making love with soccer boss Andy Roxburgh'.

This was the main news of the day for *Sun* readers: 'The love affair will stun the football world and shatter 50-year-old Roxburgh's squeaky-clean image as a caring family man. The father of one has been married to Catherine for 27 years and was awarded an OBE for services to soccer . . . '

Oddly enough I had not heard of Andy Roxburgh. In fact the only Roxburgh who sprang to mind was J. F. Roxburgh (1888-1954), founding headmaster of Stowe, although I'm not sure I would describe his image as 'squeaky clean'.

If we ask ourselves what possible motive the *Sun* might have to destroy the marriage of this humbler Roxburgh, humiliate his wife Catherine, and upset his only child, we might find the answer in a leader which appeared in Monday's edition of the *Sun*'s sister-page *The Times*, also published in Wapping.

*The Times* chose to publicise the claim of an American academic that Benjamin Disraeli had two illegitimate children by two different mothers. It was 'the latest sexual scandal to rock the political boat' it said, explaining that the Victorians 'kept their gossip private for men of the ruling class in clubs and smoking rooms . . . the difference today is that the media have shone the floodlights into the smoking rooms. So democracy gains what hypocrisy loses.'

I cannot imagine that the clubs and smoking rooms of the ruling class would have been much interested in the private affairs of Mr Andy Roxburgh, or the degree of satisfaction recorded by his former girlfriend, Jane Nottage. The *Sun*'s spiteful behaviour towards one of its own kind is typical of the sort of hell the working classes create for themselves when they are given a free rein. Hypocrisy gains what any sense of decency or decorum has lost.

# Dear Paul

FOR the second year running we are solemnly assured by a magazine called *Business Age* that Mr Paul Raymond, the Soho landlord and club-owner, is the richest man in Britain. I refuse to believe it.

If I had thought there was any truth in this rumour I would long ago have written to him inviting him to take a friendly interest in another Soho enterprise, *Literary Review*, which adds distinction and respectability to the whole area. But Mr Raymond is not even in *Who's Who*. I would scarcely expect him to answer a letter addressed to Raymond's Revue Bar in Walker's Court.

Either there is a conspiracy by the toffee-nosed establishment to keep this admirably rich man out of the society of his peers, or there is a conspiracy among tin-pot moralists to convince us we live in a sex-mad society. I do not believe that there is all that much money to be made from charging middle-aged gentlemen to watch ladies take off their clothes, although I have often wondered whether there might not be money to be made charging middle-class housewives for taking their clothes off in front of a hired audience of middle-aged men. Many women, I believe, suffer from frustrated exhibitionist urges.

Be that as it may, we often publish what we call life studies in *Literary Review* to illustrate learned articles. The older readers seem to like them.

I'm sure Mr Raymond could be helpful providing models, and would gain further respectability by the association. If he is half as rich as *Business Age* claims, he really should be a duke. Perhaps, if he reads *The Daily Telegraph*, he would like to get in touch.

## 29th September, 1993

### Show a leg

ONE might not suppose that the name Brian Mawhinney would go down in English history, but this little-known minister in the Health Department, who has previously been able to draw attention to himself only by fatuous and alarmist comments on smoking, threatens to inflict a grievous harm on us all.

Whether responding to lesbian activists in the nursing profession, or because he is himself married to an American nurse, Mawhinney has thrown himself behind the campaign to put nurses in trousers and sloppy jerseys instead of the delightful uniforms which have raised the morale of sick nd dying Britons for as long as anyone can remember.

The justification is that back-strain injuries – not infrequent among nurses required to lift patients – are more likely when a nurse is anxious to avoid exposing a thigh. There might have been some truth in this 30 years ago, when they wore black stockings, but nowadays, when they all wear tights, it is an absurdity.

No doubt many young nurses would prefer to slop around in casual clothes if they could get away with it. The minister's job is to keep up standards. What sort of deathbed can any of us look forward to, surrounded by these horrible American-style nurses in trouser suits? I think I shall start a campaign in *Oldie* magazine urging elderly male patients to empty their bed-pans over this obnoxious politician if ever he dares show his face in their wards.

## Sarnies before statues

MODERN Britain does not want Canova's *The Three Graces* to remain here. When the sixth Duke of Bedford brought this delightful group of nudes from Rome in 1819, it stood for over 160 years in a temple at Woburn, a monument ot the social system which once made Britain rich as well as powerful, civilised as well as rich.

Ever since 1985, when the Duke's descendant, Lord Tavistock, took it out of its temple at Woburn and sold it, the statue has lain in a packing case, awaiting a government export licence. When an appeal was launched, it raised less than atwentieth of the sum needed.

Modern Britain does not wish to be reminded of its aristocratic past, any more than African countries wish to be reminded of their former colonial status. In the New World Order, we send our treasures to the J. Paul Getty Museum in California, and California sends us its beads.

It is from California that Mr Murdoch manages to keep us happy. Yesterday he decided to give a "FREE Coronation chicken sarnie" to anyone in Britain who would buy his disgusting newspaper, the *Sun*. Many Britons must have been puzzled by this offer, but I have noticed how the *Sun* tends to believe that "sarnie" is lower-class slang for a sandwich. Perhaps Murdoch told them this was the case.

He may be right about sarnies, but I have never heard the xpression, and doubt whether many people in Somerset have any idea what it means. Coronation chicken refers to a particularly horrible kind of filling. Anybody who ate one of these sandwiches may be in considerable pain today. I hope the Prime Minister and the Archbishop of Canterbury are all right. It would be terrible if we lost them, too.

## Youth tax

IT IS all very well us telling Mr Clarke to close down the National Health Service, sack the police and kill all the lawyers, but we don't have to sit through the consultation procedures required before anything can be done in this country.

Perhaps he will have to think of some new taxes, after all,

against the £50 billion deficit he has inherited. As a newspaper man, I am bound to see the proposed Value Added Tax on newspapers and magazines as a form of genocide. Any tax on information is calculated to keep the masses in ignorance, in servitude. No British citizen should be taxed on essential information about which footballer's ex-wife is denouncing her former husband as a lousy lover.

I wonder if Mr Clarke has ever seriously considered my suggestion of a nipple tax. If a weekday newspaper selling four million copies chose to print two nipples a day at a penny a nipple, this would bring in £80,000 six days a week or £24,960,000 a year – from one newspaper. Multiply this by all the papers which print nipples, add the Sundays and the magazines (perhaps 2p a nipple for colour) and you have a nice little earner.

The outcry would be deafening ('Tax on Beauty!') but many men and most women would be grateful to see fewer nipples around. If Mr Clarke funks that, he must face up to the children's clothing tax. In the global warming perspective, children do not need clothes any more. They are a bourgeois luxury. Any parent who is so snobbish or so cruel as to buy children's clothes must expect to pay tax. Above all, there is no need for schoolchildren to wear clothes in class, since state schools are always heated to the temperature of a Turkish bath.

## Work makes healthy

I WONDER if it is this rash of nipples throughout the media which explains the extraordinary rudeness to women – especially prettier, younger women – which is such a feature of the New Britain. When nurses complain of the revolting manners and insulting remarks of some male patients, I tend to believe them.

Perhaps the right response is to withdraw medical services (and presumably let them die, or at any rate suffer pain) as proposed by the Swindon Health Authority. However, this does not seem the ideal arrangement. We should reflect on the undoubted presence of a man-hating, lesbian faction within that angelic host (although I am quite prepared to believe that many of the nurses agitating for trouser suits suffer from no worse a problem than bad legs).

To give nursing staff the right of summary execution without trial (where any male patient is suspected of a mildly flirtatious manner), would be an unwelcome extension of the right claimed by surgeons and general practitioners, to deny medical services to anyone who smokes. There is enough health fascism in the system already. The South Glamorgan council which sacked two foster parents because they were too fat ('There is no way I can approve the couple until they have reduced their weight') is only the tip of an iceberg. The real chill comes when we hear Mrs Bottomley, the Health Secretary, solemnly assuring the Confederation of British Industry that British industry pays £1 billion a year for drinkers.

These senseless and deliberately misleading statistics have been cooked up by the departments of Health and Transport for as long as most of us can remember. Their purpose is to increase the departments' available resources for repression. Against them all is the perceivable fact that Japanese workers, the most efficient in the world, drink twice as much as we do. The difference is that they do not have Mrs Bottomley breathing down their necks, pressing sick notes on them whenever they don't want to go to work.

## *4th October, 1993*

### The true embodiment

AN ENGLISHMAN asks a Scotswoman out to drink champagne and whisky and dance reels on St Andrew's Night in London. She asks him back to her bedroom, shows him a sofa, undresses in front of him and goes to bed. He then tries to climb into bed with her, desisting after six seconds by the Englishman's account, between 10 and 15 seconds by the Scotswoman's. After the Englishman has desisted and gone to sleep on the floor, the Scotswoman has hysterics and calls the police.

Found guilty of 'attempted rape' by an Old Bailey jury in front of a Welsh judge, the Englishman is then summoned to Swansea to be sentenced. The judge says he had no doubt the Scotswoman suffered 'a terrifying and degrading ordeal' within that 15-second period. Despite having received abject pleas for mercy from the terrified Englishman, he sentences him to three years in prison.

Perhaps this story illustrates no more than a difference between the three cultures of England, Wales and Scotland. There must be few Englishwomen who have not had a similar experience, at one time or another, and few Englishmen who have not suffered a similar embarrassment through a misreading of signals. They do not normally expect such misunderstandings to end in a three-year prison sentence. One reason for the severe sentence may be a new judicial guideline that no distinction is to be made between 'attempted rape', such as this bungled session, and real rape.

Nobody needs feel surprised that the law passes into greater and greater disrepute when burglars, muggers and car thieves are not charged, let alone convicted or, if convicted, sent to prison, and few country dwellers dare go out to lunch with their neighbours for fear of the Police Terror. But as the law falls into ever greater disrepute, lawyers become more and more determined to protect their privileges, their restrictive practices, their wigs and other paraphernalia which make them the laughing stock of Europe.

I have no desire to be dragged, trembling, before some Irish clown in Belfast and sentenced to life imprisonment for impugning the dignity of a judge, so I shall refrain from suggesting that this sentence is monstrous. I shall confine myself to observing that all these clumsy, hysterical and sadistic interactions took place between lawyers. It is only when they start turning their attentions on the rest of us that the time will have come to take action.

## Spare this poor man

A WONDERFULLY horrible picture in Saturday's newspaper seemed to show the Princess Royal being kissed on the lips by John Prescott, Labour spokesman on Transport. A headline beside the large colour photograph read: 'Fairytale ending – but will kiss turn princess into a frog?'

In a terrible sort of way, this metamorphosis seemed to be happening before our very eyes. I have nothing against Mr Prescott, who once put in some useful work as a steward on a passenger ship. What worried me was the suspicion of having read somewhere that one of the three offences which still carry the death penalty is the crime of kissing the Princess Royal. To turn the Princess Royal into a frog must surely merit the

traditional penalty for High Treason of being hanged, drawn and quartered.

It was only after studying the text that we learnt the woman in the photograph was not Princess Anne but Margaret Beckett, visually challenged Deputy Leader of the Labour Party. Even so, one cannot help wondering whether he had asked permission to kiss her, and if so, if he had specified that he wished to kiss her on the lips.

This is the new code being enforced on American students in Ohio. Although none of these brave new ideas is yet incorporated in the laws of England, it requires only a judicial guideline or two and we can send for Judge David Williams QC to come up from Swansea: John Prescott could easily find himself sentenced to surgical castration, in the exciting new spirit of the times. I would be sorry to see this happen to poor John Prescott. He once did a useful job as steward on an ocean liner.

## Support the fatties

A TAILOR once described me as possessing the fuller figure, so I suppose I should welcome the latest proposals from Harvard University to combat discrimination against the fat.

According to three eminent academics, Dr Dietz, Dr Dortmaker and Dr Stunkard, discrimination against the overweight is rampant. They have coined the inelegant expression 'fatism' to describe prejudice against those who are quantitively challenged, pointing out that fat women, in particular, are only half as likely to get married.

'They are freely discriminated against,' says Dr Dietz. 'These data indicate that obesity may be an important determinent of economic status,' says Dr Dortmaker. 'One of the last acceptable forms of prejudice is that against these persons,' says Dr Stunkard.

The obvious solution is to pass a law against such discrimination. In the checklist culture of Ohio, for instance, would-be lovers should be required to ask each other not only if they are prepared to advance a step in the direction of sexual intercourse, but if not, why not. If the reason is that they find their would-be partner too fat, they must be subject to the same disciplinary sanctions as the date-rapist. Without some such ordinance, the fate of the quantitively challenged female teenager in the United States – and there are many of them – is too sad to contemplate.

## 6th October, 1993

## Hunt the muntjak

IT IS bad news that Leicestershire should join the roll of dishonour – it already includes Hampshire, Hereford and Worcester, West Sussex and Somerset – of counties which have allowed themselves to be taken over by anti-hunting fanatics, but I do not think we need despair.

The problem which these wretched counties are now beginning to appreciate is that enthusiasm for banning the hunt is not sufficient qualification for running a county. Local government will be in an appalling mess for as long as it continues to attract this sort of person.

The solution is to pass a simple law requiring local authorities to sell all their tenanted land, which they have no business to own in the first place, and spend the money on better prisons, hospitals, schools, mayoral limousines, etc.

But the main thing is to popularise hunting and spread its appeal. On Saturday a one-day conference organised by the Forestry Commission in conjunction with the British Deer Society will be held in Cambridge to discuss the new menace of the muntjak. These repulsive little animals, which come from South China, are deer only in name, and certainly bear no resemblance to any British deer. They resemble very large rabbits, except that they have horns like a goat and tusks like a boar. They are being deliberately spread around the south of England by animal extremists, and it is thought there may be 100,000 of them on the loose.

Apart from killing young trees, these animals rejoice in attacking suburban gardens, going for the flowers first, then the vegetables. They can't eat large carrots or parsnips because their jaws are too small, so it looks as if we will soon be limited to growing large carrots and parsnips in our gardens, if nothing is done.

I would hesitate to pursue these miserable animals on a bicycle with pekingeses, fearing my pekingeses would despise me for it. But it occurs to me that many pensioners might like to have a go. Muntjak hunts could add a new dimension to old age.

## 9th October, 1993

### No conferring

AN ARTICLE by the City Editor, Mr Collins, in Thursday's newspaper said more than all the speeches at Blackpool. Delegates have huffed and puffed and postured and performed to each other all week, but the simple truth of our predicament is that government expenditure is now hopelessly out of control. Welfare and health have run amok. However thrifty and hardworking we may be, Government will succeed in ruining us all by the classic ruse of spending 25 shillings for every pound of national income.

Although delegates and humble backbenchers must be permitted to say whatever they want – that is the price we pay for democracy – ministers should not be allowed to open their mouths on any subject unless their proposal includes the sacking of at least 500 public employees and saving of £7 million. If they wish to speak for 10 minutes or more, they should propose the sacking of 5,000 public employees and saving of at least £70 million.

Yet almost every time they speak, these people promise further increases in public expenditure. Last week I drew attention to a minister in the Health Department called Brian Mawhinney who had made some foolish and irritating remarks about nurses' uniforms. This week I read that a hospital in Northern Ireland has spent £50,000 putting its nurses in pink, green, lilac and blue pleated skirts, to replace the old straight ones.

Patients have to wait as long as eight months for treatment in Londonderry's hard-up Altnagelvin Hospital, but of course they cannot expect to come before nurses and other employees of the welfare state. The scandal is that Mawhinney's fatuous ideas about nurses' uniforms should provide a further excuse for spending more money.

I feel that Mr Collins should be asked to take over the management of this country.

## What we believe

IT LOOKS as if the Church of England's compromise settlement on the vexed question of the ordination of women may have come unstuck. The Movement for the Ordination of Women has written to the House of Bishops urging that no one be ordained in future who is not prepared to affirm his sincere belief that women can really be priests.

This is not the same as affirming that women can be legally and canonically ordained, which the compromisers have said they were prepared to do. It also seems strangely at odds with the whole spirit of modern Anglicanism. A Christian church which does not require its clergy to declare belief in the divinity of Christ, let alone the Virgin birth or the Resurrection, suddenly requires them to swear allegiance to this bizarre quasi-biological proposition.

It can only be a matter of time before the Animal Rights people jump on this dogmatic bandwagon on the question of the ordination of animals. It is hard to see how anyone can be acceptable for ordination if he is not prepared to aver that animals make perfectly good priests, often better than many humans. All the worst priests of history were humans. As I reported at the time, Australia blazed the trail by ordaining some male kangaroos, and I hear of quite satisfactory results with female chipmunks in Tennessee.

# 11th October, 1993

## Wrong crackdown

HISTORY will judge Mr Major's speech to the Conservative conference on Friday, but I was puzzled by his reference to the law and order issue. 'Don't let us pretend we have been idle over the last 14 years, we haven't,' he said. 'We've increased sentences, built more prisons, spent more, recruited more police . . . '

Splendid stuff. By this time, I imagine, the cheers were deafening. But the one specific area which Mr Major chose for Government action was less predictable:

'There is one . . . issue on which I feel very strongly. We plan a big crackdown on the loathsome trade in pornography. There will be new powers of arrest and search; new powers to seize material; and – something I personally particularly support – a new offence to make possession of child pornography a crime which can lead to imprisonment.'

I forget the exact number of new imprisonable offences created by the Conservatives in government since 1979, but I think it is around 6,000. Never mind that no prison space is available. What is worrying about the present state of the law is not pornography, but the soaring rate of burglary and car theft.

Burglaries were running at 1,219,500 a year in 1991, up from 451,500 in 1971. Car thefts were running at 581,900, up from 167,600. The rate is now probably about 1,500,000 burglaries and 750,000 car thefts a year. The police seem to have given up in both these areas. On the few occasions that the miscreants are caught – usually by accident – they are seldom charged, even less likely to be convicted, and pretty well certain not to be sent to prison. Prisons must be kept for whatever small minority it is which wishes to possess photographs of naked children.

## Congratulations

LIKE every editor in the country, I pondered for many hours

whether to print a pirate edition of Lady Thatcher's memoirs in my magazine, *Literary Review*. Eventually, I decided it would annoy the readers too much. Practically nobody in Britain is interested in politics, and even fewer are interested in reading the endless self-justifications of yesterday's politicians.

Presumably the *Mirror* hoped to stir things up at the Conservative conference by printing some of the juicier bits, but even they were pretty dull. It is all very well for her to call that nice Mr Major 'small-minded, politically naïve and an intellectual lightweight', but we all know it tells only part of the story. No politician will ever do more than that.

The nicest thing about the whole episode is the evidence it affords that gratitude is still a factor in British politics. Mr Murdoch may have reckoned that few of the people who buy *The Sunday Times* actually read anything except the TV programmes, so it does not really matter what he prints. But he is rumoured to have paid his friend Lady Thatcher £3.5 million for book and serialisation rights in two continents, and that is a lot of money.

It is true that her government was very kind to him, allowing him to flout all the rules against press and broadcasting monopolies as well as preparing the legal foundation for his heroic flight to Wapping. But such generosity is still admirable, particularly from anyone as debt-ridden as Mr Murdoch.

Which raises the other big question: how long can he last? It is said that that BSkyB now makes a small profit to count against its hundreds of millions of pounds of losses, but the fact remains that Murdoch must renegotiate (that is re-borrow) $4.9 billion of loans in February.

If nice Mr Major puts up interest rates by only two or three points, as he will have to if he wants to be re-elected and ought to anyway, then the Murdoch empire will have to be broken up and sold. What a pity.

## *13th October, 1993*

### Take your pick

SO MUCH has been written about the agony of the Church of England as it wrestles with the problem of whether women can really be turned into priests that nobody has paid any attention to the state of the Roman Catholic Church, as it joyfully scoops up refugees from the Anglican fold.

Now we learn of a serious bid by the Catholic hierarchy of England to kill off the country's only intelligent Catholic newspaper. They have found a grey-bearded, pipe-smoking journalist in Manchester to launch a weekly rival to the *Catholic Herald*, the newspaper in which I wrote my first weekly column more than 30 years ago.

The purpose of the new newspaper will be to show unswerving support for the hierarchy, to be authoritative and orthodox in all things, with no frills, no arguments and no debate. All of which might have been admirable enough in earlier times, but the new orthodoxy coming out of Liverpool and Westminster is what emerged from the disastrous papacies of Popes John XXIII and Paul VI: the banal language, the despoiled liturgy, the politically correct theology of the kindergarten.

By contrast, the *Catholic Herald*, under its new and personable young editor, struggles to put a little salt in the holy gruel. She offers a reminder of the time when the Catholic Church offered a home for intellectuals, for men and women of the world, as well as for woolly, born-again sheep.

Catholics now have a clear choice between the glamorous, intelligent, 32-year-old Cristina Odone and this amiable, 65-year-old north countryman called Norman Cresswell, who looks like the best sort of sheep farmer. I wish them both well but feel the bishops may be making a mistake. To produce a newspaper for sheep may be a brave idea, and sheep may have many qualities, but their interest in newspapers is limited.

## *16th October, 1993*

### Close them down

MARKET forces, according to the new Commissioner of the Metropolitan Police, Mr Paul Condon, cannot apply to the police. There has to be recognition of the basic difference between the private sector and the public services. The same might be said of the National Health Service, which now employs a million people and costs £30 billion a year, nearly three quarters of it spent on wages. The trouble with public service employees is that they see their role in such an exalted light they lose all touch with reality.

This week alone we saw the commissioner pay £25,000 plus £7,000 costs, without admitting liability or apologising, to a Lambeth woman convicted of insulting behaviour on false evidence, while the West Midlands police paid £70,000 plus £250,000 costs in a record out-of-court settlement for false arrest and malicious prosecution, again without admitting liability.

Is this really the best way to spend taxpayers' money in the fight against crime? In the National Health Service, the position is if anything even worse. Doctors have become so over-excited by the value of the public services they provide that they threaten to withdraw them at their own discretion.

This lunacy could exist only within a service which pretends to be free. In fact, of course, it is not free; smokers and drinkers pay more for it than anyone else. But imagining they dispense a free service, these doctors have gone mad in their conceit and self-importance. If they had to ply for trade like anyone else, they would be out in the streets, cap in hand, trying to attract smokers and drinkers to their lists.

## New image

I AM sure Gus O'Donnell is a thoroughly nice man but there was a whiff of aggressive mediocrity coming out of Downing Street while he was Press Secretary. If it was his idea that the Prime Minister should take half a dozen schoolchildren with him on his disastrous visit to Japan, that says it all. The British don't like children nearly as much as they pretend they do. We all knew Mr Major was a decent chap, but we needed to be convinced of his other qualities.

It must have been a blow for him to lose O'Donnell. Now he must prepared to lose his only other friend. Sir Norman Fowler has been a disaster as chairman of the Conservative Party. We all knew the modern Conservative Party was mean, lower class and born in Essex, but did not need to be reminded of it.

Mr Major needs to touch the chord of anger running through society. To inspire loyalty he must be divisive but it is important to know where to insert the knife: not against the poor or unemployed (welfare scroungers), because it doesn't work. Not against the rich (chinless snobs), because it hurts too many Conservative feelings. Not in favour of the garagistes and computer programmers of Essex, because everyone hates them. Not against pornographers, because there are too few of them.

Not against single mothers, because there are too many and we all know a few. To capture the hearts of the nation he needs to be brave and more controversial, even a trifle bizarre and surreal.

I would like to see him in a pink coat out with the hounds. He would not be interested in foxes or stags or rabbits, all of which have too many supporters. He would be after the hairiest young hunt saboteur he can find, as representing all the welfare scroungers, burglars, muggers, unmarried mothers, crooked lawyers, students and pornographers in the land. Then he will have earned his equestrian statue in Whitehall.

## Beacon of hope

ON THURSDAY I went to North London to unveil an English Heritage blue plaque to the novelist Evelyn Waugh (1903-1966) in the house called Underhill, 145 North End Road, built by my grandfather, Arthur Waugh (1866-1943), the publisher and book critic of *The Daily Telegraph*, in 1907.

The house is now divided into three flats, and the garden where Waugh filmed *The Scarlet Woman* with parts taken by Alec Waugh, Elsa Lanchester, John Sutro, Terence Greenidge, the Earl of Wicklow and himself, has been reduced to a quarter of its size.

Underhill had a profound effect on the novelist in his twenties, chiefly in the desire to get away from it into the elegant salons of Brideshead. Ancient libels recycled occasionally by the journalist Alan Brien insist that Waugh was born in a flat over a dairy in Finchley Road, and that he used to walk half a mile from his home to post a letter so that it had a Hampstead postmark rather than one from Golders Green.

I was happy to learn that this second story is also untrue. A kind lady who lives in one of the flats told me that North End Road used to be in Hampstead, and was officiously moved to Golders Green after the Waughs had left. In later life, my father had warm memories of a childhood spent in rural Hampstead, with milk collected in a churn from the local farm, amid bucolic scenes of ploughmen homeward plodding their weary way, lowing herds winding slowly o'er the lea.

Perhaps this recollection was no more accurate than Brien's. There can be no doubt that Waugh was born in humbler circumstances than he later attained. I would like to think that the plaque will act as a beacon of hope to the people of Golders

Green, assuring them that with honest effort and application they too can end their days in a West Country manor house.

# 18th October, 1993

## Dozy ones are best

MANY citizens will sleep easier to learn that three MPs – two Conservative and one Labour – have accepted an apology and undisclosed libel damages over an article in the *Evening Standard* listing them among a 'Dozy Dozen' who had 'failed to shine' in Parliament.

Even a brief examination of the sort of people who choose to stand for Parliament might undermine our belief in democracy. Criticism of MPs cannot be allowed because it strikes at the very roots.

Minette Marrin, in these pages recently, said she found it unfathomable that so many MPs should fall in love with their secretaries or personal assistants. The explanation is simple. These women are the only people prepared to take them seriously. Everybody else walks out of the door when an MP walks in.

There is no end to the nuisance MPs have inflicted on us in recent years. Under the Noise at Work Regulations 1989, I can face two years in prison if I do not make staff at the Beak Street Academy wear earmuffs if ever the noise in the club reaches a certain level. The law that barmen must wear gloves to handle money is more pernicious, because it needs only one environmental health officer with toothache to close down the premises.

Nearly all these absurdities are home-grown, and nothing to do with Brussels. When I congratulated Mr Major on proposing the 6,001st new imprisonable offence since 1979 – possessing photographs of naked children – I forgot that this had already been made an imprisonable offence, in 1978, under the Lib-Lab pact. So did he, no doubt. But there is nothing to choose between Tory, Labour or Liberal MPs in their passion for sending fellow citizens to prison. Under the circumstances, the kindest thing you can possibly say about an MP is that he (or she) is dozy, and fails to shine.

## Feel free

PERHAPS it is the case that laws passed nowadays have a shelf life of only a few years or so, for as long as people remember them. After that, if they still seem a good idea, the next wave of politicians can exercise their power urges by passing a new law, as if they had just thought it up. This would explain Mr Major's reference to child pornography in his Blackpool speech – something he apparently feels very strongly about. The shelf-life scheme would save our liberties from being destroyed for ever by every passing hysteria arising from the day's headlines.

This may be happening already. After all the silly and oppressive laws laying down what can and cannot be said in job advertisements, I was delighted to read some which appeared in the *Guardian* for the St George Community Trust. Not content with saying that people from minority groups were positively encouraged to reply, 'especially lesbian and gay men who are currently under-represented in the workforce', St George advertises one job for a 'Black Female Housing Worker'. Another is for two locum workers, 'one of whom must be black'.

I am glad that all the rubbishy restrictions proposed in the Race Relations and Sex Discriminations Acts no longer prevent employers from expressing a simple preference. It would never occur to me to wish to express a preference for white heterosexuals of one sex or the other, but I always resented the suggestion that I couldn't even if I wanted to.

## *20th October, 1993*

---

## Help us understand

AN UNFAVOURABLE version of contemporary life is given by an American television programme in which two cartoon characters, Beavis and Butt-head, represent the generation of American teenagers which delights in stupidity and cruelty, loathing the older generation, rejoicing in arson, petty theft and any other anti-social activity.

In one episode the two 14-year-old boys buy a gun in a pawn shop and shoot down a jumbo jet. In another they steal a monster truck and run over a hippy singing save-the-earth songs.

Many parents wish to see the programme banned, as taking

an unacceptably negative view of American kids. Beavis and Butt-head are the losers in American society. They have no ambition, no conception of the American dream.

No doubt there will be strenuous efforts to clean it up since MTV has brought it to this country, but I feel this would be a mistake.

In the present lamentable state of relations between our two great countries, anything that adds to our understanding of the American reality must be welcomed.

It has been pointed out that the present generation of American 14-year-olds has fewer prospects than any which preceded it: one in five Americans who graduated between 1984 and 1990 now holds a job which does not require a college education.

Who can blame these 14-year-olds if they are unmotivated, delinquent and glorify in stupidity? It is a very shocking figure, reminding us irresistibly of the situation in Bombay, where the municipal corporation hires self-employed night rat killers, at 55 rupees (£1.10) a night for catching and killing 25 rats apiece.

The job is much sought after. Of 31,000 people who applied for 71 posts as night rat killers, 40 per cent were graduates. Beavis and Butt-head might quite enjoy the job, if they could beat the competition.

## Oops!

READING about Saturday's violent demonstrations against the British National Party by the Anti-Nazi League and other organisations, I felt a strange unease. Some time ago, writing about a BNP victory in local government, I repeated what I had read somewhere, that the BNP was opposed to hunting. Reports at one time suggested that a BNP activist was engaged in recruiting mentally retarded and delinquent schoolchildren to help sabotage hunts.

After the piece appeared, a member of the BNP queried whether there was anything in the BNP constitution which specifically committed the party on the matter, and I have to admit I may have been wrong. If it was in response to my claim that 20,000 Anti-Nazis decided to march on Welling, then I feel I owe everyone an apology.

The German Nazis were very much opposed to hunting, although I am not sure they went as far as Liberal Democrats proposed, and actually banned it. Hitler himself, of course, was a vegetarian, and fanatically opposed to hunting. I can understand that the Anti-Nazi League would wish to tackle this sort of thing at its roots, but feel they might be on safer ground if they direct their attentions to the Hunt Saboteurs Association, or the League Against Cruel Sports, or even Mr Pantsdown's Liberal Democrats.

## 23rd October, 1993

### All they understand

I DON'T think we executed any soldiers during my army service in Cyprus in the emergency, although there was a theory around that Queen's Regulations still prescribed the firing squad for anyone who fell asleep on sentry duty. Even if we had executed a few, I don't see that it would do much good to give them a free pardon now, as a Labour MP proposed this week.

Perhaps the episode explains a recurrent nightmare that I am in prison awaiting execution. I never have the slightest curiosity about the crime I am alleged to have committed, or whether I am innocent of guilty of it – only a sick dread of the approaching event. Others try to commiserate, but I reflect bitterly that it is not they who are going to be hanged.

In fact, I would like to think that if ever the readers of the *Sun* come to power with their loutish parliamentary clones to restore the death penalty, all of us called upon to do so will go to our deaths bravely, our heads held high, whistling *Auprès de ma blonde* nonchantly and putting the louts to shame.

Incidentally, I see that the Attorney General, Sir Nicholas Lyell, has just been given permission by the High Court to seek Mr Kelvin Mackenzie's committal to prison for something the *Sun* is alleged to have printed in August 1991 under his editorship. I am not sure exactly what offence he is thought to have committed, and journalists tend to look askance at attempts by politicians to send them to prison for practising their trade. Where Mackenzie is concerned, there is bound to be the additional anxiety – whatever he is accused of having done – of whether prison would really be the right sentence for him.

## Keep them busy

AFTER all the millions of pounds in police time wasted by Mrs Thatcher trying to find Second World War criminals in Hampstead, we should not be too disappointed if they all turn out to be dead. If we are prepared to countenance posthumous pardons for executed prisoners, why should we not also have posthumous convictions, prison and even death sentences?

There are many questions about our conduct in the South African Wars of 1879 and 1899 which remain unanswered. If I were a descendant of Brigadier-General Reginald Dyer (1864-1927), who was held responsible for the Amritsar Massacre of April 1919 in the film of Gandhi by Richard Attenborough, I think I should imitate the heroic Austen Donnellan and *demand* a police inquiry in order to clear my ancestor's name. While we are on the trail, we might ask the police to investigate conditions in the British fleet which sailed under Admiral Nelson to the Nile in 1798.

Anything, really, which will give the police something to do which will keep them out of danger from drug dealers, and discourage them from making a nuisance of themselves to country dwellers who might like to go out to lunch with a neighbour.

## *27th October, 1993*

## Duke of Amalfi

FOR the past two years, I learn, I have been living in a fool's paradise, chuckling quietly to myself about the City's refusal to allow Lord Palumbo, the old Etonian friend of Jocelyn Stevens, to destroy a beautiful Victorian building opposite Mansion House and put up a new office block by the German modernist architect Mies van der Rohr.

Now I learn that, while I was chuckling, Palumbo, whose family comes from Amalfi, approached James Stirling, architect of the hideous Clore Wing which houses the Turner collection at the Tate, and asked him for another office block.

While England slept, he appeared to the House of Lords and

obtained permission to put up the alternative office block, more like a 1930s wireless set, perhaps, than a glass stump from downtown Manhattan, but equally objectionable from any aesthetic point of view, and equally ruinous of the site, one of the few remaining areas of dignity and grace in the City of London.

Unless somebody does something, demolition of the Mappin & Webb building will start next year. They claim the new monstrosity will be in place in 1996, although I have my doubts. The oddest feature of this whole episode is that, as everyone knows, there is practically no demand for new office building in the City.

For 38 years Palumbo has been buying leases on the site and plotting its demolition. People assumed that this was a result of his eccentric admiration for Mies van der Rohr. Now it appears that this admiration was transferable.

It will be a tremendous shame if he succeeds in ruining this last corner of the City. It there are any patriots left in that area, I hope they will put a curse on the venture and see to it that no enterprise which moves into offices on the despoiled site is allowed to prosper.

## Send in the tanks

THE DREADED knock on the door has been sounding in Ryedale, Yorkshire, where a couple were summoned from their beds just before midnight by a persistent knocking and bell-ringing to find two policemen at the door.

It appeared that a local conservationist had informed the police that David and Sylvia Wood had blocked the eaves of their house to a family of bats which might have wanted to roost there.

Mr and Mrs Woods were unaware of the bats, and had blocked the eaves that morning to repair damage from nesting birds. The conservationist, whose name has not been revealed, said she had been monitoring bats in the neighbourhood and thought she was doing the couple a favour by tipping off the police.

I do not know why the police had to call at midnight. Perhaps it was something to do with overtime. At least nobody was shot.

### Spare them the worms

MANY people in Somerset go mad worrying about the National Debt or the education of the young. Perhaps it was coincidence that the school inspectors' report on the hopeless state of our urban schools came out on the same day as Judge Stephen Tumim's report on the hopelessly overcrowded prisons. But the connection is obvious.

Our children learn nothing in these schools and progress inexorably to the prisons where, if Judge Tumim has his way, they might stand a chance of a little education. Might it not save a lot of trouble and expense if they were sent straight to prison, rather than first waste their time in these idle institutions?

Two years ago we set up a National Commission on Education under Sir John Cassels to discover why English children were the 'worst educated in Europe'. It did not need a National Commission to establish what we all know, that English boys, in particular, are peculiarly resistant to education in any form and will accept it only under duress, which involves constant, savage beating. That is how the public schools maintained their lead. Perhaps it is in response to this situation that teachers out of training colleges no longer try to teach their charges. Instead, they provide play groups and behavioural counselling sessions, being trained only to simper, look compassionate and patronise.

Despite all these disadvantages, English schoolchildren often emerge as the best makers of Plasticine worms in the world. Their early training with Plasticine can make them particularly skilful at rolling their own cigarettes in later life, but this is its only application. I feel we should spare our prisoners the humiliation. Let them take lessons from the prison warders.

### A new offence

'I COULDN'T stop thinking about jail,' said 21-year-old David Dunn, falsely accused of rape by a 27-year-old woman called Susan Gooch. 'It's one thing for a hardened criminal, but I'm just a run-of-the-mill bloke.'

On the say-so of this mischievous woman, Dunn was thrown into a cell, quizzed for 13 hours and sacked from his job, being reinstated six days later only when Gooch, of Pinner, admitted she had been telling a pack of lies.

Newspapers seem full of frivolous or vexatious rape prosecutions at the moment. The new doctrine that women who complain of rape must be believed involves great suffering for their male victims, who have no redress. It is only in the rare event of a prosecution for perverting the course of justice, as happened with Gooch, that we are even allowed to know the name of the woman concerned.

Perhaps we could use this rare opportunity to coin a new word in the English language – to gooch, meaning to accuse a man of rape without the faintest justification. MPs might introduce a Bill establishing the gooch as a criminal offence in its own right. That should keep them busy for an hour or two.

## *1st November, 1993*

### Questions of gender

MPs who voted overwhelmingly in support of the proposition that women can become priests were demonstrating what might be called democratic fallacy: that the power of people (whom they represent) is absolute.

An exact parallel may be found in the vexed question of transsexuals: men who decide to be castrated and have all other physical characteristics of masculinity removed, usually on the National Health Service. Whether what remains is a woman, as they maintain, or something quite different, may be debated endlessly, but I am certain of one thing: that a vote in the House of Commons would make no difference to the point at issue.

It is equally foolish to suppose that 215 Members of Parliament – of many religions and of none – can determine that whatever the Church of England proposed to do to these women will somehow turn them into 'priests'.

The same House of Commons allows the National Health service to perform 'sex change' operations on men – at taxpayers' expense. We must agree that MPs have the absolute power to vote themselves as big a pay rise as they choose. When they decide they can also ordain which sex we belong to, they are simply demonstrating their own foolishness, or impudence, or both.

# Real news

THE MAIN news item in Saturday's *Sun* was contained in a front-page picture showing what might have been a cow or a sheep in the foreground and the silhouette of a cat-like object behind. It was captioned 'The beast of Bodmin: first photo'.

The story told how the *Sun*'s intrepid cameraman, Colin Shepherd, had been summoned by a local farmer, Rosemary Rhodes, who explained: 'I saw a sandy-coloured puma walking across my fields with a black cub beside it. It seems obvious that a panther is mating with other species of cat in the area. It is quite scary.'

I once saw the beast when it was called the Beast of Exmoor, later identified as the Black Panther of Combe Florey. This was in the summer of 1972 when a cricket team from *Private Eye* came down to play a local team from Nettlecombe. Five or six of us were standing at an upstairs window – at least one was a teetotaller – when we saw a large black panther lope across a field at the bottom of the property.

Nobody felt like pursuing it and eventually we retired to meditate to ourselves about what we had seen and what it had meant to us, in the manner of the times. A few weeks later I identified the animal as a not particularly large black cat belonging to a tenant. Distance had magnified it, by some strange trick of perspective.

For this reason, I remain sceptical about Mr Shepherd's Beast of Bodmin, particularly as he owns up to having used a magnifying lens. I do not doubt it was some nice old lady's pet pussy-cat. But the *Sun* was quite right to treat it as the main news of the day – much more interesting than Mr Major's suggestion for a revival of peace talks in Ulster.

# There must be a reason

I REFRAINED from commenting on the tragic news that a two-year-old boy in Staffordshire, himself the product of *in vitro* fertilisation, had inexplicably dropped dead in a hamburger bar in Lichfield. However, since the tragedy, I learn that parents have been jamming the *Sun*'s switchboard in Wapping with stories of how their toddlers have had similar accidents, always in a hamburger bar.

Joseph Hurrell, two, of Chingford, Essex broke his head open

346

after falling from his chair. Eleanor Walls, five, of Wokingham fell off her chair backwards, and banged her head, knocking herself out completely for one or two minutes; eight-year-old Lee Finch, from Quedgeley, Glos fell over when emerging from a lavatory at his hamburger bar and was discovered to have a blood clot on the brain; Laura Searle, two and a half, from Collier Row, fell out of her chair, screaming with pain . . .

The *Sun* chooses to blame the design of the furniture, floors and fittings in the nation's hamburger bars, but I feel this explanation is unlikely. I have written at some length about the terrible effect which a diet of hamburgers has had on the young people of America, and how hamburger gases were found to be destroying the ancient buildings of Rome.

The Government seems determined to hold no inquiry into the effect of hamburgers and hamburger gases (HGs) on human beings. Perhaps it will now institute a public inquiry into why so many of our toddlers are falling over.

## *3rd November, 1993*

### Prevention is better

THE HOME OFFICE informs us that it is 'looking at' the results of an investigation into burglary carried out by Hertfordshire police and probation services. The survey confirms what we all knew already, that practically no burglars are ever caught, and only 15 per cent of victims ever get any of their property back, but adds further information which was new to me.

Although the growth in burglaries has been spectacular, a comparatively small number of criminals is involved. Twenty-five burglars surveyed had committed 1,124 offences between them. It follows that it requires only a comparatively small number of people to be taken out of circulation to make a significant impact on the problem. Another fact to emerge is that most burglaries take place in the afternoon when the house is empty, its occupants at work.

It is illegal for a householder to take even a rolled-up newspaper against these intruders, which is an obvious absurdity, to be explained by the government's zealous protection of is own powers. Since the police are obviously no longer competent to do anything about burglars, and the legal system lets them off with a warning time and again because the Government cannot afford to lock them up, it looks as if we must resign ourselves to a life without personal possessions.

However, it would be helpful – and cost the Government nothing – if we were allowed to set booby-traps when the house was empty. So long as a householder left clearly visible notices that the house was booby-trapped, the burglar would have only himself to blame if he was electrocuted by a door-handle or decapitated by some refinement of a mousetrap. After a few had suffered in this way, the others might become discouraged and settle down to fiddling the Welfare like everyone else.

## Conspiracy of silence

IT IS puzzling that a famed American actor should suddenly drop dead at a party, apparently from cocaine poisoning, when he had publicly announced that he was one of the few American actors who never took cocaine. 'I don't do drugs. I get a big enough high from life,' explained Mr River Phoenix a few months before he expired.

I expect Mr Clinton is very sad, but I wonder whether he should look more closely into the circumstances of Phoenix's death. When the famous popular singer called Freddie Mercury died two years ago, everybody said he had died of the American disease. But there are similarities in these events which makes one wonder what is going on.

Meanwhile, the *Sun* continues its file of strange accidents in English hamburger restaurants. Wendy Graves, seven, of Dartford, broke two front teeth when she fell over. Claire Tate, nine, broke four teeth when she fell off a table in a hamburger bar in Corby.

Victoria Davis, three, broke her collarbone when she fell off her seat in Folkestone. Mrs Lynn Griffiths saw two daughters injured on separate occasions when they fell off their chairs in the same hamburger establishment in Barkingside. The *Sun* hotline is still active.

I am not saying that hamburgers or hamburger gases (HGs) are responsible for all these tragedies, but it is odd that we do not read of such accidents in America. It makes one wonder whether the whole United States hamburger culture may be too terrified to face the truth.

## 8th November, 1993

### Isolating the cause

ALL President Clinton's shortcomings derive from having had a drunken stepfather, claims Dr Janet Woititz, acknowledged authority on ACAS, the Adult Child of Alcoholics Syndrome.

Classic symptoms are a craving for approval, a need to be taken seriously, an inability to relax, a propensity to tell unnecessary lies, an inability to think things through . . . many of these things are evidenced by his blockade of Haiti in order to restore a Marxist fanatic who calls himself 'Father' Aristide. Or so they say.

It is a tempting theory but I feel Stephen Robinson, our Washington correspondent, who raised the matter in Saturday's newspaper, lets Mr Clinton off too lightly. Why should Americans be able to blame everything on their home background?

Discussing the matter, my wife and I went through a roll call of our friends and acquaintances who were the children of alcoholics. It was an amazingly long list. None of them is remotely like Bill Clinton. Dr Woititz, a psychologist, is typically unfair to alcoholic parents.

In fact, most politicians show exactly the same symptoms: craving for approval; need to be taken seriously; inability to relax; propensity to tell lies . . . Where Clinton is concerned, the explanation is very simple. I don't know if there was much there in the first place, but whatever there was has been completely wrecked by hamburgers.

## 10th November, 1993

### No time to bend genders

LUDICROUS Andrew Neil made some curious boasts about his shameful rag this week. 'The readership of *The Sunday Times* is growing and getting younger, more female . . . ' he trumpeted across the top of one of his news pages.

Neil must speak for himself. Perhaps he is getting younger and growing at the same time, but few of his male readers will be grateful to be told they are getting more female.

Perhaps they are. I wrote recently about the distressing new

fad (no doubt sympathetically discussed in that newspaper's *Style* pages) for men to be castrated and have all other male organs removed – usually at the taxpayers' expense – so that they can pretend to be women. If that is what *Sunday Times* readers are doing, I feel they should be discouraged.

Fortunately, Way of the World sells three times as many copies every week as Neil's horrible ragbag of a newspaper, with all its advertising supplements and comics for moronic American four-year-olds. We must use what influence we can.

Recently I sent a circular letter to selected readers of the *Spectator* bringing the good news that the time had come for them to cancel their subscription to *The Sunday Times* and take *Literary Review* instead. This would save them a lot of money, since *Literary Review* costs only £22 a year, against £46.80 for Neil's lower-class filth. The telephones in Beak Street have been jammed ever since.

Neil can make his own arrangements. If he likes to think he is growing, getting younger and more female, that is his affair. I promise that reading Way of the World has none of these effects.

## *In hoc signo*

MOST of us, I hope, will feel sympathy with both parties in the storm which has broken over Greenwich council's refusal to register a child-minder after a council inspector found a golliwog in her collection of toys.

The inspector, Mr Lonnie Lane, a Rastafarian, was apparently offended by the toy. The child-minder Mrs Deena Newton, who had been looking after children of all races for 25 years, was aggrieved to be accused of racism.

She can reasonably point out that golliwogs are lovely, friendly creatures, certainly not objects of hatred. They could not have been intended to mock Rastafarians, since the Rastafarian religion emerged only in the 1930s, whereas golliwogs first appeared in a picture book by Florence Upton in 1895. In fact I have often wondered whether the Rastafarian dreadlocks may not have been modelled on Florence Upton's golliwog, as establishing humour and amiability, as well as pride in racial difference.

On the other hand it would be possible, if one were sensitive, to imagine there might be an element of mild derision there. It is all very well to say that anyone who comes to live in England must be prepared for a certain amount of good-natured ribbing – something the Scots have never understood – but where there are also racial animosities, I suppose it might be uncomfortable.

On the other hand again it is rather tough on the English to have to give up their traditional dolls in case a local government inspector on routine inspection of children's toy cupboards finds a golliwog and uses it to make trouble. I think I have a solution.

Rastafarianism is a serious and respectable religion. Its elders do not need to inveigh against fox-hunting, or attack nice Mr Major, in order to attract a loyal and devout membership. I think they should take a leaf from the early Christians, who adopted the pagan Roman feast of Saturnalia for their own Christmas, and adopt the golliwog as a symbol of their religion, as Palestinian Judaeism adopted the Star of David, Islam the Crescent, Christendom the Cross, Marxism the hammer and sickle.

This would demonstrate not only pride in their racial identity and defiance of those who would belittle it, but also the sweet-natured patience of their long exile and the fact, which we all know, that Jamaicans have a sense of humour.

## Four sad stories

SATURDAY was rather a tearful day, with the sad obituaries of Jill Tweedie, Anna Ford's moving description of the death of her husband, Mark Boxer and, in the same newspaper, the account of a memorial service in Clapham for PC Patrick Dunne, shot down in the street by laughing drug dealers.

Tweedie and Boxer were friends and colleagues, but PC Dunne was unknown to me. He seems to have represented the very best in the police force of which we were all so proud – and proof that some of the best and kindest people in the country are still to be found in it.

It was a shame that the same day's newspaper also carried the story of how a neighbouring farmer in Somerset, Mr Mark Purdey, had been double-crossed by the police. Their latest trick in the unofficial campaign to prevent farmers having guns for use against swarming rabbits and other vermin, is to refuse to send a reminder when the gun licence is due to expire. Then they wait until he tries to renew it, confiscate the gun and prosecute the farmer for having a gun without a licence.

I was aware of this secret agenda arising from Douglas Hurd's hysterical gun control legislation in other police authority areas, but I am very sorry to see it creeping into Somerset and Avon. If this sort of behaviour continues, the police will be left without a friend in the country.

# *17th November, 1993*

## These are the worst

'FEARFUL and womanish menkind' was the heading which the *Observer* put on its discussion of the latest suicide figures. 'Male suicides have nearly doubled in the past decade. Rosalind Coward considers the reasons why more men are turning their aggression inwards.'

Coward found a Jungian analyst who thought the increase in male suicide might be the negative side of a positive shift – female suicide has reduced: 'Men are halfway down the road to change.'

Elaborating the point, she went on: 'In a post-feminist culture, externally directed male aggression is much more problematic in relationships. And if aggression cannot go outwards, it sometimes turns inwards. Every therapist knows that suicide is an act of violent aggression. The real increase among male suicides has occurred among young men. Interestingly, it is the same group whose violent aggression also causes problems elsewhere. Directed inwards, this aggression can become suicidal.'

Everything seems to hinge on what 'every therapist knows' – that suicide is an act of violent aggression. It is curious how many of these things which every therapist knows turns out to be complete twaddle.

Coward does not go on to make the point that it might be rather a good idea if more men committed suicide. This shows commendable restraint on her part. Therapists in California take their enthusiasms rather more seriously. Under therapy, children are persuaded to 'remember' incidents of sexual abuse, torture, diabolism, even murder, which enable child-care experts to lock up pretty well any male they want.

Last year, in the US, there were 2.9 million complaints of child abuse. After the current farce in San Diego, where a Sunday school caretaker was accused of stabbing an elephant and a giraffe, as well as killing four children and drowning two rabbits in a font, it looks as if America may be about to return to its senses.

But I wonder if the real message is apparent. I used to think that counsellors, with their fatuous dogmas, their low-grade intelligence and their cocksure opinions, were the most irritating people in Britain. Now I begin to suspect that psychotherapists are more dangerous.

## Unfair criticism

ONCE upon a time I might have been prepared to believe that Chairman Mao Tse-tung was a practitioner of group sex, that every Saturday evening, until he was well into his seventies, he would summon three or four young women to his bedroom for what the *Observer* calls 'sex sessions'.

Or so we are to be told on a BBC TV 'Timewatch' programme which will be shown next month on the 100th anniversary of Mao's birth. I might have believed this when I was an idealistic young man who wanted to think there could be some purpose to a life in politics, some hope of reward. Of course no English prime minister would ever have the same opportunities, but the dream was still there . . .

I might also have been prepared to believe these rumours because we all enjoy gossip. Nothing on earth will stop people speculating about the intimate details of their rulers' lives. A cat may not only look at a king, it can also meditate on what the king looks like without any clothes on. It is only in middle age that one becomes sceptical.

Even so, I would have been happy to believe that Mao was a secret sex maniac when he was preaching family values – but then I read that the same programme is going to accuse him of condoning cannibalism, and a dreadful boredom sets in. In a longish journalistic career I must have accused at least a dozen Third World leaders of this crime. The charge won't stick any more. Cannibalism is a rare taste. It is no good pretending that politicians such as Idi Amin, Jomo Kenyatta, Jean Bokassa, Tony Benn etc indulge it just because we disagree with their policies. I am afraid that Mao was really just another boring, self-important politician like the rest of them.

## *20th November, 1993*

### The Sun King

EVERYBODY in my health resort sat up to watch Hanif Kureishi's 'The Buddha of Suburbia' on BBC2 after I showed them the front page of Wednesday's *Sun*, denouncing 'Porn filth shame of BBC play. The worst ever full frontal telly':

'Fury has erupted over tonight's screening of a BBC drama crammed with full frontal nudity, orgies and perversions,' the *Sun* exclusively claimed. I do not know where fury erupted, but it certainly was not in Shrubland Hall, Coddenham, Suffolk. Most of the inmates say they fell asleep before reaching the dirty bits, which were in any case short and quite inoffensive.

There is something demented in the *Sun*'s inconsistency which makes it prepared to denounce the 'worst ever full frontal telly' on page one while relentlessly printing inmodest pictures of young women exposing their breasts for money on page three. Sometimes bonking is what every fella does to every chick when

354

the coast is clear; at other times, especially if a television actor, football manager or other celebrity is involved, it becomes a vile and wicked act which has to be exposed.

Presumably some of the *Sun*'s oddity comes from the puritanical urges of its proprietor, the strange, debt-ridden gambler Murdoch, in his Los Angeles eyrie. Does he supervise the *Sun*'s manhunts, I wonder. The current one, which is worldwide, is for Michael Jackson, the American singer, who is seeking privacy for personal reasons. *Sun* readers are offered £10,000 for a reported sighting.

The last manhunt was for James Gilbey, an Englishman of respectable family. Backstairs gossip had linked him with some wretched celebrity or other in the public eye. Is it right that the most powerful Australo-American in the world should be able to organise manhunts of Englishmen in their own country? The manhunt for Jackson is conducted with a sadistic relish which only the born-again Murdoch could inspire: 'You'll have to strip, my old cock,' the *Sun* gloated this week, revealing that 'police plan to make Michael Jackson strip so they can see the colour of his manhood'.

Jackson is said to be suffering from total nervous collapse and breakdown, which is easy to imagine. Is there to be no pity for this poor hamburger victim?

## Spend a penny

THE PROPER response to Mr Ashdown's call for a special penny-on-the-income-tax to improve education is the little gasp which a pantomime audience used to give when they brought a Shetland pony on stage. Isn't our Paddy *twee*? Isn't he *clever* to think up something as simple as that? Won't someone give him a pat on the head and a barley-sugar?

Nobody could be so mean as to begrudge one penny in the pound if it gave Our Children a Better Future, don't you agree? The truth is that in a situation where public spending is completely out of control, the extra penny would disappear without trace into the black hole of Mr Clarke's deficit.

Even if it reached the Department of Education, it would be no help. Mr Patten's school tables were good at proving that the worst-run, worst-behaved schools with the worst results were, for the most, in the poorest areas. What he failed to supply was the cost per pupil in each school listed. Some years ago I saw a table covering the Inner London education area which showed that the state schools on which most money per pupil was spent had the worst results.

Normally, one would not object to Mr Pantsdown striking his pretty attitudes and exciting little coos of admiration from the womenfolk. Live and let live, that's my motto. But only if they agree to stay in their own muesli-eating, *Independent*-reading worlds. As soon as they come streaming out of their cosy corners to prevent people they have never met doing things they have always done and which have nothing to do with anyone else – I refer to hunting, rather than sodomy – the situation changes.

The next time I see a photograph of Pantsdown's sweet little face in the newspaper, I am going to be sick all over it.

## *24th November, 1993*

### The Duke of Hamburger

FRESH from my life of voluntary restraint at a Suffolk health farm, struggling patriotically to keep within government guidelines on personal bodyweight, I was shocked to see a photograph of the Duke of York in Monday's *Sun* which, if true, would seem to suggest he has decided to defy Mrs Bottomley as flagrantly as may be.

The *Sun* quotes *Slimmer* magazine as suggesting that the Duke's many chins and dramatic increase in weight from 13 stone to over 15 stone in 12 months are the result of eating hamburgers.

If this is true, I suppose we must start taking the Duke of York's problems seriously. It may just be part of the campaign against the monarchy being waged by the entire Murdoch press in tandem with its campaign for still lower interest rates. Am I the only person in the country who sees that any further cut in interest rates would be a disastrous mistake, encouraging slackness and inefficiency in business, as well as being a further slap in the face for the nation's savers, who outnumber borrowers by seven to one? Both these Murdoch campaigns must be frustrated if possible.

But if the Duke of York is seriously caught in the hamburger addiction syndrome, then the future for our monarchy may seem bleak. A poll in the *Sun* showed more than 65 per cent of its readership opposed to the idea of the Prince of Wales succeeding to the throne. On the other hand, a dummy run on Murdoch's BSkyB television of the Queen Mother's obituary led, by an odd sequence of events, to half of Australia breaking down in convulsive sobs.

But we must decide what to do about the Duke of York. It may not technically count as high treason for him to put on weight, but by defying Mrs Bottomley in this way he threatens a Crown versus Commons civil war which the Crown is in no better position to win than it was in 1642 when Charles I raised the Royal standard at Nottingham. Perhaps the best thing to do with Prince Andrew would be to send him back to Germany with some new, foreign-sounding title – the Duke of Hamburger would be as good as any. Germans are not shocked by the fuller figure in the way that English people are.

## End of the road

TWO BURGLARS in Hull walked free because the Hull police said they could not afford to send blood-stained clothing for forensic examination. Home Office laboratories charge £178 for each item, and police funds would not run to it.

In the same way, police charge the Home Office an average of £350 a night to keep a remand prisoner in a police cell. Where do these ludicrous overpayments between police and Home Office, Home Office and police go to?

Last September I found myself suffering from a chronic headache, and rather than visit my neuroses on the taxpayer, decided to have a brain scan as a private patient in my local London hospital. Although nothing of interest was revealed, when a bill for £80 arrived from the surgeon next day, it seemed a reasonable charge for what had been a pleasant and instructive half-hour of medical attention.

Now, two months later, a further bill arrives from the Hammersmith Hospital for £265 for use of machinery. When I ask whether this is what they charge Mrs Bottomley for a brain scan on some poor person unable to pay for it herself, they brazenly reply that it is indeed.

When Mrs Bottomley announced her intention of closing down the Hammersmith Hospital last year, I urged her to think again. Now I see she was absolutely right. She should close them all down. Public employees are out of control in every department of government. Our post-war settlement has reached the end of the road.

## Are they all guilty?

ANN-MARIE Thompson, 41, a single mother of seven, obviously thought she was speaking for a wide spectrum of Liverpool mothers when she said: 'You name one kid of 10 who doesn't tell lies, doesn't swear, doesn't smoke, who doesn't go in the shops robbing.' She agreed that her boy, Robert, regularly 'sagged off' from school to go shoplifting, but objected to his conviction for the sadistic murder of two-year-old James Bulger.

Many Liverpudlian mothers would question these assumptions, but it seems to me that those pockets of proletarian culture which survive, mostly in the North, are so far removed from the rest of our humane, bourgeois liberal society they might belong to another country.

Another illustration comes from Leeds, where Mr Justice Mitchell ruled inadmissible a murder confession which had been obtained by improper and oppressive means. There being no other substantive evidence against him, Mr George Heron was duly cleared of stabbing seven-year-old Nikki Allan to death.

Heron has been a hate figure in Hendon, Sunderland, since his arrest. An angry mob marched through Wear Garth Estate attacking the homes of family friends. Others stormed the dock in Sunderland magistrates court, and a fire bomb was thrown through his solicitor's office window. These people seem incapable of opening their minds to the possibility that Heron is innocent.

Even more shocking is the reported statement of a Northumbria detective chief superintendent to the effect that the Wear Garth community had been 'let down by the criminal justice system'.

On the point of oppressive questioning, he said: 'It would be entirely wrong to be pussyfooting about – we have a responsibility to search for the truth. If we are talking about oppressive behaviour, it occurs every day in the courts, not just in the police station.'

If this man is so stupid that he cannot tell the difference between a cross-examination in open court and a police interrogation in private for the purpose of obtaining a confession, it is doubly worrying that local people assume anyone arrested by the police must be guilty. Instead of sending proper judges up there, perhaps we should leave them to dispense what justice they choose in the stupid, brutal atmosphere of their own creation.

## Save the Wigton One

TUESDAY is a rather frivolous choice for Mr Clarke's Budget, since we can now think of St Andrew's Day only in the light of last year's events, when Angus Diggle's unfortunate efforts to seduce a Scottish solicitor after the St Andrew's Ball in London landed him with a three-year prison sentence for 'attempted rape'.

It was proposed at one stage to name the *Literary Review* Booby Prize for Bad Sex in Fiction after Angus Diggle, but this seemed in bad taste while the poor fellow is still incarcerated. There is talk of equipping prisoners with condoms to discourage American disease in the prisons, but I doubt whether they will be green ones, and the whole thing seems a grotesque injustice.

The Bad Sex Prize itself was accepted with panache and grace from the hands of Sarah Miles, the actress and autobiographer, by Melvyn Bragg, for an extract from *A Time to Dance* (Hodder & Stoughton) which was read with great verve by Mr Clive Anderson, the celebrated barrister. The ceremony closed with a short but searingly relevant song from Mr Peter Bottomley. And all this time poor Diggle lay in jail.

Now we learn that Melvyn himself is to be pursued through the courts by a furious fellow writer called Michael Dobbs. Poor Melvyn, I hope he will not turn out to be another victim of injustice, like Angus Diggle.

Before he emerges as the Wigton One, let all parties reflect. Whatever the rights and wrongs of this libel action, it must be capable of friendly settlement. Any writer who invokes our monstrous libel laws against a fellow writer forfeits any claim to sympathy or respect from his colleagues. Give him a nice apology, Melvyn. Chuck it, Dobbs.

## *29th November, 1993*

## Lumley for PM

THE GOVERNMENT's new crackdown on truancy, launched by John Patten at a school prizegiving in Towcester, Northants, on

Friday, is to rely on a voluntary 'Truancy Watch' scheme, whereby public-spirited citizens are urged to keep an eye open for children wandering abroad in school hours.

Typically, he does not specify what action we should take. When identified, should they be approached and apprehended? If so, how? Some of these young people are violent; others will run away. Moreover, children are trained to be rude to strange grown-ups nowadays, for fear of pederasts.

It would be a shame if Mr Patten's brave idea for a Truancy Watch turned into a Pederasts' Charter. Equally, I do not suppose it would work for Mr Patten to ask the Home Secretary for a Bill allowing private citizens to shoot any children they see on the streets in school hours.

That is the Brazilian solution, but I don't think even Mr Howard would approve it, keen as he undoubtedly is on law and order. This is because the police are terrified of allowing Englishmen to own guns for fear we would decide to shoot at policemen instead of pigeons, or pheasant, or truant schoolchildren.

The prospect for young people looks rather bleak, but good

things are happening in New College, Oxford, whose undergraduates have voted to change the name of their Junior Common Room from the Nelson Mandela Room to the Joanna Lumley Room.

Now that Mandela has been released from prison we can all admit what has long been apparent, that he is not a Tembu tribesman, in fact he is not an African at all. He is quite obviously Chinese. Nothing wrong with that, of course, but it makes those who persist in seeing him as a great African statesman look rather foolish.

After the events in Tiananmen Square, Oxford undergraduates may have rather confused ideas about the Chinese. Whereas Lumley is undeniably a member of an oppressed minority, being a woman. At last Oxford is coming to its senses.

# *1st December, 1993*

## Out of date

FOR THOSE with the survival of the monarchy at heart, it will be gloomy news that five of the nine rooms destroyed by fire in Windsor Castle are to be rebuilt in the modern taste.

'We said: why not have confidence in our own age and put something back which represents the best of contemporary architecture, design and craftsmanship,' explained Michael Peat, who is the Royal Collection's director of finance. I am sorry to say I think this foolish sentiment comes from Prince Philip.

Exactly the same rhetoric about 'confidence in our age' and 'best of contemporary architecture' was deployed in support of Sir William Holford's repulsive 'piazza' in the precinct of St Paul's, now mostly knocked down, and Basil Spence's monstrous Hyde Park Barracks, which still disfigure the entire southern prospect of the park.

The function of monarchy in the modern age is not to lead us into further utilitarian or brutalistic experiments, but to keep us sane by reminding us of the continuity of history, that we are still essentially the same people as once ruled an empire and fought two world wars, our country is still essentially the same place, despite temporary modern accretions. Modernism offers nothing to the monarchy apart from the endless exposure, resentment and hatred. It may be true that any monarchy wishing to survive should be at least 60 years behind the times, but the 75-year-old 'modern movement' in art is one cultural cul-de-sac which it would be well advised to ignore altogether.

## Goose steps

THERE are strong rumours that the director of the Consumer Association, Mr John Beishon, is looking for a new editor of the *Good Food Guide* who will make it more politically correct, recommending cheaper meals where margarine is regularly served instead of butter, and where emphasis is given to diets of salad and uncooked fruit, well calculated to ruin the digestion and induce an itching all over the body.

It is hard to judge how much threats these food fadists represent. Having attacked tobacco and alcohol, they will soon be moving to prevent us eating meat. A terrifying photograph in Sunday's newspaper showed a woman called Amy Bertsch of Peta (People for the Ethical Treatment of Animals) with a T-shirt declaring 'Meat Stinks'

Formed in America in 1980, Peta now has nearly 400,000 members – mad, unpleasant vegetarian women and bearded, disease-ridden American males – and a budget of nearly $10 million. Bertsch is part of a vanguard setting up offices in London, Amsterdam and Hamburg. Her first assignment is to organise a Peta demonstration on Thursday which will attempt to stop Harrods from selling *pâté de foie gras*.

It is interesting how sentimentality about animals has given way to a general hatred of mankind in the ordering of these aggressions. For years animal sentimentalists have regaled themselves with stories of how geese are nailed by their feet to a board to be force-fed.

Perhaps such outrages occurred once or twice in history, to become part of the mythology of *foie gras* production, but anyone who has taken the trouble to visit a *gavage* in south-western France will know that geese adore being force-fed on maize corn, and line up, honking, for their turn.

I do not know what Mr Fayed proposes to do about these impertinent American women setting up office in London to try to stop him selling *pâté de foie gras*. I think I would set a flock of geese on them. Even one goose, I dare say, would scare them out of their wits.

## *4th December, 1993*

### A job for everyone

I FIND it hard to understand why the City continues to greet Kenneth Clarke's Budget with euphoria. Perhaps it was the prospect of 250,000 citizens losing their entitlement to welfare benefits which cheered the markets, but it is infinitely cheaper to keep people on welfare than it is to equip them with offices and pay them salaries for public administration, inspection and control.

The only way to judge any government initiative nowadays is on the extent to which it tackles this dead weight of 5.2 million public employees on our collapsing economy. Unless we can sack 1.73 million of them before the end of the century, we shall find ourselves in exactly the same position as the Russians are now in after nearly 75 years of socialism.

We must all be prepared for sacrifice. This week we learnt of two environmental health officers who took it on themselves to investigate a complaint from Mr Alan Stewart and his wife, Margaret, at Wakefield, West Yorkshire, that a neighbouring farmer's cockerels disturbed their morning sleep.

The two environmental health officers left their beds to sit with microphones and recording equipment between 4 am and 7 am on five days in April, July, October and November, monitoring the noise of cockerels. It is hard to think of a future when we will not be able to call out inspectors in this way.

When we think of the dedicated work of all these public employees administering, inspecting and regulating us the whole time, as well as providing clerical services and creating new jobs for each other, we can scarcely imagine being able to manage without one of them.

That is Clarke's problem. So far as I can see, he does not propose to sack a single public employee. Perhaps he is too tenderhearted. Under those circumstances, he has no alternative but to sack himself. When I come to power, it will be written into the constitution that one in three public employees must be sacked every 20 years.

## No carpets today

IN PAKISTAN, hundreds of religious enthusiasts have surrounded the district court of Gujranwale demanding that a 12-year-old Christian boy, Sulamet Masih, should be hanged for blasphemy. Never mind that the poor youth, accused of writing anti-Islamic slogans, was illiterate and unable, in fact, to write his own name.

Much of the same problem arises for poor Bill Clinton, husband of President Hillary, who has been called the most hated man in Islam since he received Salman Rushdie in the White House.

I am sure that Clinton, like most of us, has never read a word of Rushdie's novels and probably thought he was a carpet salesman. That won't save either of them from the fundamentalists. In Egypt, the fundamentalists have taken to murdering anyone they suspect of being lukewarm towards the Mohammedan religion. Once again, they claim that under Islamic law, Muslims have the right to kill any apostate.

As Britain seems set to become a Muslim country some time after the turn of the century, it might be prudent to establish if this is true. Many of our clubs and secret societies – from the Garrick to the Masons – have strange rituals and practices, but none claims the right to kill anyone who threatens to resign membership. I am not, of course, suggesting that the Government should do anything about it, but I feel we should be told.

## The joke continues

COMING so soon after the annual farce of the Turner Prize, the sale at Sotheby's of a pair of wooden blocks by Carl Andre for £28,750 proved too much for many people's sense of humour. It is time they realised that the joke is not about art. Art has nothing to do with these events. The joke is about money.

There are two sorts of money. The first is what we earn and spend or (if we are mad) save. The second exists in the accumulation of other people's savings, perhaps, but has no real existence outside the ledgers and VDU screens on which the digit appears. It is the money in government and corporate accounts, putative sums borrowed and lent on margins, bad debts, notional loans chasing a gambler's intuition on the international currency market, now appearing as Japanese yen on a screen in Sydney, seconds later as Australian dollars in London or Saudi ryals in Hong Kong.

When this bogus money is taken out of the VDUs, the trouble starts. In America, technological capitalism has created more wealth than there are goods or services to spend it on. Hence the great international modern art joke.

The biggest joke of all is to find honest Americans who think they really like these blocks of wood and have a bargain when they buy one for £28,750. Nobody in the modern-art world is going to laugh at the Americans, and there is no danger of them laughing at themselves. All those straight faces are what make the modern art scene irresistible.

## Getting above themselves

TWO developments in the medical field must convince us that medicine has gone far enough. Ever since doctors started discouraging the use of aspirin – sovereign remedy for nine out of 10 ailments – and urging the relatively more risky paracetamol, I have suspected that the medical profession was growing demented in its conceit and self-importance. Soon it will be spending more than our gross domestic product on itself and its footling experiments.

The latest absurdity is to suggest that healthy women should have their breasts removed if genetic tests suggest they might be more liable than most to develop breast cancer. If they refused, they would find it almost impossible to get life insurance, and employers would be reluctant to hire them (assuming that our medical histories are generally available on some national data bank).

Even more sinister than this, virologists are demanding that the smallpox virus, eradicated as one of the great scourges of mankind within living memory, should be kept alive so that they can continue to study it.

Perhaps they feel sentimental about these malign organisms in the same way that foolish people nowadays pretend to feel sentimental about bats. We are confused by quasi-religious green propaganda. It is all a bit of a shame. Doctors used to be such pleasant people. It will be a sad day when I have to advise that they should be treated like modern architects and punched in the face on sight.

# 8th December, 1993

### Albert the Golden

I SUPPOSE it is good news that work is to be resumed on restoring the Albert Memorial in Kensington Gardens after it has been hidden from view for six years and shrouded in a plastic box for three. This development follows English Heritage's decision to contribute £1 million towards the £11 million needed.

All these figures are nonsense, of course. If the Memorial was in private ownership, it could be patched up for £20,000, magnificently restored for £250,000. The plastic box and scaffolding which covers it now costs £80,000 a year to maintain. Its cubist effect is more pleasing to the 'modern' aesthetic than Scott's monument could ever be. For some time I have suspected a secret agenda, a deliberate act of sabotage, on the part of modernist aesthetes within the Heritage Department.

Even after spending £11 million, they will not restore the gilding to the central statue of Prince Albert. In God's own socialist republic of Burma, which I visited some years ago, I was told they spend a sixth of their gross national product regilding the various Buddhist shrines and pagodas. As a result of this, the Burmese can walk tall and proud in the company of their neighbours, whether Thai, Laotian, Chinese, Tibetan, Indian or Bangladeshi.

The English, by contrast, creep around their European partners with piteous faces and terrible whingeing noises. I am almost tempted to launch a public appeal to re-gild the statue of Prince Albert of Saxe-Coburg and Gotha, husband of our beloved Queen Victoria and great-great-great-great grandfather of Prince William. But perhaps, in the new spirit of Europe, we should ask the Germans to pay for it.

## 11th December, 1993

### In place of Christmas

IF IT is true that Lord Bristol spent £7 million feeding his drug habit, we should reflect that this represents £7 million paid straight into the criminal fraternity, sustaining it in life's struggles. Next we may take into account the hundreds of millions of pounds of taxpayers' money we spend on the war against drugs, through police, Customs, special drug enforcement agencies and now MI5 and MI6. On top of that we must take into account the cost to taxpayers of keeping Lord Bristol and about 12,000 other drug offenders in prison.

There was no need for Mr Carman to tell us that poor Lord Bristol was forced to wear long white gloves as a boy. There is no need to appeal to any bogus libertarian philosophy to establish the common-sense absurdity of trying to forbid people from killing themselves with drugs. But no government will ever voluntarily reduce the state's role in controlling private activities. Nor, I am sorry to say, will there ever be a sense of proportion when the state feels it is being defied.

Wednesday's picture of about 200 Metropolitan policemen in uniform who turned up to clear protesters from a 250-year-old chestnut tree threatened by a motorway in Wanstead, east London, inevitably made me wonder how many of them were on overtime. Was it really necessary for them to turn up in such numbers? Might they not have been more usefully employed elsewhere, for instance catching car thieves?

This week Mr Robert Key announced the opening of our annual festival of Abstinence and Immobility, whereby the entire population is forced to stay at home and watch whatever sickening rubbish the television controllers choose to send us. It is all very well for the police to say they are bound to enforce the law on drink driving at Christmas, but there are about 20,000 laws they do not enforce at any time of the year, among them the laws against stealing motor cars.

Of 580,000 cars driven away every year, about 200,000 disappear. The vast majority are sold in Britain on the second-hand car market with new number plates and forged registration documents.

But if any car submitted for the MOT test has a registration number which fails to conform with its chassis number on the central registration computer, or if its chassis number has been tampered with, or if the registration number, when checked, is that of a stolen car, then the game is up. Police could put a stop to the trade in stolen cars tomorrow if they had a mind to it. Instead we spend our law and order resources sending junkie marquesses to prison, terrorising motorway protesters and enforcing an annual anti-police festival of fear and loathing in place of Christmas.

## 15th December, 1993

### Protection needed

AMERICAN women are buying themselves life-size plastic replicas of men for Christmas to put in the car seat beside them. It is thought they will scare off muggers, rapists and burglars and also prevent car-jacking, which is said to be America's latest criminal craze.

Most Christmas presents bought in America nowadays are for people to give to themselves. This is a sad reflection on the breakdown of personal and family relationships, brought about in part by language difficulties, in part by the generation gap, in part by sexual anxieties, but chiefly by the inability of young Americans to be interested in anything but themselves.

'You're Never Alone With a Safe-T Man' says the advertising blurb for these plastic models, complete with designer stubble or optional moustache, looking like a really tough guy at $99.95 (£67) a time. 'Designed for use as a visual deterrent, Safe-T-Man tricks people into thinking you have the protection of a male guardian.'

Would it not be more satisfactory for these American women to have the protection of a real male guardian, instead of a 4lb plastic mock-up? Perhaps not. American women are reluctant to associate with American males nowadays without extensive legal guarantees.

But I doubt whether plastic replicas of American males would sell very well in this country. Car-jacking by male rapists has not yet really caught on, although there might be a market for female models to put in the car seat next to lone male drivers.

These would discourage women who jump into cars and threaten to cry 'rape' unless they are paid £50. Since every policeman and every judge in the country is obliged to believe any woman who complains of rape, an investment of £67 might make sense. The only alternative is to deny everything and face three years in prison, like poor Angus Diggle, the Bolton solicitor.

## The hidden people

IT IS encouraging that English country houses and estates are selling again, as the new rich discover the joys of privacy and space. Even before people started talking about the world population explosion, A. L. Rowse had pointed out that the best form of human existence known in the history of human civilisation was that of the English country house between the wars.

Some of the gilt has been lost with the disappearance of domestic servants, once the biggest single sector of labour in the country, but the horrors of noise, smells and enforced proximity in the world outside have increased a hundredfold.

Perhaps the English have always hated each other, and this is the explanation for our country house tradition. It would also explain the fact that we have the highest proportion of ex-directory telephone subscribers in the world, with a staggering 43 per cent of London subscribers choosing to have their numbers unlisted. Some say they are frightened of sex maniacs, others that they are irritated by unsolicited direct selling. A few pretend to themselves that they are celebrities, keeping an intrusive world press at arm's length by being unavailable.

No doubt some are genuinely on the run from past entanglements, others feel strangely more important for being hard to contact. But the real explanation, I feel, is the urge to shun human society as much as possible.

This passion for privacy is something which seems embedded in the English character. As the world population increases by some 96 million people every year, as more housing is built and more and more people expect to be allowed to make as much noise and as many smells as they can with cars, television sets and blaring hi-fi equipment, the unlisted telephone is the only symbol of privacy which survives, our only way of telling the rest of the world we do not want to know it.

## *18th December, 1993*

### Time to make friends

ALTHOUGH there is an understandable tendency to count our spoons, hitch up our trousers and tighten our belts whenever a new charismatic Liberal Democratic leader emerges, I cannot help feeling that we have over-reacted to the arrival of Vladimir Zhirinovsky in Russia.

He has been a familiar figure at Liberal International conferences and some of the ghastly bossiness and arrogance of these modern Liberals may have rubbed off on him, but it is over-reacting to describe him as fascist or, more insultingly, a neo-fascist, on the strength of the unpleasant anti-semitism which is a distressing feature of Russian politics.

Zhirinovsky's popular appeal has been described as xenophobic, but on analysis his xenophobia reduces chiefly to anti-Americanism. This is an interesting and important phenomenon.

I have no doubt that if the Russians knew about America, and if they were given the choice (which they can't be), they would vote for motorway food, canned music, moronic television programmes, junk art, the general glorification of stupidity and all the other cultural deformities which democratic capitalism imposes. However, that choice is not immediately available and Russia is now on the threshold of a historic decision.

They have experienced socialism and seen where it leads. Glimpses of America's mass entertainment culture in the McDonald's hamburger bars installed by Gorbachev, and in the antics of the new rich under Yeltsin, may persuade them that there is greater comfort to be derived from nursing their national pride and sucking their thumbs.

If so, it is an example which the rest of Europe could follow with advantage before our educated, bourgeois societies are all swamped in the horror of the new American people's culture. In the fulfilment of De Gaulle's dream of a *Europe des patries* stretching to the Urals, we have much to teach the Russians as they return, blinking, to the light, and much to learn from them.

## *22nd December, 1993*

### A pompous gesture

AT THE time of the publication of Andrew Morton's *Diana: Her Own Story* and the subsequent announcement of a royal estrangement, I vowed never to mention his subject again in this column. Now I feel the time has come to make a new resolution, not to mention any members of the Royal Family in the year ahead – unless some unfortunate development calls for a short obituary notice.

My reason for this is not hostility towards any member of the family, still less hostility to the monarchy, which may yet prove the only focus for a national identity in our sadly Americo-Murdochised world.

My fear is that this constant over-exposure which creates boredom and contempt in equal measure, whether its intention is adulatory or malicious, will finally succeed in transforming the monarchy into its own image – a plastic sideshow in the great Disneyworld of the mass entertainment culture – even if it does not succeed in destroying it outright.

In happier times, we might have prepared to rejoice at what would appear to be well-founded rumours of a romantic attachment in the life of Prince Edward. Even those of us who have been unable to feel any great personal curiosity about the young man would have welcomed the opportunity for a national celebration. London rejoiced, as I remember, even at the wedding of the Duke of York. Now we can look ahead to the tabloid coverage only with feelings of dread.

Three months ago, as that great chronicler of our times, Sir Nigel Dempster, reminds us, the *People* ran a 'world exclusive' story that the Princess Royal was pregnant. The Queen was 'delighted', the Princess Royal herself was 'absolutely thrilled' and Commander Laurence (her new husband) was 'ecstatically happy'. The baby would be a boy and born in February.

Now we learn the whole story was a complete invention. The tabloids could perfectly well make up these stories about an imaginary Royal Family, but it is hard to see how the monarchy can survive treatment of this sort. I do not expect all editors to follow my example. It is a personal, pompous gesture.

## Towards a new wormlessness

EVERY Christmas, with the regularity of the annual Police Terror and Crackdown, the *Sun* launches a bitter complaint about prisoners being given turkeys for Christmas. This year it picks upon a murderer called David Edwards who will 'tuck into a five-star Christmas feast beyond the wildest dreams of his victims' hard-up relatives'.

This five-star feast will consist of turkey, Brussels sprouts, carrots and Christmas pudding. Is such a Christmas meal really beyond the wildest dreams of those on the dole? Even if it is, I still do not think that prison authorities should be forbidden to budget for a Christmas treat, even if it means less gruel for the prisoners during Advent.

But this brutal attitude of vindictiveness towards anyone in prison seems commonplace in modern Britain. At the other extreme we have the humane tradition producing even greater absurdities. A 17-year-old awaiting sentence on charges of ram-raiding and burglary has been unable to attend court because he is still on an 80-day foreign tour paid for by Gloucester social services.

Its idea was to rehabilitate him by taking him away from the negative influence of his peer group. With a £200-a-week companion he has visited the pyramids and temples of Egypt on a Nile cruise, and spent months on safari studying the wild life of Tanzania, Kenya, Zambia, Malawi and Zimbabwe.

Is there any middle course between the brutality of the *Sun* reader and the barminess of the Bryn Melyn therapy centre in North Wales, which takes mollycoddlying criminals to the heights of a new art form?

It sometimes seems to me that the brutes and the loonies are chiefly concerned to establish some sort of barrier between them, such as used to be provided within the old class system. Commonsense has nothing to do with it. Nobody could have guessed what a can of worms Mr Major was opening when he announced his goal of the classless society.

## *1st January, 1994*

### Protection notes

MY NEW Year resolutions, already announced, are not to mention any member of the Royal Family for a year, and not to mention one particular member ever again. I have also resolved never to fly by British Airways, if I can possibly avoid it, for as long as the new ban on smoking, even on long-haul flights, remains. This ban comes into force today, and should successfully turn away not only the 27 per cent of long-distance air travellers who smoke, but also those who wish to travel with them.

My final resolve, in the light of Mr Howard's funking of police reform, is to keep up a regular Police Watch. This was originally prompted by the scandalous sums charged in police stations for the use of a police cell – a product of even more scandalous police overtime rates. It is also prompted in part by the new accent on harassing law abiders and ignoring criminals. Now I hear curious stories from all over the country.

Bedfordshire police, I have been told, charge the sum of £111.63 for every stolen car that is recovered. They authorise a local entrepreneur to tow these cars into a compound before notifying the owner, and will not release the car unless they are paid.

A slightly more sinister development is that police chiefs in the same county are planning to hire out constables as security men outside pubs and nightclubs. The price is £31 per hour per officer. The rub is that if publicans or club owners refuse to pay, the police will oppose licence renewal on the grounds of inadequate security.

I do not say that anything improper is going on, merely that it needs watching. Perhaps I might take this opportunity of thanking the West Mercia Constabulary Traffic Department for its delightful Christmas card, showing a traffic squad singing carols beside their squad car, and wish all good policemen everywhere a merry New Year.

## *3rd January, 1994*

---

### Lockerbie's last victim

THE SAD story of David Flannigan should be set to music and sung wherever British teenagers congregate. Leaving home after a quarrel with his father at the age of 16, David was thinking of going back to them two years later when an American airliner exploded over their home in Lockerbie, killing both parents and a young sister.

Given £1 million compensation three years later, he was stricken with remorse – 'I don't like being called a millionaire even if it's true,' he explained. 'Money can't replace a family' – and went off on a series of wild binges. On Wednesday, five years after the Lockerbie tragedy, he died aged 23, alone in a hotel in Thailand, the result, it is thought, of drink and drugs.

Many teenagers will have been intrigued by the idea of receiving £1 million after having their families wiped out, but the moral of David's sad story is that they should not be rewarded in this way. I made myself unpopular in Liverpool at the time of the Hillsborough disaster by urging that apart from dependent widows and orphans, relatives of the deceased should not receive compensation. It seemed an unhealthy principle, as well as inviting the sort of tragedy we have just seen overtake David Flannigan, to give them large sums of money in exchange for lost relatives.

With the arrival of the National Lottery, there can be no further excuse for these bonanzas. Let the nation's teenagers dream of winning their millions that way. It is much healthier.

# 5th January, 1994

## Stay as we are

SWITZERLAND, with its population of six and a half million, remains the richest country in the world with an average income of £24,153. The United States comes eighth with an average of £15,413. It is beaten by Iceland (pop. 247,000), Norway (4.2m), Denmark (5.1m), Sweden (8.3m) and Luxembourg which, with an average income of £23,500, has a population of 366,000.

Six of the seven richest nations in the world have an average population of little more than four million. The odd man out is Japan, which rates third, a long way behind Luxembourg. America and Japan are much less highly taxed than we are, requiring an average of 121 and 122 days' work each to pay the taxman, against 145 in Britain and 165 in the European Community as a whole. Apart from these two, the general tendency in the larger democracies is for government to grow and grow and grab all the money for itself and its employees.

The optimum population would appear to be around four million – almost exactly the combined populations of Cornwall, Devon, Dorset, Wiltshire, Gloucestershire and Somerset plus Bath. It is a tempting idea, but then another thought intervenes. Do we really want the new Britons to be much richer than they already are? They lack the discipline of the Swiss, the restraint of the Japanese, the cleanliness of the Swedes, the good taste of the Luxembourgeois, the manners of the Danes . . . and the American example is not really one which any reflective person would wish to follow. Think of the noise they would make, the smells, the ugly buildings. Perhaps we should stay as we are.

# 8th January, 1994

## Shopping news

NOBODY should be surprised that the Government proposes to crack down on car boot sales, invoking every sort of planning law in its gigantic armoury of oppressive and unenforceable legislation. Of its vast army of 5.2 million public employees who are slowly throttling the country to death, a huge proportion is employed to make a nuisance of itself in the field of shopping.

This army determines what can be sold, when, to whom and under what circumstances. In support of the forces of inspection, regulation and control, sycophantic press, radio and television reports call for further controls, whether on children's toys or sheep medicine. The *Independent* recently reported demands for control on the sale and advertising of sweets to children.

Against this, the car boot sale seems our only guarantee that commercial life will survive. It offers an escape, however illegal, from Lady Thatcher's determination that Britons should derive no benefit from membership of the European Community. Perhaps it would be extreme to suggest it offers an escape from local councils' crooked and extortionate hold on the adoption market.

The great case against car boot sales is that they provide an easy outlet for stolen goods. However, since the police are no longer able to do anything to discourage theft, and few of us can reckon to keep our ancestral knick-knacks for long, one might say that car boot sales at least offer us an opportunity to replace them with someone else's ancestral goods at a reasonable price.

## Some modern mums

AFTER the devastating news that around seven children were left alone over Christmas by neglectful parents – there were immediate cries for an increase in government supervision over every human activity to ensure this could never happen again – we learn that 800,000 children aged between five and 10 are left alone at home every day.

I must confess I am not surprised. Ever since the cost of housing caught up with the two-income family 10 years ago, it has been obvious that couples must either wait until they are 59 before having babies, or they must leave their children alone while both parents go out to work. The idea of socialist creches where toddlers were taught to read the *Guardian* and sing songs in praise of Polly Toynbee was always absurd. Socialist carers tend to be devilishly expensive.

The question we must ask ourselves is whether it really does children much harm to be separated from their parents. A few will always have dreadful accidents with toasters and carving knives, but we cannot organise a national way of life to cater for parents who are unable to put these things out of children's reach.

It is my observation of modern parents that by responding to a child's every whim or whimper, they do little but harm. They will create a race of whingeing egocentrics.

Left alone, children might have time to meditate on the human condition. More likely, I agree, they will watch television or play computer games. The American example shows how these can have appalling results, but our television is less bad than theirs and I do not think that even computer games can be worse for them than some modern mums.

## 12th January, 1994

### The next scare

AN ARTICLE by Matt Ridley in the *Economist*'s annual supplement, 'The World in 1994', lists all the discredited environmental scares of the past decade. Global warming, towards which, when it was at the height of its fashion, Mrs Thatcher proposed devoting £250 million of public money, has been shown to involve a change of one degree a century. Acid rain, said to be killing a third of Germany's trees, has been exposed as a total fraud, not killing trees at all.

But it took a $1 billion, 10-year official American study of acid rain by non-partisan scientists to reach this conclusion and refute the claims of partisan scientists within the environmental lobby. This lobby can raise enormous funds from any area which catches the popular imagination.

Between them, the scientists and environmentalists seem to be carving out a rather cosy corner for themselves. Ridley shows that because the sentimental public wanted an ivory ban, the green lobby suppressed a study showing that the ban of 1989 actually harmed elephants.

Where should the environmentalists turn next for their greens? Ridley suggests there might be some mileage in the theory that cellular telephones cause cancer. This seems a thoroughly good cause, but I feel we must stress the dangers of passive cellular telephoning – cancer caught from people using their machines next to one in the train, or in the same carriage, or restaurant.

In scares of this sort, no amount of scientific debunking makes the slightest difference. Day after day we hear government ministers making claims about the dangers of passive smoking which are not so much unproven as proveably untrue. They are fed these lies by partisan scientists and accept them uncritically. In fact, many scientists now believe that the commonest cause of cerebral cancer in the 25-50 age group is passive cellular telephoning, caught from the electric field around cellular telephonists in a confined space. At least it should justify a £500 million government-sponsored scientific inquiry. But the oddest thing about Ridley's brilliant treatise is that he nowhere mentions the environmental threat from hamburger gases (HGs).

## The deterrent principle

PUNISHMENT enthusiasts should be encouraged to learn that the convicted teenager sent on a £7,000 tour of Egypt and Central Africa at public expense, before being sentenced for car thefts etc, did not actually enjoy his treatment. In fact he described the three-month trip as 'weird and stupid', complained that the Pyramids were 'nothing special', the food was 'rubbish' and declared: 'I'd rather have been in prison.'

The great thing, we must all agree, is to make these young offenders suffer, however much it costs. Many would be deeply humiliated and offended to be sent to the opera, let alone the ballet. Others could be shut into the Saatchi collection for a month or sent to New York's Museum of Modern Art.

Really serious offenders could be required to listen to lectures on Picasso and the Modern movement by Wolverhampton arts graduates employed by the Arts Council, or readings from their poetry by poets of the calibre of Michael Horowitz and Alan Jenkins.

But no. We must not allow ourselves to become sadistic. Justice must be tempered with mercy. Spare them from Counsellors and Poets; send them to eat snails in Brussels.

## *15th January, 1994*

## Forever playing leapfrog

TRY as I might, I cannot make up my mind about this month's parliamentary vote on the homosexual age of consent. Perhaps it is because it does not concern me that I have no desire to settle the matter and tell people firmly what they should do.

Let us thank heavens for the Anglican bishops. 'Can the bishops lead us back to basics?' asks Margot Norman in *The Times*. 'Once again the Church is giving moral guidance while the Government displays moral confusion.' The bishops of Edinburgh and Monmouth, we learn elsewhere, favour a reduction of the homosexual age of consent to 16, in line with that for heterosexuals, but St Albans wants it kept at 21. York, Bath and Wells and Oxford all favour a compromise, reducing the age to 18.

Have they considered that it may not be just the very young who need protecting, but also the very old? Many old people become confused and do not really know what they are agreeing to. But this is only part of a much greater confusion. Many people of both sexes and all ages are constitutionally incapable of making up their minds either way.

And all this time poor Angus Diggle, the Bolton solicitor, rots in Usk prison, serving a three-year sentence for trying to climb into bed with a woman who had invited him into her room, stripped naked and climbed into bed in front of him.

At what age do the bishops feel this sort of thing should be allowed?

## *26th January, 1994*

### Lennon's death explained

MY NOTE on the dreaded Beatles Reunion next month prompts one correspondent to ask why there has never been a full inquiry into the circumstances of John Lennon's death, as there has been into every detail of the shooting of John Kennedy. Lennon was just as famous as the American politician – he once said The Beatles were more popular than Jesus – and his death was every bit as important. Can anyone seriously believe it was the unaided work of one deranged man?

Where Kennedy's assassination is concerned, the conspiracy theory has become a major industry, but I would be surprised if there was anything in it. Much may be made of the fact that Lee Harvey Oswald once visited the Soviet embassy in Mexico City. I once visited the Soviet embassy in Manila, being taken there by my taxi driver in mistake for the British embassy residence. The Soviet embassy was holding a reception for the Red Cross, and it was half an hour before I realised my mistake.

There is no need for any conspiracy to explain Oswald's behaviour. The most significant fact about him, which is only seldom mentioned in books on the subject, and never given due weight, is that he lived exclusively on a diet of hamburgers and soft drinks.

Of course the man was deranged. The only surprising thing is that he managed to shoot straight through all the gases swirling around him. Where Lennon's assassin, Mark Chapman, is concerned, I would not be in the least bit surprised to learn that he, too, subsisted on hamburgers and sweet, fizzy drinks.

To those who object it is inconceivable that two deranged hamburger eaters would be able to hit their targets within a space of 17 years, I would point out that Chapman was standing much closer to his target than Oswald was. Furthermore, I would not be surprised to learn that Chapman, the deranged CIA operative, had, in fact, missed. His victim, Lennon, also a hamburger and fizzy drink man, expired on the spot out of fright and inner corrosion.

## 2nd February, 1994

### Sending it up

EXCITING new religious tensions produced the rock musical performed in an Islington Congregational Church between services, with a chorus line of nuns in suspender belts and a scene of simulated rape on the alter; the Pope collapses and dies after being seduced by a naked nun.

The church's minister, the Reverend Dr Janet Wootton, explains that she is anxious to carry out her religious duty to care for the community: 'The arts are part of this mission. I can't see anything wrong with sending up religion.'

No doubt she is right, but sinister cries of 'no Popery' and rumblings of a new Popish plot can also be heard. The parts of Lord George Gordon and Titus Oates are taken by Ferdinand Mount, a lapsed baronet, writing in *The Spectator*, and Dr Tim Bradshaw, Dean of Regents Park College, Oxford, writing in *The Times*.

Bradshaw has uncovered 'a powerful corps of Right-wing Catholic journalists committed regularly to write corrosive articles' about the Church of England. 'The clear message has been that Anglicanism should be replaced by Romanism as the nation's primary expression of Church life'. A 'huge media assault on the Church of England by this group' is to be expected at Easter.

The main features of the original Popish Plot, uncovered by Titus Oates in 1678, were a rising of the Catholics, a general massacre of Protestants, the assassination of the King (Charles II) and the placing of his brother James on the throne (although I suppose the modern equivalent would be the replacement of the Queen by the Duchess of Kent).

Speaking as one of the conspirators identified by Dean Tim, I can only assure the world that I have no such intentions. In fact I have the greatest affection for the Church of England. It is only on the subject of its primate, Dr Carey, that I have reservations, but my doubts are those of the ordinary sceptic, rather than those of a militant Roman Catholic.

It has often been my observation that people of Dr Carey's background, when promoted beyond their reasonable expectations, sometimes become insufferably conceited. See what happened to Wolsey. I simply do not believe that Carey has this quasi-miraculous power, which he claims, to turn women into priests. Why should he? None of the 264 Popes and 31 Anti-Popes in two millennia of the Church's history claimed to be able to do that, not even the fictional ninth-century Pope Joan.

That is why I urged his Australian colleague, the Archbishop of Perth, to try it out on kangaroos first, to see if it works. If it doesn't work when Dr Carey starts trying to turn women into priests, he will make his church look foolish. That may not matter much, but he will also make the women look foolish, which is inexcusable. Far better to let them dress up as nuns in suspender belts and mock religion that way.

## *7th February, 1994*

### Never the same

ABOUT 20 years ago, I was given the task of investigating the claim that bad housing is responsible for the anti-social and criminal behaviour of people who live in it. My conclusion, after some weeks of interviewing slum-dwellers in London, Liverpool and Manchester, was the opposite: slums did not produce delinquency in their inhabitants; it was the delinquency of the inhabitants which produced slums. Respectable families put into the same buildings kept clean, respectable homes, where children were as likely as not to be honest and hard working.

Even so, it occurred to me that families in such restricted accommodation were unlikely to know about the benefits of the crying room, where babies or children who wish to cry can be put until they have decided to stop crying. These are of tremendous benefit to everyone. In modern flats or houses, babies or children who cry must be picked up, coddled and instantly obeyed to stop them crying. Hence the present generation of unemployables.

Some years ago, Staffordshire County Council tried introducing the crying-room principle in its children's homes. Delinquent behaviour was punished by sending children to their bedrooms. When word of this got out, there was a great outcry. It was called 'pin-down', like some Japanese torture, and huge sums of money were later paid in compensation to anyone who had suffered it. This compensation usually has terrible results.

One such victim was up before Stoke-on-Trent Crown Court last Saturday. The court heard how single mother Sarah Flynn, 21, blew her £18,000 compensation on drugs within five weeks, before embarking on a life of crime to feed her newly acquired habit. As her defending council said before she was sent down for 18 months after pleading guilty to 24 charges:

'The £18,000 pay-out was supposed to help her adjust, but, as in the case of many others, it has not helped her at all. The money took her into areas of illicit drug use that she would not have been able to go into.'

It is not sending children to their rooms which does them harm. It is the compensation you have to pay them afterwards.

## *9th February, 1994*

### Not a good idea

AT A party to celebrate Adam Sisman's excellent new biography of A. J. P. Taylor, held at the Imperial War Museum, I bumped into Paul Johnson, the crusading journalist and fellow member of the new Popish Plot to take England back to Rome.

When I started making secret signs at him however, he stared at me blankly and asked what I was doing. Rather to my embarrassment, I had to spell it out. Our plan was to arrange an uprising of Catholics who would kill all the Protestants, remove the Queen from the throne and replace her with the Duchess of Kent, I explained patiently.

Johnson heard me out and thought about it for a while. 'I don't think that's right,' he said. 'No, I don't think that's a good idea at all.'

Of course, I was tremendously disappointed at the time, especially after all the work that I and other members of the committee had put into the plan. But brooding about it afterwards, I began to think that Johnson may be right.

There is a tremendous amount of aggression around these days. Ambulance crews in Manchester now have to wear bulletproof vests to go about their work of mercy. Wherever I go I meet foolish people saying we should join the civil war in Bosnia. Pressure for intervention is growing, they say. What does this mean? Pressure has nothing to do with it. Bosnia is none of our business.

Our greatest test will come with the Russo-Ukranian war, which I have been predicting ever since the break-up of the Soviet Union. This strange urge to join in any scrap, anywhere in the world, must come from some semi-conscious desire for a new world war, a new holocaust. Meanwhile, it might be good training if we left the Protestants unkilled, the throne undisturbed.

## *12th February, 1994*

### Worrying

I SUPPOSE we should all rejoice that up to 100,000 American teenagers have signed 'pledge cards' to remain virgins until marriage. They would not understand if we murmured Horace's exhortation, *Carpe diem*, but we might try the poet Herrick:

> *Gather ye rosebuds while ye may*
> *Old Time is still a-flying*
> *And this same flower that smiles today*
> *Tomorrow will be dying.*

It may have been terror of death and of the dreaded American disease, as much as religious conviction, which persuaded them to sign the pledge in the first place. Either way, they face a gloomy future, eating hamburgers and waiting for someone to propose marriage as they endlessly worry about dying.

The latest lunacy on this score, reported in the *International Herald Tribune*, is a Bill before Congress to ban all smoking in any public building, whether privately or publicly owned.

For the purposes of this prohibition, a public building is any building (except a private residence) which more than 10 people enter during the day at least once a week. Smoking will be permanently banned in any such building, or in the vicinity of its entrance.

It would be nice to think there is enough spirit left in the country for Americans to rise up, drag these wretched Clintons from their smoke-free White House and throw them into the Potomac with all their ethnically selected staff, their pet lesbians and shredded documents.

## Silence of the lambs

ON WEDNESDAY Lord Justice Neill, Lord Justice Hoffmann and Lord Justice Waite allowed an appeal by Central Television against a gagging order by the High Court Family Division designed to protect a five-year-old child from learning disagreeable truths about her father. A child's privacy was less important than the principle of free speech, they decided. Lord Justice Hoffman went further, in words which should be printed in every legal textbook on any subject. Comparing freedom of speech to a trump card, which must always win, he said:

'A freedom which is restricted to what judges think to be responsible or in the public interest is no freedom. Freedom means the right to publish things which government and judges, however well motivated, think should not be published.'

No freedom was without cost, he pointed out, but the judiciary should never whittle away freedom of speech in exceptional cases. What a pity the Attorney General, Sir Nicholas Lyell, could not have read these wise words before deciding to ban *Maxwell: The Musical*, on the grounds that it might prejudice the eventual trial of Maxwell's sons on charges of conspiracy to defraud.

Sir Nicholas sought the injunction 12 months after the

musical was announced (and 18 months after the Maxwell brothers were charged) when the theatre had been hired, the cast paid, programmes printed and 4,000 tickets sold. To many, his timing will seem almost deliberately oppressive.

Most annoying of all is that I and many others were really looking forward to this musical. For more than 10 years Maxwell terrorised the press and bludgeoned it into silence with the threat of libel writs, while be pursued his various activities. He even took a former Lord Chancellor on his payroll.

Now that Maxwell can no longer issue writs for libel, the Attorney General keeps us quiet with threats of action for contempt of court. Damn Sir Nicholas Lyell. I was *particularly* looking forward to this musical, which uses tunes from the Savoy operas of Gilbert & Sullivan to put across its message, whatever that might be.

## 14th February, 1994

### Watch how you toss

TOMORROW is Shrove Tuesday, last day before the miseries of Lent. For many centuries, Shrove Tuesday has been thought a suitable time to eat pancakes, but there is no human activity nowadays without its health and safety ramifications. This explains a fax which arrived on my desk from the Somerset Red Cross: 'Red Cross Advice for a Safe Pancake Day.

Toss your pancake on Shrove Tuesday, but don't throw caution to the wind, warns the British Red Cross. Make sure you take proper safety precautions when preparing pancakes.

The very hot fat which is needed to make the traditionally thin pancake can cause extremely serious burns . . .'

The Red Cross experts give the following advice for avoiding a Pancake Day crisis:

• 'Prepare the pancakes in advance when you have the kitchen to yourself and are not likely to be interrupted.

• 'If this is not possible, keep children and any other visitors out of the kitchen.

• 'Never leave hot pans unattended.'

This is followed by advice on first aid to anyone suffering from pancake burns. Obviously, we cannot laugh at these anxieties. I would not be surprised to learn that two or three people die every year from pancake-linked accidents on Shrove Tuesday. This is against 1.8 policemen killed on duty, 46 prisoners who commit suicide and 150-200 who die from this newly discussed danger of auto-erotic asphyxia.

## 16th February 1994

### Medical mystery

MANY commentators have expressed surprise that no blame appears to attach to anyone in the National Health Service over its employment of the mad Beverley Allitt as a student nurse. She attacked or murdered 13 small children in a Grantham hospital before being discovered.

The incident reinforces an impression among these who still remain outside public employment that the nation's public employees are engaged in a conspiracy not only to grab all our earnings and throttle the economy, but also to cover up for each other on every occasion.

Recently I decided to put this theory to the test. On January 22 I received a letter from a local NHS panel addressed to Mrs Rose M. Kennedy, at my address, inviting her to attend for a cervical smear test. On January 28 I wrote to the Director of the Somerset Family Health Services Authority pointing out that there had been no Rose Kennedy at my address for the past 38 years.

It occurred to me that Rose Kennedy was the mother of a former President of the United States, and this might explain the confusion, just as Fleet Street printers used to invent shifts for Mickey Mouse and Donald Duck in the bad old days. But it would be a pity from the point of view of NHS budgeting, I pointed out, if doctors' panels were to draw money from the NHS in the name of the Mickey Mouse patients.

On February 1 the Patient Registration Manager of the SFHSA wrote back to suggest that the patient must have moved out of the area, and said it had now arranged for her name to be removed from the practice's patient list. On February 5 I wrote back to the PRM of the SFHSA:

*'My point was not that Mrs Rose Kennedy might have moved and registered elsewhere, but that she had never existed at this address, at any rate in the last 38 years when we have been living here, and she must therefore be a complete invention. I was alarmed to think that the Somerset Health Authority had been paying for a patient who never existed. She can scarcely have moved out of the area if she was never in it. What was worrying me was whether there might have been an element of fraud involved which, perhaps, you might investigate.'*

On February 11 the PRM of the SFHSA wrote:

*'Mrs Rose Kennedy registered with the . . . practice 40 years ago, in 1954, and gave Combe Florey House as her address. I must therefore assume that she lived at that address for a short time before you lived there.'*

Which, if true, would explain everything – she might, I suppose, have been a housekeeper to the previous owners – except why the local panel should suddenly invite her to a smear test after 38 years' absence. Personally, I feel I have not got to the bottom of the mystery.

## A question of survival

IF A single item from the week's news captures our contemporary British predicament, it may be the story of a patient in St Mary's Hospital, Paddington, who was stuck in the lift for 26 hours before anyone noticed. Mr. James Wataroh, 29, was missed from his ward at 1pm but was not found until 3 pm the next day, when engineers turned up to fix the jammed lift.

By the same token the shoot-out at a Tulsa, Oklahoma hamburger store might serve as the equivalent American experience. Marcus Muriel Thompson, 26, a disgruntled employee of Wendy's Hamburgers, shot four high school girls and two fellow employees.

One would have thought that with the terrible example of J. F. Kennedy and John Lennon in their minds, Americans would have come to terms with hamburger-linked violence. Yet still they seem strangely ashamed, strangely secretive about it.

Why, do we suppose, has Chelsea Clinton, the Clintons' teenage daughter, disappeared from the news since she was first presented to the world at the Clintons' famous smoke-free inauguration ball on January 20 last year?

An entire section of the White House pubic relations department is devoted to supplying news about Socks, the Clintons' cat. But there is no equivalent fan club for Chelsea. One can only hope she has not been murdered, like poor Vincent Foster. The explanation for her disappearance, I suspect, is to be found in *raisons d'état*. When she was presented to the world, instead of expressing feelings of compassion towards this classic hamburger victim, the world recoiled. We did not ask whether her condition was hereditary or environmental, whether Mrs Clinton had eaten hamburgers when pregnant, whether her nursery had been properly ventilated to remove hamburger gases at night.

It was at that point, I feel, that the Americans began to take stock. If the rest of the world rejects hamburgers, it rejects the whole of American Culture, the American Dream. After the Cold War, the United States can survive only by selling this American Dream. Chelsea Clinton, in so many ways a typical American teenager, represents a big obstacle to America's survival in the new world order.

## Vespal Virgins

IT WOULD be a tragedy if nice Mr Major dropped his Back to Basics campaign at this bleak time in our nation's history when it is providing so much laughter and fun for the rest of us.

The surviving hero of the Family Values section so far is still Mr David Ashby, Conservative Member for Leicestershire NW, who chastely shared a bed with his male friend on holiday in France in order to save money.

But Mr Hartley Booth must run them a close second. His four-month friendship with the Left-wing 22-year-old Emily Barr involved no sexual impropriety, although she claims to sleep with a condom on her bedside table and, according to the *Sun*, they would register together in hotels under an assumed name.

A question arises in the councils of the Venerable Society for the Protection of Adulterers (VESPA), of which I have the honour to be president: whether we should exert ourselves also to protect these non-adulterers. I think we should. Our purpose is to protect people in the public eye from the prurient vindictiveness of the gutter press. Non-adulterers such as Mr Booth (wittily known as Vespal Virgins) certainly qualify.

The time may have come to move our campaign into the enemy's camp. In a circular message from the chairman, all members will be advised, when booking into an hotel with their lawful husbands or wives, to book under an assumed name. Then they should pay with their proper credit cards.

It needs only a tip-off from a hotel receptionist to the *Sun* or the *News of the World* and a successful libel action seems assured. I do not normally advise people to sue newspapers for libel, but until Mr Murdoch drops his dirty habits, we have no choice.

## Somebody loves them

ON SATURDAY, two days before the feast of St Valentine, the *Sun* sent a special message to those of its readers who were in prison, tipping them off about a baby batterer sent to prison for three years:

'The sentence is an insult. Baby batterers should get a minimum of 10 years. Fortunately, there is still justice in the world. The thug will get a rough time in prison. *Sun* readers in the nick might like to know his name is . . .'

This is an open exhortation to *Sun* readers in prison to beat up a particular prisoner. If Mr Howard, the Home Secretary, had half the courage of a drunk chicken, he would ban the *Sun* from all prisons immediately.

On Monday, St Valentine's Day, also celebrated as National Impotence Awareness Day, the *Sun* addressed its readers again: 'Did you get a Valentine card today? If you were forgotten, don't worry. *Somebody loves you. Everybody here at the Sun.*'

## 5th March, 1994

### An English Munch

IT WILL take us some time to recover from the huge photograph of an English boy – or possibly girl – eating a hamburger on page 21 of this week's shock issue. The text article by Dr Theodore Dalrymple suggests that criminality among young people need not always be blamed on their diet. Idle and over-indulgent parents are just as much to blame, he argues, but the camera cannot lie, and his ingenious argument is belied by the picture chosen to illustrate it.

In this haunting photograph by Eric Roberts we see how the hamburger has in some mysterious and terrible way become part of the English child's mouth. The split bun has replaced its lips, the meatloaf has become its tongue and a large onion round represents a swollen, toothless gum. Some chopped lettuce would appear to be what this abominable mouth is eating.

Just as Edvard Munch's famous picture of *The Scream* sums up all the desperation of life in Oslo at the end of the last century – the boredom, the gloom, the Scandinavian madness – so this photograph sums up all the degradation of our present state.

Dr Dalrymple may claim that much of our allegedly healthy food has equally harmful effects. I am certainly prepared to believe, from my own observation, that too much salad can drive people mad, especially young women. But, so long as Mr Roberts's photograph remains, we will know where the truth lies. It is infinitely more horrifying than any photograph to have emerged from the Balkan conflicts.

Entitled *Good Grub*, perhaps, or just *England 1994*, it would easily become as famous as Munch's *Scream*. Best of all it should be magnified 40 times and put behind the Speaker's chair in the House of Commons as a reminder to our legislators of the sort of society they are creating.

## Speak, Bradford

IN MY recent diet of American newspapers I came across an article in the *Herald Tribune* on the subject of Britain's policy in Bosnia. It was headed 'An Equivocating Britain Leads the West Down the Slippery Slope'. Its writer, Tom Gallagher, explained:

'British policy towards the war in the Balkans has been based not just on ignorance and prejudice, but on the short-term interests of a floundering political élite in London. The élite, largely isolated from the public and insulated in its outlook, feels more affinity for Russia . . . than it does for its main West European partners. This helps to explain why Britain supports a Russian role in Bosnia . . .'

One might suppose that this drivel was written by some Irish American Noraid fund-raiser in New York, except for the dateline: Bradford, England – and the note at the end: 'The writer is a senior academic in the Peace Studies Department of Bradford University, England.'

Gosh. If Gallagher is a senior academic in Bradford's Peace Studies Department, I wonder what the junior ones are like. But it is alarming how all these Peace Students seem to feel that wherever there is a war between nations or even a civil war, as in Bosnia, it is the duty of every other country in the world to decide who are the goodies and who the baddies, then pile into the war on that basis.

This seems to me not only stupid and wrong, but also a possible recipe for world war whenever fighting breaks out between two gangs of hooligans anywhere in the world.

Is that what we want? Is there a conscious desire for another major war ever since the near-success of America's disgusting campaign in the Gulf?

# 7th March, 1994

## Angry thoughts

I WAS sorry to learn that Andrex, the makers of lavatory paper (or toilet tissue, as they prefer), have caved in when threatened by a Greenpeace advertising campaign which would have linked the firm with the destruction of rainforests.

Why must we all care about rainforests? Am I alone in thinking that it is for countries which have these wretched things to decide what they want to do with them, that it is none of our business? Where Andrex was concerned, it has cancelled wood pulp contracts with companies logging around Clayoquot Sound, Canada, described as the largest remaining area of temperate rainforest in the world.

Temperate or intemperate, why must poor Canadians be saddled with these useless things? People used to blame bad weather on destruction of the rainforests, but responsible scientific opinion is coming round to the view that this is probably caused by hamburger gases issuing from the North American continent and now swathing the globe like some enormous piece of dirty underwear. For my own part, I will buy no more Andrex.

# 14th March, 1994

## Publishing opportunity

IT IS sad that the best-selling book in Japan at the moment is a detailed guide to suicide, listing 11 ways of killing yourself and assessing each method in terms of its dignity, efficiency and the amount of nuisance it creates for others.

Of the 11 methods discussed – they include freezing, electrocution, jumping from a great height, self-immolation, various forms of poisoning, hanging, drowning, cutting arteries – hanging seems to score highest marks.

Nobody knows why 550,000 copies of *The Complete Manual of Suicide* have been sold in Japan after a first printing of only 8,000 copies. One explanation points to the economic recession, another to general gloom about the modern world.

I think there is a more specific reason than either of these. The

Japanese have suffered a particular tragedy in recent history. Twenty years ago, when I first visited Japan, their womenfolk, who subsisted on a diet of raw fish and seaweed, were not only highly intelligent but also tiny. Infinitely delicate in every limb and graceful in every movement, they controlled their men by charming them.

Even then, I noticed some extraordinarily large schoolgirls and feared the worst.

Now, after 20 years of eating American-style breakfasts, they are no smaller than women from Barnsley or Bootle, and scarcely more intelligent. They boss their men and box their ears like French housewives.

It has been a sad moment for the Japanese male, to lose all pride and self-respect at the same time as losing his greatest sensual pleasure. Even so, I do not think suicide is the answer. One way to score off these bossy, charmless women would be to send for the Bishop of Bristol to come and 'ordain' them all. Then the warriors of Japan could sit back on their red velvet cushion and laugh at them, as we have been laughing at Bishop Barry's gang all this weekend.

I hope we go on laughing as the mass 'ordinations' proceed. About 1,300 are planned for this year, but I rather fear that, like Nazi executions, the numbers will grow.

Then we shall become bored, and sad, too, and it will be time for some enterprising London publisher to inquire about British rights to *The Complete Manual of Suicide*.

## Chat-up line

MR JUSTICE Waterhouse was obviously right to disallow a husband's alleged murder confession which had been taped by an undercover policewoman. The husband was trying to get the policewoman to bed with him when he said he knew his wife was dead because he had personally strangled her and put her body in an incinerator.

Many men will say anything to get a woman into bed with them for the first time, but no woman in her senses would be taken in by such a chat-up line.

It is a shocking waste of police time when we send policewomen to extract confessions in this way. They could be digging for bodies in Gloucester or using the Metropolitan Police helicopter to arrest ginger tom cats in North London. The fact that eight North Londoners reported one to the police for looking like a lioness shows how well the Crimewatch campaign is working.

But we really don't want policewomen promising to marry us if only we confess to murder. It makes me wonder how far they would be prepared to go for a bank robbery confession, or what sort of confession they would demand for a quick cuddle behind the bus shelter. This is not what law enforcement is all about.

## 16th March, 1994

### Serve them right

WHENEVER the Government, or most especially Mr Major, announces a 'crackdown' we should fear the worst. They are nearly always silly, and very seldom work. On Sunday Mr Major announced a crackdown on seaside dole hotels. 'Small hotels have been advertising specifically to attract benefit claimants,' he said. 'It tends to change the character of the area and gives rise to huge complaints.'

He is thought to have been put up to this by Sir Teddy Taylor, Conservative MP for Southend East, who said the town had suffered from a 'nightmare of problems caused by drugs and petty crime'.

I don't know. These people have to live somewhere, and I don't see why they should not live in Southend East. In fact it seems rather a good place for them. In Combe Florey, for instance, there are no hotels, no seaside amenities at all, only a little hunting on offer. Sir Teddy does not care much about other people's pleasures, as he demonstrated by voting with 27 other 'Tories' to ban the ancient English sport of foxhunting in the Commons on February 14, 1992.

Perhaps he is proud to see himself up there with Captain 'Paddy' Stinker-Pantsdown and the Liberal Democrats of Somerset. For my own part, I hope every welfare claimant in the South of England goes to live in Southend taking with them as many problems caused by drugs and petty crime as they can carry. If the voters of Southend complain, I can only suggest that it serves them right for choosing such a vulgar and unpleasant little Scotsman as their MP.

# 19th March, 1994

## Only joking

ON TUESDAY night we were once again burgled in Somerset, but the burglars were frightened away and did not penetrate far into the house. In fact we have been very lucky – our last burglary was six years ago, despite the best efforts of Somerset County Council to turn the county into a haven for New Age travellers.

It is an encouraging development that the Children of the New Age turn out to be too nervous and disorganised to make convincing burglars. When they run away in terror, they often leave poignant little souvenirs. If they had penetrated further and encountered some of the practical jokes I have prepared for them, they might have left fingers, hands, whole limbs behind, as well.

The problem will then arise whether to donate these odd appendages, organs and limbs to the NHS, or whether to sell them to hospitals in London which look after visiting Arab sheikhs and their relations. One's first instinct, of course, is to offer them to the National Health.

Unfortunately, there are rumours that after their crackdown on middle-aged and middle-class drivers, the police are planning a crack-down on householders who protect their own property against burglars.

Almost any form of self-protection against thieves is strictly against the law. It won't look good if I turn up at the local hospital with a spare leg or head wrapped in a blanket. But if anyone sees an Arab sheikh driving around London with the head of an English New Age Traveller perched precariously on his shoulders, he will know which way the decision has gone.

# 21st March, 1994

## Time for a rethink

I HAVE seen no mention in any national newspaper of a new hazard that has been discovered in relation to aerobic exercises. Perhaps I am being unjust to the national press, but it took the Evening Gazette of Blackpool to express alarm.

It reports that an aerobic group in nearby Thornton has been barred from the St John's Church Hall in Station Road because of the disagreeable smell it left behind. Complaints had been received both from the Women's Institute and Girl Guides, who used the hall afterwards.

This puzzled aerobics organiser and medal-winning swimmer Lesley Iredale. 'I took being called smelly personally,' said Mrs Iredale, who won a gold medal in swimming at the World Transplant Games after a kidney swap four years ago. 'I use the class as part of my stamina-building programme. At the end of the day, it is a church organisation which is supposed to help the community. We are not a bunch of yobs playing loud music and leaving the place in a mess. We are only jumping up and down on boxes.'

It may be part of the church's mission to suffer these terrible smells in the furtherance of aerobics, but surely the Women's Institute and Girl Guides have a right to be consulted, too? These aerobic classes go on all over the place but nobody outside plain-spoken Lancashire has ever dared mention it.

As a nation, and as a community, we must re-think our attitude to exercise classes. The latest health theory is that a fish supper once a week halves the chances of suffering a stroke. Mrs Bottomley should concentrate on supplying every citizen with a fish course at every meal, instead of employing 1.2 million people to give us useless and unpleasant medicines at enormous expense.

## 23rd March, 1994

### Top dogs

AN AMERICAN called Stanley Coren has written a book comparing the intelligence of 133 breeds of dog. When it is released here in May, I am afraid it will cause more fisticuffs than any religious or doctrinal squabble since Henry VIII's invention of the Church of England in 1531.

When I reveal that border collies are chosen as the most intelligent of all dogs, followed by poodles, Alsations and golden retrievers, while Pekingese come 127th out of 133 breeds, I trust I will have said all that needs to be said.

Border collies, while amiable and pliant enough, are

notoriously stupid, while Pekingese vary from dog to dog. Of my three Pekingese, one is only fairly intelligent, I agree, but another, to judge by his wisdom and benignity as well as his appearance, might easily be a reincarnation of Confucius himself. He can understand every nuance of a conversation between three or four people: he recognises and welcomes those he has met only once three years earlier. He reads *The Telegraph* and treats *The Sunday Times* with loathing and disdain.

It may seem odd that an American should presume to judge the intelligence of dogs, but the mystery is explained when we learn that Stanley Coren judges intelligence by success in obedience tests. Pekingese may be the cleverest, most fearless and most original of dogs, but they are also the most disobedient. They will spend some time working out what you want them to do, and then do precisely the opposite. Perhaps it is an American trait to confuse obedience with intelligence. I do not know.

## *26th March, 1994*

### Europe: a statement

NOBODY in politics seems to have any awareness of how profoundly uninterested we all are in voting arrangements within the European Union. There is nothing so special about Britain that different arrangements must be made for us, except that we have the silliest and most self-important politicians among the 12 members.

For nearly two years our rulers have cited non-existent or inappropriate EC directives to justify their own fatuous and repressive actions. We are now not only the most foolishly governed but also the most over-governed country in Europe. Most of these insane new regulations – forbidding us, for instance, from burying a dead budgerigar in our own garden – come from bossy, ignorant, often semi-literate officials in our own ministries.

The one advantage of joining the Common Market – the reason I and millions of others voted for it – was that the price of drink and cigarettes would come down to European levels. This would have had a major and beneficial effect on my life in 1975, when we were asked for our opinion and voted two to one in favour of joining.

It was always a humiliating absurdity that we had to pay twice as much as anyone else for drink. Since the British Government's refusal to harmonise excise duties – to which it is still committed – the betrayal has been all but complete. Now British grocers like Sainsbury are setting up shops in Calais to sell Scotch whisky and English beer to britons, who then have to bring it back to this country, ruining half the retailers in the South of England at the same time.

The lesson is obvious. We have not only the wettest and most unpleasant but also the most incompetent politicians in Europe. The more power that is taken away from Westminster and given to Brussels, the better we shall all be. One day, perhaps, we shall be in a position to hang the present House of Commons for treason, betrayal and oppression of the people. Until then, the great thing is to weaken it by removing all its powers.

Europe might well be better off if its finances were looked after by the Swiss, its foreign policy by the French, its business affairs by the Germans, its sexual behaviour by the Italians. The great thing is to remove all power from London.

## *30th March, 1994*

### O Chelsea we love you

SOME residual sense of fair play tells me we should lay off the Clintons. Mr Clinton may not look very nice, but nothing has been proved against either of them. It would be foolish to start a Bill and Hillary fan club in Britain just in case the rumours turn out to be true, and I can understand the attempt to divert some of the adulatory attention which traditionally attaches to the presidency to the presidential cat, Socks. Three White House staff are employed to answer Socks' fan letters.

But it seems rather strange that the mantle should pass to a cat rather than to the Clintons' daughter, Chelsea, whom nobody has accused of anything shameful. In a culture obsessed with youth, Chelsea should be seen as a very positive signpost to the future.

If we can start a Chelsea Clinton fan club over here, it might make the point that the future belongs to the young, and Chelsea is a resplendent example of what young America is all about. She is as normal as blueberry pie, the product of an All-American diet – her father is rumoured to have been eating a hamburger and watching TV when he begat her.

If she were not the President's daughter, she might qualify to take over the main Pepsi-Cola promotion spot after Michael Jackson and the new super-chimp. But her real purpose will be to show us that there is still a New World out there, a land of instant food and soft drinks, multi-flavoured ice creams, jumbo sandwiches and 24-hour, 100-channel television, an alternative to Europe with its nasty foreign food, its fusty old buildings and boring history. Chelsea shows the way.

## Stronger man needed

'I WANT the House to know I have never eaten and never will eat a horse,' said Nicholas Soames, the Food Minister. I can understand why anybody should feel squeamish about eating horsemeat, although it is just as good as beef and less fatty. I should imagine that in my time I have eaten enough horses to provide a royal escort. But why does Mr Soames want the House of Commons to know this dingy fact?

It often occurs to me, as I eat snails or frogs' legs, that somebody must have tried slugs and spiders, bats and toads, to discover they were no good. These are the great unsung heroes of culinary history, the pioneers. As a conscientious Minister of

Food, Soames should be in the forefront of experimentation, eating grass snakes and slow worms on television, showing owners of condemned rottweilers how they can be cooked to provide several meals for an average family.

Perhaps he would be happier in some other ministry. I know plenty of people who would like the job. If I were chosen, I would take my ministerial portfolio on a world tour, letting it be known that in Australia the minister would like to eat a koala, in Russia a wolf, in China a giant panda. The job is wasted on a timid man.

## 2nd April, 1994

### Meditations for Easter

THERE is an old story about the boy at Eton who committed suicide. The other boys in his house were gathered together and asked if any of them could suggest a reason for the tragedy. After a long silence a small boy in the front put up his hand: 'Could it have been the food, sir?'

Last week I found myself staring at the terrible photograph of a Glaswegian said to be suffering from the stigmata – the wounds of the crucifixion on hands, feet and side. *The Observer*'s picture of George Hamilton, a Catholic former steelworker, showed abominable wounds also on the face.

Many Catholics who saw the picture, as well as thanking their lucky stars that no such suffering had been visited on them, must have pondered on the cause of these terrible wounds. It crossed my mind to wonder whether the atrocious standard of singing in Catholic churches might have anything to do with it.

John Gummer found himself embroiled in a great row about the standard of singing in his parish church within weeks of announcing his submission to Rome. There can be little doubt in my mind that the defection of Caroline Waldegrave, wife of Privy Seal, to the Careyite faction is explained in part by the rotten singing in so many Catholic churches.

For Catholics, a further problem must be the new hymns which are inflicted on them: tuneless, almost wordless, specially written for retarded children. These are the things we might meditate about this Easter, as nearly all the Catholic public schools are threatened with closure and it seems more and more probable that only the kindergarten version of Catholicism will survive in this country.

I am sure there are hundreds of potential converts trembling on the brink if only Catholics could get their singing together: Michael Portillo, Paul 'Gazza' Gascoigne . . . It would be a very bad advert for the Catholic church if Mr Gummer developed signs of the stigmata.

## *4th April, 1994*

### Non-native species

WHEN Mao wished to rid China of small birds he ordered the entire population to stand out of doors from dawn to dusk, clapping its hands. The idea was that the birds would fly from perch to perch until they all dropped dead from exhaustion.

Now word has gone out that all members of the British public are to concern themselves with killing grey squirrels. The Forestry Commission, backed by the Department of the Environment and conservation groups, urges the public to use any means for this urgent task.

Grey squirrels originally came to this country as visitors from the United States in the last century. Now, after vigorous breeding, they are thought to threaten our broadleaf woodlands. Mr Ron Melville of the Forestry Commission is organising a pilot Grey Squirrel Control Group, possible along the lines of Mr Lilley's crack SES, or Suicide Enforcement Squad.

Mr Melville encourages members of the public to destroy the grey squirrel by saying to them that if they catch one in the garden, 'You must kill it because it is a non-native species, and cannot be returned to the wild.'

But I wonder whether many Englishmen or Englishwomen are capable of killing squirrels any more. Forbidden to carry arms or any offensive weapon, we have only our hands left. Perhaps we should start clapping them.

### Inappropriate and belittling

SO AT last a politically correct word processor has been invented which will automatically warn the writer against any form of words likely to give offence to those worried about their sex, race, age, shape, religion, marital status or what have you.

Gender-specific expressions such as 'wife' cause the machine to object on about five points: 'Expressions that refer exclusively to one sex may offend some readers . . . it is preferable to use terms which do not imply gender.' Wife is not only gender-specific but may also be sexist – for example, 'I need to call the wife'.

This excites the rebuke 'Sexist expression. Avoid using this phrase'. The term wife is 'considered by many to be inappropriate and belittling when used to refer to women'. The machine still acts in an advisory capacity, but the day may well come when it simply refuses to print anything it judges 'inappropriate'. Then everything published will read like the *New York Times* and we will all die of ignorance and boredom.

There is just one hope. News of this fiendish invention appeared in the newspaper last Friday, which was also April Fool's Day, along with the advertisement for a 32lb Mars Bar. Much of the news nowadays leaves one hoping it is just a practical joke. Six days earlier we learnt that the Ritz Carlton Hotel in Washington had sacked a 30-year-old female employee for growing a moustache. That sounds more like the America we know and love.

## *6th April, 1994*

### A tricky character

IS IT wise to bombard the general public with pictures of luxury beyond their means? In Monday's newspaper there was a photograph of a pretty young woman holding a giant egg from the Great Elephant Bird of Madagascar, to be auctioned at Bonhams on Friday. I found myself burning with desire to own it.

Of these eggs, the largest ever laid, only three survive in private ownership, and Bonhams expect theirs to realise between £20,000 and £30,000. Alas, I cannot afford it. This does not seem fair. Everyone should have the right to his own Great Elephant Bird egg, should he not? In this field, the gap between rich and poor, haves and have-nots, is particularly wide, since only three people in the world have a Great Elephant Bird egg, while the rest of us – some five billion people in all – have not.

Brooding on this sort of injustice, as the Archbishop of Canterbury has done, may drive people to desperate acts, like voting Liberal Democrat next month. I must urge them to resist the temptation. The Liberal Democrats include many of the most unpleasant and conceited people in the country. Under their dreaded leader 'Paddy' Pantsdown they are committed to closing down all the hunts and banning free Englishmen and Englishwomen from their centuries-old national sport. Whatever he may say, 'Paddy' Pantsdown is in no position to distribute Great Elephant Bird eggs among the population. He should be denounced as a liar if he promises to do so.

A correspondent asks why I always put the name Paddy in inverted commas, as if it was not his real name. The answer is that it is *not* his real name. He was christened Jeremy, just like his predecessor as Liberal leader.

Presumably he asks everyone to call him 'Paddy' because he does not wish to be confused with Mr Thorpe, but this seems a curious way to set about things. Perhaps I should call him Mr Jeremy Pantyhose to make the point. Nobody should believe him, either, if he claims to have seen a great Elephant Bird in Madagascar. They have been extinct since Napoleonic times.

## Uninteresting times

I NEVER really believed the story of William Tell. A similar story is told in the Danish chronicle of Saxo Grammaticus written nearly a hundred years before the alleged incident in Altdorf.

When I was a boy a group of Poles decided to shoot at apples on each other's heads in my uncle's house after Christmas lunch. Luckily no one was hurt, but an arrow remained embedded in the front door for many years afterwards.

However, they were not trying to make any anti-colonialist points. They were just having a good time. Now some boring Swiss historians have announced that William Tell never existed, the cruel Austrian governor called Gessler never existed, nor was there any 13th-century war of liberation against the Habsburgs because the Habsburgs had never bothered to occupy the area in the first place.

William Tell is the only hero Switzerland has ever produced, and the apple-shooting episode is the only memorable thing in Swiss history. Now we must suppose it is a country without heroes and without any history to speak of. Perhaps that is the proudest and happiest boast of all.

## Heritage notes

THE OLD ghetto in Cracow has long been one of the most haunted and terrifying sites in Europe. Now, since the success of the film *Schindler's List*, the Poles have set up a major tourist industry, selling souvenir T-shirts, with ice cream parlours in the streets where the massacres of children originally took place, later tastefully filmed by Spielberg.

One guide, Dariusz Kuznial, is quoted (admittedly in the *Sun*) as charging twice what he could get for showing visitors round Cracow's cathedral and castle:

'By the time I've done that, and taken them to the two Auschwitz camps, I'm a much richer man.'

Some time ago I reported a quarrel between Poles, Germans and Jewish groups about who should pay for the maintenance of Auschwitz and other Holocaust monuments in Poland. The Jewish groups did not see why they should be expected to pay, the Poles said it was nothing to do with them and the Germans, no doubt, pointed out that they had no further use for them. History has shown this to be a short-sighted view. There is good money to be made from the exploitation of history.

It would be absurd to talk of any American equivalent to these sites because the United States has never known anything like the Nazi experience. But a similar debate has arisen over the fate of the oldest McDonald's hamburger bar in the world, sited in Downey, California.

One of the last with McDonald's original golden arches piercing the roof, the restaurant is 41 years old. This, in California, gives it the antiquarian value of Westminster Abbey or Notre Dame. Despite an impassioned appeal from the Governor of California, the local McDonald's *apparat* insists that this important piece of American social history is not equipped to meet the needs of today's consumer. They have no further use for it. I feel they may be right, and all these relics should be cleared away.

### Too drastic a measure

I KNOW we are all supposed to support the reintroduction of compulsory games at schools as being the only way to teach the new generation of unemployables about team spirit, discipline, etc, but I don't think it will work. As someone who always detested school games – soccer, rugger *and* cricket – I feel I should speak up.

Team spirit is an excellent idea when we all have to pull together in wartime, but as we approach the fifth anniversary of the Hillsborough disaster on Friday, when 94 football fans perished, we might query the wisdom of too much group involvement in sport under present conditions.

Violence and vandalism appear to be endemic in our society. My original proposal for the nation's redundant churches which the Church of England can no longer afford to maintain was that they should be set aside as places for quiet meditation, away from the babbling clergymen. Under those circumstances, they could be maintained on the rates, but supervision would still be needed. An alternative might be to turn them into expensive karaoke bars, inviting exhibitionists to preach a sermon from the pulpit rather than sing a popular song.

The new violence and vandalism are most apparent, it seems, in places such as schools and hospitals. A new idea is to turn

them into fortresses, with armed police patrolling the grounds and corridors, ready to escort any pupil or patient who wishes to go to the lavatory.

This seems a good idea if it keeps policemen out of mischief, unable to harass motorists and other threatened groups. I am almost sure it is not necessary to re-introduce compulsory school games.

## 16th April, 1994

### Pack up your troubles

AS SOMEONE who was only slightly alarmed by scientific claims that the Western male could become sterile in the next century, I can express only modified rapture at the latest scientific assurance that it is all a load of rubbish. The original survey, by Prof Niels Skakkebaek, of Copenhagen, was used to support the popularly held idea that women using the contraceptive pill are polluting the water supply. Oestrogen in the water, as we all know, makes men's genitalia shrink and causes them to grow breasts, just as excessive use of testosterone causes women to grow moustaches and, in extreme cases, beards.

Now Prof Skakkebaek's figures have been re-examined in Warwick University, and it appears that he did his sums wrong. This will disappoint those who like a good medical scare. Prof Dennis Lincoln, of the Medical Research Council, replies that it is hard to count spermatozoa per millilitre of sperm, adding rather grumpily:

'What's more important is the rise in testicular cancer, the increase in the number of babies born with undescended testes and the increase in congenital abnormalities of the male foetus.'

So we can all worry about those things instead. Oddly enough, the rise in all these afflictions marches hand in hand with the decline in smoking. In the *Guardian*'s correspondence column, I learn that breast-feeding babies can give them HIV. That should give the *Guardian*'s readers something to worry about. Anything to keep their minds off the dreaded tropical rainforests.

I read somewhere that these tropical rainforests act as some sort of global air filter, protecting us from CFC, carbon-monoxide, hamburger and other man-made gases. I don't believe

406

this is true. We in Britain are blessed by these wonderful winds, which blow all our atmospheric pollution to Sweden.

## The best we can do

THURSDAY was made hideous for my fellow readers of the *Sun* by the news that a six-year-old boy had been thrown out of a hamburger bar in Chiswick because he was judged too ugly to eat there. Little Daniel Stanley-Clarke wept as staff forced him to leave his half-finished cheeseburger and marched him outside.

His mother, Jenny, claimed that Daniel had been suffering from chickenpox, and pointed out that there were 'several smelly tramps at nearby tables, but nobody complained about them'.

The reason for this, I suggest, is simple. The tramps' faces were not covered with livid spots. Among possible explanations for livid spots are acute food poisoning and an infectious disease. No restaurateur likes it to be thought he is poisoning his customers, and in the new atmosphere of health awareness, few customers wish to catch the more virulent forms of infectious disease.

There must be a message of hope in this somewhere. Parents who wish to exercise some sort of control over the number of burgers their children eat (if this is still legal) might consider painting their faces with large spots in indelible red ink. If we can spare our children even one burger a week by this means, they might yet grow up with that slight edge over their contemporaries which will enable them to secure one of the few jobs left – probably something to do with beefburgers.

## 18th April, 1994

## Send a letter

'PREPARE ye the way of the Lord', sang the prophet Isaiah. 'Every valley shall be exalted, and every mountain and hill shall be made low: and the crooked shall be made straight, and the rough places plain'.

These activities are all the more useful if the Lord concerned is in a wheelchair. But Lord Tebbit was spared such a fate, after the unforgettably poignant moment when television viewers watched first his toes, then his feet, then his pyjamaed body emerge from the rubble of the Grand Hotel, Brighton.

It was not on his own behalf, but gallantly on behalf of his wife, an even more innocent victim of the bomb outrage, that Lord Tebbit wrote an angry letter to *The Times* on Saturday:

'Sir, May I suggest that Mr Simon Jenkins should sit himself in a wheelchair and without raising his backside from the seat try to use the telephone in one of the BT red boxes he so admires.

Yours faithfully,

TEBBIT,

House of Lords'

Jenkins's crime had been to admire the old red telephone boxes designed by Sir Giles Gilbert Scott, and lament the new booths replacing them throughout the country.

We must suppose that these new booths, although hideous and unpleasant for everyone else, are more convenient for people who have the misfortune to be confined to wheelchairs.

That is a point in their favour, but people in wheelchairs survived somehow during the 60-odd years of the handsome Gilbert Scott design, and I am not sure that their greater convenience is sufficient reason to pepper the whole face of England with nasty, vulgar plastic capsules.

Above all, I am sorry that Lord Tebbit should seek to advance the cause of the handicapped by adopting the mendicant's snarl, rather than the voice of sweet reason, the appeal to kinder and more generous instincts. Since the philistines appear to have won this battle, as they nearly always do, he might attract greater enthusiasm for his cause by being a little more gracious.

## Holiday plans

TOURISM, we are told, will be the world's biggest industry by the turn of the century. I can see nothing but sorrow resulting from this. Tourists are bad for the commercial honesty of the countries they visit, but they also destroy that basic benevolence towards our fellow men and women which is the foundation of all civil society.

In the past few weeks we have read how the Irish, who are desperate for tourists, have set up a tourist victim support service to counsel visitors who are robbed, raped or murdered during their stay in Dublin. We have also read how British women visiting Greece are so often raped that few of them bother to report it.

Visitors to America are as likely as not to be shot out of hand. Americans in Singapore are liable to be caned and we all know what we in Britain do to foreign tourists, although it might be better not to spell it out here. Nor is it very wise for Britons to move around their own country too much. Any day now American jets based in Turkey will start bombing anything that moves in England in the belief that it is either a part of Serbian-held Bosnia or part of the exclusion zone in northern Iraq.

One day the realisation may be born that we would all be much happier staying at home. Those who have the misfortune to live in horrid homes might spend their holiday time improving them, with potted plants and the occasional medlar tree in a window box, as well as ingenious anti-burglar devices vaguely based on the mousetrap idea.

## *27th April, 1994*

### The battered husband scare

POLICE have expressed alarm over a claimed increase in battered husbands – the number of reported cases has doubled in five years – but I remain sceptical, fearing a repetition of the ritual child abuse fiasco. Until fairly recently, the police did not concern themselves with quarrels between husbands and wives, unless serious harm resulted. Now they have set up domestic violence units specially for the purpose.

It seems to me that any husband who allows himself to be systematically beaten up by his wife probably enjoys it. If he doesn't, he should go back to his mother. Police must not be encouraged to go barging into private houses when they should be making life difficult for car thieves, house burglars, muggers and street hooligans.

Any man who turns up at a police station to complain that the woman in his life has boxed his ears, or thrown a saucepan at him, or chased him round the kitchen table with a carving knife, should be made to take lessons in unarmed combat and sent home with the laughter of the constabulary ringing in his ears.

Mr Gerry Bermingham, Labour MP for St Helens South, said the problem was now so serious that he will ask the Home Office to start keeping records of domestic attacks on men. In that one suggestion he encapsulates all the fatuity of modern government. If the problem was, indeed, a serious one, what possible good would it do for the Home Office to collate figures?

Perhaps it would provide employment for a couple of score extra civil servants. Then we might have a White Paper, Mr Major would announce a crackdown and his ineffable Home Secretary would add another section to his Criminal Justice Bill increasing the penalties. Women's prisons would fill up with bad-tempered housewives and the police would announce they were alarmed by children who leave toys on the stairs.

## A great headmaster

THURSDAY'S *Times* was full of letters from former public schoolboys testifying to how they had been beaten by Anthony Chenevix-Trench, the great educationalist and flagellant who died in 1979 after being headmaster, in succession, of Bradfield, Shrewsbury, Eton and Fettes.

As a student of the press, I find this revealing. When the *Independent* was launched, it made a deliberate and successful effort to steal male homosexual readers from the *Guardian*, where they had previously resided. I was working for the *Independent* throughout its first year, when it soon became apparent that any reference to those of the Bulgarian tendency had to be written in terms of the warmest approval and encouragement.

This did not worry me in the least, although it sometimes occurs to me now that the *Independent*'s present declining circulation may have something to do with the dreaded influence of Aids. *The Times*, by contrast, has often seemed to me to be lacking a sense of direction. Now we must suppose it has been quietly setting its cap at the masochists and 'correction' fetishists – although, of course, none of its distinguished correspondents falls into those categories. I am afraid that with the decline of corporal punishment in schools this may well prove to be another shrinking market.

Chenevix-Trench is one of the most interesting figures of our time. A brilliant teacher, he was deeply affected by his experiences as prisoner of the Japanese on the Burma Railway project, and returned to England with an apparent mission in life to beat English boys.

Although I was never his pupil, many of my friends had that experience – Richard Ingrams, Paul Foot, Christopher Booker, even Willie Rushton who so kindly illustrates this column. None of them is likely to forget Chenevix-Trench's enthusiasm.

If there are any Chenevix-Trenches left, I feel we should send them to the Far East where they can exercise their skills on all the American students who seem to be settling there. This may annoy President and Mrs Clinton, but most of America will applaud, as will the Far East and the rest of the world.

## A glint of light

SOMETIMES this column is accused of being unfair to the police. At least we must congratulate the East Sussex Constabulary on their spectacular arrest of Mr Stephen Grant, a 39-year-old businessman who disturbed three suspected burglars at his home in Hove and after a 30-mile chase in his car, arrested two men, bundling one into the boot of his car and delivering both to the police.

Mr Grant was promptly arrested and has now been released on police bail. He may be charged with abduction and firearms offences, since the suspected burglars accuse him of firing a cap gun at them. Well done the East Sussex Constabulary! They also arrested and released on police bail the three suspected burglars, but I do not think the police can take quite so much credit for that, as Mr Grant had done nearly all the work for them.

Perhaps we will never really be happy until suspected burglars are raised to the dignity of a protected species, like bats and vipers. Then it will not only be a criminal offence to prevent them burgling your house. It will also be an offence to disturb, annoy or frighten them in any way.

Suspected burglars who report unco-operative householders will receive money from the informants' fund, but any householder who telephones the police to inform on a suspected burglar will be arrested and charged with wasting police time.

## *2nd May, 1994*

## Mistaken identities

THOSE of us with a certain idea of England will have been shocked to learn that the name of a 20-stone brute, sent to prison

411

for 28 years after repeatedly raping two young girls, is Adrian Mole, just like the hero of Sue Townsend's fictitious diary.

Many of us had identified the fictitious Adrian Mole with all that was nicest, kindest, most middle-of-the-road and anxious-to-be-good in modern Britain. On the strength of this, *Private Eye* has been running a *Secret Diary of John Major* for many years, where the distinction between the fictitious John Major and the fictitious Adrian Mole becomes ever more blurred.

Now we have a real Adrian Mole in this 20-stone multiple rapist one cannot help wondering whether the real John Major has any surprises in store for us.

I do not see the faintest possibility that he will turn out to be a multiple child rapist, as I feel sure that our vigilant tabloid press would have discovered it long ago. But we have been warned that he 'will fight like an alley cat' to keep his job, and the tabloid press claims he would be prepared to take us out of the European Union rather than resign with dignity and decorum, as his predecessor did.

Time will tell. As we wait in dread for the results of Thursday's local elections, it is curious to think that the South Africans have gone to the polls to elect their first black president.

Which of us, I wonder, will look the biggest fools at the end of the day: we, who thought when we elected John Major, that we were electing a sweet fictitious Adrian Mole and found we had chosen a ferocious alley cat; or the South Africans, who think they are electing a black president, when all of us outside the fevered atmospheres of Cape Town, Johannesburg and Pretoria can see perfectly well that Nelson Mandela is Chinese.

Perhaps it is rude to point this out, but one can't help laughing.


## *7th May, 1994*

### Foot inspection time

I WONDER if the new compulsory curriculum for the teaching of history in government schools will include information about Hitler's feet. As we know from the published reminiscences of Eva Braun, Hitler suffered from terribly sore feet which required him to sit night after night with his trousers rolled up and his feet submerged in a footbath.

Medical science has now identified this as cheiropompholyx, a recurrent condition in which the arches of the feet are covered with deep-rooted, itchy blisters. I pass on this piece of information, because it seems to me we should all be worried about young people's feet. The new generation of semi-literate unemployables created by modern teaching methods tends to wear these horrible rubber shoes which they call 'trainers', although goodness knows what they think they are training for,

A shoe salesman once explained to me that rubber does not allow the foot to breathe. Every sort of rot and fungus develops under those conditions. I have often expressed the fear that when New Britons reach the age of 40 or 50, they will turn out to have lost their feet, and will be even more dependent on public charity than they are now.

Recently a document came into my possession from the headquarters of an organisation called Animals' Vigilantes. It was in the form of a begging letter:

'Many view the world today as a place where standards are being lowered and those high ideals of which we were once proud losing their values. Therefore it is hoped you will be interested in the work of Animals' Vigilantes . . .

'In the last one hundred years there has been a loss of hundreds of species of wild life and youth today we hope for a better world as they become the adults of tomorrow.' *[sic omnia]*

The signatory, needless to say, is called Tracy. My own reaction is to disregard the request for money and say: 'Tracy, show me your feet.' The great debate about education is a waste of time. What schoolchildren need is constant foot inspection. Enough trouble has been caused in this century by one man with bad feet.

## *9th May, 1994*

---

### Shopping the wrinklies

CHILDREN in Salisbury, Wilts, have been asked to report their parents' drink and drugs habits to a panel of counsellors on a 'hotline' subsidised by the Wiltshire County Council. The counsellors, who call themselves a Drugs and Alcohol Liaison Project, offer only a weekday 'hotline' service.

This seems rather slack to me. Some of the heaviest consumption of drink and drugs takes place at weekends, and the charity is designed to protect children aged nine to 14 from

413

the consequences. It promises confidentiality unless the counsellor feels the caller is at serious risk, when the helpline will pass details to the police.

Many will find it shocking that they confine themselves to drink and drugs. Obviously, children should be encouraged to report much more than this. They should report of their parents' consumption of tobacco, fatty meat, butter, sweets and all non-salad food.

Above all, they should report any unacceptable or ethnically inappropriate conversation they hear. This may explain why, two weeks after opening, the Liaison Project had not received a single telephone call. But the first step must be to extend the project to provide a 24-hour seven-day a week service. Hotline telephones must be installed in the homes of all children who do not already have them.

Ideally, all parents and all children should be personally attended by at least two counsellors every hour of the day and night. That goal may seem distant at present, but it is the one we must work towards.

## Sense of fair play

IT IS easy to sneer at the French National Assembly's panic measures to keep the French language pure. These culminated in last week's Bill making public use of English liable to a fine of £2,400 where there is a French equivalent. But as Jacques Toubon, the Culture Minister, made clear, it is not the language of Shakespeare from which he hopes to protect his countrymen. It is the language of Brooklyn.

Even the language of Brooklyn, it might be said, has its own richness and vitality, but Toubon is playing a subtler game than his critics allow. He reckons very few Americans speak any French and his real purpose is to discourage Americans from visiting France. His anxieties are quite simply commercial.

Give Americans a lift in your car in Normandy, offer them a cigarette in Provence or propose some sort of romantic involvement with them in Paris, and you must prepare to be sued for every farthing you possess – in the American courts. One of the most heartrending things I have read recently was the statement by the young doctor who arrived first on the scene of the M2 disaster, when he discovered that most of the victims were American.

Although anxious to do what he could for them, he was terrified 'It is a standing joke in medicine that the last thing you want to encounter is a load of Americans who are likely to sue the pants off you if you get things wrong.'

Now we learn that British Airways is being sued for millions of dollars because it flew the victims to Europe. Whatever happens, it all seems to end up at Lloyd's, which is why half the country houses of Somerset are for sale. Most of the wealth of England, accumulated over many years, is being shipped to America to console Americans for some of the revolting diseases they pick up at work, or for the emotional pain of losing an aunt or uncle, a nephew or niece.

## *11th May, 1994*

## The war against crime

NOBODY could possibly object to policemen being given cudgels two feet long if only we could be sure they would be used on burglars, car thieves, muggers and street hooligans, but the police do not often seem to be around when such people are in evidence. I fear we shall see them used only against people who are alleged to have attacked a policeman, and am not sure they will add much to our happiness or peace of mind.

Mr Howard proposes to combat the general outbreak of burglary, car theft, mugging and street hooliganism by making it compulsory for all citizens to carry an identity card at all times. If ever we forget or mislay it, the police can arrest us and keep down crime that way.

But the police are very much against Mr Howard's plan to have private citizens patrol the streets under the umbrella of Neighbourhood Watch. Street patrolling is a highly skilled and very dangerous job, they point out, which should be undertaken only by policemen at the appropriate wage level.

I think it unfair to expect the police to interest themselves in ancient laws against burglary when there are so many exciting new laws to enforce. The best way to discourage burglars is to allow householders to shoot them. There would inevitably be a certain number of casualties from accidentally discharged weapons in the home, but burglary is becoming a serious nuisance nowadays. Perhaps my solution may frighten the police; in that case we should all be given truncheons. They would be considerably cheaper than identity cards, and possibly – who knows? – more effective.

## 14th May, 1994

### African lunchtime

THERE was a certain fragility, I thought, as well as poignancy in Nelson Mandela's memorable promise, 'Never, never, never again will this beautiful land experience the oppression of one by another', delivered at his inauguration. South Africa, or whatever they may choose to call it next, is indeed a beautiful country, and everybody must wish it well under African rule, but it is also richer and more complicated than any other African country. Something of the complications ahead may be foreshadowed by arrangements for Mr Mandela's inauguration banquet.

A vast marquee was put up outside the President's palace in

Pretoria to receive the 1,200 most important guests. They were served an elaborate meal inside the tent, while outside an 'African lunch' was served to some 5,000 minor functionaries and others who had flocked to the ceremony.

Because of a transport failure, the Duke of Edinburgh, representing the Queen, and Douglas Hurd, representing the Government of Great Britain, arrived too late for the banquet and instead had the African lunch outside. It include springbok paté, smoked ostrich, crocodile and, by one account, different types of worm.

No doubt they made the best of it and said it was all much more interesting and enjoyable than the conventional meal on offer inside. If they had managed to get inside, they would have risked meeting Mrs Clinton, Fidel Castro and other undesirables.

No doubt there have been many embarrassing mishaps with heads of state at royal banquets in London. Even so, I am prepared to bet that in the long history of Buckingham Palace there has been an occasion when a visiting royal consort and a visiting foreign secretary, arriving late at a banquet, have been required to stay outside and eat worms.

## *16th May, 1994*

### Puritan zeal

WHEREVER I go I am asked for my advice about whom we should have as the next leader of the Labour Party, but I'm afraid the question rather embarrasses me. It is not just that, like everyone else, I have a certain difficulty in telling these people apart. For the first time in the recent history of this once-great party, I simply do not know any of the candidates.

John Prescott, at 55, is at least a respectable age. He is said to have been usefully employed as a steward on passenger liners for eight years before deciding to lead the country. I have never heard anyone suggest he was anything but a reasonably competent steward, but one can't be sure. Why, in that case, did he throw it over to go into politics, the most rackety and uncertain business of all?

This leaves Anthony 'Tony' Blair and Gordon Brown. I once saw Brown on *Question Time* and took a great dislike to him, but that need not influence anyone else. This sentence, from an assessment in the *Daily Mail* may be more significant: 'A workaholic bachelor – he is said never to have recovered from rejection by Princess Margarita of Romania – he has a Scots puritan zeal for the truth.'

If true, this statement will set several alarm bells ringing. Lovelorn workaholic bachelors are all very well, but it would not do the Labour Party any good if its leader became involved in a repetition of the Stephen Milligan tragedy. This taught us that auto-erotic asphyxiation was not just another schoolboy joke but a serious risk in the life of the ambitious, unmarried politician.

Moreover, I do not know anything about Princess Margarita of Romania, even if she exists. But she sounds as if she may be a foreigner. In that case, we are bound to ask ourselves why, if Gordon Brown was not considered good enough for her, he should be good enough for us.

This leaves Tony Blair, who is at least a public-school man, and who, at 41, may attract the vital teenage vote. But it is a bewildering variety of choice for Labour. The Tories, by contrast, have no choice at all. If they do not choose the fragrant 50-year-old member for Sutton and Cheam, Lady Olga Maitland, as their next leadeer, they will ensure that they disappear down the waste disposal pipe of history, while the whole nation laughs sarcastically.

## Dog food days

I WAS sad to learn that we can no longer afford to send the King's Troop of the Royal Horse Artillery to the Royal Windsor Horse Show. The reason may be that everyone nowadays seems to overcharge the government for their services.

It started with lawyers and spread to the police, who can charge as much as £1,200 a night for keeping one prisoner in a police cell. Now it has spread to the Army, which would have had to pay £12,000 to take 85 horses from London to Windsor and back.

The event was sponsored by Harrods, owned by members of the Fayed family, who were invited to drinks at Windsor Castle over the weekend in recompense. Unfortunately they do not appear to have sponsored it quite enough. So instead of the famous RHA gallop, spectators were able to watch the Pedigree Chum Royal Army Veterinary Corp dog display team go through its paces. One wonders if this will be the pattern of future royal events. At the State Opening of Parliament, Her Majesty will be seen to carry the Pepsi Cola sceptre, along with an orb sponsored by McDonald's. The mace may come from Mars Bars, but I would hesitate to award the honour of sponsoring the crown itself, symbol of all temporal power in the land, to any firm less well established in the affections of the nation than Pedigree Chum.

## Just look at her

NOBODY has yet tried to start a chapter of the Hillary Clinton Fan Club in Britain, to join the 20 chapters already existing in the United States and others in Japan and Austria. It is not a work to be undertaken lightly. Ruth Love, who started it all with her husband Eugene, from their homes in Florida and Maryland, explained:

'It has almost taken over our lives. My husband has no time for golf; I have had to give up country dancing.'

What worries me most about this energetic couple is that, when they get around to organising a Hillary Clinton Fan Club in Britain, it will interfere with my own plans for a Chelsea Clinton Fan Club among our despondent teenagers.

For two years I have been trying to interest these incurious, apathetic, semi-literate people. It would not require them to sing, or jump up and down, or demonstrate against smoking, or even tie difficult knots in pieces of string.

All they would be required to do would be to carry a photograph of Chelsea Clinton with them and study it from time to time. If they wished to listen to something on their Walkmans while they were studying the picture, it could not be the voice of Chelsea Clinton herself, because I do not think she has ever been heard to speak in any audible or comprehensible way.

It would be the voice of some famous actor – Gielgud perhaps, or Guinness – pointing out that this is where we will all end up, this is where Western society, Western culture, Western civilisation, are heading. Many teenagers will be quite cheered up by the message.

## Keep demonstrating

OTHERS have commented on the extraordinary pomposity of students at the Liverpool John Moores University who objected to the offer of an honorary fellowship to Cilla Black. One of them said:

'It's absolutely absurd. We have to work hard for three years to get our degrees, and this devalues the whole thing. We can't associate the host of *Blind Date* with anything academic.'

But what decided Miss Black to refuse the fellowship was when she saw a group of students demonstrating outside the Central Social Sciences Department. She decided they must be demonstrating against her, and announced: 'I won't be accepting the fellowship.'

In fact they could have been demonstrating for hundreds of causes. Young Liverpudlians are not always easy to understand when they speak. My own feeling is that they were probably demonstrating in favour of Lady Olga Maitland as the next Prime Minister and leader of the Conservative Party. She is understandably popular in Liverpool, where they are fed up with people pretending to be disabled. More than half the 6,500,000 allegedly disabled people in Britain are thought to live in Liverpool.

Equally, they may have been demonstrating with the new Fat Liberation Movement, demanding new legal rights for themselves and 700,000 other obese Liverpudlians. This is another good cause. Many would not be so fat if they had not been given too many sweets as children. No legal aid is yet available for them to sue their parents.

All in all I feel Miss Black should accept her fellowship – unless she is hoping to be the next Warden of All Souls. Somebody told me that the job was up for grabs.

## Stop this breast feeding

WHENEVER the Government has anything particularly irritating to say, it seems to ask Lady Cumberlege to say it. Cumberlege, a junior health minister, has now urged cafés, restaurants and other places of common trade to encourage mothers to breast feed their babies in public.

Why? What business is it of hers? Many men are made to feel

uncomfortable by the spectacle, either jealous of the baby or because they prefer to see the woman's breast as an object of erotic veneration rather than in its less interesting role as a teat or udder. This is especially true where other people's wives, other people's babies are concerned.

Speaking at the start of National Breast Feeding Week on Sunday, Lady Cumberlege said it was the best start in life a baby could have to be fed instantly on demand whenever and wherever it was. Nothing could be further from the truth. Even the American Dr Spock, who invented this mad doctrine, had grave doubts about it by the end of his dreadful life.

He was responsible for the generation which lost America the war in Vietnam, and may lose it in Haiti, if Mr and Mrs Clinton decide to invade. Nobody seems certain what the Haitians have done wrong, but it is thought Mrs Clinton may be displeased with their policy on smoking – particularly their toleration of cigarette advertisements with a humorous concept.

Experts are divided on whether it was the Sixties' fad for breast feeding on demand, or the Shirley Williams educational reforms of the Seventies, which account for the present generation of unemployables in Britain. Perhaps Lady Cumberlege will open Child-Centred Education Week next.

## *21st May, 1994*

### Daffodil peril

AFTER years of agitation, the Consumers' Association has prevailed upon the Horticultural Trade Association to set up a working party of doctors, botanists and horticulturalists to produce a list of garden flowers and plants which should not be eaten, rubbed into the skin, pushed up the nose or into the ears or otherwise ingested.

So now voluntary health warnings will be attached to daffodil bulbs, snowdrops, lilies of the valley, hyacinths, honeysuckle cuttings and about 50 common trees, plants and shrubs.

All those busy people, how they manage to create work for themselves and others! But has there been a single case in recent British history of any child eating even the most notoriously poisonous plant (as opposed to a chemical preparation) and suffering more than temporary discomfort?

It appears that there was once a case in Illinois where someone mistook daffodil bulbs for onions, made them into a soup and was very ill. Now daffodil bulbs sold anywhere in the Western world had better be labelled under penalty of enormous damages, in case an Illinois housewife eats them by mistake.

## 23rd May, 1994

### Do as you please

TO TAKE the place of a member of the House of Laity in the General Synod of the Church of England who considered that her Church no longer preached the Christian Gospel, a candidate called Eglah Jeannette Bond put herself forward under the following manifesto:

*'Dear Electors, I offer myself as a candidate for the House of Laity of the General Synod because of my interest in the Diocesan policies. I have particular concern for the Church of England's smoking policy, which is virtually non-existent . . . I do have some other ideas on policies, but this is the strongest point I wish to make now.*

*'Passive smoking is a serious health risk and many smokers do not realise the danger in which they are putting their fellow-worshippers, and those that do conveniently turn a blind eye.*

*'The question is:*

*1. How many Parishes find themselves operating a "Do as you please" smoking policy that could lead to them finding their covenant money being frittered away to pay for possible future lawsuits for claims of lung cancer, asthma and other illnesses?*

*2. Is the Church keeping up with the new Health and Safety Act laws, updated in 1993?*

*3. Do we want to find ourselves, once again, in a similar financial situation like the Church Commissioners put us, in which millions of pounds could be lost due to the Church's failure to keep up with the code of practice on smoking in public places?'*

Eglah Jeannette Bond was not elected, I am sorry to say, but if anyone knows of a London church where smoking is permitted during services, I would be delighted to hear of it.

# 28th May, 1994

## Terror in the countryside

AS SOON as I saw a headline in the *Daily Express* to the effect that Mr Major was personally intervening to save us from the flesh-eating bacterium necrotising fasciitis, I knew that we would be safe: 'MAJOR ACTS ON KILLER BUG . . . Deaths from the flesh-eating killer bug rose to 12 last night as John Major pledged to do everything possible to tackle it.'

In the nicest possible way, Mr Major is something of a necrotising agent himself, in that he dries everything he touches. Our enthusiasm for this newly discovered health hazard, familiar to everyone as galloping gangrene since long before the Great War, cannot long survive Mr Major's interest in it.

However, one serious new health hazard has been played down. Many newspaper did not even carry the story of a four-year-old girl in Nottinghamshire who was attacked by a fox while in bed. A spokesman for the RSPCA expressed 'surprise', saying foxes were normally shy and nervous creatures.

By nature, the fox is greedy, ruthless, cruel and furtive. It is only by hunting the brute for hundreds of years that we have introduced a note of 'shyness' into its foul nature. The new animal sentimentalism which seems to affect many town-dwellers nowadays threatens to spoil all this.

Liberal Democrats take these dangerous animals into their homes, say 'goo goo' and no doubt try breast feeding them. Mark my words, it will all end in tears. The wretched Michael Howard is waiting until a baby has been eaten before grabbing the headlines with some new 'crackdown' legislation.

The point about foxes is that they are supportable members of the ecological community only if they are hunted four days a week. Now we shall have to have a 15-year sentence for sabotage of a hunt, and five years for speaking disrespectfully of a Master of Foxhounds.

## A question of manners

'MADE to Crawl by Lady Olga's Tories' was the *Mirror*'s headline under a most unpleasing photograph of allegedly disabled people on all fours on the pavement outside Parliament, wearing rude T-Shirts printed 'Piss on Pity'.

If that is to be the new language of politics, then so be it. The tactics of these protesters, invited to Westminster by Dennis Skinner, are exactly the same as those adopted by north African beggars should be treated like North African beggars, who exhibit their amputated limbs and other sores with furious grimaces, as a way of exciting guilt, rather than pity, in the onlookers.

It might work over here, but I am not sure. It would be easy to say that people who behave like north African beggars, propped against the nearest wall to have the occasional coin tossed in their direction.

I think we are kinder than that, but it is an unfortunate truth that many people who have the misfortune to be confined to wheelchairs become bad-tempered, self-pitying and extremely unpleasant in the course of it. They need – and often find – saints to look after them.

But most people are not saints and, rather than be seriously inconvenienced by the need to flatten every mountain in their path, and fill in every valley, they would be quite happy for the disabled to stay in their bedrooms, or in special institutions, if the money were available. It must all depend a little bit on their comportment.

I think I know what Mr Skinner and the *Daily Mirror* hope to gain by exploiting these wheelchair crawlers, some of whom had to be brought overnight from Glasgow and Cardiff. I wonder if the invalids themselves have any clear idea.

## *30th May, 1994*

### Outing the Papists

LATE on Saturday evening, a rumour swept through the Dordogne that Tony Blair, Mr Major's heir-apparent, is a Roman Catholic. I think it may have been started by his reported complaint that there were not enough bedrooms in 10 Downing Street for all his children, or perhaps it referred to his wife's religion. At any rate, it seemed a good rumour to encourage.

At Ruskin College, Oxford, where Labour leaders of the future are sent, they recently prevented the college's Catholic Society from affiliating with the students' union on the grounds that Roman Catholicism was 'an oppressive, patriarchal religion'. In a dignified letter, the College's Women's group explained that 'women, under popery, are not free to decide on their own fertility' and suggested they were reduced to 'little more than grow-bags for more Catholic children'. I hope that Mr Blair takes note of these reactions.

A good way of scotching the rumours would be if he announced that the next Labour government will put a stop to child benefit. Most parents do not need it and those who do should receive it least of all. These are the people who are producing an ever-growing army of unemployable criminals and louts. Isn't that right, Tony?